DISCOMBOBULATION

WHEN CLANS COLLIDE UNDER THE INFLUENCE OF URBAN RENEWAL, BABY BOOMERS, KNUCKLEHEADS, AND STUPIDVILLE

WAYNE RUDOLPH DAVIDSON

abbott press

Abbott Press books may be ordered through booksellers or by contacting:

Abbott Press
1663 Liberty Drive
Bloomington, IN 47403
www.abbottpress.com
Phone: 1 (866) 697-5310

ISBN: 978-1-4582-1912-1 (sc)
ISBN: 978-1-4582-1913-8 (hc)
ISBN: 978-1-4582-1914-5 (e)

Library of Congress Control Number: 2015910740

Print information available on the last page.

Abbott Press rev. date: 9/4/2015

Also by Wayne Rudolph Davidson

Manufacturing African American Self-Employment in the Detroit Metropolitan Area

When Clans Collide: The Germination of Adam's Family Tree through Surname, Life Experience, and DNA

Dedication

To my Savior, Jesus Christ
To my parents and my siblings
To my wife, Bertha
To my daughters,
Treasure, Lydia, Lynette, Jeanne, and Kalyn

There are two great days in a person's life—the day we are born and the day we discover why.

—William Barclay[1]

There is no greater agony than bearing an untold story inside you.

—Maya Angelou[2]

Contents

Also by Wayne Rudolph Davidson v
Dedication vii
Foreword xiii

Preface 1
Acknowledgments 19
Prologue: Spilled Milk 21
Timeline 27
Key Events and Considerations (Macro Level) 1941–1976 28
Key Events and Considerations (Micro Level) 1977–1979 31

Chapter 1 State of Urban Renewal and the Great Jim Brown 33
Milestones and Knucklehead Incidents 122
Chapter 2 State of Superfly and Chaos 126
Milestones and Knucklehead Incidents 189

Key Events and Considerations (Macro Level) 1980–1990–2000 ... 192
Key Events and Considerations (Micro Level) 1980–1990–2000 193
Chapter 3 State of Redemption and a Man's World 194
Milestones and Knucklehead Incidents 338
Chapter 4 State of Connectivity and Personal Development 347
Milestones and Knucklehead Incidents 420
Epilogue: State of Reorientation following a Devastating Blow 428

Foreword

"I did the best I could with what I had," exclaimed Reuben Alfred Davidson, husband and father of four children and member of the African-American family unit of the Alexander Davidson II family tree and the Thomas Davison family tree of Barren County, Kentucky. Alexander Davidson II was a signer of the 1799 Kentucky state constitution. Thomas Davison of Scotland is connected to the George Washington family tree by marriage to Anne Alexander Lewis, the granddaughter of Betty Washington, the sister of General George Washington. Ms. Lewis's father is Fielding Lewis, a distant relative of Meriwether Lewis, the explorer. Her legal guardian at the time of marriage was Brigadier General Alexander Spotswood, offspring of the first royal governor of Virginia and a prominent English family.

The surname Davidson/Davison/Davis is prominent in the social and economic growth and defense of this country from colony to state with the help of an industrious African-American branch. The great industrialist John Davison Rockefeller's mother was named Elizabeth "Eliza" Davison, and the great Negro educator Booker T. Washington's first wife and the mother of his two sons was Olivia A. Davidson. The family tree for the surname Davidson/Davison/Davis includes my African descendants, a Negro boy named Adam and a Negro woman named Venus, who became the legal property of Alexander "the Immigrant" Davidson on the Rappahannock River in Virginia in the mid-1740s.

Reuben Alfred Davidson migrated to the north to find work and start a family- wife Lydia and sons Wayne, Glen and Robert.

Preface

This text is the second book of a trilogy in the discovery of this author's family history. The first book, *When Clans Collide: the Germination of Adam's Family through Surname, Life Experience, and DNA*—a 2014 Global E-book Award winner[1]—resulted from a genealogy study of the surname Davidson. The findings of the study illustrated the life, times, and diversity of the Davidson/Davison/Davis family tree. The surname *Davidson* was traced through Western civilization as far back as the Middle Ages, through the discovery of the New World, through the Negro migration, and through the end of World War II. The survey found that branches of the Davidson family tree by surname featured many prominent and historical figures and introduced this author to several industrious members related by blood, and provided an understanding that the genealogical research of African-Americans is a painstaking task because of the lack of or inconsistency of recordkeeping before, during, and after the period of African slavery.

The focus of this second book is on the author's own personal branch that stems from the genealogical trunk of the Davidson family tree discovered in the first book. The journey is based on the life experience of an African-American male born in the post-World War II era and growing up in the second half of the twentieth century and into the twenty-first, as closely as it can be remembered. The research and writing have given this author freedom and a better understanding of who I am as a person.

I learned that knowledge of one's ancestral roots is a key element in the structural foundation of a person's life, which many African-Americans have been without for more than one or two generations—most notably

African-Americans who were born and raised in the domestic United States. Many have surrogates in the form of institutional roots, such as social and religious groups, fraternal organizations, the penal system, and the military.

Freedom is a relative term in my newfound knowledge, as it is juxtaposed with the Gospel of John 8:31–32 in the New King James Bible, when Jesus speaks about abiding in his word and from that truth the abider would become free. Arguably, the Holy Bible is regarded as the foundational document of historical knowledge. It has been my experience that the lack of knowledge, as described in Hosea 4:6, is in reality self-exclusion from any situation, circumstance, or demographic. Think about it: once a bit of knowledge is obtained, it should be circulated back into the community so that others may grow and reciprocate in a way arguably similar to the order of precedent set out in Cristina Lourosa-Ricardo's 2014 *Wall Street Journal* article.[2] Knowledge of one's ancestry is essential to the past, present and future, as demonstrated by Kalā Kaawa, reports Carla Herreria.[3] After receiving his diploma from the University of Hawaii, Kalā Kaawa promptly discarded his cap and gown and walked back to his seat in the traditional Hawaiian loincloth to a standing ovation from his graduating class.

Truth is also relative. I recall listening to a professional speaker proclaim that his transition into a more prosperous speaker happened when he began to speak from his own experience rather than the experience of another speaker who was world-renowned. The publication of my life experience gives to the best of my knowledge details as to

- where I came from;
- how I got here;
- where I am now; and
- where am I going

in an effort to make peace with any pitfalls I may have encountered along the way. It is my growth process that helped me to develop a more cosmopolitan view of the world and attempt to assist others through examination of the static socioeconomic position I progressed from to the more dynamic socioeconomic position I gravitated to. There are several psychological tools addressed in the text that will hopefully provide the interested party with encouragement to make change happen.

The American Dream

The post-World War II timeline in which I grew up as an African-American male was filled with great moral confusion, social contradiction, and restrictive covenants. I pondered the question, "Why is this condition so?"—most particularly in a prosperous land that has been promoting peace, love, goodwill, and opportunity since its inception.

For instance, I live in a single-family home that I purchased in 1999; it was built in 1977. The house is located in a well-managed Detroit suburb among good neighbors of diverse culture with a good school system. The house was paid for in less than fifteen years. In 1977, I was employed as a general laborer in a local automobile factory approximately five miles from where my current house is located. But in 1977, I would have most likely not qualified to purchase the same house because of a restrictive covenant established and enforced by white homeowners and the real-estate industry and the inability of African-Americans to secure financing.

In 1966, my parents, Reuben and Lydia Davidson, purchased a single-family home in the Glendale Gardens subdivision on the west side of Detroit and lived in the same house for forty years. The house was paid for under the terms of a thirty-year mortgage. The previous occupants, as told by my father, also lived in the same house for forty years. The house was surrounded by good neighbors and a good school system, but many of the white neighbors and employment opportunities were quickly moving to the suburbs. The social transition most likely made the house available for my parents of African descent to buy.

My parents' house was built in a segregated Detroit in 1922, three years before the Dr. Ossian Sweet incident ignited racial tension. Dr. Sweet, a Negro and graduate of Howard University Medical School, purchased a house in an all-white neighborhood in the city of Detroit in 1925. The terms of payment are unknown, but most likely it was a cash transaction. A short time later, Dr. Sweet had to defend the purchase with a gun.[4]

My paternal grandfather, Ernest Davidson, owned or leased a small farm in Barren County, Kentucky, as did my paternal great-grandfather, Chris Davidson, and paternal great-great grandfather, Harris/Harrison Davidson. It is believed that Harris/Harrison Davidson, a former slave, was the first person of African descent on my family-tree branch to legally own or lease property when he was recognized by the Ninth United States Census taken in 1870 as a legal citizen. His forefathers, Alex and Adam, did not have the opportunity to own land, as they labored as legal chattel on the Davidson family tree, a distinguished family tree connected by marriage to the George Washington family tree.

This family history is important to know about, because owning a home and property is the foundation for building wealth in pursuit of the American dream. In the twenty-first century, this achievement of wealth-building is equivalent to becoming a champion in a chosen sport and typically measured by the presentation of a championship ring or belt. In this case, the prize is home ownership. There has been socioeconomic change in the air since the momentous legislation of the 1960s, but for whatever reason the championship opportunity is not open to all who need it and when they need it.

GENERATIONAL FRUSTRATION

I recall that during a bus trip home from high school with a rambunctious group of kids, I inadvertently tore the blouse of a female student I remember as Wendy. She spun with the quickness of a cat and whacked me in the mouth. I became discombobulated by the force and speed of the punch. Stunned, I asked myself how in the heck that happened. I became as angry as a teenage boy could be in a public setting and made threats toward my female classmate all the way home.

Luckily, the threats I made turned out to be empty, but I had to withstand the ridicule of my fellow students for some time during and after the incident. For years, my tooth suffered from the crushing blow, and I was frustrated and upset as time went on. More than twenty years later, I went to the dentist's office where I had a root canal done, and I was all better—because I finally took a personal action to make it that way. The same type of discombobulation can be seen in my expanded life experience. It fueled my academic cultural research and genealogy study for the purpose of making it all better for some other unsuspecting person.

On Thursday, January 30, 2014, Bill O'Reilly, a news broadcaster for the Fox television network, reported the liberal dissatisfaction with President Barack Obama's proposal to exercise executive authority to raise the minimum wage. During an episode of his show *Talking Points*,[5] O'Reilly introduced video interviews featuring several black males associated with citizen action groups who expressed dissatisfaction at being unemployed and having little opportunity in the job market. From the interview, O'Reilly, a perceived fact-based conservative analyst working for a perceived conservative network, summed up the socioeconomic condition in the African-American community as being "cultural," thus implying to me that the circumstance is woven into the social fabric of the group called *African-Americans*.

The argument that black males have tenuous opportunity in the socioeconomic fabric of the United States may have increased validity, but historically there have been extenuating circumstances that made it so. For instance, since that January interview, four African-American males have lost their lives in 2014 and 2015 at the hands of white police officers in Ferguson, Missouri,[6] New York City,[7] Cleveland, Ohio,[8] and North Charleston, South Carolina,[9] sparking riots and mass protests across the country as a result of no criminal indictment of the white police officers to date.[10] In Baltimore, Maryland, six police officers comprised of black and white, male and female members have been indicted in the 2015 death of Freddie Gray.[11] In either situation police misconduct have impacted the municipal budgets greatly.[12] From my body of research and my own experience, I believe unemployment and violence have both physical and social connection in the African-American culture.

Additionally, in the Detroit metropolitan area in the post-bankruptcy era, Nolan Finley in his 2014 *Detroit News* editorial asked the question, "Where Are the Black People?"[13] The question is pertinent especially during the economic growth spurring the rebuilding of the once-barren downtown area. New business establishments, major cultural events, and professional meetings are frequented in greater proportion by white consumers than black consumers. Finley suggests that African-Americans must participate in the rebuilding of the city of Detroit because it is a city of opportunity, implying that there is no reason to complain if only few of the disenchanted are participating in those opportunities.

I understand Finley's call to action because many times in my growth process, I was the only person of African descent partaking in an opportunity. And whether or not we like it, a key element in socioeconomic opportunity is qualification. Which brings us to the question, is the apathy shown toward new opportunity in the city really a lack of interest or a lack of opportunity? Typically, opportunity does not fall in a person's lap. Generally, a person has to go out and seek it.

While there is little argument that black males have been offered limited opportunity in the marketplace, African-Americans have proven that they are always up for a social fight. There is always mass participation of African-Americans and charismatic speakers when a perceived social injustice occurs, employing outdated tactics and strategies, a protest march here and an economic strike there. So boldly have protests become that recently an African American duo overtook the podium held by Democratic presidential candidate Senator Bernie Sanders to force their message on the agenda much to the displeasure of the audience.[14] Understanding the institution of family is important, but to achieve the American dream there must be a shift from a collective focus to an individual focus,[15] as mixed views generate a multitude of directions.

Most people want change, but few people realize change begins with the individual. Racial prejudice exists but the presence of racism should not serve as the "go to" phrase for every disappointment in the life of African-American. From a researcher's perspective, I also think tragic events happen many times because African-Americans lack extensive knowledge of their own African heritage, and Western civilization does not know its culpability in the socioeconomic factors leading up to these distinct events. In my opinion, the media inferences and tragic deaths require further investigation or study from a different perspective.

FOOD FOR THOUGHT

I was raised in a liberal environment, but I have acquired a taste for conservatism through personal growth. Through that growth, I have detected that the difference between liberal and conservative is the perceived point of view on the management of available resources. I have concluded that liberals want the door to the barn where the grain is stored wide open, making it accessible to all, while conservatives want the door secured and accessible to those with a key.

I've also realized that life is an evolving human process, and my individual personal growth can be attributed to three theories learned along the way:

1. Find out who you are.
2. Find out what your aspirations are.
3. Find out what actions need to be taken to make your aspirations happen.

These three realizations are discussed in more detail throughout the book.

LAWS OF NATURE

So as to Mr. O'Reilly's quick summation, I have to agree there is a great mass of African-Americans, in particular African-American males, still struggling with what many call the American dream. This assertion may be influenced by perceived social circumstances thought to be beyond their control—identifiable with Ralph Ellison's *Invisible Man*[16]—or their lack of ability, confidence, or material resources to take personal action resulting from the frustration identifiable in the lexicon of the twenty-first century as the Angry Black Man Syndrome.[17] As well as my own academic study, many of these social perceptions have been addressed in Richard J. Herrnstein and Charles Murray's controversial 1994 book *The Bell Curve* pertaining to environmental and social factors.[18]

From my own socialization, I believe this perception is taught from birth and is carried over for generations as a continuation of a social belief system. The stages in a man's life cycle, according to Davidson Powell's 2010 article,[19] are distinct: infancy, toddler, childhood, puberty, adolescence, adulthood, and old age. There appears to be a disconnection in the tenets of sociology and biology.

The biological process is fueled by the laws of nature, whereas the evolutionary process is fueled by heritage and inheritance. Tragically, many people of African descent lack knowledge of heritage and inheritance that is prevalent in families of European descent. During the first five stages of man's life cycle as illustrated by Powell, the individual is dependent on the benevolence of a family unit. The influence of the family unit provides an environmental foundation for making career choices. In stages 6 and 7, the individual has reached a physically mature level, and the expectation is that he is responsible for the choices he makes, in most cases.

Each stage of life is therefore part of an evolution that must be nourished to maximize growth potential. If unnourished, the growth expectations are perceivably not as great. As a result of misfortune, the population at each distinct stage institutionally gravitates toward each other en masse because of similar challenges in social and economic experiences. Despite many detractors and inequities, Booker T. Washington, the great Negro educator, emphatically encouraged persons of African descent to fully engage in commerce where they stood, at every level and through every obstacle,[20] while understanding that not everyone is destined for riches and glory. I learned in my academic research that a blue-collar worker with a ring of keys hanging from his belt was once considered to be a symbol of authority and responsibility in the African-American community.[21]

It seems that only a determined few African-Americans have made socioeconomic decisions that moved them in line with the American dream. In conducting research for my academic study *Manufacturing African American Self-Employment in the Detroit Metropolitan Area*, I found that statistically, African-Americans are the most at-risk social group with many family units born from reality and social circumstances, and African-American males are its most at-risk members.[22] If the Centers for Disease Control and Prevention (CDC) data is used as the official metric, according to Caryl Rivers' *Detroit News* article,[23] this same ethnic group is distinctly targeted by gender, behavior, street apparel, and perceived lifestyle. Case in point: when the legal system posts its daily parade of faces, it is evident that the apprehended population is predominately of color, stamped with institutional stares drained of potential that emanate from flat-screen televisions and front-page newspaper panels awaiting judgment of their actions against the public. The acquaintance of Miami-Dade County Judge Mindy Glazer and her former classmate suspect Arthur Booth is a sobering visual image.[24]

Many of their actions were conducted with malicious intent and are punishable. Obviously, from the perspective of an employer, the propensity to become repeat offenders and inability to rehabilitate put a damper on their future earning power as employees. In contrast, similar lawless activity among other ethnic groups may be romanticized and then commercialized.

In reality, the daily screening makes parody of a popular national network ad of "must-see TV" instead of "too much see TV" for the general public or public at large. The institutional pool also limits eligible bachelors for the daughters of fathers like me and ensures that the already dysfunctional African-American family unit continues to be heavily populated by deadbeat fathers.

The Trump Card

As with any social group, African-American males can do better. In a game of cards, the suit that outranks all others is called the *trump card*. Relative to the socioeconomic status of African-Americans, the trump card is found in several places in the New King James Bible, most importantly in Genesis 1:26–28. The first trump card assures that the African-American male is not invisible,[25] because like the rest of the human family, he was made in God's own image. The second trump card makes it known that African-American males possess skills of survival because like the rest of the human family, they were given dominion over all the lesser creatures and situations. The third trump card is God extending His blessing and giving males and females the directive to be fruitful and multiply.

Too many African-American males have walked the same path, so it is important to know in the development process that Proverbs 22:6 says "train up a child in the way he should go and when he is old he will not depart from it." This is the fourth trump card and may be the most important card, for statistically, many African-American males have not been trained in success. The Bible as the trump card addresses who we are, how we should be trained, and how we can survive in any socioeconomic situation. In addition to the power of the trump card is the reality of the "3Ts":

1. *Talent*, where one possesses a skill, attribute or idea;
2. *Timing*, where time and space meet so the skill, attribute, or idea can be appreciate in value; and

3. *Taking the opportunity*, where a person, place, or thing executes the skill, attribute, or idea.

WHO ARE YOU, WHERE HAVE YOU BEEN, AND WHERE ARE YOU NOW?

From my academic research, I have learned in greater detail the plight and circumstances of the African-American community. In fact, since the time of African slavery, the African-American community has been culturally *discombobulated* in key socioeconomic areas. Based on scrutiny of CDC data, I learned the importance of the following factors:

- organizational structure-formation of the family unit, neighborhoods, marriage protocols, and business center;
- access to quality medical care, educational systems, and employment
- religious practices, influenced by diverse (traditional and unorthodox) belief systems;
- citizen/soldier commitment to civic and military duty and obligation.

According to the Random House Dictionary, the word *discombobulated* is interpreted to mean confused, upset, and frustrated by a circumstance or situation. Despite Mr. O'Reilly's inference, the American Negro did not arrive in the land of freedom and opportunity with freedom and opportunity. Since the first recorded arrival of Africans into the harbor at Jamestown, Virginia, aboard a Portuguese slave ship in August 1619, generations of offspring have been generally discombobulated by the institutional barriers erected long after their journeys as hijacked cargo ended in the unknown land of the New World.[26]

In lieu of fully documented history, the patchwork heritage of the American Negro evolved from an African embryo, a virtual culture filled with too many diverse personal experiences, social constructs, and belief systems to count. This much diversity makes the management of cultural change difficult to appreciate or achieve. But not so in the single fight for basic human rights for all people, where there is strength in numbers. Since the seventeenth century, descendants of the African embryo initiated civil disobedience engineered to improve basic human rights for a social group that was not observed and build bridges in the name of social injustice for the masses to cross over.[27]

Yet from the perspective of individual achievement, there remains an economic gap and disparity in creating inheritable wealth that builds and sustains African-American family units, most notably in a free economy. Even for an optimistic people, to anticipate a call to ancestral unity is unrealistic, since many times economic opportunity involves a personal preference and personal adherence to ideas that are perceived to be remedies. The personal rights that a free person or individual can exercise may be influenced by political leadership, military service, religious practice, and labor.

Aside from the direct style of military communications, I suspect the "robot community" to be a true homogenous entity only because a robot is built to fill a specific mechanical purpose or function. Robert Lee Hotz, in a 2014 article in the *Wall Street Journal*,[28] provides a vivid illustration of a group of robots assembled to carry out a command in unison, not unlike soldiers. In the anatomy of humans, the process of thought may be homogenous, but the outcomes of the thought process are different, since some humans like the color blue while others like the color green. Among the human population, powerful people, in fulfilling their purpose, have sought to create a pure line of succession to lead over a mystified and unedified citizenry as illustrated throughout traditional history books.

Adapting to Environmental Conditions

From a scientific perspective, living organisms tend to adapt to evolving environmental conditions. Alan Deutschman, in his book *Change or Die*,[29] asserts that the inability to adapt to environmental conditions leads to socioeconomic demise. Typically, as a living organism, members of the human population develop cultural core values and adapt to the environmental condition they are confronted with. My purpose here is to share exhaustive research and personal experience as a living organism that adapted to the environmental condition as the condition presented itself. The evolution of technology makes both general information and academic research accessible at a keystroke.

How do people adapt? A full assessment and understanding of the concept is in order. In times of war, combatants seek to destroy the enemy and at the same time preserve their own lives. Most recently, in Iraq and Afghanistan, American military forces have encountered the problem of improvised explosive devices (IEDs).[30] IEDs are basically homemade bombs constructed and deployed along the battlefield without identifiable markings or warnings. They cause more destruction, harm, and terror than conventional tactics and actions. Once the problem was assessed by the military leadership, a collective effort was taken in the design of defense strategic and tactical measures that limit battlefield personnel's contact with IEDs.

Relative to the domestic economy, socioeconomic IEDs loaded with compound interest[31] have been politically constructed and employed to discombobulate the dreams of the American Negro for several hundred years. For this story, the twentieth century and the continuation of mass production in the post-World War II are the principal backdrops where socioeconomic IEDs have been found that impact my personal experience, including the following:

- economics or management of valued resources in the social community—the impact of the oil embargo, raging inflation, gasoline shortages (1970s), the introduction of Reaganomics (1980s);
- technology or advancing application or endeavors that facilitate solutions to perceived human problems in the social community—in telecommunications, the advent of telephones, radios, and

televisions as consumer products (1940s); in transportation, the construction of an interstate highway system that expanded commercial capabilities (1950s); in experimental travel, the walk on the moon, space orbits, and global transport by air that exceeded expectations (1960s); the evolution of the information superhighway that expands the depth and capabilities of the knowledge base (1990s);

- politics or issues that influence the civic environment of the social community—urban renewal and transportation initiatives that displaced minority populations (1950s); the Cuban Missile Crisis and the political unrest, protests, and riots fueled by assassinations (JFK, Malcolm X, Martin Luther King, Jr., Robert F. Kennedy), the Vietnam War, the military draft, and civil rights (1960s); Watergate, Nixon's resignation and subsequent executive pardon, military draft pardons by President Ford and Carter, and the raising of the modern volunteer army, seen as compromise resolutions (1970s);
- social conflicts or ideological clashes between interested parties in the social community—second Negro migration and the civil-rights movement (1950s); Woodstock, the hippie generation, the drug epidemic, and sexual freedom that led to the pandemic of HIV and AIDS in the 1980s and 1990s and the dormant Hepatitis C virus that festered during the same period (1960s); the environmental movement, women's movement, and teenage drinking (1970s); world hunger that brought light to a global condition as the Cold War in Europe transitioned to a hot war in the Middle East (1980s); and the attack on September 11, 2001, that led to more distrust and hostility in the twenty-first century (2000s).

In the post-World War II years, the generation known as *baby boomers* was born. This group conceivably witnessed and laid claim to being the greatest agents of social and scientific change in world history.

I am part of that generation, and I was greatly influenced by the change in social behavior.

It should not be forgotten that without the internal fortitude and personal desire of migrating people of African descent during dynamic times, like my parents and extended family, seeking a better quality of life and self-improvement in spite of socioeconomic IEDs, my personal experience could not have come to life. My purpose here is to convey my life experience for future generations to use as a stepping stone to a higher plane.

I believe my research began when I asked what I thought were simple questions. I wanted answers pertaining to the state of the African-American economy in which I lived and grew up. I wanted to know where I came from, my genealogy. These questions shadowed my formal education since elementary level, and I asked them relative to the subject matter I was studying. It was in 1980 that my physical research began and my support documentation started piling up. I then researched, wrote, and published my findings on the topic of African-American self-employment and the genealogy of my surname as original works. I wrote the texts for interested parties who also sought to supplement the traditional point of view with facts not previously heralded.

On completing my work, I found revelation in American history, and my questions were addressed with great substance. I learned that African-Americans do possess the desire and attributes to operate their own businesses in the mainstream economy. The demise of African-American businesses was greatly influenced by the civil-rights movement and the apathy of minority consumers is not fully discussed in the American classroom. Its emergence and dissemination lay in the hands of traditional learning institutions retaining traditional capital resources and sponsors.

Subsequently, the first book of this trilogy, *When Clans Collide*, reduced my ignorance in my genealogy as it launched the retrieval of at least five generations lost to African slavery and illustrated how the world really turns in the matter of the family unit. I was introduced to an expanded version of both genealogy and the traditional history book. I learned more of who of I am, despite the perception of a reviewer of my work who saw the personal discovery of my African-American genealogy as too much of a shotgun blast. It is ironic that the reviewer cited very little of the historical revelations that should now augment traditional study, because it was all new and relevant information to me.

It is the scientific evidence of my DNA-test results that will influence the third book of the trilogy. These indicate my cultural heritage to be that of the Ashanti culture of Ghana and Native American. I am anxious to understand the scientific application and bring these ancestral connections to fruition.

Who Are You, Where Are You Going, and How Will You Get There?

During a change of season, a cleaning crew working about my "man cave" pondered the many certificates and artifacts on display around the room and asked the question, "Who are you?"

My reply was quick: "Who, me? I am just man. The stuff around the room helps me to recall my journey, because I am still discovering myself. I only know that when things got bleak in my life, I kept pushing." For this exposition, *Discombobulation: When Clans Collide Under the Influence of Urban Renewal, Baby Boomers, Knuckleheads, and Stupidville* is my journey and life experience as an African-American male that proves the background. John Steele Gordon in a 2013 *Wall Street Journal*[32] article points out that a writer is better served by writing about a subject he knows about, and that is what I've attempted to do.

Like the cleaning crew, my own daughters have always been inquisitive about my life, with a slight deviation in the question of why they do not know me well or why they are not close to me. For their edification, I will open the front gate to my life experience. Typically, when conveying personal experience, it seems quite normal to avoid intimate details. But in order for a reader to understand the attitudes and circumstance of the time period, I will attempt to be most candid in this autobiography. This second book captures my life experience, warts and all, in four diverse phases: naivety, chaos, redemption, and connection. As a precursor, it should be duly noted that growing up in the industrial north as a member of a matriarchal family unit, I had to change my lifestyle or I would become a negative CDC statistic. If the center of Herrnstein and Murray's bell curve[33] is the greatness number of a value, then I do believe that the period of my life experience was most likely at the front end.

Although each daughter has grown into womanhood at the time of this text, none of them fully realizes she has fewer restrictions on her growth potential, statistically in the United States domestic economy, than her father had. Much social trauma is associated with the period following World War II, and the survival rate for African-Americans, especially males, was woeful. There was a "be safe" speech given by my parents to each male sibling before leaving the house mandating that we conduct ourselves like we had home training and wear clothing that was clean and did not attract attention or have bulging pockets of stuff that did not belong to you.

Depending on the geographical location, this warning let us know that if we did not conduct ourselves accordingly, the authorities could put us in jail or worse. This experience is parallel to the one described by television moderator Don Lemon and his discussion panel on the topic on August 15, 2014, titled "What Black Parents Tell Their Sons in America"[34] when they exit the home for outside activities. Traditionally, the warning meant that it was best to build a plastic wall around my emotions as a defensive measure and lay dormant until the social trauma passed. Wait out the incident and survive. Then carry on with life in America as opportunities presented themselves. This control mechanism is important. I learned according the Federal Bureau of Investigation statistical figures for 2013 indicate that 90 percent of murder against African- Americans where committed by African- Americans, whereas, 83 percent of murder against whites where committed by whites.[35]

Historically, few African-American men get to tell their side of the story of what they encountered outside the family home without standing before a magistrate. Please note that this written disclosure will never replace the loss of quality time with members of my family unit. Conversely, this story will give my family unit a better depiction of my life experience beyond their basic knowledge of me being their primary provider that they can draw conclusions from. It is and has been my desire to be a better person, and that led me to gain knowledge on how to become a better person. In my formative years, the speed and chaos of my environment put me on the fast track to nowhere, and then suddenly the opportunity for change came and I stepped up and took action.

In conveying this story, the availability of the Internet database of both academic and general references has helped me to illustrate the themes and events of at least seven stages in my own life cycle. The musical genius of soul singer Marvin Gaye captures the political storms and chaos that had broken over the horizons of my timeline in his 1971 song, "What's Going On."[36] The comprehension of world events is interrupted by the moog of George Clinton and his funk group's 1977 psychedelic recording "Flash Light"[37] blazing across the audio atmosphere. The naivety found in the fictional character *Forest Gump*, portrayed by actor Tom Hanks, holding his mortally wounded friend Bubba, is a grand depiction of the wonderment on my face, not unlike the deer-in-the-headlights look, at what I witnessed and survived during the post-World War II years from a black perspective.

It is my hope that this response and other exhibits gives further details for Mr. O'Reilly to ponder about the discombobulated state of affairs within the African-American community and an opportunity for others to expand their own knowledge base of the African-American experience as I have.

Acknowledgments

I want to acknowledge my fallen family members, friends, and baseball heroes, past and present. Thanks to Mr. Willie "Shake" Jackson for his lifelong friendship. Thanks to my friend Josh Sidorwicz for taking time from his collegiate studies to lend an editing hand. Thanks to Wendy Bishop, English teacher extraordinaire, for her encouragement to write my story. Thanks to Ms. Davette Pittman for her encouragement to share my story and accomplishments with others. Thanks to my theatrical mentors: Marc Rattray, Kim Streby, the late Dr. Harold McKinney, Lisa Agazzi, Kimberly Louden, Cindy Flach, Dewey Scott-Wiley, Greg Leevy, Jocelyn Sanders, and Liz Taheri. Thanks to Denise Stranahan and Debbie Lafleur for their drive-by encouragement. Thanks to Rubye Mae Cheshier McTizic, Katie Bennett, Harold "Jim" Wilson, and Charlene Wood-Wilson for sharing their family heritage; Jerry Byes for sharing biblical insight; David Demers for sharing his life-changing experience; Andrea Williams for sharing her logic; and Denise Barber and Barbara Lyons for helping to keep my temperament in check. Special thanks to United States Army Master Sergeant Donald G. Smith (ret.) for his mentorship in playing the game. Thanks to my late mother, Lydia B. Davidson, a strong black woman as she was often called. Thanks to my father, Reuben A. Davidson for sharing his heritage and life experience. And to my wife, Bertha, who provided me with the freedom of expression in all my endeavors.

Prologue: Spilled Milk

One day in 1953, my father, Reuben Davidson, left Louisville, Kentucky, on a train for Detroit, Michigan, with two small children—my one-year-old brother, Glen, and me, age two—without the company of our mother, Lydia. I can only make an educated guess sixty years later that there had been a domestic dispute. My mother has since passed, and while my father reminisced about the time with an old country chuckle, he did not reveal the intimate details.

Since small children require special care, I will assume my father received proper instruction at the outset of the journey along with adequate supplies and provisions from a knowledgeable caregiver. I learned my Aunt Lucille provided my father with a glass fruit jar filled with milk for the day's ride. This was a few years before Elvis Presley and Carl Perkins made the world aware of old fruit jars in a rock-and-roll song. By train, the ride was at least six hours from Louisville, Kentucky, to Detroit, Michigan. In the early 1950s, the weary traveler to Detroit was greeted by the full beauty of the Michigan train depot in bloom, a stark contrast to the mausoleum that was sitting there in 2014. But for special occasions, the building and surrounding site serve as a memorable backdrop for photo shoots and movie sets, saved only from the wrecking ball because of its national status as a historical site registered in 1975.

It is not unusual for a traveler with small children in any era to carry multiple bags with necessary clothing and provisions. My father was undoubtedly armed with paper sacks filled with traveling stuff, but a paper sack has never been known for its durability. As I understand the story, my father was managing the bags and children pretty well until the train jerked, causing the bags to tip over. Inside a bag was the glass fruit jar filled with milk prepared by my aunt. When the bag tipped over, the glass jar hit a metal rivet that secured the passenger bench to the floor. The glass jar shattered, and the milk was lost with many miles yet to travel.

In the 1950s, there were very few conveniences available to Negro passengers. So my father had to make do with what he had, and that was most likely nothing. My father remembers a lady passenger sitting across the aisle whispering out loud, "I wonder where the mother is?" I can imagine that my brother and I probably cried, whined, and annoyed the other passengers, but we overcame the circumstances and made it safe and sound to Detroit. At the passenger gate to greet us was my mother, most likely pregnant with my younger brother, Robert. This was probably my first encounter with adversity; over time, I learned to use levity to combat it.

My purpose in conveying this story is that every day, a container of milk is spilled somewhere in the world. The thing to do once the spillage or incident happens is to keep moving down the road and overcome the subsequent state of discombobulation.

Three brothers give patriotic salute

Three brothers gardening with Dad

Three brothers smile with Mom

Mom and Dad celebrate with cake

Family celebration at Mildred and Raspberry's apartment

Mom the basketball player

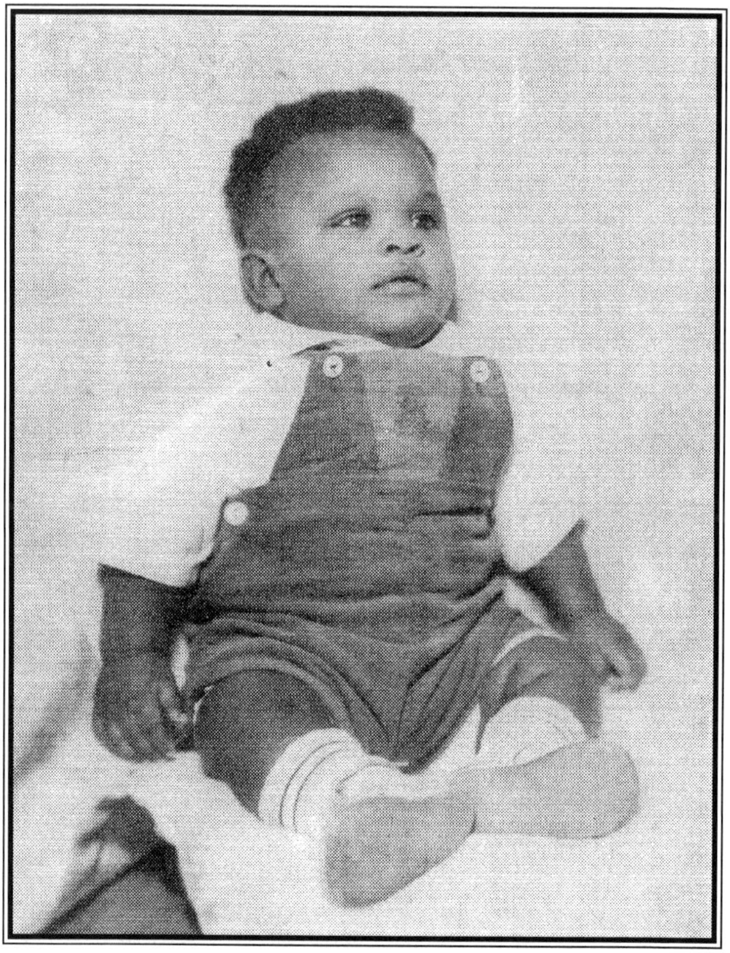

Baby Wayne Rudolph Davidson

TIMELINE

Twentieth Century[1]
The Industrial Age[2]
The Second Negro Migration, 1940-1970[3]
The Atomic Age[4]
The Age of Baby Boomers[5]
Urban Renewal Initiative[6]
The Cold War[7]
The Korean War[8]
The Civil-Rights Movement[9]
The Vietnam War[10]
The Modern Volunteer Army[11]
The Persian Gulf War[12]
The Information Superhighway[13]
Twenty-First Century[14]
Attacks of September 11, 2001 (9/11)[15]

Key Events and Considerations (Macro Level) 1941–1976

1941–1942

- Highs and lows of race relations[1]
- Executive Order 8802: Desegregated Federal Employment[2]
- Sojourner Truth housing incident[3]

1943

- Violence between blacks and whites turns into a riot near Belle Isle in Detroit.[4]

1946

- U.S. Supreme Court bans segregated interstate buses.[5]

1948

- US Supreme Court rules restrictive covenants (which limited where blacks could live) violated the Fourteenth Amendment.[6]
- Executive Order 9981 desegregates the US armed forces.[7]

1949

- Detroit mayoral candidate Cobo supports urban renewal for the area called "Black Bottom" that displaces residents and businesses.[8]

1954

- Federal injunction is issued against Detroit Housing Commission to end segregation.[9]
- Segregated public schools declared unequal.[10]

1955

- Rosa Parks is arrested in Montgomery, Alabama, as part of the yearlong boycott of city buses.[11]

1961

- Detroit mayor Miriani authorizes police to stop and frisk suspects in black neighborhoods. Four men in an unmarked car employ this "Big Four strategy" to round up targeted members at bars and among prostitutes in the community.[12]

1964

- Anti-discrimination law signed by President Johnson prohibits discrimination of all kinds based on race, color, religion, or national origin.[13]

1966

- A war protest sparks three days of violence on Detroit's eastside.[14]

1967

- A police raid at an illegal drinking establishment sparks six days of violence in Detroit.[15]

1968

- Detroit Tigers win the World Series.[16]

1973

- The military draft ends.[17]

1973

- The modern volunteer army begins.[18]

1975

- The Vietnam War ends.[19]

1976

- United States Bicentennial.[20]

Key Events and Considerations (Micro Level) 1977–1979

1977[1]

- Gasoline: 65 cents a gallon
- New York blackout
- Disco song "The Night the Lights Went Out" performed by the Trammps.
- Jimmy Carter grants pardon to American draft dodgers of the Vietnam War.
- Opium perfume introduced in France.
- Elvis Presley dies in August 1977.
- *Roots*, the TV miniseries, airs on the American Broadcasting Company (ABC).
- Hit movies: *Stars Wars, Rocky, Smokey and the Bandit.*

1978[2]

- Gasoline: 63 cents a gallon.
- Worldwide unemployment rises after several decades of near full employment.
- Japanese imports impact US automotive market following energy crises and increase in fuel prices.
- Jim Jones and cult commit suicide in Guyana.

1979[3]

- Gasoline: 86 cents a gallon.
- USSR invades Afghanistan.

CHAPTER 1

State of Urban Renewal and the Great Jim Brown

"I am going to shoot your ass!" These words emanated from the dark night and rattled around in my brain as my six-foot-three-inch frame with wild disco hair tensed up in anticipation of a sharp blow and the soft verbal response of "Oh God!" escaped my lips. The one open eye could not survey quickly an immediate escape route among the stacks of clutter in this garage lit only by the shadows in the snow.

I remember the year 1978[1] and how bleak it was. The weather was cold, and there I was hanging out with a friend named Greene Cutlass. We were both broke from factory layoffs, and the fuel gauges in both our cars were on near-empty as usual during the energy crisis of the 1970s.

Sometime during the day, I had a dare from my brother, Glen. There was an abandoned house across Grand River Avenue that was easy picking for pulling a "rip"—a street term associated with taking something that belonged to someone else. I was never any good at taking physical things that did not belong to me, just maybe a kiss from somebody's girl. But I told Greene about it, and we waited for dark to walk up the alleyway to the house.

The dark came, and we parked the car and walked up to the house through the alleyway. We entered the garage looking and feeling about in the dark for something of value. We'd started to pick over stuff when suddenly someone yelled out, "Who is out there?"

Greene and I were stunned. The house was supposed to be empty.

Then the person yelled, "I got a gun, come out with your hands up!"

Greene and I looked for an escape route, but there was no place to go. All we could do was slink slowly out of the shadows and into the moonlight toward the voice.

The man holding the pistol was angry and said he was tired of people ripping the house off. He told us that this night was going to be our worst nightmare. He planned to call a friend to help get the message out to leave this house alone, and the two of us would be the message-carriers.

Greene and I were subdued in our responses, because we did not want to fuel the man's anger any more than it already was and have the pistol go off. He held the gun and told us to go into the house so he could call his buddy for assistance in taking care of us. Of course, at this point, my mind was thinking the worse. It appeared that I was either going to get shot dead or pistol-whipped to a pulp. I was not happy. I was also afraid and angry at my brother for getting me into this mess. I calmly prayed and asked for God's help through the name of Jesus Christ.

The guy placed his call with the pistol still in his hand. When he finished the call, he started to ask us why we were in the garage. I told him that we'd heard the house was abandoned, and we were looking for something of value to take. He got upset again, shouting loudly that this house was *not* abandoned. Greene and I made our apologies, but the guy said he was waiting for his friend to determine the next step. The tone of his statement did not sound very encouraging to either Greene or me.

Shortly thereafter, there was a knock on the door. Another man entered carrying a pistol down at his side. As he walked into the room, the first guy updated him on what had been taking place in the garage. The situation did not look good for Greene and me. Again, Greene and I apologized for our actions, but the situation looked grim. The second guy said something to the first guy that I could not make out, but I could now see his face in the light. It was Cleve Childs, a friend from high school and the Big Boy Restaurant. It had been nearly nine years since

I had seen that face. My only hope now was that he remembered my face from back in the day.

I gained his attention and told him that I thought I knew him.

He grimly muttered back, "Yep!"

I said from work and school.

He grimly muttered back again, "Yep!"

Cleve never said much, but when he did, people always seemed to listen. Cleve said a few words to the other guy; the guy put his gun away and then Cleve put his gun away. Now all the guns were put away, and the situation was becoming less tense. I think it is fair to say that when Cleve walked through the door that wintry evening, God had answered my prayer.

Now I was just waiting for word to take leave of my captors, because I was ready to get out of there and never look back. My first stop would be to find my sibling and wring his neck.

The evening had turned benevolent, as our captors suddenly became our hosts. They offered us some of their powdery stash. I was in shock; I partook of the hospitality, but I was still uncomfortable. I did not want the air to change back to hostile. Greene, on the other hand, was acting like he lived there, and in my opinion was getting too damn comfortable.

In my view, we'd literally dodged a bullet, so I thought it was time to go. They shared their stash, and Greene and I stayed about another thirty minutes. During the whole episode, Cleve and I did not say much to each other, and when Greene and I left, it was the last time I ever saw Cleve Childs. Finally, Greene and I headed to the car, and I was relieved. We had an unbelievable story to tell, and without a doubt we were grateful for the absence of malice in the hearts of our armed hosts.

My prayer had been answered, but I was still angry at my brother for planting the seed of thievery and angry at Greene because he wanted to hang around a volatile situation. I was not raised a thief. I received my "be safe" speech before I left the house. I am grateful that I survived this harrowing encounter, and I hoped that the rest of 1978 would not have so much potential for disaster.

THE SECOND NEGRO MIGRATION

"Ain't nothin' to do in the country but look in the mailbox!"

That was the complaint of my Aunt Wadean during my interview with her, the youngest daughter of my maternal grandmother, Roxie. She headed toward the industrial north from Bolivar, Tennessee, looking for domestic work alongside her sisters and brothers in the 1940s. However, Wadean told me many years later that she was a bit bewildered because her journey started at age fourteen, much earlier than her older sisters'.

According to my Aunt Rubye and my mother, Lydia, Wadean was a rambunctious teenager running wild about the countryside instead of hitting the schoolbooks. The family was concerned because my grandmother, Roxie Jones Cheshier Sherley, was getting on in years and still raising children from a second marriage. As a result, she could not keep up with Wadean. The family was determined that since Wadean did not attend school, she needed to grow up and get a job in the real world of the 1940s just as her older siblings had to do.

Grow up Wadean did, first heading to Louisville, Kentucky, for a few years and then north to Detroit, Michigan. For my maternal family, Louisville, Kentucky, served as a stopover along the way under the mentorship of my great Uncle Maston Jones, the headwaiter at the famed Brown Hotel.[2] Once Wadean reached her final destination of Detroit, she gained steady employment on the factory floor of the automobile industry and then rose to the position of foreman. At some point, Wadean earned the equivalent of a high-school diploma. Steady employment allowed her to become a homeowner and a car owner, living single and fancy-free. As a result of her good fortune, she sent money back home to her mother in Bolivar and helped her siblings in financial distress whenever she could. I am sure my maternal grandparents would have been proud of Wadean's accomplishments.

Although Wadean lived out her American dream,[3] she died alone and in need of medical care. She had acquired material goods and personal freedom but had no husband and no children, just her legal guardian, my mother. From a religious standpoint, it was awkward at her funeral when my mother stood at the podium in front of the sparse group and wondered whether or not her sister Wadean was a Christian and had been saved. I was shocked when the question was raised in a public ceremony. Personally, I did not think that was an issue for others to question. For me, it was an issue to be discussed between the person and the Almighty, not a third party.

"Boy! When you get up to Cincinnati, you can sit anywhere you wanna!"

That's what my paternal grandfather, Ernest Davidson of Rocky Hill, Kentucky, shouted to his eldest son, O'Neil, to prepare him for the road north a few years short of the start of World War II. For the Negro rider using public transportation as a means of travel in the segregated South, whether to and from work or for a journey of leisure, it was understood that he would move from the front of bus to the rear in a timely manner as required. If it got to the point that the Negro rider heard the phrase "Get to the back of the bus!" it was too late to avoid rebuke.

It really did not matter that the Negro rider was exhausted from a tough day of physical labor, or heading off to church or to meet friends wearing his favorite suit of clothes. He was required to make way for others who had privilege. And if he didn't, the Negro rider was subject to penalty of mental or physical ridicule. If the Negro rider became uncooperative or belligerent about the law of the land, the Negro rider could ultimately face the rap of a white policeman's nightstick or, even worse, fines or jail time.

Now the Negro rider, scarred and exhausted of strength in free fall, knows if the flight is survived then he could make it back to the neighborhood. Once there, he could seek cover among the ethnic terrain, mend his wounds, regain his strength, and cling to life in the period of segregation. Most importantly, this lone survivor can preserve his personal dignity and fight another day.

O'Neil told me that he conformed to the travel conditions as he headed north. On the farm, it was O'Neil's job to pick up a small-caliber rifle each morning and head off into the woods seeking meat for the table. "A possum would do," he told me, "but a groundhog would be even better."

Like many young men of color in rural communities, O'Neil was ready to leave the farm and head to the big city during the Negro migration. In O'Neil's master plan, the target destination was Dayton, Ohio, a few hours north of Kentucky across the Ohio River, a way station for my paternal family. He had two aunts in Dayton who owned and operated a restaurant. So O'Neil headed north on segregated transportation during segregated times to seek his fortune.

After O'Neil crossed the Ohio River, his master plan began to take shape. He started doing chores in the restaurant and other odd jobs in the Dayton area When World War II began, O'Neil enlisted in the army as part of his investment as a citizen. As a black American soldier serving with the engineers in support of the predominately white military fighting force, O'Neil stated, he was treated as a second-class citizens on the battlefield and during garrison duty.

After the war, O'Neil returned to Dayton, where he worked on the factory floor of General Motors for the next forty years. He achieved his American dream, becoming a property owner and raising a large family. O'Neil passed on in his nineties with his large, loving family surrounding him.

Relative to life on the farm, the 1984 movie *The Natural*[4] follows a mature farm boy—Roy Hobbs, portrayed by actor Robert Redford—following his dream of playing baseball. At one point, Roy asks Iris, the character portrayed by actress Glenn Close, the big question: did she sell the farm?

Iris's response to Roy was, "No, I will always have that!"

Roy replied, "Good. It's home!"

It should be noted that the lead characters in the movie are white, and this eloquent statement may be marked by sharp contrast with the African-American experience of farm life.

Although the ground is considered God's green earth and a gift to man, according to my father, Reuben Davidson, a man of African descent and a farm boy of the 1930s and 1940s, it still required material resources: livestock and machinery to work and keep the earth green and make things grow. Historically, few Negroes owned or had access to the resources needed to cultivate the land they owned, and as a result, thousands of them departed the land for the north.[5]

During the first half of the twentieth century, thousands of Negroes migrated from the agricultural south to the industrial north looking for greater economic opportunity in metropolitan cities. It was not uncommon during the migration process for blacks to use cities, homes, and hospitality of friends and relatives who had settled from earlier journeys as a way station or rest area along the way to their final destination. This was a reality of the segregated times: the Negro of the South had to be self-sufficient, because many of the basic human services and products needed to live and raise families were not available to them outside of their own collective community.[6]

According to Booker T. Washington, in the 1890s, the Negro of the South owned or operated nearly 22 percent of the farmland in the South Central states and 30 percent in the South Atlantic states.[7] The Negro of the post-Civil War era had a huge political investment in the Republican Party, the party of Abraham Lincoln, until the depression caused 30 million workers to become unemployed in the 1930s. Washington also cited that Negroes represented 19 percent of all homeowners in America during the time period,[8] but with such affirmative statistics, why leave the South? The simple answer is probably that each new generation looks for something different from the generation of old. It appears that formal education could have been a contributor. Historian George W. Williams suggested that young educated Negroes in the post-Civil War era believed that farming was below their dignity.[9]

The mass exodus from the South to the North took its economic toll on the white population in both agricultural cities across the South and industrial cities in the North. First, in the South, there was no longer a concentrated and controlled labor force to maintain the agricultural infrastructure. On the other hand, in the North, swelling populations consumed available resources, including food, water, and shelter.[10]

In a "Raw Data" chart for the *Detroit Free Press*, Kristi Tanner cites a statistic that in 1914, the Detroit population was at 675,000 and then peaked to 1.8 million in 1950 before the drastic decline began that still continues.[11] After the turn of twentieth century, the black population in the city of Detroit expanded more than thirty-five times, from a community of approximately four thousand people to a massive community of 150,000 people over a period of fifty years.[12]

Looking at the surnames Davidson, Davison, and Davis, the 1900 US Census shows approximately fifteen African-American families with the surname Davidson or Davison living in Michigan, compared to the 1930 US Census which shows approximately thirty-six African-American families with those surnames living in Michigan. The 1900 US Census shows approximately 140 African-American families with the surname Davis living in Michigan, compared to the 1930 US Census showing approximately 1,753 African-American families with the surname Davis living in Michigan.[13] The small sampling indicates an increase of more than double over a period of thirty years.

Detroit brought people together through mass production and music. The city was already an industrial center during the nineteenth century. In the twentieth, it became the epicenter of the automobile manufacturing industry. The city attracted people from different walks of life and cultures, and it steadily grew into the fifth largest metropolitan city in the United States,[14] a figure displayed at the Detroit Historical Museum in Downtown Detroit. Ford Motor Company opened up the pay window and offered five-dollar-a-day wages for laborers.[15] For the Negro, the thought of trading a job pushing a plow in the fields for a job on a fast-moving assembly line was inspiration enough to make the long journey from the South. However, discrimination was prevalent, and the general hiring rule was that Negro workers were hired in quotas and assigned to perform the most dangerous jobs as general laborers.[16]

During World War II, additional manpower was required in mass production, so much so that women entered the labor market for the first time outside the home. Still, the heavy influx of Negroes caused a population shift in the industrial north that fueled both friction and fear in the white population. The first recorded race riot in Detroit occurred in 1863.[17] Fueled by the Civil War, the riots resulted in at least two deaths and the beating of a number of Negro inhabitants, as well as destruction of numerous properties. From the violent event, the role of Detroit's police force expanded to uphold the peace.[18]

Housing became the kindling leading to the combustion of social unrest in Detroit in 1941 and 1942. As the World War II production of war materials ramped up, employing a diverse production crew, whites made threats to keep blacks from expanding nearer or into white neighborhoods. The battleground was the Sojourner Truth Homes located near Nevada and Fenelon Streets on Detroit's north side.[19]

The spark ignited as blacks seeking to maintain residence paid rent to white landlords who in turn knew they were in conflict with the restrictive covenant on residency. Area white residents staged a protest march that turned into a fight despite the presence of two hundred area policemen on duty. The confrontation resulted in more than forty blacks injured but no deaths. The violence became front-page news. The federal government intervened, and the housing units were formally opened to black residents in 1942.

The flames continued to be stoked. Detroiter Marvin V. Arnett cites the riot of 1943 as the most violent event in Detroit's history. Arnett gives an account of the incident in her book *Pieces from Life's Crazy Quilt*. Young blacks and whites engaged in fights and riotous behavior near the MacArthur Bridge leading to the park of Belle Isle, ignited by the spread of rumors.[20]

Belle Isle is a beautiful island in the Detroit River and has always been considered a jewel of the Detroit metropolitan area, although its beauty has been blemished for a long period of time.[21] It has been the home of many civic monuments and recreational facilities and wonderful tourist attractions, such as the pony carriage, the zoo, and the giant woodstove that once sat off Jefferson Avenue near the entryway; I remember them well as a young boy of the 1950s and 1960s. These valuable city assets have been under scrutiny in wake of the city's financial trouble that is still front-page news.[22]

Arnett goes on to explain how civil disturbance contributed to public unrest, violence, and property damage over the course of three days in June 1943. Many of the thirty-four causalities and those incarcerated were Negroes who had to fight and defend themselves against both the whites directly engaged in the fight and the Detroit police who should have been acting to protect *all* citizens from harm.[23]

Racial tensions in the Detroit area remained high over the years from volatile social issues: police brutality, education, employment, and housing to list a few. All of these led to the next event of civil disturbance that ignited in 1967 when a police raid of an illegal establishment hosting a welcome-home party for two Vietnam veterans in a black neighborhood resulted in destruction of property in the millions of dollars and more than forty deaths.[24] Federal troops were called in to restore order in both cases. During the 1967 riots, I was to remain at home, instructed by my father to paint the house as chaos in the streets spread all about me, as I will explain later in greater detail.

Arguably, and in the view of many black residents in 1967, the dispatched troops caused the most intentional damage and destruction to local buildings and establishments, such as Central High School, than did those engaged in riotous behaviors.[25] Nonetheless, in the healing process, the words Father Gabriel Richard penned when the city of Detroit burned to the ground as a result of a fire in 1805—"We hope for better days; it shall rise from its ashes"—serve as a reminder of peace and optimism.[26]

PARADISE VALLEY/HASTINGS STREET

The influx of Negroes to the Detroit area had few neighborhoods to choose from by law. Many settled in the Paradise Valley/Hastings

Street area on Detroit's eastside, while others lived in scattered ethnic enclaves around the metropolitan area. Ernest Borden, in his 2003 book, *Detroit's Paradise Valley*, explains that the community of Paradise Valley began in the 1920s and was home to four square blocks of Negro businesses: lawyers' and doctors' offices, real-estate offices, restaurants, and nightclubs. It was a center for entertainment for white patrons and hosted notable Negro entertainers when they visited the city.[27]

Paradise Valley was also the home of numerous black churches and the Detroit Urban League. The neighborhood provided an ethnic foundation where the black community could obtain business experience and training, just as Corktown did for the Irish community, Greektown for the Greek community, or Chinatown for the Asian community. However, R. C. Goodspeed, in his academic case study on urban renewal, suggests that Paradise Valley was demolished by the bias and prejudice of the municipality disguised as an initiative of urban renewal for the public good. Simply put, the city fathers thought the community to be an eyesore. Arguably, the Negro community has to share in the blame because of the lack of leadership, understanding, knowledge, and participation concerning the integral aspects of civic planning on a larger scale.[28]

In the 1950s, as the Negro migration continued to grow, the black population grew with it. Yet Hastings Street, the incubator for black economic growth, was earmarked to be dismantled as a public eyesore, resulting in a horde of displaced persons. A second thriving African-American community in the Warren-Tireman District, home to many African-American professionals, appeared to remain intact. The remaining Negro population lived sparsely and restrictively across the Detroit area.[29]

The urban-renewal initiative[30] did create some public housing units in Detroit in the 1950s, including the Jefferies Projects[31] on the west side of Woodward Avenue and the Brewster Projects[32] on the east side of Woodward Avenue. The construction of these units during the rock-and-roll era resulted in almost every bright street lamp on every corner of public housing communities filling up with groups of young blacks, including myself, practicing musical harmonies in the form of doo-wop.[33]

In Detroit, this music phenomenon led to the creation of the Motown Record Company by Berry Gordy Jr. and the music labeled the Motown Sound.[34] The new genre paved the way for social change in what were previously split communities across the country. Detractors called music of this type just plain "howling at the moon"; nonetheless, today those same street corners in the remaining housing areas have been renamed in honor of those who once practiced on them:[35] Contours Lane, Temptations Lane, Miracles Boulevard, Four Tops Drive, Marvin Gaye Drive, Martha Reeves Drive, and Aretha Avenue. Don't forget Diana Ross and the Supremes, and Smokey Robinson, who wrote "My Girl,"[36] in my opinion the greatest song ever written and performed.

I remember the 1960s as tumultuous. Local stores and banks began to outfit their places of business with plexiglass.[37] I recall a popular movie in 1967 titled *The Graduate*[38] that featured a memorable line spoken to Dustin Hoffman's character, Ben, by a family friend: "I just want to say one word to you, just one word, Ben … Plastics … There is a great future in plastics!"

The speaker of that prophetic line was correct, because sheets of plexiglass sold well in Detroit and went up everywhere. The new age of plastics provided merchants with a higher degree of protection from the angry public and criminal elements. Of course, it also created a barrier between merchant and customer in urban areas, where there was already an existing barrier between the population of blacks and whites. The arrival of Chaldean Christians[39] seeking their American dream as new merchants in urban areas added a third barrier between Christians. Since the plastic sheets have gone up, several generations have grown up with this clear artificial barrier placed between themselves and others. This disconnection is still evident today and offers little encouragement to future generations to rebuild Paradise Valley from a business perspective.

Historically, it was always tough for Negroes to buy a house in the Detroit area because of the discriminatory redlining policies[40] supported by the federal government. It was equally tough to get a mortgage loan from a metropolitan-area bank. As an alternative, many people of color who were seeking home ownership faced the unfortunate reality of having to borrow from a questionable third party, who then abused the legal practice of contract sales housing. In her 2009 book, *Family Properties*, Beryl Satter provides insight from her father's perspective as a businessman on how Negroes in Chicago were forced to use contract sales to obtain financing to buy homes. Typically, this method of real estate always turned out to be a disaster for the Negro buyer. If a single payment was missed or late, the legitimate third party possessed the right to foreclose immediately.[41] My parents may have experienced this type of sale with their home on South Patricia Street, because the topic seemed to be taboo and sparked quiet debate between family members.

As I learned in my research study years later, Booker T. Washington exclaimed in 1907 that home ownership in the South at the turn of century was a crowning achievement that Negro people could be proud of despite restrictive covenants. Many Negroes during the migration followed that accomplishment, and upon reaching the industrial north, sought to buy and maintain a home of their own.[42] In the American dream, home ownership had always been seen as a sign of wealth that resulted from hard work.[43] In addition to ownership, new homeowners augmented their homes with bountiful gardens using agricultural skills previously learned in the South and their country of origin.

Shamefully, the real-estate association in the metropolitan area used fear tactics to create widespread panic in white communities, fueling throngs of white citizens' flight from the city to the suburbs.[44] The result: several apathetic generations of white offspring who most likely have never been within the Detroit city limits during their lifetime. Negroes were able to work in neighborhoods like Dearborn and Warren, but only a few lived there. When the workday began and ended—as depicted in the revealing 2012 movie *The Help*[45], hundreds of Negro workers in service uniforms would stand at local bus stops in soldier-like formations, heading back home to the inner city to the elation and bias of city fathers like Orville Hubbard.[46] This is how I remember it in the 1960s as I traveled through these neighborhoods. The municipal motto inferred that to keep Dearborn clean meant keeping Dearborn white.[47]

Heading into the 1970s, Detroit was influenced by greater social and economic changes. The city was slowly losing its distinction as the epicenter of industrial dominance, as evidenced by the many shells and remnants of industrial buildings that once housed its manufacturing power. The domestic automotive industry has steadily lost market share and profits to foreign manufactures over my lifetime.[48] By way of comparison, Arnett asserts in *Quilt* that the true event that triggered financial decline in Detroit really began two years before official recognition of the Great Depression in 1930. During that time, the Ford Motor Company suspended production of the Model T automobile at the Highland Park plant and closed all of its manufacturing plants for a significant period of time.[49] That would have been in 1928, the same year my father was born in Barren County, Kentucky; his personal destiny was to migrate to the industrial North for greater economic opportunity.

Based on Arnett's assertion, Dad's American dream had already started to vaporize long before he started out on his own personal journey.

NAIVETY: LIFE AND RELIGION IN THE GREAT INDUSTRIAL NORTH

It is 4:44 a.m., September 8, 1951, a Saturday morning in the Negro migration period of 1940–1970. I am the first grandchild in the union of the Davidson and Cheshier families born in the industrial North at Trumbull Hospital. Delivered into the world by Dr. I. H. Friedman—not by midwife,[50] as members of colored families traditionally were. The building located at 3966 Trumbull Street that housed the hospital still stands today. Just down the street, on the corner of Trumbull and Michigan Avenue, stood Briggs Stadium, home of the Detroit Tigers.[51] In 1951, Trumbull Hospital was not considered a segregated or colored hospital; it was simply a hospital.[52]

In anticipation of my birth, my maternal grandmother, Roxie Jones Cheshier Sherley, hitchhiked with relatives to Detroit from Bolivar, Tennessee, to help with her second youngest daughter's firstborn child. Lydia, or "Ly-dee," as she was called, had suffered a miscarriage the year before and needed help. Roxie had plenty of experience with children. She came from a large family and over her lifetime had given birth to twelve children: four boys and eight girls in two marriages. In addition to her own children, Roxie had helped raise a large number of stepchildren, grandchildren, nieces, and nephews.

My healthy birth was a good start for my mother and grandmother. I had all my fingers and all my toes, for which I am grateful, and my physical senses were working. I can still hear my grandmother's weary meticulous Southern drawl ringing in my head:

"Ly-dee, lay that boy down here."

"Ly-dee, this is the way you keep that boy clean."

"Ly-dee, tell Dave to go down to the store and pick up some things!"

A quick trip to examine my maternal roots: My maternal grandfather, Wade Cheshier, an extraordinary citizen of Hardeman County, Tennessee, died in 1926. His black-and-white photograph was prominently displayed as a dignitary in many of the homes of my maternal family I visited. I was told there was a tremendous turnout by the community for his funeral. Wade Cheshier caught pneumonia and laid in fever for more than a full week after he escorted some workers home on horseback in a torrential rain. The trauma from the event forever affected his oldest daughter, Lucille, who was barely fifteen years old at the time. In her testimony, she said "Papa" lay on his deathbed talking out of his head until he succumbed to fever a little more than a week later.

Another daughter, Rubye, who was barely six years old at the time, remembered the event clearly. She reached out to touch the body of her father but was quickly whisked away by family members at the behest of her mother, Roxie. My mother, Lydia, was barely two years old and a "knee baby" because she was at the right age to bounce on Papa's knee, but not old enough to remember events of this magnitude. The youngest child, Wadean, was still in the womb at the time of Papa's death.

Grandma Roxie's second husband, George Sherley, was a widower with two daughters and six sons. Their union around 1928 or 1929 produced three sons: Ulesser, James Gaston, and Edwin Maston. Before my mother, Lydia, passed away in 2011, she inferred that George Sherley may have been related to Wade Cheshier. It was not uncommon in rural communities that if a spouse died, the widow or widower would remarry in order to maintain the land and the family unit.

George Sherley was called "Pa" by the members of his new family and is described as a strict disciplinarian. This strictness is evident in a story told to me by my Aunt Rubye about my mother, Lydia, and her feistiness. As a young girl around five or six years old, Lydia fell off the wagon as they drove in from the fields after putting in a long tiring day of work. It could have been because she was tired and sleepy, or she could have been playing as young children do. My mother proceeded to tell her stepfather what was on her mind and placed the blame for her falling off the wagon squarely on him driving the wagon. Not good for Lydia. Pa left her right where she fell off, which meant my five- or six-year-old mother had to make her way home on foot.

Using the 1930 US Census to research the Sherley family was challenging. It was not unusual for census takers wrote down what they thought they heard on the census forms. For example, the 1930 census listed the head of household and family members as George Shelley; his wife, Rand Shelley; the children each brought to the marriage; and the son, Ulesser, who was the first produced by the union. The research challenge was the misspelling of names associated with this record. The surname *Sherley* was misspelled along with the first name of my grandmother, Roxie.[53]

THE LINE OF REUBEN "THE MIGRANT" DAVIDSON

The US federal census of 1930 listed my father, Reuben Alfred Davidson, son of Ernest Davidson, as a two-year-old male child named Alford.[54] The spelling of the child's name is wrong, just another case of census workers writing down what they thought they heard.

My father, Reuben Alfred Davidson, lived and worked as a general laborer from Barren County, Kentucky, a place in the back country called Rocky Hill. He was the fourth of five children born to Ernest and Flossie Davidson, and his nickname was "Hon." He received a fourth-grade education and worked chores around the farm. When his dad went to town on Saturdays, he and his younger brother, Buddy, went along so they could sit in the balcony and watch cowboy movies at the picture show for twenty-five cents while my grandparents shopped.

As mentioned earlier, the eldest brother, O'Neil, had the responsibility of hunting game for the family table. O'Neil said that it was not advisable to take his younger brothers, Reuben and Buddy, hunting with him. They played all the time and most likely would have chased the game away. However, for those living in the back country, hunting was a way of life.

Dad described the shooting prowess of a relative, considered to be an uncle and grandfather, who raised my paternal grandmother, Flossie. Zach "Buck" Davidson walked with a limp but was an eagle-eye dead shot with a 32-20 rifle, especially if birds of prey attacked his livestock. The story goes that Zach shot a red-tail hawk in flight that was attempting to steal a chicken. He also had dogs—bloodhounds he used to track foxes. From the movies, I understood foxhunting to be a sophisticated gentleman's sport. Not for Zach; he had his hounds scampering after foxes every chance he got. The fox would be cornered and then shot for his fur pelt, which would be taken to town for sale.

Dad recalled that Zach loved to sit on the side of the road and have a conversation with anybody who walked by, and one of his favorite subjects was baseball. In farm country, there was little or no time for sports activities—and in most cases, no money either. Nonetheless, it was my father's recollection that Zach had the opportunity to attend a World Series game sometime during his life, in either St. Louis or Louisville. In any case, it would have probably been the Negro Leagues World Series. No matter, in the age of technology, watching television became Zach's favorite thing to do, so much so that he died sitting in his comfortable chair watching it. Anita Roddick writes that the television wields an incredible passive power, making the twentieth-century contraption a pacifier for the human mind.[55]

Typically, Negroes who migrated to the North to earn a living came back to the South to visit with new cars, new clothes, and new wives. That is why my father, Reuben, decided that he wanted off the farm. From the age of fourteen, he worked strenuous odd jobs to earn wages in and around his hometown of Rocky Hill and nearby Glasgow. Notably, my father's physique was not one where muscles protruded from his shirt and his work jeans. He would be considered by most to be an average-size man with high hopes. Dad wanted to leave what he called "The Po House" with the ambition to get a new car, new clothes, and a new gal. I heard my father used the term "The Po House" all my life. It is ironic that Barren County was historically home to the County Farm, known as the poorhouse or "The Po House" in many counties in Kentucky. It housed those who could not take care of themselves because of poverty, handicaps, or other causes for many years.

TIME TO GO!

My father's aspiration was the first step in his journey. Dad knew once he left home it would be for good, because a return trip could imply failure. As a young man, he could not afford to fail, and if he did have to return home, it would have to be for a short time only. Dad knew he could not live off his folks at home in Rocky Hill; their only income was the equivalent of "egg money."

Rocky Hill wasn't far from Glasgow, Kentucky. According to my father, Negroes in the larger city of Glasgow lived in an area dubbed "The Kingdom." The name is a euphemism that probably derived from Kentucky's wondrous caves and lakes, or as the population center of Negro families, schools, businesses, and churches. Dad told me that he could not just stand around on a street corner in town. In those days, a young Negro boy could be easily locked up as a person of no means or vagrancy and spend a long time in jail, subsequently working on a chain gang. The chain gang had been a common and accepted labor practice in Southern states since the time of the Reconstruction.[56]

Spending time in jail or the chain gang was not in Dad's master plan. It was his time to fly the coop, just as his older siblings, relatives, and boyhood friends had done before him. All had reached the age when they would begin their migration to the North seeking fortune. With haste, Dad anxiously made his preparations to go north around 1945. His destination was Louisville, a few hours away. His father's brother Garland worked in the stockyard up in Louisville. Dad thought Uncle Garland's house was a good place to go and get started on making his fortune.

His father, Ernest, tried to help; he said, "Hon, if you'll wait until next week, I'll get you a new pair of shoes and better suitcase when I go to town on Saturday."

Dad replied, "No, Papa! I'm all right, I will wear what I got and carry anything else in the suitcase that is here."

That suitcase was brown with worn edges and two tie-down straps around it to keep it closed. The pair of brown and white shoes on his feet had holes in them, but they were filled with wadded newspaper to provide more wear. My father, Reuben, described his father, Ernest Davidson, as a kind, loving man who taught his children to respect their elders. He passed on to me what his father passed on to him when he said, "Be careful, you can get in more trouble in five minutes that will take you a lifetime to get out of."

So the trip began. Dad got up early in the morning to begin his journey north to Louisville, about a hundred miles away. He had less than ten dollars in his pocket and a wrapped sandwich in his suitcase. Luckily, he was able to hitch a ride on a truck carrying hogs. The two Negro men yelled from the truck cab, "Where are you going, boy?"

Dad replied, "To my Uncle Garland's house in the projects up in Louisville!"

It so happened that the truck was headed to the hog pen north of the city, so they told him to hop on the truck and gave him a ride. The heavy smell of livestock was familiar to all on board, and the crew of three talked and laughed all the way on their journey north.

When they reached Louisville, the men dropped Dad off in the area of town around 10th Street and Warren Avenue, and then they headed off to the market with their livestock. Meanwhile, Dad stood there on the street lugging his brown tattered suitcase with the two straps holding it together, with holes in his shoes, trying to get his bearings. A little old lady walked up to him and asked, "Can I help you?"

Dad replied, looking about, "Yes, I am looking for my Uncle Garland, he lives in the projects."

"What is his address?" she asked.

"I don't know," Dad replied as he scratched his head.

Then she asked, "What is his telephone number?"

"I don't know," Dad replied as he shook his head.

During the conversation, a Negro policeman walked up to the two on the street. The old lady asked him to assist Dad, but it was no use.

My father learned a lesson that day. When you live in the back country, addresses and telephones are generally not required, because everybody knows everybody. In rural areas, the person, place, or thing you are looking for would generally live over yonder and be within hollering distance. But when you visit or live in a large metropolitan area, current addresses and telephone numbers are important bits of contact information you need to know.

Louisville was his stated destination, but Dad couldn't find his uncle's house. The day grew shorter as he sat there on the side of road perplexed, understanding that he could be picked up for vagrancy. Then suddenly, *beep, beep, beep!* Dad looked up. "Hey boy, did you find your uncle?" It was the two Negro men in the hog truck he had hitched a ride up to Louisville with.

"No, I didn't, I couldn't find his house!" Dad replied.

They yelled back, "Boy, get on this truck so we can take you back home before they come get you and put you on the work crew!"

Disappointed, Dad ran over to the truck with holes in shoes, tossed in his worn brown suitcase with the two straps holding it together, and hopped on the back of what was now an empty but still smelly hog trailer. The three souls headed back, laughing and talking about the events of the day all the way to Barren County.

The return home to Rocky Hill was the safe conclusion to Dad's first attempt to migrate north. On this first test the water was a little cold, but it provided Dad with a life experience invaluable to a boy from the back country of Kentucky. Dad was fortunate that the truck drivers, old lady, and policeman had looked out for his welfare. In the big city, there have always been "city slickers," or people who act with malice, on the lookout for naive human prey coming into town from the countryside without much knowledge of how fast life is in the city. Fortunately, Dad survived this time.

Dad quickly pondered a second trip north. This time he hitched a ride with the Shaw family, relatives living in Louisville. They knew where Uncle Garland lived and offered to drop him off. However, shortly after he arrived, Dad found out that you have to be careful what you wish for. Dad lived with Uncle Garland for only a few days before he decided he could stay no longer; Uncle Garland's wife was just too mean. Lucky for Dad, the Shaw family, who had driven him to Louisville, agreed to take him into their house as a boarder. The couple had two sons who were about the same age as he was. Apparently it was a good deal all around, because Dad stayed with the family for a good while.

To earn his keep, Dad worked odd jobs washing dishes and doing construction. He later learned the trade of mattress-making while he prepared for his next trip, which would take him beyond the city limits of Louisville toward the Kentucky state line, north and across the Ohio River. Learning a skill or trade was a necessary part of his plan.

During this preparation period, my dad engaged in many of the popular antics and fads of the time, including having a distinct hairstyle held together with Murray's Pomade[57] and wearing jazzy clothes. On a visit to his older brother's house in Dayton, Ohio, Dad got a gold crown put on his front tooth. Back then, a gold crown was seen as a symbol of prosperity. The hairstyle, the clothes, and the gold tooth helped him look hip and made an impression on his dates to the movies or to see Harlem Globetrotters and Meadowlark Lemon when they came to Louisville.

Years later, I asked my father why he chose to go to Louisville, which was more than a hundred miles to the north, rather than Nashville, Tennessee, which was less than a hundred miles to the south. His response was that he did not know anything about Nashville. Being in the South, all the good news he heard about came from Louisville to the north. It was the segregated South that motivated Negroes to move north; typically, the belief was that the further south you traveled, the worse it got.

My father recalled an incident at a local White Castle hamburger restaurant in the mid-1940s when he and his two friends were driving about the rural countryside of Barren County. The three Negro youths attempted to enter the restaurant to place an order. The waitress told them, in her long Southern drawl, that they had to go back outside and order through the window. Upset from the exchange, they hopped back into their car and drove off, vowing never to let that happen to them again while they lived in the South.

THE HONEYMOON TRIP

It was my father, Reuben, who told me the story about my mother on their honeymoon trip in 1949. My father met my mother, Lydia Cheshier of Bolivar, Tennessee, in Louisville through a mutual friend. The story goes that Lydia and her sister Wadean were up from Bolivar and staying at the home of their sister Juanita in Louisville. Dad went to the house on Cedar Street with his friend, Floyd Bale, to visit Wadean but came away with Lydia. It seemed that during the introduction, a brash Wadean insulted my father at this first meeting by calling him an adolescent. I can relate, because Aunt Wadean used to call my brothers and me "squirts" as young boys growing up. Wadean was probably too fast and too brash a woman for my father.

During their courtship, Dad and Mom walked to the movies. Walking to and from social destinations was a common activity during the time of segregation. Sometime later, they decided to get married. My father arranged for his cousin, James Shaw, to drive them across the Fourth Street Bridge over the Ohio River from Louisville, Kentucky, into Clarksville, Indiana, to the justice of the peace to get married in 1949.

At that time, the justice of the peace was located in a municipal building in the middle of the city square not far from the end of the bridge. The union was witnessed by Warnell King and James Lockhart. The newlyweds headed south from Clarksville in Clark County, Indiana, back over the bridge in Shaw's 1939 royal blue Chrysler automobile to Rocky Hill, Kentucky, to meet my paternal grandparents. In those days, few luxurious honeymoon destinations were available to Negroes, but in Michigan there was a place called Idlewild,[58] a black resort area also known as the "Black Eden" that catered to Negro clientele and featured Negro performers. A good thought; however, Michigan was way up north, and it took money to get there. So the first leg of their trip as a married couple was to the backwoods country home of my paternal grandparents.

The second leg of the trip was further south to Bolivar, Tennessee, to visit my maternal grandmother. To get there, the newlyweds had to take the southbound bus from Bowling Green, Kentucky. In 1949, transportation rules in the South operated under segregation.[59] Few full-service rest stops of the kind seen in later years as the highway system became commercialized and open to customers of all walks of life were available then. At this time, during rest stops, passive Negro riders had to patronize fruit stands owned and operated by white vendors for refreshment of limited choice. Of course, the restroom facilities were separate, or in some locations not accessible to Negroes. In keeping with the rules of the road, Negro riders sat in the back of the bus and were required to give up their seats to white patrons accordingly.

"I ain't sitting in the back of the bus," my mother shouted out in defiance on her honeymoon trip.

My father, a passive person, had to quickly spring into action to calm my mother down. Before this day, my father had never been farther south than Bowling Green, Kentucky, but he clearly understood the harsh penalty for not conforming to the transportation rules in the era of segregation. Those rules would be struck down in later years as a result of the civil-rights movement, but this was 1949. After a few anxious moments, Dad was able to calm his new bride down and convince her to comply.

From my perspective as the eldest son, this is probably the only time in their sixty-plus years of marriage that my mother ever complied with my father's instruction. Later, my maternal Aunt Rubye recalled the story and admitted that she, as a woman of color living in those times, did not possess the kind of moxie or the feistiness in her personality to buck the system that my mother possessed. A few years later, in the 1950s, Rosa Parks becomes the symbol of the civil-rights movement for her noncompliance with segregated public transportation.[60]

NORTH TO DETROIT

On a journey that began in the summer 1945, Dad finally made it to Detroit, Michigan, on July 3, 1950, by train with my pregnant mother. The next day, the Fourth of July, he and my mother attended a barbeque at my Aunt Rubye's house in Southwest Detroit to celebrate. My mother was evidently athletically inclined, a former basketball player, and she enjoyed tossing horseshoes that day. My dad told her not to strain herself in the activity. Maybe it was the joy of being around family, but my mother did not heed my father's warning. Subsequently, the celebration was too great for my mother's condition. She suffered a miscarriage shortly after their arrival in Detroit, a subject not widely discussed by immediate family members over the years. In the family Bible, written in my mother's hand, is "Miscarriage, August 5, 1950."

The day after the holiday, Dad found employment as a mattress-maker in a local bedding factory. He had learned and worked the trade for five years in Louisville, Kentucky. The shop also made soft feather pillows. I know, because, for many years, I clung to a feather pillow in a similar manner as Linus van Pelt, a cartoon friend of Charlie Brown in the popular *Peanuts* cartoon series, clung to his blanket.[61]

When they reached Detroit, my father and mother lived with relatives, a common practice in the migration. On occasion, Dad worked two jobs to build a family nest egg. He would leave one job, hop the trolley, and head over to the next job just as the start work whistle blew.

Hourly wages were fifty cents, which was too low for the standard of living Dad had heard about and the one he wanted to achieve. The wages paid in the automotive factories, seventy-five cents per hour, were higher and included employee benefits for being a member of the collective-bargaining union.

One day in 1953, Dad and a friend got word that Briggs Manufacturing Company—which had a history of exploiting its labor force, especially Negro workers—was hiring. The company was sold a short time later to the Chrysler Corporation, which had plants on Jefferson Avenue, Mack Avenue, and 8 Mile Road. In the heyday of the automotive industry, the foreman had the power to hire men on-site by sight. Dad said that he stood in line waiting his turn with many others seeking employment.

The foreman stood in front of him and asked "Who did you work for last?"

My father replied, "Ford Motor Company!" Of course, the Ford

Motor Company was a competitor. My father had not really worked there, but that was the tall tale his cousin, Ervell, told him to tell.

The foreman grumbled back, "I can't use you. Next!"

Rejected, my father stepped away from his position in line. But as he was leaving, he overheard the guy behind him going through the same drill. That person happened to be white. The foreman stood in front of the guy and asked him, "Where did you work last?"

The guy replied: "Bud Wheeler." Bud Wheeler was a local supplier to the automotive industry.

The foreman said, "Okay, fill this form out, you're hired!"

My father marched to the end of the line and got back on again. When he reached the front of the line for a second time, the foreman looked at him, did a double take, and then asked the same question: "Who did you work for last?"

My father replied, "Bud Wheeler!"

The foreman grumbled back, "You cats are all alike. Okay, fill this form out, you're hired!"

Now, my father must fancy himself a risk-taker. For a man with limited formal education, he is always etching out on a paper pad probability and risk factors involving winning lottery numbers for a small reward. In this case, he figured out that he could never be mathematically eliminated if he kept getting back in line, time after time after time. From that day, my father worked for the Chrysler Corporation, formerly the Briggs Manufacturing Company, for thirty years. Or as he so proudly calls it, "30-30"—thirty years and thirty days!

His first job as a general laborer at the Mack Ave. assembly plant was washing cars after they were sanded in preparation for the first coat of paint. He also did a little metal finishing using a screwdriver and hammer at his station. His second job was as a sander on a four-man operation using a tool nicknamed "Jitterbug" because it shook as it crossed the automobile body seeking to smooth out imperfection. He was now part of the union workforce, but he ended up laid off for thirteen months from that job. His third job was as a "hooker," hooking up lathe die equipment to an overhead crane. Because he did so well in that position, his fourth job was a fulltime promotion to overhead crane operator at the Twinsburg, Ohio, plant. There were very few Negroes operating overhead cranes in automotive factories. Dad stayed at the Twinsburg plant for about eight years until he could transfer back to Michigan. Listening to his stories, he was glad to leave Ohio. He said it was a Republican state, and he thought they did things backward.

Once the official records become available to the public, the US Federal Census of 1960[62] should show Reuben Davidson, son of Ernest Davidson, and family living in Cleveland, Ohio, as follows: Reuben Alfred Davidson, 32, male, black, general laborer; Lydia Beatrice Cheshier, 36, female, black, spouse, and keeping house; and four children, Wayne Rudolph Davidson, 9, male, black; Glen Alfred Davidson, 8, male, black; Robert Cheshier Davidson, 7, male, black; Glenda LeNette Davidson, 1, female, black.

MY MOTHER, THE BASKETBALL PLAYER

My mother, Lydia Beatrice Cheshier, was school-trained in domestic homemaking to take care of white families and their children. Traditionally, Negro women were just as limited as Negro men in career opportunities, so domestic homemaking and providing child services to white families were common occupations long before and long after the Civil War. Before my mother met my father, she worked as a domestic homemaker for a white doctor and traveled with his family to New York and Canada caring for his children. Nonetheless, when it came to starting her own family, my mother told me that she was afraid and felt it necessary to have help with the birth and care of her firstborn child. A trait I remember vividly. That is why her mother, Roxie, came up to Detroit.

My mother said her proudest moments as a youngster growing up in Bolivar, Tennessee, happened on the basketball court in the late 1930s. She earned athletic honors playing the guard position for the Bolivar Industrial School and the Allen-White High School girls' basketball team. This was probably why we looked at life differently. She loved basketball, and I love baseball. Of course, the game of basketball played in the 1930s was not as fast as the modern game. However, she said her coach, Samuel Jones, helped shape the minds and bodies of many Negro students who attended the schools. The average students attending the schools from rural communities were children of local farmers. The students attending school from the city had mothers and fathers who worked either in the homes of white families or as laborers on the railroad. With athletes, frustration can set in once a career is over.

As mentioned previously, my mother, Lydia, was called the "knee baby" because she was the second to last child of Wade and Roxie Cheshier. She was always on the knee of either my maternal grandfather or one of the other older children. Later in life, my mother returned the kindness by helping her siblings through difficult family matters, aging, and death.

My mother said she enjoyed her large family. They did so many things together: going to church, having picnics, cooking big Sunday evening dinners, and small-town shopping on Saturday. On a farm, my mother had numerous chores at age six, from milking cows to feeding chickens, hogs, and calves. One day she broke a cardinal rule: obey your parents. Her mother sent her to the store to pick up an item for dinner, but she did not buy what she was supposed to buy; instead, she spent the money on candy. She was embarrassed, and she cried all the way home, thinking her mother would whip her and everyone would laugh at her. When she got home, she was reprimanded, but she didn't get punished or spanked.

In school, she found music and reading to be her favorite subjects and algebra to be the hardest. As she grew in wisdom, her words conveyed that children should obey their parents, listen to elders, go to church with people who believed in God, and be honest. You know: the standard mother stuff.

THE BLACK FRYING PAN AND URBAN RENEWAL

When I was born, I am told, my parents split time living at the homes of my mother's sisters, Rubye and Mildred, and their spouses. I am told the address 5710 John R Street was my parents' first apartment. I remember vividly standing at the cross streets looking at the big shiny cars go by. That corner would have been Palmer and John R, and it was located near an area many people called the Black Bottom.

Now, contrary to popular belief, the area got its name not just because of its residents but from the dark color of the soil. The area was rich with black soil, and that is where the name originated. The early French settlers used strip farming so that the community could access water from the Detroit River and cultivate the soil in the eighteenth century.[63]

The area served a large African-American community just east of downtown Detroit in the mid-1920s. It did not feature a grand landscape of architecture, but it did host sixty square blocks of black commerce. The main thoroughfare through the Black Bottom was Hastings Street. Paradise Valley/Hastings Street was considered a cultural center for blacks during the Negro migration. On St. Antoine Street, hundreds of business owned by merchants of color—like barbershops, restaurants, theatres, and various stores—provided services to patrons. The revenue from these business ventures generally returned to the African-American community.[64] In his book *Temptations*, Otis Williams remembers from working odd jobs and shopping in the district that the area of commerce could be tough, as Detroit mobsters controlled many enterprises in the area.[65]

My mother, for her part, was proud to make her purchases on Hastings Street. One such purchase in April of 1951 was a black frying pan bought for my parents' first apartment together as a couple. Since taking their marriage vows in 1949, they had been living with family members, and the privacy of their own apartment must have worked because I was born soon after. The black frying pan served as the centerpiece of my mother's gift for cooking and feeding her family and friends. In remembrance of those happy times, she gave me the frying pan as a memento, and I still have it.

In describing the commerce of Hastings Street, my mother said even the bums on the street were courteous when a woman with children shopped along the commercial thoroughfare. Typically, my father has always been one who never goes grocery shopping, but I am sure he enjoyed the commerce of Hastings Street, maybe getting a haircut where he could play a number or two with the local numbers runners. Few remember that "playing the numbers" generated millions of dollars in the black community nationwide for generations that was returned to the community and its commercial enterprises until the operations were taken over by outside influences.[66]

Aunt Rubye worked in a beauty shop in the Hastings Street community, getting both the local ladies and their out-of-town guests ready to attend Sunday church services—what Dr. Martin Luther King called "the most segregated hour in America."[67] New Bethel Baptist Church[68] was located in the Hastings Street district where the dynamic ministry of Rev. C. L. Franklin[69] resided. Rev. Franklin is the father of the Queen of Soul, Aretha Franklin, a close childhood friend of Smokey Robinson.[70] As a community leader, Rev. Franklin helped to obtain housing and jobs in the automotive industry for many during the Negro migration. A friend of Dr. King, Rev. Franklin played a significant role in the civil-rights movement in the Detroit metropolitan area. The local black church was often a contributor to the local community, with the pastor providing the daily lottery number from the pulpit.

Paradise Valley was the entertainment district, and John White's Gotham Hotel was the center of hospitality to world-famous celebrity entertainers of color who came to Detroit to visit and perform. Performers included Billie Holiday, Sammy Davis, Cab Calloway, Redd Foxx, and many others.[71] They all came to Detroit to share their gifts and their dreams.

Personal freedom and opportunity to sow a seed that bears fruit from the land is a promise of the American dream. For a business to exist and grow, it must have a seedling. It must have thoughts, ideas, and suggestions planted in the free-enterprise system that ultimately bear fruit. Like many other ethnic communities in the Detroit area, Paradise Valley offered plenty of opportunity for merchants of color to build their foundation and continuously serve the surrounding community. Aunt Mildred owned and operated a small restaurant called the Do Drop Inn in the vicinity of Pingree and Brush Streets. My father called it an old hamburger joint; my mother worked there and often spoke bluntly, calling it hard work.

Historically, the Negro business class has faced economic challenges from the lack of potential customers and adversarial and destructive environments like that of Rosewood, Florida,[72] and Tulsa, Oklahoma.[73] Later, I found in my research that many businesses owned and operated by Negroes and frequented by Negro shoppers could not operate with as wide of a credit base as did white-owned businesses. As a result, the proprietor of color had limitations in marketing and selling his goods or services. Few white-owned banks extended lines of credit to Negro merchants because the consensus view was there was little need to improve Hastings Street as a permanent fixture or investment.[74]

For many black families, it was the duty of the black woman to interface with local merchants as the black male awaited her return in the car with the kids. This social posture is still prevalent today, with many of the males awaiting their spouses giving the appearance of getaway men. This course of action may have been less intimidating, but only one person gained knowledge of how commerce worked, and that was the black female.

After World War II, the CEOs of the Detroit municipality quickened the demise of Paradise Valley. Under the guise of urban renewal, a master plan to showcase the automobile and eliminate blight plowed under this economic venue. The project was the construction of Interstate 75 traveling south to north from downtown Detroit to communities in the greater Detroit metropolitan area. Just like that, urban renewal cut a path across the community where many African-Americans lived, where

African-Americans enjoyed social events, where African-Americans went to church, and where African-Americans shopped.

The renewal project created a horde of displaced persons. Few African-American residents and business owners knew in time how an urban renewal project in the form of federal construction would impact the entire neighborhood or how to properly muster enough support to stop the project.[75] Later, I learned that the intent of the social policies envisioned by the Roosevelt administration[76] and the Truman administration[77] was to build upon existing structures, not demolish and displace.

The second place I remember living is 1342 South Patricia Street in Southwest Detroit. I do not remember details of the house very well, but I remember the house had a fence, and we had a small dog. There was also a lot of noise. The large street under construction in the back of our house turned out to be a southwest section of Interstate 75. Southwest Detroit was also home to many large industrial complexes, most notably the Ford River Rouge Complex,[78] Great Lakes Steel on Zug Island,[79] and the Marathon Oil Refinery.[80] They all contributed to the smelly air and pollution associated with Southwest Detroit. There is always smoke and fire in an industrial zone. I know—I lived in an industrial zone for many years.

On the plus side, these manufacturing complexes brought thousands of jobs to the community. Today, the house still stands, but a majority of the jobs have faded away. I believe this house led to a bad time in my parents' financial life that has yet to be fully shared.

Aunt Rubye lived only a few short miles away. When we traveled to her house on 3138 South Beatrice Street, it was a greatly anticipated journey for me and my brothers because we would play a pointing game called "I Got That!" I remember riding down Fort Street with the Greyhound bus station on the right, a large truck depot on the left, and the Woodmere Cemetery on the right, and then we would cross the drawbridge over the Rouge River. Sometimes the bridge would be in the up position to let ships pass through.

My brothers and I would spend a lot of days at Aunt Rubye's

house. I remember she had a large piece of furniture with a small picture screen in the middle called a television in her living room. As children, we watched cartoons and kiddie shows for hours. We were dazed and amazed by the antics each character went into and the elasticity of the bodies as the characters got out of trouble and the orchestra music played in the background.

As we grew into puberty, we watched the rock-and-roll stars of the 1950s, Elvis Presley or Ricky Nelson, sing their songs while the audience danced and screamed. We mimicked their look as we winked our eyes and put a smirk in our smiles. Then we watched them hug and kiss the beautiful female movie stars, so we would act as if we were in love too, and hug and kiss the television screen. As we moved into adolescence, it was the local television movie hosts that caught our attention: Bill Kennedy on CKLW across the river,[81] Rita Bell on Channel 7 in Detroit,[82] and Cleveland's ghostly host "Ghoulardi."[83] They entertained and informed us, making our lives more diverse and complicated. At the movies, we caught the original 1960 film *Ocean's 11* [84] with Frank Sinatra, Dean Martin, and the gifted Sammy Davis Jr.

It seemed that everybody on the television looked different than we did, and they certainly acted different than we did.[85] The white faces possessed extraordinary attributes, skills, and endurance. They were young and full of vigor and vitality, with names like Annette or Frankie, always supported by a slightly older white person who appeared to be sophisticated, worldly, and of means. There was constant interaction and dialogue between the characters. It seemed no matter the type of show, everybody had a smile on his or her face, and any despair was quickly remedied within a period of sixty minutes.

There were no black heroes or seductive black women on television in the 1950s and early 1960s. When a black character showed up, there was no quick remedy, and the despair always carried over from show to show. The characters of color always came in second place, no matter the storyline. Sammy Davis Jr. was the first black actor to possess hero power in his portrayal of a black Westerner in episodes 131 and 151 of the hit television show *The Rifleman*.[86] The images seen through my young eyes were of black women dressed for church, dressed for housekeeping, or dressed as a "good-time girl," as my mother called the scantily clad ones. All of the ladies had a slow, struggling, dependent black male in tow and under control.

In later years, I learned that black culture greatly influenced the socioeconomic structure of the US, most profoundly as the artistic foundation for the performances of white artists in music and theater. White artists would model their style after a black performer and then introduce their act to white audiences as new and original. A white artist, Pat Boone,[87] recording the songs of a popular black artist, Little Richard,[88] comes to mind. Who knew the difference? In times of segregation, black performers had little access to white audiences.

DEGREES OF KNUCKLEHEADEDNESS

At this point, I want to address the term *knucklehead* in context. For me, the term indicates how innocent and naive my brothers and I were about what was going on in the world as we were growing up. No matter, it was still fun for three little boys. We three would lay down on blankets and pillows on the floor to nap. I was labeled *silly* because I enjoyed humor and laughter. We enjoyed visiting Aunt Rubye's house, especially on holidays. The scariest Halloweens I remember were spent walking through Aunt Rubye's neighborhood, but when we returned to her house, our bags were filled with goodies.

I believe the term *knucklehead* can be measured by degrees, on a scale of 1 to 4, with the lowest degree being the worst offender:

- Fourth degree identified as the baby or infancy stage of right or wrong behavior, with a childlike innocence.
- Third degree identified as the elementary stage of right or wrong behavior, inquisitively testing the water for boundaries, or just plain stupid people who forgot their home training.

- Second degree identified as the high school stage, where the deviant behavior has become chronic and on the edge, set to cross over to the point of no return voluntarily.
- First degree identified as the graduate stage that is habitual, where the deviant behavior is manifested with intent to do harm.

The most extreme degree of knucklehead would end up as a long-term resident at the state prison in Jackson, Michigan.[89]

The World's Greatest Grilled-Cheese Sandwich and the Hobo Cocktail

My brothers and I fit right into the fourth-degree category because we did nothing outside the authority of our parents. During the summer, my brothers and the Bradley brothers from the house next door played sandlot baseball on the vacant lot next to Aunt Rubye's house. Man, I could hit the ball over the fence. I believe I had natural ability, and as a result, the game of baseball became my first love. I read all about it, and I watched it on television and never found the game to be boring.

There were many family gatherings over Aunt Rubye's hot brick BBQ pit in the back of the house. It would overflow with pork ribs, steak, and hot dogs, and it was where visitors on the maternal side of my family argued about being a Cheshier, Sherley, or Jones. This was also the forum that kept family members in touch with the folks back home in the South, across the local Detroit area, or wherever a traveler had ventured to or from. My father always watched and listened intently with a full plate of food and a beer in his hand alongside my mother's identical twin brothers, Mas and Gas. The two were former soldiers who now spent their time under the influence, driving erratically and biting me and my brothers on the ears. The family story goes that as they progressed in their daily drinking routine, they ended up driving into every ditch between Bolivar, Tennessee, and the surrounding areas of Hardeman County.

Speaking of a ditch, I remember an incident that happened in Detroit when I was very young. A car driven by one of my uncles, not one of the twins I learned later, did not make the curve on the Ford Freeway around Schafer Road near the Ford River Rouge plant in Detroit, most likely going too fast. I remember my grandmother Roxie, my mother, my brothers, and one of my mother's sisters were also in the car. I remember my grandmother speaking about the incident in the same tone that has rang in my ears since my birth. But later in life, when I inquired about details of the incident from the surviving passengers involved, it seemed they had developed selective amnesia.

Aunt Rubye's house on Beatrice Street is long gone, as are many of its former visitors. Around 1956 or 1957, my parents moved the family into a public housing complex named the Jeffries Projects on West Canfield Street[90]—on the tenth floor of 1231 West Canfield Street. The Jeffries Projects opened for residency in 1953. The complex had at least six tall apartment buildings with twelve to fourteen floors that were surrounded by a number of low-rise apartment buildings. I remember the rooms to be small and box-shaped with sliding screen windows. From a tenth-floor window, a person could survey the landscape across to the other large building and down at the smaller buildings. The world was shaped like a box from that vantage point, but it was home.

Because of the large number of occupants and the maintenance workload, the buildings fell into disrepair quickly. Residents had to be careful as they headed outside and be sure not to walk into an empty elevator shaft.

I remember that when I walked out on the grounds of the Jeffries Projects as a kid of six, seven, or eight years old, the air was always filled with the aroma of roaring engines and baking bread. That was because the buildings were located near a motorcycle shop and a bakery on Grand River Avenue. Today, that smell is long gone, and a large hotel and casino occupies the lot. In the evening, as previously noted, the air was filled with groups of men and women with shiny hair standing under the lampposts "doo-wopping"—singing, harmonizing, and snapping their fingers.

It was typical for a family to be outside during hot weather because of the poor ventilation and smallness of the apartments. Today, many of those same folks under the lamppost who achieved fame from their musical talents are remembered on the street signs, as the lampposts represented the first step on their long road to fame and fortune.

The Jeffries Project sat right in the shadow of Wayne State University. I always wanted to attend Wayne State. I lived in the shadows of the campus, and I always told people that the school was named for me. I remember sharing that in a job interview at the university some years later. I did not get the job.

Sometime in 1957, my father had to transfer to Twinsburg, Ohio, to keep his job at the Chrysler Corporation. He split his time between Cleveland and Detroit. Dad said that he had to take the job because he needed the work, and being laid off was no good ... although it did have some perks if you had buddies. Unemployment benefits were paid on different days of the week, so Dad and his buddies developed a system. According to my father, it was the responsibility of the person who received his unemployment benefits that day to buy the drinks. For example, if Dad got his check on Tuesday he would buy, and in return, when his friend got his benefits on Thursday the friend would buy. Since they had very little money coming in, the participants would buy the cheapest ingredients available to make what was called a Hobo Cocktail during their drinking days. The mixture was cheap wine and a forty-ounce beer. A later generation called the concoction Sneaky Pete. No matter the name, personalities tended to change after a few swigs.[91]

My mother and brothers would take long walks around the neighborhood with my youngest brother, Bobby, in his stroller. Other times we would cross the bridge over the John C. Lodge Freeway and head for the swimming pool on the corner of Forest Avenue. Sometimes we would walk to pick up an allocation of government surplus; we called it "commodity cheese." My mother made the greatest grilled-cheese sandwiches in the world from that surplus.

On occasion, we walked down Trumbull Avenue south to the corner of Michigan Avenue where Briggs Stadium was located, toting a full picnic basket. My friends Chili Carlson, Eric Inkster, and Alvin Tucker would sometimes walk with us. We were good friends, fourth-degree knuckleheads, and we all attended Poe Elementary School on West Canfield Street. Okay, there is that word association again: po, Poe, poor.

THE DISGRUNTLED MOVE TO CLEVELAND, OHIO

For my father, driving between Cleveland and Detroit took its toll. In 1959, he made a decision to move the family to Cleveland. Notice I said my *father* made the decision. That meant trouble with my mother. Years later, my mother disclosed to me that she was not a listener, and as I remember, she is right. She did not listen too much to what others had to say. My mother resisted the move for a million reasons known only to her, but the most obvious were my little sister, Glenda, who was an infant, and the fact that most of my mother's siblings lived in Detroit. There were a few of her stepfamily members living in Cleveland, but most of her blood relatives lived in Detroit.

One day after school ended for the summer, Dad pulled up in the parking lot of the Jefferies Project with a rental truck for loading up the household goods, but according to Dad, my mother would not budge. Time was a-wastin', and it took several hours to convince her that moving to Cleveland was the right thing to do. Finally, the rental truck was filled with our stuff. My father drove the truck with my brother Glen and me right there on the front passenger seat. The marching orders heading east on Route 2 to Cleveland, I was told, was my mother following behind us in the car with my brother Bobby and my sister, Glenda, driven by my father's cousin Doris and her husband, Paul McClain. Doris was also from Rocky Hill. She moved to Detroit with her siblings Alberta and

Ervell and her mother, Nora, in the late 1940s. Her late sister Alberta would have been a great contributor to this effort on family heritage.

Once we got to Cleveland, my father took us to a small house on Decker Avenue he'd rented from a fellow worker. This small house was located in the back of the main house and had a 1/2 in its address. This place was small for a family of six, and it was home to giant water bugs that appeared in the bathroom sink every morning. I remember, because at the time I was the only child old enough to go to school, so I had to get cleaned up and then head off to Wade Park Elementary School.

THE LONGWOOD PROJECTS

Sometime later, Dad moved us to another public-housing complex, the Longwood Projects.[92] These projects were tri-level buildings constructed between the years 1957–1958 along Scovill Avenue as a Cleveland urban-renewal project. We lived on the third floor at 3652 Scovill Avenue. Our unit was not as high as in the Jefferies Project in Detroit, but it had the same ventilation flow. I remember there were two streets named Scovill. The commercial businesses and public housing were located on what was called "long Scovill," whereas "short Scovill" led to the Woodland Cemetery. The projects were brand new, clean, and free of giant water bugs. But forty years later, when I returned to Cleveland for a visit, the complex was in ruins.

During the 1950s and 1960s, the United States and the Soviet Union were highly engaged in the Cold War.[93] The people living in the apartment complex all seemed to be very civic-minded and felt a need to exhibit good citizenship. I remember going to meetings hosted by the Civil Air Patrol and learning what to do in time of disaster. Although we lived on the third floor, I remember having a small garden in the rear of my project building down under the shadow of our kitchen window. I was in the Boy Scouts, and I was trying to earn a merit badge. It was from this agricultural project that I learned that I did not acquire a green thumb from my ancestral tree. That garden was the only real disaster I experienced during that period of the Cold War. I do remember kissing my first girl in the bushes not far from my garden spot. I think she was probably trying to show me her garden.

The businesses operating on "long Scovill" filled the street with sights and smells that attracted customers. People always seemed to line up to buy food at the Red Devil BBQ Hut, especially on the weekends. Then there was the man pushing his food cart and shouting "Hot tamale, hot tamale, here!" There was also a place that sold ice cream through a walk-up window. Once I saw a Great Dane dog that was so long that he could touch the top of the ice-cream place with his paws when he stood.

My brothers and I found new friends: Marvin Burge, Babe, Cleo, Tweet, Rob, Donald Perry and his brothers, Bruce and Robert. All were fourth-degree knuckleheads. Most of us attended Longwood Elementary School, where the strict Mrs. Olivia Schneider was the school principal and my mother was involved with a lot of school activities. If the main baseball diamond was occupied, we would play ball in the school playground—and yes, I could hit the ball way over the fence.

We got together and rode our bikes through a place we called Hobo Junction. It was located near a large open-air fruit and vegetable market. This section of ground was an open field filled with vagrants and people without steady work, all living and sleeping mostly in makeshift quarters outdoors. There were broken glass bottles everywhere. We would ride with agility to avoid the glass and speed to avoid the outstretched hands of vagrants. In another open field, a church building had been torn down to make way for the building of a new college. We would catch grasshoppers and roast them on an open flame, just for mischief, not for supper.

My closest friends were my brothers, Glen and Bobby, and it was my job as the oldest to watch out for them. As I recall, we were always together, either in our own room sleeping or playing; when we visited relatives, we slept on the floor together. We ate together, and we watched our favorite vampire show on our black-and-white television together. At

Christmastime, we enjoyed opening our gifts together in the early hours of the morning.

In the 1950s, as we grew up, there were few dolls, toys, games, television programs, or movies I recall that were Afrocentric. All of the dolls, toys, games, movies, and television programs were Eurocentric. For the growing mind of a young black kid, it seemed as though all of the stuff considered to be beautiful was represented as white, and all of the stuff considered to be ugly was depicted as black.[94] There were no heroes with black hats or black faces; all of the heroes were white. I think social media and marketing strategies have made inroads on changing attitudes as society progressed into the twenty-first century.

My friends and I got into very little trouble, except for lightweight rock-throwing fights with a group of boys living in a project complex across East 40th Street. I could run pretty fast. I tossed my rocks and was halfway home, but I could not go home without Glen and Bobby. Man, they were the slowest runners in the whole world. I would have to go back to help them move along. Once I got hit with a brick in the back and limped home. My mother took me to a lady in the building who was a nurse, and she patched me up. If I would have left my brothers, the pain would have been much greater.

KEEPING THE FAMILY CAR ON THE ROAD

As stated, my father grew up on a farm in the back country of Kentucky, and he was always working on either his job or his car. The story goes that the first car my father bought from a used-car dealer in Detroit broke down as soon as he drove it off the lot with me, an infant, and my mother inside. The car was a 1950 Buick Super, two-tone green in color. Evidently, the car looked magnificent sitting there on the car lot, but when it was cranked up to be driven it was a piece of junk that needed engine oil, transmission fluid, and coolant every day of the year.

My parents laughed about that incident years later, but I am sure it was not so funny at the time. There was very little a consumer of color could do about poor quality or service in the 1950s. There were few or no Lemon Laws or guarantees on consumer products at the time.[95] Poor-quality products and untrustworthy shady salesmen were the primary reason, I learned, why Negroes did not trust people in business.[96]

The city of Cleveland sits right on Lake Erie, and the winters can be very cold. My father did not have any hobbies that he shared with us. On many days, he was bundled up from head to toe repairing his car, a black Oldsmobile with the word "HAWK" etched across the hood in white, so that he could make it to work in Twinsburg, Ohio. I learned later the etching on the car was a nickname given to him at the plant. He did not play with us that much, and he was not the hugging-and-kissing type, but I do remember that he held me up as I learned to ride a bike in between the time he was making car repairs. One thing I do remember is that we always drove in the family car on a Sunday outing after church, to family friends' houses or family trips to Euclid Beach.

BLACK ASPHALT AND BASEBALL CARDS

The project grounds featured a large black asphalt recreational area in back of the complex with a baseball field, basketball court, and playground area with swings and things. A track ran between the baseball diamond and the housing area. I was a good all-around athlete, but I was turned off by basketball. I could play the game pretty well, but we could not play on Sundays because all of the cool cats—guys who worked blue-collar jobs all week—gathered in their cool clothes to drink alcohol, gamble, and fight in front of the basketball nets until the cops came. At the time, I was not a cool cat, so my love for the game of basketball was impacted by callous behavior that was ego-driven and whining.

There was a grassy area on the corner where football or soccer was played. One of my friends, Larry Battle, broke his leg running into a tree when he slipped on the grass adjacent to the asphalt playground. He was our first casualty. The second casualty was probably a result of our inquisitive minds. My friends and I were too aggressive with the playground intern and her body. She was young, shapely, and black. That behavior of the 1960s—the encroachment of personal space by a healthy growing boy—would surely not be tolerated in this day of women's rights. Maybe that is why I got bit in the butt by a German shepherd one summer on that asphalt baseball field as payback for my inquisitive but aggressive behavior.

My friends and I played baseball on a black asphalt baseball field. If you fell, slipped, or slid on that hot asphalt, you were scarred up pretty good in the spot that hit the ground. I remembered an older kid named Jackie Thigpen threatened my life when he informed me that no matter how hot the asphalt was, if I missed a baseball, I'd be dead. I quickly became a better ballplayer.

We collected baseball cards with bubblegum inside. Long before there were automated video games, we would make baseball cards come alive under the big beautiful Cleveland sky in the summertime. Our imagination allowed us to become Willie, Mickey, Al, Johnny, or whatever name was on the baseball card.

I was a rich young man because I had a ton of valuable baseball cards, and all the gum that came with them. Of course, I paid the price for the gum in later years at my dentist's office. I went to the poorhouse—okay, there's that word again—when my mother threw my cards away claiming they attracted roaches. Truly, she did not understand the value of baseball cards. Today, those same cards in mint condition would be worth hundreds, if not thousands, of dollars.

The Longwood Project complex was located close enough to Cleveland Municipal Stadium that when the American League Cleveland Indians hit a home run, we could hear the fireworks. When you were headed downtown to attend a game, the first sight you would see was the giant face of Chief Wahoo on the side of the stadium. Sometimes we got free tickets from a community organization to go to the ball game. One year I remember seeing the great Willie Stargell as a rookie for the National League Pittsburgh Pirates play an exhibition game at Municipal Stadium. Then, another year, the National League

Cincinnati Reds came to play an exhibition game in Municipal Stadium. But I do not recall seeing the banished Pete Rose play that day.

I dug the National League because each year John H. Johnson's *Ebony* magazine[97] would feature the pictures of Negro ballplayers, and it was obvious the National League had more Negro ballplayers than the American League. There were two black ballplayers who played for the Indians, Willie Kirkland and Willie Tasby, who lived in the same project I did. We would run up to their doors, ring the bell, and run. Of course, we were just stupid little kids.

I remember many of the other Cleveland players, including Leon "Daddy Wags" Wagner, Jim "Mudcat" Grant, Luis Tiant, Vic Davalillo, Max Avis, Jim Perry, John Romano, and Big Joe Adcock. Then there was Vic Power at first base, always trying to pull the hidden ball trick on the opposing team's base runner. The television announcers for Cleveland were Ken Coleman and Herb Score. The most dramatic baseball game I witnessed at Cleveland Municipal Stadium was in the summer of 1962 when Mickey Mantle hit a tape-measure pinch-hit home run in the eighth inning to dead center field, way back in the bleachers. It was amazing. I know Mickey Mantle was paid to swat home runs, but I learned later that he had been injured or was maybe even under the influence of alcohol when he was at bat.[98]

Marriage or Matrimony: A Strategic Alliance in the Civil-Rights Era

My parents were raised as Christian people, and as far I know, they never engaged in criminal or profane behavior. They smoked cigarettes, I presume because smoking was popular. They ultimately quit that bad habit over the years. When it came to alcohol, my father agreed with Ray Charles's 1966 hit recording "Let's Go Get Stoned,"[99] especially when Ray sang the line, "Ain't no harm, to go out to get a little taste!" To the chagrin of my mother, there were many days when my father arrived home from work under the influence of alcohol. Then he would ask, "Somebody put Joe Simon[100] on the piccolo!" That really meant he wanted to hear his favorite singer on the stereo.

Growing up, I remember that my father did not speak very much unless he did have a little taste. He always seemed passive in nature, only worrying about tomorrow until it was here, saying, "We'll see how the wind blows tomorrow," until the cap on the bottle or can was snapped or uncorked. In later years, my father disclosed that he was not a public speaker. On the occasion when he did speak wisdom, it was proverbial: "Boy, the old folks say ...!" My father would get a little upset when people misspelled his name. He would correct them by spelling his name out, "R-E-U-B-E-N," and then say, "like in the Bible!"

In contrast, where Dad was not much for words, my mother made up the difference. A woman of power in red lipstick, she participated in many community activities in Cleveland. She was an active participant of the Parent–Teacher Association, the Cub Scout and Boy Scout programs, and the church choir at Triedstone Baptist Church down the street. On one occasion, she met Dr. Martin Luther King.

My mother represented the family on all formal or business matters, either in person or on the telephone. She would use or speak her husband's given name, "Reuben Davidson," in a manner of precise enunciation. Years later, in my academic work, I learned and wrote that when women are in charge, as it is in a matriarchy, the leadership attributes in males are not developed. Having a mother who was not a listener and a father who was not a public speaker could be a challenge to the development of any type of personality, especially the alpha male.[101] Typically, this type of male is seen as aggressively competitive in acquiring position or standing, human resources, and social contact.

"Hey Baby, You Got Any Bread Over There?"

I am sorry to say that I don't remember my parents sharing a laugh, kidding around, or taking part in horseplay just between each other—as couples in love do—in front of my siblings and me. On Sunday, Dad would tie the dress ties my brothers and I wore to church if the selected tie was not a clip-on. Then he would sit back down in his chair dressed in a worn-out undershirt, have a "taste," and relax. My mother would be upset at my father for not going to church. Dad said he was tired from working all week and that he wanted to sit and watch cowboy movies—or "shoot-'em-ups," as he called them—on the television, a pastime that he enjoyed all of his life. In this state, my father was kind of a quiet and dormant person. But if he had a "taste," he seemed more jovial, humorous, and conversational.

My mother addressed my father as "Dave" when talking to him at home. My father called my mother using the following phrase: "Ly-di-ah!" If he was talking to us kids, he would say, "your mother."

My father is a meticulous eater. One could even say that he is a connoisseur at the dining table. He used sophisticated skill to cut his entrée and to mix and mash his potatoes with his vegetables. As a younger man, he did not care much for salad and called the green stuff "rabbit food." On the other hand, bread has to be his first love when he sits down to dine, especially cornbread. That is when the most anticipated phase uttered at the Davidson dinner table was heard. He would call out to my mother, "Hey, baby, you got any bread over there?" This was his routine even when he was in hot water for not bringing all of his earnings to the house. When that event happened, my mother did not cook for him. Nonetheless, Dad maintained his sophistication, eating canned tuna or potted meat with crackers instead. My father still salivates over my mother's culinary skills more than three years after she passed on.

PRESIDENT KENNEDY; THE DAY THE VOICE STOOD STILL

On Friday, November 22, 1963, I was a seventh-grader at Kennard Junior High in Cleveland, Ohio. At the beginning of the afternoon, my teacher, Mr. Calhoun, a very light-skinned Negro with straight hair, rushed back in the classroom and told us that President Kennedy had been shot and later died in Dallas, Texas.[102] This event greatly impacted my life, not necessarily because of the murder of the president, but for what Mr. Calhoun said to me.

After Mr. Calhoun reported the event, I evidently had a nonchalant smile on my face and said, "Aw, you're joking!" Mr. Calhoun quickly rebuked me with a tongue-lashing that I still haven't recovered from to this day. After that incident, I never spoke in another class the rest my academic life, as an adolescent or teen. I resigned from speaking and only spoke when spoken to. Johann Wolfgang von Goethe, a German philosopher, stated "the person born with a talent they are meant to use will find greatest happiness in using it."[103] But my vocal talents went dormant and hid in a shell. That nonchalant smile became my natural expression and later served as a lifesaving asset.

Despite this tragic event and personal embarrassment, I still enjoyed going to school. Although I suddenly became a quiet person, I was a good student and participated. I got stars on my report cards to prove it, but over the years my mother threw my old report cards out. I especially enjoyed field trips to the symphony to hear the orchestra play *Peter and the Wolf.*[104]

My two favorite teachers were black females: Ms. Keith, who was tall and lean, and Ms. Peck, who was short and vivacious. Both were nicely proportioned. They weren't my favorites because of their academic presentation, but because they surely were the finest-looking teachers I ever saw. At that time, in the Cleveland Public System, it was acceptable to punish students using a paddle, rod, or stick to rap on the knuckles, the open hand, or the buttocks to get their attention. Both women reprimanded me at least once, and it still stings today. In the words of risqué soul singer Millie Jackson, "It hurts so good!"[105]

The Great Jim Brown

Another event that impacted my life enormously was meeting Jim Brown, the great football player for the Cleveland Browns.[106] He is considered by many to have been the greatest football player ever and a real live superhero. As a kid, I attended only one football game at Cleveland Municipal Stadium. It was the Cleveland Browns versus the Pittsburg Steelers featuring Big Daddy Lipscomb and John Henry Johnson. I remember that game well because Big Daddy died a short time after. As a fan, I watched the Cleveland Browns on our black-and-white television purchased from Western Auto all the time. One Sunday, early in the history of the Dallas Cowboys, I remember watching Jim Brown run through and around the Cowboys defense like they were not even there, as I ate my mother's Sunday savory pot roast.

There was one cold and wintery day in Cleveland when my brother Glen and I were outside playing football with our friend Biff. My favorite player at the time was Johnny Unitas of the Baltimore Colts, so I wore my "Johnny U" helmet, a white football helmet with a *U* painted on each side. After tossing the ball around a few times and tackling each other in the snow, Biff said, "Jim Brown is up at my house visiting my sister."

Of course, who is going to believe another eleven- or twelve-year-old making a claim like that? We shouted back, "Jim Brown ain't at your house!"

He said it again: "Jim Brown is up at my house visiting my sister."

Then came the challenge. My brother and I shout back to Biff, "Okay then, show us!"

So we walked over to Biff's apartment complex and up to his apartment on the third floor. Biff opened the door and we walked inside. On the couch was a neatly dressed Negro male. Biff shouted, "I told you Jim Brown was at my house!"

When Jim Brown stood up from the couch and extended his hand to shake mine, I realized I had come upon the tallest and most chiseled black man I had ever seen. Years later, in my memory, I am still looking up at him, and I was a tall boy who grew to be six foot three inches.

As we shook hands, Jim Brown said, "Howdy partners!" We talked with him for a few more minutes and then the three of us—Biff, Glen and me—headed back downstairs and outside with excitement and glee. We had just met the world's greatest football player, and he was built solid as a stone wall. When we got outside, we looked over into the parking lot, and there was a beautiful green Chrysler automobile that looked special-parked there. The car looked like money, and it belonged to Jim Brown, the greatest football player who ever lived. We admired the car, but we did not guard the car. We headed back onto the frigid football field to practice our own skills so we could make money and buy our own set of wheels.

FIRST TRUE LOVE

If the truth be told, I liked football, but I loved baseball. I liked the Cleveland Indians, but I loved the Detroit Tigers because the team reminded me of home. Especially the 1961 Detroit Tigers[107] featuring Al Kaline, Norm Cash, and Rocky Colavito, who won over 100 games over a 154-game season yet still came up short, losing the American League pennant to the powerful New York Yankees. I remember the game announcer would always say that the girls came to the baseball game to see the handsome Rocky Colavito. This was also the year when several players on both teams challenged Babe Ruth's home run record of sixty-one finally broken by Roger Maris of the New York Yankees on the final day of the regular season.

Each summer the gang played Little League baseball. We got up early in the morning, hopped on our bikes, and headed to the baseball diamond, where we would spend most of the day. I was a good ballplayer. I learned to be a good player because remember I told you about the older kid who told me one day after a ground ball rolled up and hit me in the throat that he was going to kick my ass if I missed another ball? I have had zero errors since that day on a dirt or asphalt field.

As I got better, my favorite position became centerfield, and I was selected to play on the Little League all-star team. I was happy, excited, and preparing for the big leagues, but my joy was short-lived. During the summer is when my father took his vacation, and the summers were the only time my parents had the chance to visit their families living in the

South. There would be no all-star game for me. I loved to play baseball. I was my team's best player and I wanted to play in the all-star game. I have not forgotten, and I am still haunted by the missed opportunity to this very day.

Visiting the Folks Down South

Okay, it is June or July, time to take a disappointed me and head south with the family on our annual vacation trip. When my family headed south, it was to one of three places:

1. Barren County, Kentucky, where my father's family lived;
2. Hardeman County, Tennessee, where my mother's family lived;
3. Louisville, Kentucky, where those from both families who got off the farm first but chose not to cross the Ohio River for whatever reason lived.

Of course, I would rather be playing baseball, but my complaints fell on deaf ears. Instead, I looked for ballparks from the backseat of the car as we headed south. If I saw a ballpark along the way, we did not stop. This was the 1950s and 1960s, and we were not tourists stopping to sightsee as we tried to make our way south in one piece.

A big green Buick sedan had by now replaced the big black Oldsmobile sedan. Another interesting story for later is that my father worked for the Chrysler Corporation but owned General Motors automobiles. This was an interesting observation. Years later, as an automotive worker in my own right, I learned that Ford workers owned Ford products, General Motors workers owned General Motors products, but Chrysler workers owned Ford and General Motors products. It suggests the question, if the cook does not eat his own cooking, then why would anyone else?

Anyway, my two brothers and I sat in the back jockeying for a window seat. Bobby was the smallest and always ended up in the middle, wielding some rapid-firing toy gun and causing destruction. Glen sat on the rear passenger side reading books, and I sat on the rear driver side thinking about a baseball diamond or women. Dad was the primary driver; my little sister, Glenda, sat in the middle clinging to our mother, who sat in the front passenger side.

My father might have been the primary driver of the vehicle, but wherever my mother sat was the primary command control seat. From this location, she controlled all of the goodies: food, water, and money. Road cuisine included snacks of convenience: fried chicken, boiled eggs, potato chips, and select fruits, all washed down with a swig of Kool-Aid. My mother also maintained authority on when and how the automobile was to be driven, to include direction, speed, and the interval between other vehicles, plus when to stop for gas. I think my mother controlled the whole world of her family, including the intimacy.

The primary control seat also provided Mother with easy access to highway foliage that quickly became switches if she thought we were getting out of control with our behavior. If you do not know what a switch is, it is a long, lean, sturdy limb from a wild bush that grows along the highway. When it was swung against the air current with female force, it left a whelp on a kid's unprotected legs that left the kid crying. My mother would say, "Dave, pull over!" She would get out of the car to pull a firm branch from its roots or stalk and then get back in the car and start thrashing it about the backseat.

I was a witness to the potential destructiveness of a switch and the sound it made as it cut through the air to strike human body parts. I cried before she even started. Ironically, my brother Glen never seemed to cry after getting a whopping. He always seemed to block the switches with the comic books he was reading. Then he seemed to defiantly stare back at my mother. Glen was an avid reader of everything from Spiderman[108] to Iceberg Slim[109] to Donald Goines.[110] The use of a switch was Parenting 101 in the pre-21st-century era. Today, the act of spanking may bring a criminal indictment on the parent.[111]

Another aspect of the time in which I grew up was the contrast in the way families on the television interacted and conversed versus the way my family interacted and conversed. Television families always held conversations that appeared to include both characters. The role of the father was much greater and clearly defined. For example, television shows in 1950 and 1960 like *Leave it to Beaver*[112] or *The Adventures of Ozzie and Harriet*[113] featured a father, a mother, two sons, and their friends interacting with each other. Of course, it turns out that utopia communities on which the television families are modeled do have social ills, and the real residents are not so squeaky clean. Exhaustive investigative reporting in the twenty-first century indicates that bad behavior does exist in the white community.[114] But in either case, there was little resemblance to me and my family.

In my family, I felt there was very little conversational dialogue among family members because my father was busy fixing the car and my mother was busy cooking, leaving little time to learn or understand who a person was or aspired to be. Unlike the families on television, my mother's role always seemed greater in the reality of my family circle. Additionally, in my youth, there was no television show that featured the interaction of black family members until *Good Times*[115] and *The Jeffersons*[116] in the 1970s and *The Cosby Show*[117] in the 1980s.

As previously mentioned, when my family traveled, my mom controlled all the assets, everything, the food, the water, the money, the switches, and the conversation. She also controlled the map and made the decision of the direction in which she wanted the car to go. I often pondered why this was so and why we were often herded as a group instead of nurtured as individuals. When there is herding going on, in my opinion, there is no opportunity for individual expression. My mother subscribed to what she called the Bible adage that children should be seen and not heard. However, I learned later that this adage was not from the Bible but from the time of the Middle Ages in Europe, and it meant young maids should be seen and not heard.[118] Later, I found that the Christian Bible actually encouraged the free expression of children. Relative to Negroes, this adage was probably modified for the Negro child's own protection during the time of slavery, just for a disciplining

Negro parent's convenience or part of the "be safe" speech before kids left the house for outdoor activities. I conclude that there was lots of love in my parents' house but very little romance.

Taking a Safe Southern Route

For years, African-American families had to be selective of the route they took and the places they stopped, especially in the South. During the Eisenhower administration, the Interstate Highway system was under construction to accommodate travelers.[119] However, people of color understood they had to be selective, because they did not have the liberty to stop off on many primary and secondary roads or anywhere they pleased to seek supplies and services, especially if they were males. This understanding was well known among the black entertainment population as they traveled from venue to venue.[120]

As I described in the part I of this trilogy, since the Reconstruction period, thousands of black males and some females had been lynched in South and select Northern states for reasons unknown, other than the color of their skin. The Tuskegee Institute reported that from 1872 to 1946, there were at least 3,455 recorded lynching in the United States, with the 1890s being the most brutal.[121] Recall that the census of 1890 was destroyed by fire. Then there was the matter of vagrancy. If a black person was just standing about a public thoroughfare, he or she was subjected to incarceration for vagrancy and sent to the work crew or chain gang for a time period unknown. A black person always had to be in motion, especially a black male. From research and experience, it seemed that the greater role of a black woman was less threatening to a white public than that of a black male.

In our travels south from either Detroit or Cleveland, we always seemed to stop in Dayton, Ohio, first. For our family, it was the planned stop in the North before we crossed over the big river into Kentucky. That is where my father's older brother, O'Neil, and his family lived.

Although O'Neil was my father's older brother, he had children who were younger than we were.

After a short visit in Dayton, we would continue down to Louisville, Kentucky. When we arrived in Louisville, it was probably not right to call the city "country," because it had the same hustle and bustle of any Northern city. There were areas with nice houses, and there were areas with houses that were not so nice. There was no utopia—the South had knuckleheads too!

LOUISVILLE KENTUCKY AND NO RED MEAT

While in Louisville, my mother always seemed to have us under even more strict control, regulating our conduct and whereabouts because we stayed at the houses of her older sisters and the houses were very nice. My mother did not want us to get her on their bad side. We had to eat everything on our plates. What we did not know was that her eldest sister, Aunt Lucille, was a vegetarian and did not eat or serve red meat. Hey, what up with that? My brothers and I—not to mention Dad, a meticulous carnivore—did not sign up for that.

I wondered how I could become the home-run king being a vegetarian, or how Dad could work on automobiles at the factory without a slice of meat on a plate, because meat was a source of protein for superheroes. I learned later it was Aunt Lucille who raised my mother while my grandmother, Roxie, worked in the fields. Subsequently, it was my mother who helped watch over Lucille's children occasionally as they grew up in the 1930s and 1940s. That old adage that children should be seen and not heard may have incubated in my Aunt Lucille. We could not touch anything, and we had to eat what was placed before us simply because my mother did not want us to embarrass her. Well, little did my mother or aunt know that my older male cousins, Charley and Buford Jr., had adult magazines hidden in their rooms that kept my brothers and I occupied and quiet during our meatless visit.

ROCKY HILL, KENTUCKY, BY THE LIGHT OF THE FIREFLIES

After a few days of visiting Louisville or Dayton, we would head further south to Barren County, Kentucky. Barren County, the ancestral home of my father, is—as I remember it as a youngster—definitely the back country. There were trees, rolling green pastures, crops, and animals everywhere. I remember when my father drove by a familiar stockyard, he began hollering at the mules and the other livestock walking around in between the fences. My brothers looked at each other and wondered if Dad had lost it, talking to the farm animals out loud. Then he talked about who lived here and who lived over there. A mile or two later, we turned into a long gravel driveway up to my grandparents' house in Rocky Hill, a long way from Detroit or Cleveland.

There were no skyscrapers or freeways as a backdrop. My grandparents' house sat alongside the wood line. To my brothers and me, the forest was a little creepy because it was alive with strange sounds both day and night. Rocky Hill is located in the vicinity of the Mammoth Cave,[122] which was established as a national park in 1926 and is officially known as the world's longest cave. Before my father learned that he had grown up near a national park, he remembered when he was a child playing and exploring caves and their entryways with his brothers. The spookiness of the forest probably came from the inhabitants of the cave: bats, crickets, salamanders, water creatures, and surface animals. At night, it seemed that fireflies were the only source of light.

This area is truly dangerous. In nearby Bowling Green, at the National Corvette Museum, a sinkhole swallowed no less than eight classic Corvette cars in 2014.[123] I know now that when my father was growing up in Rocky Hill, there was no place for a young black kid to play sandlot or organized basketball or baseball. As a result, my father acquired no boyhood love of sports.

GRANDPA ERNEST: LIVING AND WORKING IN TOBACCO COUNTRY

I'm not sure that my paternal grandfather, Ernest Davidson, knew of his Ashanti roots or his slave ancestors, or knew that his surname was connected to the George Washington family tree.[124] I remember him as a quiet, stoic, and slender man with glasses and noticeably grey hair. I was told later that he was very talkative, a stern disciplinarian, and a man of great moral conviction. From that background, I learned Ernest also smoked a pipe that may have contributed to him having only one lung and a number of other ailments at the time of his death. Barren County, after all, was tobacco country since colonial time.

Uncle O'Neil said that my grandfather enjoyed reading the newspaper while patting his feet. The patting of his feet may have become habit when white soldiers took his blankets and boots in France during World War I, or so the story goes. According to O'Neil, the hottest topic for my grandfather was how bad things were down South, in terms of civil rights, in states like Alabama, Georgia, Arkansas, and Mississippi, which were further south than the border state of Kentucky. My uncle's interpretation indicated that my grandfather was concerned that the civil-rights movement and marches were upsetting to what he knew as the status quo, and directing Negroes into even more of the unknown and uncertainty. I asked my father years later about why he did not get involved in the protest marches of the 1960s and 1970s. His reply, in summation, was that he had a family and he had a job, and he needed to go to work to keep both his job and his family.

My father remembered his father, Ernest, as a kind and loving man who took his boys with him everywhere in his old Model T automobile or walking. He also had the boys working odd jobs around Rocky Hill to keep them out of trouble. Ernest Davidson grew up in the middle of tobacco country and served the community in the military and as a devoted and respected church leader at Rocky Hill Baptist Church. Although Ernest had medical issues from World War I or his work as a laborer, I am told that he rarely got angry. He understood his limits as a Negro living in the South, but he stood his ground whenever he could.

As a community leader, he had input on who became sheriff, even though the sheriff would always be white. One day the local sheriff accosted a young black male during the investigation of a crime. The young man was hurt pretty good. Ernest Davidson rebuked the officer and stated that he was "hired to maintain the peace, not cause a riot!"

O'Neil tells about one trip to the mill to grind some corn for bread. That cornmeal would then be used by my grandmother, Flossie, to make biscuits. You may recall that bread has always been a staple on the Davidson table. According to my father, Reuben, biscuits were a family favorite, and some of those biscuits were called Cathead biscuits because the biscuit top had baked to a large oval shape the size of a cat's head. That delicacy would be capped off with a swig of Blue John. According to Dad, "Blue John" was the bluish-colored milk that was left after the butter was removed from buttermilk. Cathead biscuits and Blue John—what a life in the back country!

O'Neil continued on to say that, for whatever reason that day, the grinding machine would not start. But instead of finding out what the problem was with the grinder, the mill owner, a white person, cursed and blamed my grandfather, Ernest, because the machine did not work at his request. O'Neil said that my grandfather remained passive throughout the incident, understanding his limitations in dealing with white merchants. He picked up his corn and took his boys home because his goal was to feed his family and keep them safe.

My grandfather worked as a farm laborer nearly all his life. He supplemented his income by cutting and selling hogs for the winter, be it his own or for others. He also hired out and worked all day for a fee. My father tells a story of when my grandfather had hired himself out working around farm equipment. My father had brought him his lunch, and while the white crew took their lunch, my grandfather began servicing the equipment. The story goes that he was inside a machine that tied and bound wheat together, cleaning out the debris and preparing it for the rest of the day. One of the workers returning to the work site noticed the machine was turned off. He was in the process of turning the machine back on when the foreman yelled, "Hey, don't turn that thing on, Ernest is in there!" Without that warning, my grandfather would have been the victim of an avoidable farm accident.

My grandfather appears to have lived a blessed life. My dad tells of another incident when my grandfather was cutting a dead tree down along the side of a hill expecting the dead tree to fall down the hill away from where he was standing. Instead, the tree fell up the hill toward him. My father said he cried out a warning, "Run, Papa, run!" and my grandfather got away to safety in time.

GRANDMA FLOSSIE AND HER WATCHFUL EYE

I remember my grandmother, Flossie Pulliam-Hibbitt Davidson, as a dark, medium-build woman who wore glasses. Born and raised in Barren County, she kept house, raised the children, and wrung the necks of chickens for supper. Dad recalled that they had plenty of chickens, but his father seemed to like the chicken wings and his mother the feet and necks. He wondered why when there was very little or no meat on those chicken bones. Dad deduced that his parents must have eaten those parts of the chicken so that the children could have a larger portion of the chicken meat. If they were making that sacrifice for their children, everything had better be eaten on your plate after the meal was done.

In observing his mother running the household, my father stated that she was quiet in nature, an attribute he received from her. She often provided him with proverbial encouragement like, "Don't worry about the mule going blind, just keep holding the line!" I interpret her saying to mean, "Don't stop, just keep on going!" She seemed to be well liked by her neighbors, both black and white. One day, she was given an item that was very nicely made. When she came home, she showed her family and exclaimed, "Look at what my good white folks gave me!" A young boy at the time, my father responded, "Mom, there ain't no good white folks!"

Besides keeping her own house, she worked as a domestic for local white families. Uncle O'Neil said that she had to keep a very watchful eye over her children, because she understood the volatile times in which she and her family lived. O'Neil said there was a white family who lived close by with two boys and two girls who would play with O'Neil and his brothers on occasion. He said that his mother was constantly calling to her children to be careful playing with those girls. She knew the slightest provocation or misunderstanding could cause an incident across racial lines that could escalate. Her watchful eye was the equivalent of a "be safe" speech.

FARM CHORES

In fact, volatile times dictated everyone's conduct. O'Neil told me about a white employer named Mr. John Young who would never give him proper breaks from doing chores during the work week or sit at the table at the same time as him when he was being fed. He told of the time he asked to listen to the Joe Louis fight on the radio at the home of the white family he did chores for. His parents did not have a radio at the time. O'Neil said that he did not even remember who Louis's opponent was; he just wanted to hear the fight. He said the family was really nice to him until the bout ended in a Joe Louis victory, and then the family turned the radio down and told him abruptly to go home.

My grandfather kept his sons busy and out of trouble. Sometime later, when he was a little older, O'Neil worked on the railroad as a porter, which was a tough job. He recalled that the railroad conductor told him to get better at doing the job, because if he quit this job, he was going be in the army because a second war in Europe was brewing.

"Go Get 'Em, Boys!"

The family diet included rabbit, chicken, goat, and groundhog, but the primary meat staple was a cut of the domestic hog. The family owned milk cows but no beef cows. Since there was no beef, my grandfather would bring my grandmother beef stew from town when he could. There were, however, plenty of squirrels. My father tells the story that my grandmother loved the taste of squirrel.

On occasion, my grandfather would sit on the porch with his small-caliber rifle and shoot at the squirrels along the tree line of the forest near the house. When he hit one or two squirrels, he would yell, "Go get 'em, boys!" The boys would then run into the forest to retrieve the squirrels. Dad said that in the barn was a nail that was used to skin each squirrel along the back. The fresh kill of squirrels then went into the hands of my grandmother for the evening dinner table. The animal skins would be taken to town and sold.

I recall my grandparents had a wood-burning stove, and of course, when it was hot, the doors and windows were opened for ventilation. That gave more opportunity for flies to attack my food from all angles, especially my watermelon slices. It did not help that the outhouse was in the back of the house near the tree line where my grandfather shot squirrels.

I grew up in the city with indoor plumbing. In the country, water was drawn from a well or a creek for cooking, the rain provided water for bathing, and the outhouse was the place to relieve oneself. My cousin Charlie Lewis recently reminded me of the procedures for and experience of using the outhouse. There were two holes in the outhouse that could easily be occupied at the same time. For safety, we would put kerosene around the hole first before we released our waste product, because you never knew what critter might crawl out from below. Of course, I tried to hold my bodily functions, but holding it was only a short-term solution especially after eating a piece of wild game or drinking a tart country drink.

On each trip down South, I continued to learn that farm hygiene is different from city hygiene. We bathed in a large no. 3 washtub and then rinsed from a small can with a spout. In the summer, the tub was left outside so that it would fill up with rainwater for bathing. In the winter, the same tub would be filled up with heated water from the stove. I learned that my father's namesake, Alford Barclay, passed away while taking a bath, and from my experience I could understand why. This was culture shock. I was missing the city and the conveniences, because at the time, Rocky Hill in Barren County, Kentucky, was hardcore country, harsh as the down-home soap used to scrub with.

Although my mother was raised in the country on a farm, I don't think she cared too much for the ruggedness of my father's home. We never seemed to stay long when we visited Dad's family; we always stayed longer when we visited my mother's family. I do remember my paternal grandparents as nice people, and I also remember when my father received the call at our apartment in Cleveland that my grandfather had passed in 1962. I can still hear my father grieving and my mother trying to console him.

The Southern Davidson Family

One of my father's two other brothers, Rogers Charles ("RC"), and his sister, Earlene/Earline, lived in the larger metropolitan city of Bowling Green in Warren County. Coincidentally, "bowling green" is the name of the green acres that lay in front of George Washington's Mount Vernon estate in Virginia.[125] It is ironic, as the colonial lawn remains pristine to this day; three of my daughters have had the opportunity to run and frolic on the colonial turf in the twenty-first century.

I vaguely remember that my uncles, RC and Buddy, both served in the military. RC served in the army in World War II, and Buddy served in the navy during the Korean War, but their lifestyles did not lead to long-lasting success. RC died in 1990; he was the second eldest son. As I understand it, he was diabetic and had a taste for hard liquor that often kept him from following his prescribed diet. Buddy, whose real name was James Edward, was the youngest son. The story goes that he enjoyed drinking, fighting, and playing with knives. I remember when I was about ten or eleven, my father and Buddy had an altercation during one of our visits to Dayton, and liquor was involved. Later, I learned the squabble happened over the philosophy of their father, Ernest Davidson. I remember my brothers and I helped to extricate my father from the altercation with our baseball bats. We felt pretty brave that we, little kids, could help our father.

One day the combination of drinking, fighting, and playing with knives caught up with Buddy. He died as a result of a knife wound in 1977 on New Year's Eve. He was allegedly stabbed by a lady friend, and he ran out of the house for several blocks before he fell in a yard or alleyway. Normally a prayer is said when leaving a gravesite, but before leaving Buddy's on an extremely cold day more than forty years after his death, my father said painfully, "If you had listened to Papa, you would not have gotten in the mess you are in!"

As a result of the altercation, I remember my mother vowing never to return to visit my father's family ever again. My mother was very hard person to sway once she made a decision, right or wrong. Dad told me some years later that my mother sat in the car for hours rather than go inside Aunt Earlene's house.

I do remember my aunt Earlene. She and her husband, Fred Lewis, were married for sixty-four years and had seven children. I was grateful to visit with Aunt Earlene prior to her passing, because she was very helpful in remembering my grandmother. Growing up, she spent most of her time with her mother, helping with the household chores. She also worked as a domestic while she raised her own family.

From my aunt Earlene I also learned that my grandmother Flossie truly loved and missed my grandfather Ernest. Aunt Earlene found letters my grandmother had written after my grandfather passed that showed she was heartbroken and longing for his company. She was lonely for him nearly ten years before she died in 1971.

TENNESSEE-BOUND AND CHICKEN MAN

After our visit to see my paternal family, we drove south to Bolivar, Tennessee, the ancestral home of my mother's family. I never met my grandfather, Wade Cheshier; he died in 1926. However, his black-and-white photograph has been prominently displayed in many of the homes of my maternal family and friends I visited. I am told that I was named Wayne with him in mind. The story goes that Aunt Rubye suggested I would be named Wade after him, but my mother decided on Wayne. As cited earlier in the chapter, my maternal grandfather was considered a special servant to his community in helping them seek and obtain both educational and occupational opportunity.

My maternal grandmother, Roxie L. Jones Cheshier Sherley, and the Jones family are of Native American[126] descent. This fact was only oral history before DNA testing became available to the public. I remember my grandmother, Roxie, as very light in complexion, with long black hair and a strong chin.

As I said before, I remember her voice in my infancy talking to my mother, saying, "Ly-dee, lay that boy down there," "Ly-dee, this is the way you keep that boy clean," "Ly-dee, tell Dave to go down to the store and pick up some things."

When we reached Hardeman County, Tennessee, it became my mother's turn to recall her days growing up in the community. She talked about who lived in the houses we passed, where they worked in the fields, and how far they walked to school. Then we reached the city of Bolivar, and in the vicinity of her mother's house she pointed out what relative lived here and what relative lived there. My maternal grandmother's surname was Jones, and over the years I met many of my grandmother's siblings and offspring. They all had strong Native American features. I never realized that features other than skin color or hair were obvious until one day a white lady told me, out of the clear blue sky, that she knew that I had Native American heritage because of my high cheekbones.

My maternal grandfather was a Cheshier, but I do not recall meeting many of his siblings or their offspring in Bolivar. They would have been darker in complexion. I could not obtain any DNA samples to identify their African heritage. My mother stated over the years that her mother's house suffered from several fires and that a lot of family documents and history went up in smoke. My mother did not elaborate on how the fires got started, whether they were set accidentally or by arson.

My mother's second oldest sister, Oziel, lived next door. She was widowed and had given birth to four children very early in life. The first child was a girl born with a broken neck. The story goes that my grandmother, Roxie, gave instructions to two very young boys, my Uncle Robert and a nephew, to dig a grave in the Cheshier Cemetery and take the child's body for burial.

The second daughter was named Shirley Mae, and she may be my eldest cousin. A third daughter, Gloria Jean, drowned as a young girl. I remember as a boy of six years old when my mother received the phone call with the sad news. The youngest daughter was Virginia, and she has a booming voice. She said she developed it from yelling from house to house in the country. Later, she came to Detroit with her booming voice and met her future husband, Willie Scott Jr., and together they formed a gospel group called the Scott Singers. I remember them practicing on Belle Isle in Detroit as a teen. They sounded pretty good; I do not know why they did not become rich and famous from their talent. Maybe the market was oversaturated.

In the country, the basic ingredients for dinner were either growing in the garden or walking around near the garden. My younger brother Bobby chased chickens around the barnyard long before Sylvester Stallone, as Rocky Balboa, contender for the heavyweight champion of the world, did.[127] Bobby ran those chickens so hard that Virginia nicknamed him "Chicken Man," but he never caught them. However, those same chickens could not escape the clutches of Aunt Rubye. She simply selected the hen she wanted, snatched it up, and wringed its neck, all in a compact motion. The next thing you knew, dinner was served. This city boy learned there is a difference in the way dinner tastes when you know it came out of the store versus when you know it came out of the backyard just a few short minutes ago. Nonetheless, when you are hungry, you eat what is set in front of you or you have to deal with my mother.

When asked, Aunt Rubye stated that she chose not to have children because she spent too much time raising younger brothers and sisters. As a young lady, she had plenty of suitors, because she had the look of a Lena Horne. "I'm not married" is the lie young Frank Murphy told my grandmother, Roxie, so that he could sneak Rubye off to Detroit. I am told Frank was hell-bent on splitting up Rubye and her beau, James McTizic. He succeeded; Rubye married Frank Murphy in 1941, and they went to Detroit as a couple. But soon after, Rubye had the marriage annulled. It seems young Frank Murphy had not told the truth, and he was still legally married to his first wife.

A few years later, Rubye married a man named Dukes Holland, and as my mother told me, Uncle Dukes took a shine to me as a little boy and acted as if I was his very own. My father said Dukes's favorite saying was "little poor living," for whatever that meant. Notice, there is that word *poor* again.

In the meantime, James McTizic, Rubye's childhood sweetheart, married a friend of both his and Rubye's, and their marriage produced two children. Around 1960, James became a widower; sometime after, Rubye and James rekindled their childhood affection, married, and raised the two children in Washington, DC. In late 1969, Aunt Rubye and James returned to Bolivar, Tennessee, and invested in the community. Together, "Mr. and Mrs. Mac," as they were called by the locals, opened and operated a grocery store and established a Baptist church and a day-care center over a period of thirty years.

THE LONG QUEASY DRIVE HOME

I remember once we traveled back to Cleveland from the south through a very heavy downpour that made the driving slow and dangerous. As prescribed, my father was careful where he stopped to get gas or a nap.

If he got tired, he would pull up in the hotel or motel parking lot and take a peek into the lobby from his car window, and then ask my mother, "Well, do you see any spooks in there?" What my father meant was, *Do you see any Negroes in that place?* My mother, always excitable in this situation, replied, "No, Dave, just find a quiet spot on the side of the road and rest!" And that is what he did.

In the late 1950s and early 1960s, the prime spot for resting would be near the Greyhound bus terminal and White Castle restaurant, especially if you had children. There was access to a bathroom and a hamburger.

It was tough riding behind the driver seat when the goal was to make time and ride through without stopping. For boys riding in the backseats and sitting in close quarters, there are always bodily functions happening along the road to make you sick. It could be the leaking of human gas or spittle from a fellow backseat rider, or even spillover from the front seat. Once my father spat out his open driver's window and the residue hung on my closed rear window for hundreds of miles. Truth be told, my stomach is still queasy today from that trip of more than fifty years ago.

TEENAGER: PONDERING THE NEXT STEP

In 1964, I had become a teenager preparing for my next step: high school. The school I attended, Kennard Junior High, was a feeder school to East Tech High. Two Olympic gold medalists in track and field, Jesse Owens[128] and Harrison Dillard,[129] had both attended East Technical High years before. I recall Dillard provided inspiration to our student endeavors when he spoke during an assembly one day and emphasized focus because the world is conquerable.

I was excited when one day in swim class, the Kennard coach recruited me for East Tech football. Subsequently, my mother took me to my preliminary physical examination, where I learned I had funny-growing knees. Evidently, my height had grown faster than my knees could catch up. What a bummer! I had already been wearing glasses for a year or two that I hated. Believe me, wearing glasses of any kind was not as popular as the many fads that followed. Now I couldn't ever become a cool cat. I had great hands, so I still played sandlot football for a short while, until the pulling guard reminded me baseball was my true sport by sticking his helmet in my stomach on an end run.

During the summer of 1964, I smashed my left hand through a window while chasing my brother Glen during a visit to Aunt Rubye's house in Washington, DC. We had taken a family visit to John F. Kennedy's grave site. My brother Glen and I stayed for the remainder of the summer. After the accident happened, my cousin Towana and my brother wrapped my hand with a towel while Aunt Rubye rushed home from her place of business to get me to the hospital. The closest hospital did not take me for whatever reason, I did not know, I was a juvenile from out of town. So Aunt Rubye took me to another hospital, where I ended up getting twenty-five stitches in my lower left hand and baby finger. I learned later that Washington, DC, was a segregated city, may be the most segregated in the nation in 1964. Instead of just getting ice cream to ease the pain, Aunt Rubye and Uncle James took us to Coney Island, New York, later during our visit.

When I returned to Cleveland from vacation, I remember lying around the swimming pool at the recreation center staring toward my next destination: East Tech High School. No matter the physical condition of my knees or my new glasses I was a good athlete. Still, I was unable to get my parents to sign the athletic consent form, my youthful aspiration to be a hometown sports hero was in jeopardy. Well, I guess it really didn't matter. Not long after, my father got a transfer back to Michigan, and he took the whole family with him on the return trip at the end of the school year.

Back in the Motor City

I don't remember the trip back to Detroit in 1965 to be as chaotic as the trip eight years before. I don't recollect that my father had to pry my mother from the apartment in Cleveland for the return trip. Although we'd visited Detroit off and on during our eight-year absence, moving back to the Motor City was a little different. We had become outsiders, and ever since then I've come to ponder that I may have left my true peer group in Cleveland.

We moved to a rented apartment in a four-family flat located at 1965 Blaine Avenue between 12th and 14th Streets. My mother's sister, Mildred, and her husband, GW Raspberry, lived on the same block, two streets over on Pingree Avenue. We'd visited them and Aunt Wadean often when we made our many trips to Detroit and played up and down the halls of their apartment buildings. At the time, we owned a green 1962 Buick four-door sedan, and I remember when the Rolling Stones' recording "(I Can't Get No) Satisfaction"[130] blared out of the radio. My mother would say it was noise and turn the radio to a gospel station, and then start singing and clapping along as if she was in church. I learned later that Mick Jagger, the lead singer for the Rolling Stones, was greatly influence by the music and performances of James Brown, the great soul performer.[131]

I attended Hutchins Junior High School, located on Woodrow Wilson Avenue, as Otis Williams, cofounder of the Temptations, the deity above musical singing groups, and Lamont Dozier, a popular singer and songwriter, did in the early 1950s.[132] Years later, I learned that in his day, President Woodrow Wilson was not a great friend to the Negro people. But the street the school and the recreation center were located on was named after him, and both were in walking distance of our apartment building.

I mentioned that the environment in Detroit was a little different from the one in Cleveland. Maybe Detroiters lived in a little faster lane than Clevelanders. This was the first time I heard a group of kids my own age giving descriptions of a sexual act they had witnessed, or capping on somebody, the verbal practice on urban street corners of talking about somebody's family member, most often the mother.[133] I did not feel like part of the group, and I do not recall making many friends at either the school or the recreation center. I am probably wrong, but at the time, the black folks in the area seemed less prosperous than the black folks in Cleveland. The Detroiters I encountered were proud of Motown, but instead of reading, writing, and math, the focus centered on whether the Temptations or the Four Tops was the better singing group.

I loved Motown! It seemed each Sunday on our way to the church we would drive past the 20 Grand Night Club,[134] located on 14th Street and Warren. The marquee seemed to always headline a great Motown act that I was familiar with. I could only peek out from the backseat and stare at the glitter and dream. At age fourteen upon our return to Detroit, I had no idea that Hitsville USA was located at 2468 West Grand Boulevard and its family of performing artists lived within walking distant of the recording studio, most notably Otis Williams on Philadelphia Street, David Ruffin on Euclid Street, and Eddie Kendrick on Hanover Street.[135] The remaining group members, Melvin Franklin and Paul Williams, were most likely in the same vicinity of the music mecca. Berry Gordy, the creator of the Motown Sound, took residence on Blaine Street and at 1719 Gladstone Street.[136] Who knew that in 1965, I lived with a 1.2-mile radius of a Detroit music factory and its talented staff that made dreams come true? Man, if I'd known, I could have walked over myself. This was a missed opportunity.

In Detroit, there was always tension between folks living on the east and west sides of the city. There also seemed to be more criminal elements, activities, and malicious behavior in the neighborhood in which I lived. I remember there was a young man wearing heavy chains around his neck walking hastily across 12th Street with a chained and fierce-looking dog. The young man appeared to be beyond a fourth-degree knucklehead. He appeared to be looking for something or somebody for that German shepherd to sink its teeth into. Otis Williams remembered in the 1950s that 12th Street was known for its population of street players who had criminal intent.[137] I concur, and sadly, poor economic conditions have not allowed the street to change much since the 1960s. Another day, a group of guys we did not know tried to intimidate my brother Glen and me on the way home from school. They were around our same age and ready to begin their journey as knuckleheads through intimidation. Nonetheless, we stood our ground there just off of 12th Street. That was a day I missed both living in Cleveland and my friends.

Home Ownership

In January 1966, my parents became homeowners. They purchased a wood-frame house at 12682 Pinehurst Street on the west side of Detroit. I remember vividly when my family got out of the car to check our new home out. Across the street stood two white ladies talking. I do not recall seeing those ladies ever again after that day. No matter, my folks owned a piece of the American dream.

At the time, I was too young to know or understand that the Detroit population and housing market was in the middle of a social process called *white flight.*[138] As Negro families moved into neighborhoods, white families who could afford to move quickly crossed 8 Mile Road to suburban neighborhoods. The timing for this purchase must have been right, as I learned later that the real-estate association put great pressure and fear in the buying and selling of homes in the Detroit area.[139] Nonetheless, our new house in our new neighborhood made my parents feel prosperous.

I too felt prosperous, and I became pretty industrious. I owned a bike that took me where I needed to go. I delivered the morning newspaper, I delivered Twin Pines Milk in the morning, and I cut grass and shoveled snow around the neighborhood whenever I could. I also worked on a grounds maintenance crew at the Redford Golf Course near Redford, although I didn't really know anything about the game of golf.

On occasion, I worked at my Uncle Raspberry's Fuller Brush[140] store on Grand River near West Grand Boulevard. I would sweep the floor, dust off the stock, and run errands. Uncle Raspberry was a great fan of Berry Gordy,[141] whose Motown Studios was just up the street on West Grand Boulevard. I worked at a grocery store, Wrigley Supermarket, on

Livernois Avenue between 6 Mile Road and Curtis Avenue that some of the Motown entertainers frequented.

Later, I worked at the Elias Big Boy Restaurant on Plymouth and Telegraph Road in Redford. It is fun reminiscing about this particular job. I worked there from about 1966 until 1969, maybe not that long, but if I did not know better I'd think the popular 1970s television show *Happy Days*[142] used the atmosphere of this restaurant as its model. It was a little like a family. I remember the owner, Mr. George Curis (who may have been of Jewish heritage), the rest of employees, and the patrons were primarily white. Mr. Curis always seemed to have a cigar in his mouth. When they were not attending college, Mr. Curis taught his two sons how to run the business. Years later, when I returned to the city, I read where one son became a prominent figure in the civic renovation of East Jefferson Avenue near Belle Isle.

On Sundays, it seemed that Mr. Curis's whole family ate at the restaurant. The regular supervisors were two good-looking females: Polly, who was petite, stacked, and blond, and Cathy, who was tall, stacked, and brunette. The cooks and waitresses were mainly students working their way through college. One cook who acted goofy all the time was studying to become a medical doctor.

I remember the waitresses who worked in the dining room would get angry if somebody messed with their tips. Some of the blue-eyed carhops wore roller skates to deliver orders to the modified automobiles blasting the latest record hits on their car radios in the parking lot. Everyone appeared to be very close, working together in a cordial and friendly manner.

Hobart the Dishwasher and the Strawberry-Pie Rule

The only blacks on the premises were the busboys and dishwashers, including my friends Cleve Childs and Chili Carlson and me. All three of us attended David Mackenzie High School.[143] I'd known Chili since we were kids living in the Jeffries Project and going to Poe School in the

1950s. It was Chili who recruited me for the job. Later, other guys from the neighborhood also worked there.

I knew Cleve from high school too. Cleve was what you would call a super-cool dude who none of the extreme crazy dudes would bother. Cleve was mature beyond his age, and all the ladies seemed to like him. Plus, he knew a bit of martial arts. If there was a person a young guy would want to imitate, it would probably have been Cleve. I would not say that I was close to Cleve, but I found out he was a good person to know. Remember, it was Cleve who would later step in to save my life from an armed property owner in a dark garage.

As busboys and dishwashers, our primary job was to clear tables and wash dishes in Hobart, the commercial dishwasher. We also performed miscellaneous jobs as assigned, such as refilling the soda or milk machine, making a salad or pie, keeping the floor clean, and cleaning the kitchen when we closed. On occasion, we would help out cooking on the kitchen grill. Ultimately, Chili was promoted to cook, and Cleve was promoted to management. For a time, he managed the Big Boy restaurant located across from the MacArthur Bridge leading to Belle Isle, a location that was prevalent during the 1943 Detroit riots.

I did not progress as well as the others, but some days I had a little fun, especially when asked to make a strawberry pie, a featured dessert on the Big Boy menu. It was easy to make. The pie shell, the strawberries, and the glaze sat right there cooling in the basement storage locker. I would gather up all the contents and put them on the table and make strawberry pie. I would make a strawberry pie for them, and I would make a strawberry pie for me. I learned that everything had a price tag, however, and the philosophy I dubbed the Strawberry Pie Rule has been applicable to life situations over the years because of its mutuality. In the matter of employment, "give the man what he wants so I can get what I want."

I guess the most fun we had was when Cleve, Chili, and I got together washing dishes. Along with Hobart, the commercial dishwasher, we would harmonize and sing "doo-wop" songs in the dishwashing area. We called ourselves the Hobarts, and one of our hits was a rendition of the 1968 Temptations hits "Runaway Child"[144] or "I'm Losing You"[145] while we did the Temptations Walk in a circle with Hobart. Sometimes we would do other artists, like the Esquires' "Get on Up"[146] or Marvin Gaye and Tammi Terrell's "Your Precious Love"[147] when we took the trash out to the dumpster. A couple of us guys sounded pretty darn good.

Speaking of sounding good, in the days of Motown in Detroit, you never knew what famous star would walk into a business establishment, because the restrictive covenant applied to the rich and famous as well. A few months later, I worked at the Wrigley Supermarket on Livernois Avenue between 6 Mile Road and Curtis Avenue in Northwest Detroit. I worked as a stocker, a bagger, and a housekeeper—you know, "Clean-up in Aisle 5!" The surrounding residential area featured a lot of well-kept brick homes and seemed to have a different culture about it.

To me, the neighborhood residents had the air of professional people who spoke proper English, and they appeared to be mixed with ethnic diversity. The residents' kids went to Mumford High School,[148] where a number of former students have become celebrities in their chosen profession, like Jerry Bruckheimer,[149] producer of mega-television shows and movies, and Ivan Boesky,[150] who was convicted of insider trading in 1980s. I cast my vote to affirm that the Mumford High School of the 1960s and 1970s had the most beautiful and exotic women in the entire city, but that was just me. However, I had to change my vote in 2011 after I sat at a table at a popular dinner theater in the Detroit suburbs with two former Mumford ladies. While the Temptations provided first-class entertainment, in the midst of the performance they praised the Lord and then stiffed the waiter the price of dinner and tip for services rendered. The two ladies may have been close friends of classmate Mr. Boesky.

One day, Smokey Robinson and the Miracles came into the supermarket, and I bagged their groceries. In his autobiography, Smokey stated that he and his wife, Claudette, took up residence at 19357 Santa Barbara. That address is approximately a mile and a half from the store. In addition, his close friend Marvin Gaye and Marvin's wife, Anna Gordy Gaye, lived around the corner on Outer Drive.[151] After they left the store, I told my work buddy who also lived in the area about the celebrity shoppers. He nonchalantly responded, "Smokey is my neighbor." I could have hit him in the nose. I could not believe that he had never mentioned this important fact before. I surely would have stopped by his house to visit. Another missed opportunity.

I learned a lot about warehousing in that job, and I also learned that I was clumsy with sharp objects. My brother Glen and I bought switchblade knives to be cool. Glen could pop his blade out like they did in the movies. I had a little more difficulty mastering it. One day I was at work at the grocery store and I tried to pop my knife out, but it did not work out. Instead, I cut the inside of my thumb and bled all over some boxes in the storeroom. It took me an hour to stop the bleeding.

My brother Glen met his match against our younger brother Bobby, who not only popped switchblade knifes but also popped people with baseball bats. During the famous 1968 Super Bowl that featured Joe Namath leading the New York Jets to a win over the Baltimore Colts,[152] my brothers got into an altercation. I came home from working at the grocery store, and I noticed that Glen's head was swollen to twice its normal size. My mother said that Bobby hit Glen with a baseball bat during a disagreement. What fueled such stupidity, I will never know. Bobby began to build a reputation when he chased a couple of my buddies around our backyard with a baseball bat.

URBAN RENEWAL

Although my neighborhood in 1966 was transitioning, it still felt nice, safe, and prosperous. On my street, my parents joined the block club and participated in the neighborhood watch. Industrious people invested time and effort in keeping their properties up and their children out of trouble and off the streets. There was plenty of work in the factories, so people were employed and did not have time for shenanigans. We had a new set of friends, and we all seemed to get along well doing kid stuff.

We played baseball at the Monnier Elementary School yard located on Ward Street and Schoolcraft Avenue—and yes, I could hit a baseball onto the schoolhouse roof. We went to Sunday school at New Light Baptist Church, located on West Chicago Boulevard off of Grand River Avenue, just two or three miles from our house. We walked home most of the time, and we would window-shop along the way. We would stop at Cunningham's Drug Store at Grand River Avenue and Oakman Boulevard with the loose change in our pockets to sip a shake or a cool drink from the soda fountain.

Few in my circle of friends knew at the time how an urban renewal project, in the form of federal construction, would impact the entire neighborhood. The project was the construction of Interstate 96,[153] traveling east to west from downtown Detroit to communities in the greater Detroit metropolitan area. Just like that, urban renewal cut a path across where many of our new friends lived, where we played baseball, where we went to church, and where we shopped. It divided the neighborhood streets into upper and lower regions.

My family house on Pinehurst Street was on the south side of the new construction, so it was lower Pinehurst. The reason our house was not in the path was because there was a construction decision to bypass the shopping district that sat on Oakman Boulevard and Grand River. To say the least, it was pretty cruel. Residential homes that many people had waited all of their lives to acquire fell to the wrecking ball in the name of urban renewal.

Although my family can be considered fortunate, the construction displaced many incoming African-American homeowners who were unaware that the house they just bought was in the path of the construction. As a result, a short time later these families were again seeking to buy a home in a town where they already had limited financing options. Two obvious reasons come to bear: their personal research on the home was incomplete or the real-estate agent or seller of the home failed to disclose pertinent information. The Taylor family brought a home on Cherrylawn Street and then received official notice six months later that their newly purchased home was in the path of new construction.

As the existing homes fell to the construction, the remaining homeowners would salvage the debris to shore up their homes. Mr. Larry Ford Sr., father of Larry Jr., Sammie Lee, and Benny Ford, would have them take a wagon to the area and collect bricks and bring them back to their home on upper Griggs Street. All three would have the most despondent look on their faces as they executed their father's directive. The rest of us, free to ride our bikes, chuckled, making the situation worse.

Mr. Larry Ford Sr. had other idiosyncrasies that provided the guys with a few laughs. For instance, his sternness with his sons always gave license for the group to tease them. Probably the number-one thing we would get a kick out of was his relationship with the members of the Seventh Day Adventists.

These folks made their rounds through the neighborhood at least one Saturday per month. Typically, they knocked on a door to engage the person in a discussion about Jesus Christ, salvation, and becoming a member of their church organization. Many people in the neighborhood avoided this direct contact, but when they knocked on the door of the Ford house, they generally got more than they bargained for. Mr. Larry Ford was notorious for engaging them in religious theory, his doctrine versus their doctrine. Where others avoided the engagement, it seemed as if he looked forward to it. After many close encounters, the Seventh Day Adventist folks ran up the white flag. They avoided the Larry Ford household at all costs. Ironically, I learned later that many of my paternal and maternal relatives were members of this religious organization.

Another industrious Ford family (no relations) lived on upper Griggs across the street from Larry Ford. Nicky Ford was a skinny guy who took a lot of teasing from the guys for looking and acting like the Walt Disney character Bambi. His father, Mr. Ted Ford, was a city bus driver and always on a schedule. When it was lunchtime, he would park that big bus on Davison Avenue near the corner of Griggs and walk up to his house to have lunch. During his lunch break, Mr. Ford would give directions to his son on the chores he wanted done before he came home that evening.

Then he would hop back on the bus and head back onto the city streets to pick up passengers. When Mr. Ford got home, the grass was cut and all the other assigned chores were completed. The exterior of the house was well kept and worthy of having its picture taken for posterity. It is a shame that some thirty-five years later, that same house became dilapidated and serving as a lean-to over a dilapidated Nicky Ford, a veteran, sitting in a stupor on the dilapidated porch.

Nicky had sailed away with the US Navy for several years, and when he returned he had grown from the physical frame of a young deer to a young buck. He owned a motorcycle and a car, and he spoke differently. Nicky also acquired several adult habits: smoking, drinking, and doping. The new lifestyle most likely led to the erosion of his moral foundation. Today, neither Nicky Ford nor the house is there, only an empty lot.

CALM BEFORE THE STORM

It appeared to me that Detroit's west side was pretty tranquil. There was only one incident I recall prior to 1967 that disturbed me. It took place near where I attended school at Mackenzie High School. The school is located a few blocks from the city of Dearborn, and a short bus ride from the historic Ford River Rouge factory complex.[154] A few of the guys and I were riding our bikes in the vicinity of Dearborn when suddenly a car tried to run us down. The driver was white, and he was shouting at us. We took the driver's behavior to mean get out of Dearborn, which was the social attitude of the day.

Ironically, some twenty years later during the Persian Gulf War,[155] CNN[156] reported that the city was recognized as the Arab capital of the United States. During the Gulf War, I was stationed in Alaska as a member of the armed forces. I was astonished and unaware of the ethnic turnover. When did Orville Hubbard let this happen? The report stated that Arab-Americans comprised nearly 50 percent of the more than 100,000 people who lived there in Dearborn.[157]

There was another incident that happened in the neighborhood as me, my brother Glen, and my friend Terry Grittle walked to a basement party at a house on the other side of Interstate 96. Terry yelled a slur toward a house with white residents. The next thing I knew, we were running because there was an army of white boys filing out of that house toward where the slur came from. We got to the house party and told the folks what had happened. That gave the tough guys license to boost their knucklehead status when they went out to tango with the white boys.

I did not go. I was too busy trying to learn to dance about the basement floor to soulful slow records like Stevie Wonder's "Hey Love,"[158] the Artistics' "I'm Gonna Miss You,"[159] or Lou Rawls's "Love is a Hurtin' Thing!"[160] without having it be known to the other partygoers, especially the girls, that my body chemistry was rising. When Terry returned to the dance, he would cup his hand with his partner's and then swirl his thumbs to keep time with the music and make an attempt to be a cool cat.

I think the first time I saw a person who resembled what the media called a hippie[161] in the flesh was in 1966 or 1967. The guy and his girlfriend lived in the small apartment building on the corner of Pinehurst and Fullerton just down the street from our house. I had to be careful to whom I spoke. It was in the same block my Aunt Mildred and Uncle Raspberry had recently moved to from Pingree Street.

Both the man and the woman were white. They both dressed like hippies as shown on television and both talked about the wonders of drugs and getting high. I pinpoint this time frame as important because I was still riding my bike as my primary mode of transportation. It was a period of naivety, singing silly and playful tunes by some corny group called the Monkees[162] and then riding in peace to buy candy at Mr. Young's store on Fullerton between Manor and MonteVista streets, or venturing down to Casey's store a block further on Grand River Avenue, the main thoroughfare, or taking the big trip across Grand River Avenue to the Pinehurst store. Meeting this hippie should have alerted me, like an omen, that cannabis, opiate byproducts, and magic pills shaped like candy would soon flood my peaceful neighborhood.

The king of the P-Funk movement, George Clinton,[163] recalled in his memoir that in this period of time in American history, drugs were a communal activity, to be shared among friends. The community sharing circle was broken when someone introduced the entrepreneurial aspect. The drug substance became known as a drug product that required inventory and sales to the general population for the purpose of a guaranteed profit. As a result, the competitive drug industry was born, and many have suffered from its existence.

Beautiful Downtown Detroit

There was no place like Downtown Detroit. It had everything a visitor could desire to do or see. There were tall majestic buildings everywhere—the Fox Theatre, the Palms Theatre, the Wayne County Building, and Cobo Hall to name a few. Although the nickname for Detroit is the Motor City, you really did not need an automobile to get around unless you were particular or trying to impress your date. With a world-class public transportation system serving Detroiters, you could take the bus to and from downtown to all parts east and west, north and south.[164] I lived on the west side of Detroit, so I would catch the bus at the Washington Boulevard terminal on the west side of Woodward Avenue. I remember the shops on the street were very busy. There was a bakery, a Big Boy restaurant, a Coney Island restaurant, a steak place, a Chinese place, clothing stores, and a music store from which Aretha Franklin's voice would blast out toward the terminal. But it was to your benefit not to eat or drink too much and get sick waiting at the terminal, because the public restroom was horrendous.

There was nothing like holiday season in Detroit when the city was under the spotlight of national television, starting with the Thanksgiving Day parade's early morning march down Woodward Avenue to the front of the JL Hudson store, where Santa Claus would emerge from his sleigh to the roar of the crowd to wish everyone a Merry Christmas. My Uncle Raspberry, a black man, had a wig shop located right inside the S. S. Kresge store across the street on Woodward. At high noon, the Detroit Lions football team would face off with a tough opponent at Tiger Stadium. I watched all of these fantastic events from the living room of an aunt, uncle, or my parents where the holiday table, full of homemade goodies, was a feast fit for a king.

Thanksgiving was also the beginning of holiday shopping season. The streets and shops in downtown Detroit were full of smiling people looking for gifts. My friends and I took the bus downtown with our pockets bulging with holiday money earned from odd jobs, gifts, and allowances. We could only window-shop at the many exclusive stores, like Hudson or Crowley's, along Woodward Avenue. So we took our holiday money to Louis the Hatter, a clothing store on Woodward where all the black celebrities shopped. At least that is what they said, because there were pictures on the wall of all the Motown stars. We would head south down Woodward Avenue a block or two, turn right on Grand Circus Park, and there was Sibley Shoes. The local celebrities brought their shoes there—at least, that what they said because there were pictures on the wall of all the Motown stars. Who could doubt their claim?

The Motown Revue

In between these two stores on Woodward Avenue was the Fox Theatre. During the holiday season, Berry Gordy hosted a show there called The Motortown Revue or Motown Revue[165] that allowed Detroiters to see the Motown stars in action. The Motown Revue featured Smokey Robinson and the Miracles, Gladys Knight and the Pips, Stevie Wonder, the Marvelettes, Martha Reeves and the Vandellas, and many more. The girl groups were glamorously dressed in big wigs and evening gowns, and all the guys had slick hair and slick suits.

I remember when Bobby Taylor and Vancouvers[166] performed a rendition of Otis Redding's hit song, "Try a Little Tenderness."[167] Bobby Taylor sang the vocal and made that song his own when he changed some of the words to provide the audience with a little humor. Sometime later, group member Tommy Chong teamed up with Cheech Marin to form the comedy team Cheech and Chong.[168] The Motown Revue also put white groups on display like the Underdogs, singing a song called, "Love's Gone Bad!"[169] My brother Glen and his friends Clinton and Terry would mimic that song all the time.

My all-time favorite group is the Temptations.[170] These five guys were just fabulous at singing and dancing in concert. They were in sync with their every movement or action on stage. It must have been the lighting, but it seemed like they changed to a different-color wardrobe at least three times during their routine. All the girls loved them, and all the guys envied them. I remember seeing lead singer David Ruffin in a tight black leather outfit talking to the ladies along the aisle of the Fox Theatre. Man, they were going crazy! That is why I wanted to be a member of the group. It was a great time for the Motown Sound in Detroit and the surrounding areas.

The Robin Seymour Show

CKLW was a Canadian Television and Radio station that operated just across the river in the city of Windsor.[171] The radio station featured all of the hit songs of the day, including the Motown Sound, and had enough wattage to be heard as far south as Cincinnati, Ohio. Robin Seymour[172] hosted a local dance show on the CKLW television station that also featured local artists, and many of them were Motown groups. After school, a ton of teenage boys and girls would cross over the Detroit River through the tunnel or over the bridge to go on the show and dance in Canada. A zillion more teenagers across Michigan, Ohio, and Canada would be watching on television at home.

I watched the show all the time. Once I got the chance to go on the show and dance. A girlfriend of Chili's sister, Daylene, had four tickets and needed two guys to dance with two girls. Chili asked if I wanted to go. I hesitated because I was a baseball player, not a dancer, until he told me I would be escorting Jackie Smith. What! My hesitation turned to a resounding "Yes!" Jackie Smith and her older sister, Cynthia, stopped the Wyoming Avenue school bus every day with their goddess-like beauty.

Every guy's head turned to watch them get on the bus in the morning, and every guy's head turned to watch them get off the bus in the afternoon—including the bus driver. I went, and I did not care how clumsy I looked. It was great! We danced, and a local singing group named the Fantastic Four[173] performed their hits. I now had a great story to tell to my buddies.

My mother, I am told, went around the whole neighborhood telling people I was on television. Some years later, while stationed in Germany, I was at a shop on the army post and opened a *Jet* magazine published by John J. Johnson,[174] and there she was, Jackie Smith, exhaling in a bathing suit as the centerfold in the early 1980s. Wow!

SUMMER OF 1967

Sunday, July 23, 1967, began as a peaceful summer day filled with anticipation of musical excitement. My friends Chili, Clinton Delray, and I talked about what we might see at the big musical show at the Fox Theatre as we rode toward downtown from the west side on the Grand River Avenue bus line. The numerous shops and businesses that lined Grand River Avenue were closed, but not the churches—they were on high. As mentioned, the Motown stars held a musical revue at the Fox Theater during Christmas time. This show was a summer celebration.

Robin Seymour, the CKLW personality, was hosting a musical show called *Swinging Summertime*, starring some of the Motown acts. It had the makings of a great time. Smokey Robinson and the Miracles were going to be there! Martha Reeves and the Vandellas were going to be there! And there were many more super acts, including George Clinton and the Parliaments![175] At that time in their career, they were dressed in bright coats, sharp ties, slick trousers, and shiny shoes, like my favorite group, the Temptations. Their hair was shiny and straight, or better yet, "fried, dyed, and laid to the side." I remember they performed a song called "Ol' Man River,"[176] and their performance was smoking—almost as good as the Temptations themselves.

The show had started in the early afternoon, and it was rocking. Then suddenly, the music stopped, and I recall that Martha and Smokey appeared on the stage together. They informed the audience of the disturbance that was taking place in the 12th Street area and stated that many of the bus lines heading toward the west side of Detroit were closed because of the disturbance. Just as quickly as the show stopped, it resumed. Few patrons inside the show really understood that the city was under siege.

As the show at the Fox Theater progressed, we found that we had no way to get home, and that the streets of Detroit now overflowed with rioters. When the show ended, we walked outside the Fox Theater to find the air filled with the sound of armed soldiers. I do not remember panic erupting, but I do remember wondering how in the heck we were going to get home. Chili got to a telephone and contacted his stepfather, Mel Baker. Mr. Baker told us to find a safe place in the theater, and he would be down as soon as he could. When he reached us, he had a friend with him and a gun on the front seat. We made our way to Interstate 75 on the eastside of Detroit and headed north out of harm's way. Smoke could be seen in the distance both east and west. There is always smoke and fire in riot zone, I know—the next five days were filled with it.

The Detroit riot of 1967[177] began on 12th Street near where I used to live when my family returned to Detroit. It has been categorized as a civil disturbance. The initial incidents arose in the early hours of Sunday, July 23, 1967, at a place conducting illegal activities. The crowd was celebrating the homecoming of two local veterans from the Vietnam War.[178] Some may argue that these veterans were knuckleheads of the lowest degree. Subsequently, members of the Detroit police vice squad moved in and raided the place—what is commonly known as a "blind pig" or "speakeasy."[179] This was an establishment that sold alcoholic beverages illegally. Remember, during this time, there were no parades or celebrations for returning Vietnam veterans. As a result, a disturbance began, and then it grew, and then it exploded.

The riot lasted five days. The property destruction was great, with more than two thousand buildings destroyed, many along Grand River Avenue. Businesses that claimed to be black owned and operated hastily scrawled *Soul Brother* across the storefront. The term was familiar in the black community.

Then there was the violence: forty-three people died, over 460 were injured, and 7,000 people were arrested. Several of my friends were among them. They spent a few days in jail for their participation in the riot.

The riot made national news, and it was televised. At the time, my brother Glen was visiting Aunt Rubye in Washington, DC. He called home night and day for an update; he wanted to hop a plane back to Detroit so that he could participate in the riot. As for me, my father kept me out of it. He made me stay home, and we painted the house. Because I obeyed him and completed my assigned chores, I did not get in trouble. I avoided having a criminal record at the naive age of sixteen. Thanks, Dad!

In the same year, the Detroit Tigers baseball team missed winning the American League pennant and going to the World Series by one game. I watched the Tigers' season end on a somber note on the last day. I also watched the smoldering timbers as Detroit seemed to be on its last days. Some remnant of the destruction is still evident today. In the city of Detroit, there was great social and economic upheaval that musical Sunday in July 1967.

I learned years later that Detroit was declared a disaster area and eligible for immediate funds to rebuild small businesses, homes, and personal property under the Small Business Administration (SBA). Many of the merchants chose to rebuild their businesses somewhere else.[180] What happened to the initiative and the funding is a story for another day. What remains are the shells of former businesses once prosperous on vacant lots more than three generations later, providing evidence of things to come for new sites of civil disturbance.[181] The citizens of Detroit looked at a hole in the wall for a long time. The words of Father Gabriel Richard, "We hope for better days; it shall rise from its ashes," helped to facilitate the healing process.[182]

SUMMER OF 1968

In my optimistic view, the healing process for the city of Detroit began in 1968 when the Detroit Tigers major-league baseball club won the American League pennant. The city streets were once again filled with people, but these were joyous fans. Chili and I were there at Tiger Stadium with my girlfriend, Miranda Northland, and we got there in Chili's 1951 Lincoln with no floorboards. When Detroit Tigers great Al Kaline crossed home plate, I and thousands of other elated fans chasing after him stopped to slide into second base. I was not painting the house that night, I was painting the town. I recall the event as if it were yesterday.

"*Safe!*" The ump's call spread like wildfire. It signaled the release of hundreds and hundreds of glowing embers trapped behind both foul lines. The base paths quickly filled with runners. From the short porch in right field, a thundering herd of revelers stampeded across the manicured outfield grass. Once pure, this diamond now swarmed with joyous flaws. You can learn a lot about a diamond when you smash it! When the diamond was smashed at Tiger Stadium, it ignited a social phenomenon not seen at the old ballpark any of the previous twenty-three seasons. One clean base hit mellowed the tense atmosphere in Motown at the end of a long hot summer in 1968. Where were you in 1968, when the Detroit Tigers defeated a mediocre New York Yankees baseball team 2–1 to clinch the American League pennant outright that glorious night of September 17? *Man!* I was sitting right up there in the right-field stands at the old ballpark. And believe me, there is nothing like the sound of a clean base hit. *Whack!*

At 10:18 p.m., Kaline scored the winning run after third baseman Don Wert singled to right field. At 10:19, I was kissing my girl. At 10:20, I was streaking in from right center field at full speed so I could slide into second base. At 10:21, I was kissing *your* girl. At 10:22, I was ripping up the manicured green grass in center field for a souvenir. At 10:23, I was kissing *his* girl. At 10:24, I was tearing the dark green padding off the centerfield fence for a souvenir. At 10:25, I was kissing some girl. That was a wondrous night. There was a lot of people kissing 'n' hugging, caring 'n' sharing, sliding 'n' priding.

Detroit, the city of champions! After a turbulent year of civil disturbance and a close second-place finish to the Boston Red Sox, the Tigers assembled a bunch of daring men to represent the Motor City on the baseball diamond. It was like a partnership of players and fans. The partnership staked a claim on the American League pennant and then later beat the St. Louis Cardinals in the World Series. At summer's end, there was one big mess of folks celebrating at second base. This historical event helped the city rise from the ashes of 1967. I have the proof, neatly planted in my parents' manicured green backyard, and of course, a set of permanently bruised lips.

SUMMER OF 1969

In 1969, I graduated from Mackenzie High School, student number 451 out of 534 students with a grade-point average of less than 2.0. I feel fortunate and blessed that I graduated; there are many students who fell by the wayside. Growing up in Cleveland, Ohio, I believe I was a good student who participated and received academic achievement stars all the time. When I returned to Detroit, my academics became dismal. Maybe I was distracted, or maybe I missed my old friends in Cleveland where I was, on most days, the center of attention. At Mackenzie, I remember the counselor wrote on my academic folder "Not College Material" and recommended that I focus on general labor skills. I did not fully understand that phrase at the time, but more than forty years later I am pissed over what was written. This disconnection between my former classmates and faculty is still evident in my attendance at the thirty-fifth and forty-fifth class reunion.

When I first arrived as a student at Mackenzie High School, the atmosphere was similar to the popular *Happy Days*[183] television series, just like the Big Boy restaurant I worked at. Along the north side of the school, there was a residential street with an ice-cream parlor on the corner. On that side of the school grounds, the whites seemed to always be racing hot rods on the street with little incident.[184] On the south side of the school, it seemed the black kids found time to throw dice. There were a few altercations, and a squad of Detroit police always seemed to show up on scooters to break up the action.

During the same time, I remember a few guys joined the military service specifically to go to Southeast Asia to pick up a shipment of contraband, or a *package* as the cool guys said on the streets. There was talk among the teen crowd that many soldiers scheduled to return home had heavy drug habits along with a sexual transmitted disease. The disease was rumored to be a killer that restricted soldiers to a secluded island until they were cured.

Local soul singer Deon Jackson's hit record "Love Makes the World Go Round"[185] was always on the radio and imitated by students in the hallways. There were many talented people at Mackenzie High School. In my class, Eric McClindon, Cliff Moore, and Phil Taylor supplied the group harmony as Erik and the Vikings.[186] Phil Taylor became a working actor and on occasion served as a stand-in for actor Denzel Washington.

Another talent in my class was Rosalyn Bowen; she had a big beautiful voice and was a local favorite. Ms. Bowen ended up in Hollywood on a television show *Amen*[187] with Sherman Hemsley. Another classmate, Claude Thompson, married my buddy Francisco Garcia, a Motown Hall of Famer from his work with the Falcons, Ma Barker, and Leonard King and the Soul Messengers.[188] Frank is also the keeper of the archives of Detroit music with his nonprofit work with the Original Historical Music Society of Detroit and Detroit Historic Musicians Association. I too am a vocalist, but I believe I was too naive at the time to understand my gift, in addition to not having a career direction or infrastructure.

The same was true of my passion for baseball. I was too naive to understand I needed a mentor to guide me and tell me that I needed to wear my glasses when I tried out for the high-school team. As a result, I was unprepared to play in organized baseball, the defunct Negro Leagues,[189] or the Police Athletic Leagues.[190] Ultimately, it was my fault that I did not take the opportunity to earn a letter or the right to wear a letterman's jacket. The same lack of career infrastructure can be said about any other accolade or recognition or accomplishment not earned in high school. This condition was rectified some years later when my daughters, Treasure, Lydia, and Lynette, attended high school. All three earned high-school academic, band, and athletic letters for their letterman's jackets.

I was a knucklehead moving slowly to the third degree from the fourth degree, a little stupid and a lot naive. I took my girl, Miranda Northland, on a Sunday cruise to Belle Isle in my father's work car. The car had a flat, and I tried to jack the car up on an incline. A couple of guys walking by had to help keep the car from jumping the jack and rolling down the hill. That is probably one of the reasons why Miranda kicked me to the curb right before the senior prom at the historic Roostertail nightclub.[191] Instead, I took my friend Maria Washburn, which was really unfair to her because I allowed Sammie Lee Ford and Clinton Delray to ride along stag. I was a poor date to Maria, and there is that word again: *poor!*

CHANGE WAS A-COMING

The 1960s was an explosive time in the lives of many people. I was growing up, and the world was changing. On my brother Glen's birthday, July 20, 1969, astronaut Neil Armstrong placed his foot on the moon.[192] Glen, me, and our buddies ordered soft drinks and watched the event on a television set at a neighborhood bowling alley on Grand River Avenue and Fullerton Street. While we celebrated both events, many of the white patrons kept a curious eye on us from their bowling lanes.

The great Jim Brown was representative of a strong black male in sports, the silver screen, and the community. However, I believe I was unprepared for many of the things that I encountered, both good or bad. For the most part, I was naive and grew up in a sheltered and protected household influenced greatly by my mother, a matriarchal situation not uncommon in the African-American community.

In 1968, there were many explosive topics: the Vietnam War,[193] the civil-rights movement,[194] and the assassination of Dr. Martin Luther King[195] and Robert F. Kennedy.[196] As a result, there were many school protest walkouts in support or against. There was also a radical Black Power movement[197] growing in conjunction, led by notables Angela Davis and the Black Panther party. The radical call for change in African-American culture was drummed out by socially vocal artists like The Last Poets[198] and Gil Scott-Heron.[199] Heron's album *The Revolution Will Not Be Televised*[200] was profound and thought-provoking.

I remember that Angela Davis and members of the Black Panther party came to the Michigan state fairgrounds during these turbulent times. I participated in some of these activities, not that I knew any of the real facts pertaining to the social issues. I was a naive follower. Outside the school building is where I followed everybody else, especially the girls, who were so vividly depicted in the Last Poets' "Black Thighs."[201] My subpar grade-point average showed how great of a follower I was, but I was fortunate to have finished the decade with a high-school diploma.

Despite my naivety, I did get an opportunity to go to Highland Park Junior College[202] in Highland Park, Michigan, in the fall of 1969, where Smokey Robinson was an alumnus from 1958.[203] Recently, a former student of the Highland Park school system informed me that the architect who designed the school building used by the school system and the community college is the same person who designed Alcatraz.[204] I remember my mother borrowed two hundred dollars from our neighbor, Mrs. Wilson, for my tuition. My curriculum was general studies, but I got caught up in student protests and school walkouts and girl-watching. That lasted one semester, because if you dropped out of college in the 1970s, there was a complication. Your name automatically went up to the draft board[205] because your status changed from a college deferment to "IA"—eligible for military service. Of course, I tried to get back to school by enrolling in the newly formed Wayne County Community College[206] near the Northwestern High School campus in a data-processing class, but during the 1970s, draft notices had a tendency to move at light speed through the postal system.

MILESTONES AND KNUCKLEHEAD INCIDENTS

Knucklehead incidents:

- the garage incident
- rock-throwing/hit by brick
- mouthing off in class after Kennedy assassination
- switches/parental control
- rough boys on 12th Street
- junior-high students talking sex
- switchblade and cut thumb
- Dearborn driver near hit-and-run
- meeting hippies
- Robin Seymour/Detroit riots
- school walkouts/student protests
- insufficient college credits/draft status change

Milestones:

- birth in nonsegregated hospital
- doo-wop singers under streetlights
- the television set
- meeting Jim Brown.
- Boy Scouts/Civil Air Patrol
- Harrison Dillard speaks
- learning Southern roots
- parents purchase home
- performing odd jobs before and after school
- evolution of the Strawberry Pie Rule
- harmonizing on street corner
- hitting baseball over fences and school roof

- experiencing urban renewal
- the Motown Revue
- Detroit riots/painted house
- Detroit Tigers 1968 championship season
- graduating high school 451 out 534 students, subpar GPA
- enrolling in Highland Park Community College

Down south with Grandpa and Grandma Davidson

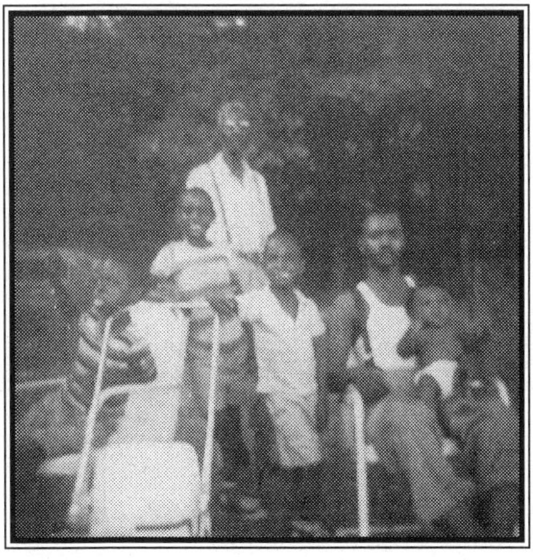

Kids with Dad and Grandpa Davidson

Mom's Sunday feast

Davidson kids off to Sunday school

Wayne dressed in nerd's clothing

CHAPTER 2
State of Superfly and Chaos

Danger was everywhere. Although they paid well, the factory jobs earmarked for African-Americans were characteristically labor-intensive and dangerous. Remember my grandfather, Ernest, barely escaped with his life from several farm incidents.

Ervell Davidson, a paternal cousin, was born in Barren County, Kentucky, in the early 1920s. Ervell worked hard, he drank hard, and he smoked a plenty throughout his lifetime on the farm, in the military and in his hazardous jobs, and it showed. I remember his hands were so tough that when he reached out to shake someone else's hand, his razor-sharp calluses could cut like a knife. Apparently, Ervell had a few idiosyncrasies or quirks. My father, Reuben, said that Ervell carried a gun in his pants pocket and always had his hand on it in anticipation of trouble. He said Ervell also loved to eat peanuts out of the bag. He would take his hand out of his pocket to get a peanut and then put his hand quickly back in his pocket on his gun.

In the 1960s, Ervell worked at Frank's Gas Station on the corner of Cass Avenue and Myrtle Street near Woodward Avenue in Detroit doing mechanic work and pumping gas. One day while performing his duties, he ignored that familiar yet intoxicating smell in the air. As was his habit, he lit a cigarette and *boom!* there was an explosion. The station blew up, and debris came falling down around him. What a sight—captured by a newspaper photo. Luckily, he was physically unhurt, but there was an immediate economic change to his lifestyle. The gas station was gone, and so was his livelihood.

My father told me another interesting story about Cousin Ervell returning to Rocky Hill for a visit. During the Negro migration, it was not unusual for Negroes who had migrated north to return home to the South on a regular basis to see family and friends. Most often, the returnee brought home purchased goods and services that might be unavailable to those still on the farm, and of course, to show off.

On occasion, Ervell would enlist my father to drive his car the highway distance from Detroit, Michigan, to Rocky Hill, Kentucky. That way, Ervell could sit in the passenger seat and sleep, smoke, and take a little "taste" if he chose to do so. However, when they were about a mile out of the town, Ervell would tell my father that he was taking over the wheel. That way he would get the glory of the conquering hero returning home in a big luxury car pulling into designated driveways with horns sounding victory over the industrial North. When it was time to head back north, Ervell would get behind the wheel, hit the gas, and make a great commotion for the folks still down on the farm. Then about a mile down the road, my father would take over the wheel for the long haul back north.

The experience of my cousin Ervell Davidson and the explosion of the gas station is a great illustration of social and economic change. The event put him out of a job, and the customer had to go somewhere else to buy gas. There were a lot of problems, challenges, and adventures that my family members faced over the course of their lives. The time in which they lived and the location in which they lived greatly influenced their ability to overcome circumstances and move forward prosperously. For me, growing from an immature youth to an immature African-American male, there were a lot of problems, challenges, and adventures as the 1960s came to an end. The narrative that follows illustrates my own circumstances and hope for survival.

UNDER THE INFLUENCE OF THE LOVE GENERATION

An old adage describes the 1960s as a party so great that if you remembered it, you were not really there. In this hazy utopia, there were too many unidentified substances being passed around under the great fog of music blasting out around the faces of captivated people. I remember the music of 1960s was electrifying and hypnotic, in particular "In-A-Gadda-Da-Vida" by the rock band Iron Butterfly.[1] The psychedelic sound led to the great cultural upheaval as the 1970s marched in. One could say the 1970s was the morning after the party, when you learned there would be hell to pay for your conduct of the previous night.

I can only take the Fifth Amendment for many of my personal experience and naivety during the 1960s, because for me there was much hell to pay in the 1970s. I became a third-degree knucklehead living a chaotic lifestyle and stumbling around with the other malcontented inhabitants in a place I call Stupidville. Where the inhabitants were all engrossed in a zombie state of bad conduct and bad habits. My best definition of this whacky spaced-out place will follow. Here in plain language, I define a third-degree knucklehead as a just plain stupid person who has forsaken home training and makes extremely poor decisions under the influence of euphoric environment but can be saved from being ordered to an incarcerated institutionalized lifestyle.

THE FLOODGATES OPEN

Seemingly overnight, lifestyle changes influenced social behaviors that brought potential danger to young naive people of diverse backgrounds across the nation. These changes came in the unidentifiable forms of powders or weeds wrapped in aluminum foil, paper products, and capsules in different sizes, shapes, and colors thought to be authentic, to bring about daily euphoric rituals as confessed by the protagonist of the 1823 classic *Confessions of an English Opium-Eater.*[2] Many young people nurtured for greatness by caring families came under the influence of the pandemic and did not survive the new decade.

The 2008 movie *American Gangster*[3] featuring Denzel Washington and Russell Crowe is representative of the transition of my neighborhood. The film provides vivid details of the drug heroin—manufactured from the opium poppy grown in foreign lands—suddenly flooding into urban neighborhoods. It also depicts the ruthless risk-taking of men seeking profits and men with guns and the law pursuing the profiteers. Among those who did not survive the destructive behavior brought about by the drug flood in the 1970s were my brother Glen and several of my friends, both close and distant.

The package of contraband just showed up one day in our newly acquired neighborhoods while the kids were out riding bikes up and down the street. This may prompt the inquisitive to ask, where did this stuff come from and how did it get here? Who knows, but one thing is for sure: a lot of societal change came with it. It seemed like one day all the young men stood upright dressed and ready for Sunday church service, and the next day these same young men looked discombobulated, dressed like a mess and heading off into the darkened streets with bad intentions.

The word *heroin* is derived from the Greek word *hero*.[4] Scientific research conducted in the nineteenth century indicates that the original intent of heroin as the "hero" drug was to ease human suffering, not create habitual users.[5] It is ironic that as a result of the research, heroin was perceived to be good for mankind. The medical world believed the drug would avoid side effects in patient care normally experienced in the use of morphine and codeine. From a biblical perspective, Ecclesiastes 1:9 tells us that "there is nothing new under the sun." So when God created the earth, it was done with due care. Arguably the problems in God's world have been created out of abuse. According to Proverbs 23:21, "For the drunkard and glutton will come to poverty and drowsiness will clothe a man with rags." Subsequently, the "hero" drug was declared a menace in the 1920s as it became a chemical cocktail and economic commodity for criminal activity.[6]

The Place Called Stupidville

For the purposes of this text, *Stupidville* can be defined as any location or place of deviant behavior where people take personal risks to gather and engage in activities that could lead to criminal associations and long-term incarceration. Negative behavior can jeopardize one's own personal health and safety and subsequently the sanctity of the family unit. In simple terms, I remember Stupidville as the place where a lot of stupid stuff took place, hosted by first-degree habitual knuckleheads. When my third-degree knucklehead friends and I engaged in risky behavior and harmful substances, our state of mind became nonproductive. Deviant behavior in the black community was treated by the media as front-page news,[7] while the deviance in white communities was not.[8]

When a chemical cocktail of harmful substances and risky behaviors is put together for sale on the public street, there is danger. How does a person really know what is in it, and whether or not the ingredients could be deadly poison not fit for human consumption? There are many vulnerable people, including those uneducated to the danger and those with a lot of idle time. At least in the hobo cocktail from the mischievous and idle days of my father, the ingredients were typically purchased from the liquor department of a store. From a contemporary perspective, a team assembled by Dr. Frank McGeorge has informed the public of the growing heroin problem in the metro Detroit area.[9]

The 1970s

The transition into the 1970s came with a heavy price, and I may be heavily criticized for my personal behavior by many people in addition to my own family members, but this was the era I grew up in. I can counter and say that there were very few Puritans during the chaotic 1970s, which featured the continuation of the Vietnam War,[10] escalation of civil disturbance,[11] and a widespread drug epidemic.[12] It's no excuse, but I had little knowledge of life in the fast lane and the reality of the streets. The everyday challenge was to just stay alive.

I should just appreciate receiving my high-school diploma, because little did I know that at the end of the decade, a sheepskin would give me options that others did not have or take. I understand now that my diploma served as a stay-out-of-jail card for me because it gave me options as I sought change.

I acknowledge my high-school years in the Detroit public school system as forgettable. But, in contrast, my father only made it to the fourth grade, and I am sure my forefathers introduced in the first part of this trilogy—Adam, Alex, Harris/Harrison, Chris, and Ernest—had little or no opportunity to attend formal schooling at all. Without a doubt, my anemic grade-point average did prepare me for unskilled labor, blue-collar positions, just as the school guidance counselor wrote on my academic record: parking attendant, delivery man, mail sorter, housekeeping attendant, warehouseman, general laborer, forklift and machine operator. None of these jobs put me on the fast track to a corporate boardroom. But I did understand the meaning of work, and that helped me to stay occupied.

BLAXPLOITATION MENTORSHIP

During these bold times, when actor Billy Dee Williams peered from the shadows to woo Diana Ross as Billie Holiday in the sultry 1972 movie *Lady Sings the Blues*,[13] it prompted me to say, "I got to get me some hair like that. I got to get me some teeth like that. I got to get me a smile like that."

When actor Richard Roundtree, dressed in a full-length leather coat, emerges from the subway and made his bodacious walk across the mean streets of New York in the explosive 1971 movie *Shaft*,[14] it prompted me to say, "I got to get me a coat like that. I got to get me a walk like that. I got to have an attitude like that."

When the voice of Curtis Mayfield coolly sang out the theme song as actor Ron O'Neal drove his pimped-out Cadillac without a care in the suave 1972 movie *Superfly*,[15] it prompted me to say, "I got to get me a ride like that. I got to get me a woman like that. I got to be fly like that."

And when Richard Pryor socialized and told jokes between the riotous musical performances of Stax artists in the 1973 movie *Wattstax*,[16] it prompted me to say, "I want to talk like that. I want to live like that. I want to make people laugh like that."

About five years later, Richard Pryor was in Detroit making the movie *Blue Collar*[17] with Harvey Keitel along the John C. Lodge Freeway. I tried to find him on the set to talk and shake his hand, but to no avail. The emergence of Richard Pryor was a phenomenon because his talent crossed all ethnic borders.

The social and economic time of blaxploitation films[18] was the decade of the 1970s. None of these films would have passed the censorship established by the Hays Code[19] during the 1920s and 1930s. All of these black movie characters took risks, lived boldly and dangerously, experienced superhuman sexual exploits, and "beat the man" on the silver screen. No matter their plight, right or wrong, death or imprisonment, at the end of the movie, in the mind of the black audience, these black movie characters stood victorious, complete with their own theme music accented with heavy funk and soul.

There was a common theme in blaxploitation films' storylines no matter the geographic location. In an urban setting, the films featured life in the crime-infested ghetto, dealing with hit men, drug dealers, and pimps. The use of ethnic slurs was a common dialectic, and corruption was a common characteristic among white cops, politicians, and criminals who were covert racists. On the other hand, if the film took place in the South, the local sheriff, local government, and business owners were all habitual overt racists. In either location, if you were not part of the hero's circle, then you were depicted as being with "the Man," and that was bad news for you. These blaxploitation films greatly influenced me and my lifestyle during the decade of 1970s.

GREETINGS, THIS IS UNCLE SAM

The Vietnam War[20] and military draft,[21] not to mention the Kent State incident,[22] resulted in civil disturbances in Detroit as well as the rest of the nation in the 1970s.[23] As a result of the raised issues, I thought myself ill-prepared to serve Uncle Sam, although I'd participated in the Boy Scouts,[24] the Civil Air Patrol[25] growing up in Cleveland, and in high school, several semesters of the Junior Reserve Officers' Training Corps (JROTC).[26] Although I grew up watching a ton of military movies with John Wayne, James Stewart, and the rest, the heroes they played got the girl but did not look like me. It was the sidekick who got dead and no girl who looked like me.

My father had not served in the military, so I was also naive about the real military. I learned that when my dad was of draft age, there was no draft in place, and when the draft was reinstated for the Korean War, married men of age with children were basically exempted.[27] I discovered later that members of both my paternal and maternal family served the country in the armed forces with distinction many times over.[28]

From my perspective, there was no mass push of patriotism in the 1970s with young men rushing to the defense of the United States as seen during the World Wars in the community I lived in. For years, there was no homecoming parade of returning Vietnam soldiers. May be because television projected disturbing images that showed suspect battlefield data and extreme collateral damage to the local Southeast Asian population and erosion within the United States military ranks into American homes. But since the 1980s, the service of the Vietnam era soldier has been given formal recognition and efforts for full accountability have been made as due the veterans of subsequent wars.[29]

As I grew toward draft age, I remember there were a number of young men who joined the military service at the earliest opportunity seeking adventure, growth, and the opportunity to marry one day. The Monitors, a Motown singing group, had an awakening hit song in 1966 titled "Greetings (This is Uncle Sam)"[30] that they performed at the

Motown Revue. The song provided an illustration of the change from civilian life to army life with an African-American point of view.

At this time, I was passively riding around the neighborhood on a bike. However, some teens had developed real plans for the future, finishing high school with the goal of joining up and then getting married and starting families. One acquaintance, Eugene Harris, followed this path when he joined the Marines and spent thirty-plus years in service. He wanted to marry the young lady who lived directly across the rear alleyway from my parents' house. I remember her vividly, because the family German shepherd always barked from the yard at people passing by or guys playing basketball in the alleyway. As far as education, a person could eventually complete his high-school education in military service by obtaining a General Education Diploma (GED).[31]

I mentioned before there were young men who had deviant plans to join the military with the premise of seeking business opportunities in the Far East. There was always slurred street talk pertaining to somebody's relative sending back a package from the Far East with goodies inside. This plan had tremendous risk.

Then there were the war stories, as told by guys upon their return home who were bragging about their active duty. They would talk about Vietnam or Germany (*Deutschland*) in broken language, if they were trying to impress, describing the women they encountered and the drugs they ingested. As a young listener, I do not recall any of the stories being perceived as positive or providing motivation for other young men like me to follow in their footsteps, other than the tales of beautiful and exotic women.

On reflection, there were very few guys I knew who took full advantage of any military-service benefits or who obtained new skills that would help them and their families. The guys I saw returned to the old neighborhood with major physiological problems and drug addictions, with bad conduct discharges or medical discharges. These veterans seemed to be out of control, and their corrupt behaviors continued to rise when they returned to city streets where the drugs were watered down a billion times from what they'd obtained overseas.

During this time, there were few heroes for a young man to emulate. Many veterans became knuckleheads from their experiences and ended up in jail for committing crimes, often crimes against their own community. Some took their own lives, jumping out of windows in the housing projects where they grew up, unable to cope with readjustment. It is ironic that the 1967 Detroit riot ignited when Detroit police broke up an after-hours celebration of two Vietnam veterans returning home.[32]

Another topic of discussion was the overt discrimination that many African-American soldiers encountered. Typically, in war, men and women achieve a special status from their deeds and sacrifice. A valid question: why were there few heroes of color recognized in this conflict? In reality, soldiers of color performed their duties gallantly without formal recognition of their deeds.[33] This situation was not new to soldiers of color who had faced discrimination in the military before.[34]

During the Vietnam era, these prejudices may have had a higher visibility because of the volatility of 1960s and 1970s that resonated with the brothers in the old neighborhood. The story I remember through the grapevine concerned my friend Cleve Childs, who had joined the service and had his arm broken in an altercation with his drill sergeant. When you hear this on the street, you wonder immediately how it happened, and how did he get his arm broken? Cleve was tough, and did he not know martial arts? Recollecting a scene from a popular movie of 1990s, *Forest Gump*,[35] the question is posed by a fatally wounded soldier of color named Bubba to Forest Gump, a white soldier who risked his life to save the life of Bubba in the jungle of Vietnam, "Forest, how did this happen?"

It Just Didn't Work Out

The lack of role models deterred many in my neighborhood from wearing a military uniform. My own lack of knowledge and immaturity dropped me out of community college, and within a few short weeks I received my induction notice that read, "Greetings, You are hereby ordered for induction into the Armed Forces of the United States, and to report to Fort Anthony Wayne on West Jefferson Avenue" in Southwest Detroit. I reluctantly went down as directed and reported for duty.

I soon learned that the folks in charge were not the friendliest of people, and they were very direct. I stood in my underwear quietly as instructed and went through the physical examination and other administrative requirements. There were a few guys in line I knew from high school. It was like a factory process, bodies in and bodies out. I found out my deformed knees were not as bad as I'd hoped, because the condition did not get me out of duty. So I signed my papers and took my oath to support and defend the Constitution of the United States, and I marched off to eat lunch.

I lasted an hour or so in service before my immaturity struck again. My friend Eric Inkster had given me the magic words if I ran into trouble, words he had used one year earlier: substance abuse. Substance abuse was rapidly becoming a huge problem in the military, and soldiers could not leave or enter the service in the 1970s unless they were clean. Soldiers under the influence were considered to be unfit for duty and of little value to the US Army if they could not pass the urinalysis test.[36] Notably, drug use among American troops had been cited as early as the 1898 Philippines insurrection[37] and the Buffalo Soldiers in garrison at the turn of the twentieth century.[38] Now drugs had crossed the American border in great number, bringing genocide to American neighborhoods and in particular African-American neighborhoods. When I invoked the term *substance abuse*, I did not answer the army's call to adventure. Instead I resigned myself to the status quo.

The genocide that substance abuse created was bad news for the family structure and for me. I ran the streets of Detroit alongside many others who were lost and under the influence, working as an unskilled general laborer throughout the 1970s as forecasted by my academic counselor. When I got paid, the few dollars I earned were basically thrown out the window as I chased after a euphoric feeling down in Stupidville that lasted a few moments. In reflection, that detrimental activity was a complete waste of time, except that the experience allows me to tell you about my journey so that you do not take a detour through Stupidville yourself. I was fortunate that I did not become a negative statistic, but even worse are the loved ones who suffered from my behavior during the time of affliction.

A year or so later, I saw one my former classmate who I'd seen in the induction line. He said that the bus he was assigned to went to Fort Knox, Kentucky, but he did not detail any other aspects of his military experience. I was too stuffed up with stupidity to listen anyway, and then I remembered that Fort Knox is where the gold supply is located.

Attitude: The Honeybee Story

One characteristic of immaturity, in my opinion, is a person's questionable ability to make good decisions. Without that ability, poor decision-making always comes back to bite the person, like those who live and operate in Stupidville. I want to expand on this thought with an incident that happened during this null period of time. As previously discussed, those in blue-collar jobs experience periods of unemployment for various economic reasons, generally out of the worker's control. During these periods of unemployment, there may be a job-related training requirement as directed by the agency. This is when I learned the first attribute to go on your way to becoming a first-degree knucklehead is attitude.

There I was sitting in the classroom by the open window being retrained, as directed by the State of Michigan, on a beautiful spring day. A honeybee flew in through the window, and I paid no attention to it. The bee did not fly toward me, so why should I care? The bee circled the room and settled on the back of the person sitting in front of me. I was apathetic; I made no effort to give warning to the person sitting in front of me that the bee was present and that it had landed on his back. I closed my eyes for one second to rest and to wish that I was somewhere else other than sitting here meeting this training requirement, and then I opened my eyes. I noticed the bee was no longer flying around in front of me. I glanced down and spotted the honeybee atop the outside lip of my right shoe, leaning over to go down inside. I clinched, but as my right ankle moved as a natural motion inward toward the encroaching bee, the bee stung and then was smashed, and my heel was swollen, leaving me in pain.

In retrospect, I should have exhibited less apathy and displayed more concern for others. At the time the bee entered the area, I should have warned people that a bee was in the vicinity and been more respectful to the bee's presence and ability to deliver a dangerous payload of pain. I learned there is danger in being an apathetic person.

THE BANK JOB

After high school, my fulltime working career began at the main branch of the Bank of the Commonwealth located on the corner of West Fort Street at Griswold Avenue. There was a branch office with both street and sublevel parking located two blocks south on Fort Street at Washington Boulevard. My friend Eric Inkster helped me get hired at the bank sometime after graduation in 1969. I knew Eric from the Jefferies Projects when I lived there, and we ended up living in the same neighborhood years later. His family moved from the projects to the Detroit suburbs where they lived for a number of years when my family lived in Cleveland. He was a year older than me, and he graduated from Mackenzie High one year earlier than I did.

Eric worked at the mailroom in the main branch on the twenty-third floor. His uncle Jim, a postal carrier, helped Eric to get hired at the bank the previous year after he graduated. The bank position had its perks, and on occasion I rode in the back of the bank president's chauffeured limousine. I looked important when the chauffeur dropped me off before we got to the main entrance on Griswold Avenue.

My primary job was to help park cars at the bank branch parking lot on Fort Street. At the parking lot, I worked with an older black gentleman named Frank. He had worked this job for a number of years, and he was from the generation that wore a clean uniform to work every day, addressed customers with an appropriate "sir" or "ma'am," and received a generous tip for his service. We operated out of a small shack built on the premises surrounded by tall buildings. The buildings tend to block out many of the local R&B radio stations that I listened to, including WCHB[39] and WJLB.[40] However, CKLW, the Canadian radio station across the Detroit River, came in loud and clear with the popular music of the day, like "In the Year 2525"[41] and "American Pie."[42]

Although the shack was close-quartered, we had great conversations, laughter, and music—at least until lunch. Frank wore dentures, and it was always a challenge to watch him eat a sandwich and drink coffee, as he made a clacking sound when he chewed. For me, I found it was best to leave the shack to Frank and his lunch.

Bank customers generally parked at the lot and walked two blocks to the main branch to attend to their business. They drove all models of cars, and Frank would park the vehicle on either the street-level lot or below on the subsurface level and then provide the customer a ticket to be validated at the main branch. Over his lifetime and employment at the bank, Frank had driven all types of vehicles, both automatic and standard transmissions, and maybe even a couple of getaway cars.

Up to that date, I had driven only one standard vehicle with a manual transmission, and that was my friend Chili's 1951 Lincoln. That monster of a car had the gear-shifter on the steering column. Surely I would have been a poor getaway man. My driving experience was primarily on vehicles with automatic transmissions.

To get me up to speed, Frank gave me lessons on driving a manual transmission so if he took a day off or went on vacation, I would be prepared for those fancy sports cars that might come in. I practiced pushing down on the clutch, shifting the gear, releasing the brake, and then releasing the clutch while pressing down on the accelerator as many times as I could. But believe me, I was real content not driving a vehicle with a manual transmission.

Well, it had to happen that the day would come when Frank would be on vacation, and there I was in charge of the parking lot. I prayed all day that no fancy cars with standard transmissions would come into the lot. Around midmorning, a bank customer pulled into the parking lot in a red Corvette. I got a giant lump in my throat and tried to swallow. I gave the customer a ticket and then I looked inside the vehicle.

"Oh my God!" This red Corvette had an automatic transmission with a gear-shifter between the bucket seats. With glee, I jumped behind the wheel and drove the vehicle to an empty sublevel parking spot. Sometime later, the customer returned to pick up his automobile. I ran downstairs, jumped behind the wheel, and drove it up from the sublevel parking with a song in my heart. I went back into the little shack to listen to more music on the radio.

A short time later, a gentleman in a beautiful late-model Mercury Grand Marquis station wagon pulled up. I came out of the shack with confidence and gave him my best greeting, a parking ticket, and directions to the main branch with enthusiasm. Then I got in the car to park it and, to my surprise, saw that this large luxury vehicle had a manual transmission, with the gear-shifter on the steering column. I did not expect a luxury car to have a manual transmission. I was in shock. It took me an hour to park that car in the sub-parking lot, in between a bunch of squeaks and screams from both me and the car. I was sweating. Finally, I got the car parked. What a relief!

Then I ran back into the shack to rest for a minute. No sooner had I sat down to recover than the car owner knocked on the door to retrieve his car. I smiled and projected my best service attitude. I went down to the sublevel, got in the car, and prayed. It seemed easier getting the car up than the hour it took me to get it down. Still in service mode, I handed over the car to the gentleman and he drove off. I thanked the Lord again and finished the workday.

About ten days later, a gentleman appeared in the doorway of the shack. I remembered him vaguely, but he remembered me specifically, and he was very irate. The man stated that I had burned out his clutch, and he continued to give me his two cents on the matter. I was just out of high school, and all I could do was listen to his complaint as I stood there like a mummy. This incident was a true sign that my career as a parking attendant could abruptly come to a close any second.

In between parking cars for bank customers, I developed my skills of observation as a parking attendant. I had a bird's-eye view of patrons of all types, especially ladies, walking by the shack or driving through the teller window to take care of their bank business. One day an early 1960s Plymouth Valiant with the push-button transmission was in the bank drive-through lane with four African-American male passengers. No, there was no bank robbery in progress. I thought their faces were familiar, but I could not remember from where. As they completed their business with the teller, I remembered who they were: they were members of the Fantastic Four, the local singing group I'd danced to on the *Robin Seymour Show* only a few short months before.

It appeared that the group had come to the bank to cash their factory checks. It was Friday, and for factory workers in the Motor City that was payday. Yes, the eagle flied each Friday, and that was a good thing for the local economy. I went over to the teller booth to speak with the teller, an African-American female, and she verified their identity because she was also familiar with the group's music. She was excited because she was single and on the lookout for a man with a job.

How do you like that? I thought celebrities rode around in the lap of luxury with rolls of green dough, not in a Plymouth Valiant, wearing funky work clothes and cashing a factory paycheck. My perception of singing stars was tarnished, but I did learn something that day: celebrities have to feed their families too, the best way they can.

Sometime later, I was assigned to drive a company vehicle, either a van or car depending on the task, around the metropolitan area delivering bulk mail to the branch offices. I would get to go inside the secured area where the bank tellers provided banking service to customers. On occasion, I got to look at a lot of the green dough they make in the back, but too bad I was not allowed to sample any of it.

I found out the hard way that driving around all day in the hot summer could be a little exhausting. It does not help if the driver did not have a good night sleep. I learned that lesson when I sideswiped another car driven by an elderly man one day in the downriver area of Detroit in a company vehicle.

In the winter, when there was a nice layer of snow on the ground, area freeways could turn quickly to heavy slush as a result of moisture and traffic. In snow, the rule of thumb is to follow in the tracks of the drivers ahead. I was driving a commercial van on newly constructed Interstate 75 North near an upgraded curve near 13 Mile Road area when I found out abruptly that a driver needs to be well rested and alert in the wintertime too.

Mr. Jim Inkster, a bank employee and Eric Inkster's uncle, was in the passenger seat of the van that day. As I reflect now, I probably was exceeding the speed limit for the driving conditions. For some reason, I wanted to pass, so I maneuvered over to the far left lane. What I found in that lane was extra heavy slush, and that slush caught my wheels and twisted the vehicle 360 degrees across the freeway. The van came to a stop across two lanes of the freeway. I was in shock, and Jim was in a stone daze. Luckily, the traffic following behind us was not as fast as we were. For some reason, I could feel my career as a company driver coming to an abrupt end.

The end grew even nearer one afternoon during rush-hour traffic when a blond lady ran into the side of a company car I was driving. One minute I had my window down and my arm hanging out of it, and then "*wham*!" A few days later, I learned from the official police report that I was cited for blocking the intersection. The door to my freedom as a company driver was now closed, and I was taken off the road.

For a short time, I worked in the mail room in the main building located on the twenty-third floor with Eric Inkster and Greene Cutlass. Greene also graduated from Mackenzie High School in my class year. I know he was much higher in the class standing than I was. But that did not matter. I was a little angry at Greene because he was digging on my girlfriend, Miranda Northland, when we were students. Then Greene moved in on my girlfriend, Gail, Eric's cousin, who lived in the Detroit suburbs.

I soon found out that if you had wheels, as Greene did, you could visit all the ladies whenever you wanted to. I walked or ran the two miles to Miranda's house to the beat of Edwin Starr's "Twenty-Five Miles."[43] In contrast, I took the bus to visit Gail in the suburbs. The round trip was nearly four hours. Anyway, that is water under the bridge, and all is forgiven. But I learned that you did not have to look like Errol Flynn to be a ladies' man because the advantage goes to the one with physical assets—a car, an apartment, and a couple of bucks. Advantage Greene. He had clear access to an automobile 24/7, and all I could do was improve my voice, so that is the name of that tune.

Bulk Mail and Pitney Bowes

Prior to the age of personal computers and automated devices in the 1990s, a corporate mail-room operation might be considered dull to some. In reality, the whole world passed through the traditional mail room, and the traditional mail-room clerk was the gatekeeper. That mail clerk probably saw nearly every bit of information in some form or fashion of regular mail, corporate mail, and private mail for an organization. I learned later that in 1810, the US Congress prohibited blacks from handling the mail[44] for two distinct reasons:

1. Whites did not want the mail to be destroyed.
2. Delivering the mail would give blacks opportunity to survey the landscape and gather information that could aid in escape attempts or insurrection.

It was not until well into the Reconstruction period that blacks could legally handle the US mail.

At this job, there were two full-time African-American postal workers who worked part-time on the night shift at the bank. As they worked, they listened to the Detroit Red Wings play hockey on the radio. This was a sport not many blacks from my neighborhood engaged in or understood; I certainly didn't. I have since gained an appreciation for the game.

In many ways, the traditional mail room in company operations was like an assembly process. When the mail came into the bank, it had been picked up in bulk from the main post office and brought directly into the mail room by mail clerks. The mail person began to sort by name or office as scribed on the mail and then opened any individual mail that was not clearly marked as necessary to determine which office the incoming mail should be directed to.

During this process, I found out that there is a reason why companies encouraged the public not to send cash in the mail. If the mail is clearly marked, it should have no problem reaching its destination. But on the occasion that the mail is not clearly marked or maybe distinctly marked for charity, the possibility is great that the mail will have to be opened, and generally mail handlers are inquisitive and have sticky fingers. When the incoming mail that is opened contains valuables, it is highly unlikely that the contents of the envelope will make it to its destination.

In 1970, cash donations earmarked for charity most likely ended up being spent at the Louis the Hatter clothing store, the Sibley shoe store, or on drugs. The regular mail clerks rarely missed a workday during the time leading up to and after a big charity event. The opportunity for substance abuse was also high, so much so that I almost fell out of the mail-room window located on the twenty-third floor of the Griswold Building one Saturday morning recovering after a long Friday night of hanging out with Greene and Eric.

The assembly process of mail continues when the corporate mail is designated and goes out of the bank. Normally it is processed in bulk through a mechanical mail-sorting machine designed by Pitney Bowes. The operator inputs the stack of envelopes on the entry ramp of the mail-sorting machine. The machine is powered up, and then each letter moves along the mechanical assembly. Each letter is weighed, and based on the weight of the individual envelope, a commercial stamp is attached. At the exit ramp, the stamped envelopes are placed back in a mailing container and loaded onto a corporate vehicle to be taken over to the main post office before the evening deadline for processing to bank customers the next business day.

One evening during this assembly process, I remember having an altercation with a white employee, a young college student. I thought him to be very slow at working the mail. One night I ended up delivering the mail to the post office by myself to meet the deadline. I was angry, and I whacked him because I thought he was jacking me around. I learned later that he had to leave so that he would not miss his bus home. Although I felt bad later, there was little training in anger management for African-American males in 1970. There was just so much to be angry about.

The First to Go Postal

The other interesting time in the mail room was when the cycle of monthly customer statements ran. These statements were processed through the Pitney Bowes mailing machine as previously described. Sometimes, there was a problem with individual envelopes that were bulkier than others. The bulkier envelopes presented a greater chance for the sorting process to fail because the weight and size of the envelope stopped the machine from processing. The alternative was to process the bulky envelopes manually.

At the time, it seemed that bulkier mail generally belonged to important high-profile customers who wrote a lot of checks. During one particular case, the envelopes belonged to Mr. William Robinson of Detroit, Michigan—better known as Smokey Robinson of Motown Records. His mail was always too bulky to go through the mailing machine and had to be weighed. Why was that? Remember, I mentioned that mail clerks are nosey, and there was always time to take a peek inside.

The Pitney Bowes machine signaled my last days as a bank employee. The end of my employment did not happen because of my driving record but because my anger and immaturity induced me to toss a wooden office chair in the direction of my supervisor. Employers beware! I may have been among the first to go postal as a result of stress in the workplace nearly twenty years before the term became synonymous with extreme behavior in post-office shootings in the mid-1980s.[45] And because I behaved badly, I soon became unemployed.

Life and Employment in the Factory Town

My brother Glen was scheduled to graduate from Mackenzie High School in June 1970, but instead he had to complete his high-school requirements in summer school. How did this happen? Glen was the smartest person I knew, and he was college material. He had received good grades throughout his entire school life. As a formality, he walked across the stage as part of the ceremony, but he still had work to do, and his alternative was to complete summer school.

Well, my brother Glen, like me, did not take advantage of his academic skill set during this period of time. We were now both looking for work in the automotive industry as physical laborers. This was the traditional path of two young African-American males in a blue collar town.

Great Lakes Steel on Zug Island

In July 1970, Glen and I were verbally motivated by our mother's repetitive words of wisdom calling for us to get up out of bed and go look for a job over and over and over. Somehow we got word that the Great Lakes

Steel Company located on Zug Island Road in Southwest Detroit[46] was hiring. We knew nothing of the company, but we got hired. This was our first real job in the industrial world. The Great Lakes Steel Company was in the business of making steel, and when steel is being made, it is serious business in Detroit. Three days later, we were looking for new jobs, and my mother was not happy.

On our first day of work, we donned our safety equipment. and the foreman took us on a tour of the industrial site. Everywhere there were mechanical gadgets and gizmos, steam and heat, and large vats connected to the operations of blast furnaces. As we walked through the plant area, I remember molten hot steel being poured into a large vat sitting on a railroad car. It was something to see.

We noticed that one side of the building appeared to have been scorched. We asked the foreman what had happened to that area of the plant. He explained that an industrial accident had happened a few weeks ago, where a vat with hot molten steel turned over and injured several employees. He stated that the injured employees were not expected to return anytime soon, so we needed to learn our job assignments. Of course, my brother and I looked at each other with dismay after the foreman's talk. We were the replacement employees.

My assignment was to don additional protective gear and then get inside an empty vat that had cooled down with a high-pressure air gun. My job was to clean the metal residue from the walls of the vat. This method of cleaning a vat may be a good industrial technique on paper, but not for the person doing the job. Once you are lowered down into the vat and the gun is turned to the "on" position, you become a target for the loose flying steel beads being knocked around. In essence, the high-pressure air-gun operator is in a vacuum with metal residue flying about everywhere. Well, I can tell you, three days of being in a vacuum was enough for both me and my brother. Time to move on!

THE FORD MOTOR COMPANY ROUGE COMPLEX

Right after Labor Day of 1970, Glen and I went over to the Ford Motor Company River Rouge complex on dusty Miller Road in Dearborn, Michigan. From a historic perspective, the Ford River Rouge was the largest single industrial complex in the world when it was completed in 1928.[47] Ford was in the business of making automobiles, and when cars were being made it was serious business in Detroit.

The Ford Rouge plant was conveniently located just a short bus ride from a convenient labor pool: my high school, Mackenzie High. For many years, there were students who, instead of getting off the bus for school, stayed on the bus for the continued journey on out to the Ford Rouge complex. They were seeking dollars instead of diplomas. One might think with my grade-point average that maybe I should have been there earlier.

When you walked into work, you could not help but feel that you were being consumed by a massive web of machines. The Rouge complex sat on more than a thousand acres paved with fourteen miles of dusty roadways, and miles and miles of railroad tracks that wove through the dark, drab, grimy factory buildings and structures. All thousand acres were controlled by electronic gadgets and gizmos, and a lot of industrial ingenuity. And over on the waterway, there were vessels full of raw materials. Those raw materials would go in through one door of the factory complex, and a short time later, a shiny red Mustang would drive out on the other side.

In its heyday, the complex employed more than 100,000 people at one time. During the great migration of Negroes from the South, many long journeys ended at this complex.[48] Again, the pay was good, but again, Negroes were typically regulated to the hardest, most hazardous, most dangerous, lowest-paying jobs in the Northern factories.

Those 100,000 folks had plenty of personnel issues concerning pay and work conditions. So the Rouge plant employed its own police force, hospital staff, and maintenance crew. Since its completion in 1928, the

Ford Rouge complex had been the center of historic strikes and, of course, layoffs. In 1937, Rouge was the site of a famous labor battle between union organizers and Ford security forces in a clash called the Battle of the Overpass.[49] How do I know? Besides what is written in history books, on the days I showed up to work, I would see the commemorative plaque as I crossed the overpass to enter through Gate 4.

As with Great Lakes Steel, the factory environment and the work process at the Ford River Rouge complex was somewhat intimidating to me. I had to get motivation from somewhere. So before I headed off to work on the afternoon shift, I had to get hyper with cranked-up high-energy songs like Steppenwolf's "Magic Carpet Ride"[50] and "Born to Be Wild"[51] or Jimi Hendrix's "Fire,"[52] all while playing my air guitar:

You say your mommy ain't home, it ain't my concern,
Just play with me and you won't get burned
I have only one itching desire
Let me stand next to your fire,
Let me stand next to your fire …

Those sweaty days working on that fast-moving assembly line, at the world's most famous factory complex, are still fresh in my mind. The first position I had as a general laborer was in the stamping plant, working as a press operator with Glen. The hours were long stamping out metal parts, but the weekly wages were pretty good for young men about the age of twenty. At that time, Glen and I did not have wives or children, so we spent the minimum time on the job, and then we would hit the streets to shoot the breeze with our friends. In those days, the automotive plants were generally working three shifts, twenty-four hours a day. Near the end of the afternoon shift, the foreman would walk through the factory line holding up two fingers representing the question of who wanted to work two hours of overtime. My brother and I declined every time, because we wanted to quickly get out of the plant and into the street.

No matter the job, factory work was exhausting and boring. On occasion, when I worked the day shift, on the bus ride home I would oversleep and snooze past my bus stop. This was the same bus stop where I'd watched the Smith sisters head for home after school a year or two before. Now I would have to walk one or two miles home, exhausted because I would not have the car fare for the return trip.

I found out it was the kiss of death to stop a manufacturing assembly line in the 1970s.[53] If the assembly line stopped, a gang of white-collared supervisors converged on that point with two objectives in mind: fixing the problem and firing the person who stopped the line. So to avoid being fired, we made sure the machine kept operating to keep the factory line running regardless of the quality of the material or product being processed. When the factory line did break for authorized lunch, employees quickly made their way to the bathroom to find an empty stall to do their business, whether relieving their bodily functions or ingesting their personal motivation—alcohol, drugs, whatever. Human consumption and waste is why it took thousands of janitors to clean the Ford River Rouge complex up each day.

Although auto factories provided steady work that paid well, absenteeism[54] was a huge problem. The adage was, never purchase a car that was made on a Friday or a Monday. The reason: most likely the person who regularly performed that assembly job was out getting a "taste" on Friday and recovering on Monday. I remember that, after a short layoff, I did not return to the Ford stamping plant where I was originally hired, but I went to the Ford assembly plant. Glen, who was also laid off, returned to the Ford steel mill. I quickly learned that the assembly-plant workflow was much different from what I was used to at the stamping plant.

In the assembly plant, I was assigned to the engine assembly line. The first thing I noticed was that the worker who regularly performed the job, who was also assigned to demonstrate the job to me, had a much larger physical build than I did. I was tall and slender. He demonstrated the requirements and activities involved in performing the job. The mount frame had to be lifted out of a rack with an overhead hoist and jockeyed into position on the line. This activity took muscle. The same action was repeated for the other side. This activity took more muscle. What made this particular job really tough and strenuous was the fact that this crucial and manual task was located at the head of the assembly line, and if the assembly line below that point was not stocked consistently, the rest of the assembly process was down, and the workers were standing around with nothing to do.

Wouldn't you know it—the next work day, the worker who had showed me the job was absent. The foreman informed me that it was on me to work that job. If I did not already know, the first thing I found out was that my physical build was not made of pure muscle. I was too tall and slender, and after nearly an hour of trying to feed the assembly line, I told the foreman I was outta there and walked boldly off the job and out of the River Rouge complex to the bus stop. The assembly line continued on without me. My mother was not happy.

I soon learned that it was a blue-collar sin to walk off a job without first talking to the shop steward. The union jumped all over me, but I still had seniority, so I returned to the stamping plant. When I returned to factory labor, I was familiar with the loud thunder of the metal presses shaping steel.

I was assigned to the Ford Mustang press line. The workers were seasoned employees, men of different backgrounds who'd come to Detroit to find their fortune. When they talked, the conversation focused on their collective appreciation for their jobs and their strong desire to keep them so they could take care of their families.

I found that factory workers are a unique breed. They may have been the low man on the factory food chain, but they were not stupid. Many of them had been born and raised in different parts of the world, but their characteristics and idiosyncrasies were the same. They were multitalented and skilled in the art of feeding their personal habits in synchronization with the machinery they operate. The best example I can give is the art of smoking. In the 1970s, smoking was an acceptable bad habit in the factory. I was amazed when I saw a press operator keep the rapid tempo of the factory line without losing one ash off a cigarette he was smoking, until he chose to flick the ashes off. In addition, many factory workers were philosophers, able to chair critical debates and discussions and present resolutions to the ills of the world while simultaneously operating a press machine.

They generally stayed on-point in their discussions. For instance, I remember working on the small machine press line that punched holes in the side panel or front fender panel for the Ford Mustang at the stamping plant. The plant had catwalks that allowed visitors to walk about above the factory floor. On many days, there were thousands of kids visiting from local schools, and other curious faces from the far corners of the world who came to watch shiny new cars being assembled at each workstation. "Wow, is that how they do that? Wow, I want one of those cars! Wow, I can't wait to drive that!"

Then there were the Japanese visitors. They too walked along the catwalks that hovered around the manufacturing floor, smiling, waving, and taking pictures of every man, machine, and operation in sight. Although many of the assembly workers had limited education, they could put two and two together. These machine operators on the Mustang machine press line felt threatened. They understood, even at their level of company, that foreign people would take over their jobs if pictures were allowed to be taken of the factory operation. How true was their prognostication? The fuel crisis of the 1970s[55] showed the deficiencies of making American cars using old technology and concepts. Around January 1972 or thereafter, I was among thousands laid off from the Ford Rouge assembly plant, permanently.

CHILDREN'S HOSPITAL

Again, I was in need of a job. Mrs. Cottonlean Anthony, the mother of my girlfriend, Jeanette, got me hired on at Children's Hospital at 3901 Beaubien Street, in the housekeeping department. Mrs. Anthony had been working there for a number of years. My job was to keep the hallway, operating, and surgical floors cleaned and buffed. I worked the midnight shift, and yes, it was a little creepy keeping the operating room shined, especially if my morbid imagination got the best of me.

However, the job lasted only a few weeks, because Jeanette wanted me to take her out and have fun that Fourth of July. I was scheduled to work, but I did not go because I was influenced by Jeanette, whom I later married and fathered a child. When I reported to work on my next scheduled day, the supervisor fired me for not reporting to work as scheduled on the holiday. I felt very bad because Jeanette's mother recommended me for the job. I let her down.

CARR-STEVENS WAREHOUSE

Again, I was in need of a job. My friend Chick Taylor got me hired at a wholesale warehouse located on Fenkell Street near Livernois Avenue. The warehouse provided industrial-sized cases and bags of foodstuffs and associated food-service equipment to local restaurants and other food-service operations.

Chick and I helped load local vendors with the stock they had purchased. We unloaded trucks with incoming inventory. The incoming inventory would be stacked and rotated with old stock accordingly. We learned to be aware that warehoused foodstuffs attract rodents—rats, mice, and the two-legged kind. On occasion, the two-legged kind set a few cans outside in the back alley for personal use. I do not remember exactly why I left this job, but I believe Chick may have hid one too many cans in the back for personal use.

THE CHRYSLER CORPORATION IN THE SUBURBS

In November 1972, my father got me a job at the Chrysler Sterling stamping plant, just before Thanksgiving. My mother praised the Lord and reminded me every day thereafter that I had a good job and I needed to keep it. She did not have a clue what my dreams and aspirations were.

The plant was located at 35777 Van Dyke Avenue in Sterling Heights, Michigan. It was the very same plant my father worked at when we returned from Ohio in 1965. I started on the afternoon shift. My father worked the day shift. At shift change, he would climb down from his overhead crane and stand at the end of the factory floor "figuring out" his lottery numbers and waiting to see if I showed up for work that day.

My mother felt compelled to drive twenty miles to the plant and back to pick up my father's paycheck each payday at lunchtime. That way a greater percentage of Dad's paycheck would get home. In the matter of paychecks getting home, the wives of automotive workers had an advocate on the airwaves. Martha Jean "The Queen" Steinberg[56] was a former disc jockey who changed her program from popular music to a help-the-community and religious theme that advocated the care of women and children. As a result, Martha Jean spoke to a huge audience of women from all walks of life. The enthusiastic women would be dressed in their best outfits to support the morning program from Monday through Friday. You might say that Martha Jean "The Queen" Steinberg was the local Oprah Winfrey of her time.

Martha Jean rang the alarm bell when the automotive industry paid their workers special payroll disbursements, such as the cost-of-living disbursement which was part of the union agreement. I recall the Ford Motor Company disbursed the cost-of-living pay as part of the regular payroll each week. On the other hand, Chrysler and General Motors paid a lump sum each quarter. From her point of view, that was income the women knew nothing about because the men would not bring that money home. So she rang the alarm.

I remember driving down the street one morning and hearing that alarm go off during Martha Jean's radio show. She shouted out over the airwaves, "You women, don't let them *mens* tell you they did not get an extra check today from Chrysler. Honey, Chrysler paid the COLA or 'cost of living' check this week, and you make sure that money goes to help the family buy food and clothes, not to the bartender or some *hoochie-coochie* girl." I later learned that Martha Jean's maiden name was Jones, and she was from the Memphis area, meaning she was probably a relative on my maternal side.

Do not worry about my mother missing the alarm; she was on it. Then, on the way home, my mother would shop for fruits and vegetables at the open-air markets near 8 Mile and Mound Road; 8 Mile serves as the border between Detroit and its northern suburbs. I must confess, my mama's cooking was great, and that was acknowledged by all those who ever sat at her table. Why was it so good? Besides the tender loving care, we will never know. I asked her to cowrite a cookbook with me, but she scoffed at the idea. From what I learned later, my mother cooked from memory and feel. She never trusted a person, friend or foe, well enough to share her secret recipes. As a result, many of her secrets followed her to her grave.

At Chrysler, I was hired as a general laborer, and in the beginning I operated a machine press. The job paid good factory wages, and after ninety days I had union seniority and company benefits. Remember, I stated that those benefits from a dangerous factory job came with a high price, especially if you operated heavy machinery under the influence. One day I was operating a large press when a metal piece, shaped like an arm and hand, reached up from the conveyor belt and smacked me on the side of the face, knocking me cold onto the floor. I was taken to the emergency room on a cart. I still have the scar across my left eye from that knockout.

Another time I was working on the lead machine press when I dropped a square metal blank on my forearm. The metal blank must have hit a vein, because the blood gushed from my forearm like a geyser. I was again rushed to the plant emergency room on a cart, and I still have the gash to prove it. I considered myself lucky, because others have been crushed in the machine press itself. *Warning!* Never operate heavy equipment under the influence.

I lived at my parents' house and paid rent. A few weeks later after starting on the new job, I bought my first car. It was an orange-colored 1970 Plymouth Barracuda[57] two-door coupe. I was not a stock-car guy or speed nut, but I used my vivid imagination as I headed down the highway to and from work and about town. Man, I just dug that orange color and the turtle-shell top!

The people I worked with were very interesting, and like the crew at the Ford assembly plant, they were philosophers, prognosticators, and dreamers. Al Grant was a dreamer; he worked as a backup singer when he could, and like Berry Gordy he wanted off of the assembly line. I remember loading deck lids with a young African-American man from Mississippi named Eddie in the mid-1970s who told me to watch for a football player coming out from Jackson State named Walt Payton.[58] He said that Payton would become a great running back and end up in the Football Hall of Fame. I have not seen Eddie since that first year we talked. Nonetheless, Payton did indeed become a great running back with the Chicago Bears, who won the 1986 Super Bowl, and he was elected to the Football Hall of Fame in 1993.

I worked with a young muscular man from Arkansas named Jimmie who was raised on a farm and had toted heavy things from one place to another since he was a kid. The lifting helped develop his physique. With his physical body, power, and strength, he looked like Cedrick Hardman, who played football for the San Francisco 49ers in the 1970s and played a tough character in a jail scene with Richard Pryor in the movie *Stir Crazy*.[59] There was no way a sane person would make jest of Jimmie's mannerism and Southern speak—like "Main!" instead of "Man!"—without expecting to suffer the consequences. Jimmie always had a lit cigarette in his mouth, and he enjoyed talking to and about the ladies as he demonstrated his physical prowess around them.

There were a lot of women working on the assembly line for various reasons, supporting their lifestyles and families. I tried to be as friendly as I could with them. I remember working on the factory line with an older lady who claimed she was the mother of David Ruffin,[60] once the lead singer for Motown's Temptations. As we worked on the line, she told me stories about many of the Motown artists. I have no reason to doubt her claims. However, as a coworker, I did wonder why the mother of a famous singer was working as a general laborer on an assembly line and not part of his entourage.

Then there was this young dude whose name escapes me, a former convict with a large Afro hair style. He favored the martial-arts champion and actor Jim Kelly.[61] We became friends at work and hung out a little. He needed a ride to work, so I picked him up and drove him once or twice. One night after work, he asked me to take him over to a friend's house to pick something up. I drove him to the location, and he got out of the car and walked toward the house.

A few minutes later, I heard a sound I thought to be firecrackers. He came back to the car breathing fast, and he told me I needed to drive away quickly. I asked him why, and he told me that the guy owed him some money. The guy did not pay him, so he shot through the front door. I drove off as quickly as I could, I dropped that guy off at his house, and I have not seen that guy again on purpose. To this day, I still wonder if the dude had the gun in his possession during our shift at Chrysler.

When You Got Good Hair

Hair has always been a touchy subject in the African-American community. Women of African descent, in their quest to achieve beauty standards, have been straightening their hair with harsh chemicals for years. From a cultural perspective, actor and comedian Chris Rock, in his 2009 documentary *Good Hair*,[62] explores the African-American world of good and bad hair—what good or bad hair is and where good or bad hair comes from. Rock traveled to various commercial locations to ask pointed questions of the buying public, beauty operators, and those in the supply chain of the wig industry. It appears from the feedback that those who have good hair have fewer issues of self-esteem and appeared to be envied. For those with the blessing of hair, the mantra is, "Those with it get it!"

The topic of hair has also been a touchy subject for African-American men. In Spike Lee's 1992 movie *Malcolm X*,[63] actor Denzel Washington provided a vivid picture of the youthful days of Mr. Malcolm Little prior to his religious transformation to Malcolm X when he undergoes the painful straightening process of getting his hair "conked." For many in the Negro community, this was a key rite of passage in the life of a Negro male because now he appeared to be part of the "in" crowd, or somebody special.

I got off the factory line as soon as I could and onto operating a forklift on the factory floor, and suddenly my social life picked up. I had a few girlfriends—Dorothy, Veronica, and Felicia—who worked in different areas around the plant. I now had the wheels to visit them when I chose to. It also helped that during this period, I had conked hair flying in the wind as I zipped around on my forklift.

Oh yeah! I was cool! My hair was "fried, dyed, and laid to the side" courtesy of the Michigan Barber School owned by the Green family.[64] The shop was located on Grand River and Joy Road across the street from the famed Grande Ballroom.[65] This ballroom is where many famous white rock stars—The Who,[66] Bob Seger,[67] and Mitch Ryder,[68] to name a few—played when they were in Detroit. At the time, there were several styles to choose from. I remember two popular styles for conked hair: the John F. Kennedy or JFK[69] or the Tony Curtis,[70] if you could stand the pain. Believe me, processed hair was an endurance test. Ask Otis Williams of the Temptations; he loved the Tony Curtis look, a style that took all day to create.[71] For years, I watched the dudes with conked hair being cool, and I guess it was now my turn.

I remember the first time I stepped out onto the street and stood at the bus stop. I swear my hair stopped traffic. Then when I stepped on to a bus, I swear people stopped talking to stare. I agree—my hair looked good, and everybody was looking! I was bad! I wore a conked hairstyle for about five years, the heavy stuff. It was not the wet look of the Jheri Curl[72] formula advertised on the popular television show *Soul Train*.[73]

Along with my slick hairstyle in the mid-1970s, I owned a 1974

Buick Electra 225 Limited.[74] On the street, it was called a "Deuce and a Quarter." Burgundy red inside and out with a white landau or El Dorado top, it was a full-size premium automobile that was as big as the Taj Mahal.[75] I would cruise about with the front armrest or "pimp post" down listening to Curtis Mayfield's *Superfly*[76] soundtrack or sit in the parking lot of the Montgomery Ward at Greenfield Road and Lyndon Avenue listening to Richard Pryor's comedy on cassette tape. I was so greatly influenced by his style of speaking that I knew every word and sketch verbatim. Today, I believe I process information using Richard Pryor as my central processing unit (CPU).

Of course, the car had room for female guests, and I extended a lot of invitations. Yes, I thought I was somebody special.

I soon learned that there are two distinct problems with conked hair and large automobiles. The first problem is maintenance. For hair to look nice, it had to be taken care of daily; if not you can become bald or nappy-headed pretty quick. The second problem is when a brother has chemical-processed hair, sometimes a brother's focus is on the cost of hair care rather than on making your woman happy in the romance department when a brother needs to. Similarly, automobiles craved oil, gasoline, and regular scheduled maintenance. In the economically challenged times of the 1970s, there were many days when I drove up into the gas station in my fancy car with my fancy hair and purchased one dollar's worth of gas in the tank, and then paid for it in nickels, quarters, and dimes.

ABSENTEE EMPLOYEES ALWAYS VISIT STUPIDVILLE

I mentioned that absenteeism[77] was an employer–employee issue in the automobile factory. The perception was to never buy a car built on a Monday or a Friday because those were the days the assembly process was shorthanded of workers. One can ask the question, why was this so? One reason is that the work was hard, physically strenuous, and mentally boring. But for a person with limited education and a lot of mouths to feed, it was heaven.

An absentee worker could cover the day that was missed for a nominal fee. Okay, what was the fee? If the absentee worker had five bucks, he could ride downtown to the office building adjacent to the Fox Theater and purchase a valid sick slip from a participating medical doctor. This practice was available to workers long before I got on the scene. For the worker, this could be a great resource, depending on how many work days a year the worker was absent.

If the worker missed five work days a year, $25 taken from the family budget might be okay. But what if the worker was chronic in missing work days? For example, missing thirty-plus work days per year took $150 out of the family budget, which may not be as manageable, plus the chronic absenteeism might jeopardize the person's job. Management was not stupid. During the economic crisis of the 1970s, automotive plants started to put sick slips under closer scrutiny.

As for me, I was a borderline chronic absentee. I had no purpose but to be free and stupid. When I skipped work, it would be on Thursday, because that was payday for the afternoon shift. I would sneak past my father and into the pay room to pick up my check, and then I'd hop into my long lean automobile and zip out of the 15 Mile Road gate. When I made that right turn onto 15 Mile Road, my tires would thump across the railroad tracks just outside the gate, and then I would zoom toward the newly built Interstate 696 heading down to Stupidville. On my radio cassette player, the rock group Bachman Turner Overdrive's recording of "Takin' Care of Business"[78] played as loud as I could get it to come out of my radio.

UNEMPLOYED PERSONS ALWAYS VISIT STUPIDVILLE

Another opportunity to spend time in Stupidville was during the cycles of unemployment[79] in the automotive industry. Some of these cycles were scheduled and others were based on the economic environment. In the 1970s, there was a long period of double-digit unemployment.[80] A job or employment represents a person's standing in the community and a stream of income. When a person is unemployed, it brings a loss of standing in the community that has a negative impact on that stream of income. Being unemployed is only funny the first day and then it gets old.

I recall that the fuel crisis was among the first major economic issues to hit the American workforce during that time frame. As a result, apathy and pain began to seep into the attitude of both employers and employees. It showed at the gas pump where many people were standing in long lines and fist-fighting over gasoline prices and product availability. I remember it well.

Economic change and uncertainty in the automobile industry led the population to shift in Detroit as the fifth largest city's lifeblood drained slowly away to other parts of country.[81] The perceived kiss of death may have happened during the election speech of Coleman Young as the first black mayor of Detroit in 1974 when he called for "all the criminals in Detroit to hit 8 Mile Road."[82] But recent studies indicate that Young's speech just reduced the white talent pool and investment dollars in the city; the criminal element remained. An erosion of civic leadership since the late 1920s may be the genesis of the problems.[83]

The Young proclamation alienated the suburbs so much that folks living there but still earning a living in Detroit took a lot of expertise and resources with them and never returned. Federal loans and insurance proceeds earmarked to rebuild burned-out city business from the 1967 riot instead were used to rebuild businesses outside the city limits.[84] The lack of a major franchise grocery store located and operating within the Detroit city limits until 2013 is a vivid example of the alienation.[85]

I recall prior to the fuel crisis, unemployment had been considered seasonal for many automobile workers. As a result of profits and ample inventory, designated automobile plants spent two weeks in the summer changing the assembly setup in preparation for the new model year. Automotive workers took advantage of the scheduled time off and many planned their vacation around seasonal unemployment.

During routine scheduled unemployment, there was an added benefit in union contracts that enabled eligible employees to receive 95 percent of their normal wages. To collect, the laid-off worker would register for authorized benefits at the local state unemployment office. The laid-off worker would be interviewed, and the benefits would be approved and generally start the following week. Depending on a worker's status, some considered the trip to a crowded unemployment office a hassle. For the state of Michigan, generally, there would be a temporary spike in the number of applicants on the state unemployment rolls for a short period of time and an assumption that the state unemployment office was prepared for the increased workload.

On the other hand, a period of unemployment could have a negative influence on the laid-off employee who now had extra time on his hands and a window of opportunity to get in trouble. With no work, many idled employees filled their time off with alcohol consumption and substance abuse and other deviant social behaviors. Annalyn Kurtz cited in her 2013 news article the statistic that one out of six unemployed person is involved in substance abuse.[86] Remember those hobo cocktails my father and his friends created in the 1950s when they were laid off? When I was out of work, I spend a lot of time in Stupidville with knuckleheads of various degrees. I was lucky my personality is laced with the fun-loving freedom of a juvenile, not a juvenile delinquent.

I found out personally that unemployment and social deviance went hand in hand in the matter of self-destruction. First, this negative behavior that transpired would be the primary topic of conversation for those employees who reported back to work. Additionally, not everyone reported back to work after the layoff. Some workers quit, some workers were incarcerated, and some workers died. The state of unemployment always generates conflict and chaos, and during idle times the company you keep is a huge factor in the lifestyle you lead and how long you live it.

The Company You Keep and the Mortality Rate

It is my belief that during my times of idleness, the company I kept hurt me. I consider myself lucky to be here to tell my tale. Sometimes idled workers gambled, and on occasion I did too. I hung out with some guys, and we gambled in the friendly confines of somebody's basement. Once during a period of idleness, I remember one particular dice game held at a house on Manor Street. Everybody there worked at an automobile factory and was collecting unemployment benefits at the time, meaning benefit payment day was high times, but the next check did not roll around until two weeks.

That day it seemed everything I rolled on the table was a winner. I threw 7 or 11 or made my point. I was happy, and I was trash-talking or talking smack. However, I quickly learned a lesson that day to never throw dice and win while in a basement of a house that does not belong to you, and where there is only one way of egress or exit. Because once you begin to win the houseman's money, that place is no longer a friendly confine.

The consequence of this layout is that you may not get outside the premises with your winnings without suffering or getting injured, or even becoming a fatality. I lived to talk about this incident because I decided it was much better not be so excited in talking smack. I purposely tossed a couple of nonchalant rolls hoping for snake eyes so that the money I was up on the house went back onto the table for some other unemployed fool to take.

Everybody Loves to See Knuckleheads in a Boxing Match

It is my belief that the company you keep can impact your life expectancy. For instance, once I got into an altercation with a person I knew by the name of Ray Moore, who was several years younger than me. First, Ray had a fine-looking older sister who I dug—her name was Marguerita. I had no game, but I remember riding around on my bike singing a song that I wrote about her. It was a couple of simple verses where I rhymed her beautiful name with "I need yah, I need yah!" To my chagrin, I shared the song and my feelings with the wrong people, my buddies.

They howled and laughed so viciously that my expression, creativity, and sharing of intimate feelings about a girl is still impacted to this day. Just think, the guys' negative hollering and catcalls may have deterred me from becoming the next Smokey Robinson.

Remember the company you keep. One night I was gathered at a place in Stupidville. For whatever reason, Ray and I got into an altercation. Initially, it was just two young men talking loud and saying nothing at each other. The altercation should have been over and done with. Of course, my good buddies did not leave the issue alone. The next day, I found myself looking for a fight with Ray. Why? Well, one could say that the group of unemployed people that I hung out with did not have any other form of entertainment.

As I remember, the agitating group of unemployed people consisted of Chick, Sammie Lee, Clinton, Pops, and my brother Glen. They ragged on me with the intent of initiating another encounter between Ray and myself. It worked. The five of us drove down near Ray's house on lower Birwood Street in Chick's sister's 1970s model gold Chevy Nova. The car seated five people, three in the back and two in the front. I sat in the front passenger seat.

Suddenly Ray appeared. We had words, and a few fists flew in the air. Of course, the guys were yelling and screaming. Another buddy named Terry Grittle, bringing the number to six guys with nothing else to do, just happened to be walking up the street during the commotion and joined right in. Suddenly, Ray broke away from the engagement and ran toward his house. The guys were sensing victory for me with high fives and pats on the back.

But Ray wasn't quitting; he was actually running to the rear of his house to release his dog, a German shepherd named Danger. The growling dog came running out of the backyard and around the corner of the house toward us at full speed. There were six unemployed guys scrambling as fast as they could to get back into the car. Again, the car is a Chevy Nova with only five seats.

When I reached the car, Terry Grittle, who had walked onto the scene, had taken my seat, making me the odd man out. The front passenger door was still open, so I grabbed on to the inside of the car door and the roof with my feet on the inside of the side floor panel. The car was moving and I was hanging on as best I could, but my butt was exposed. That was the only target the growling dog needed, because he bit me in the buttocks as many times as he could as the car moved down Birwood Street toward Grand River Avenue. When we were out of range, I was able to squeeze into the car, and we drove away.

Chick dropped me off at my house a couple of blocks away. My body was in pain, and my butt was bleeding. When I limped up to the house, my father had been working around in the yard, and he drove me to the hospital. I really did not tell my father the full account of what happened, but it was ironic that the route he took to the hospital was down the same street that Ray lived on. When we passed his house, I yelled out that I was coming back to kick his ass. My father looked at me like I had lost my mind. He was right, because if I had returned for revenge, that would have been both stupid and crazy. This was the second time my butt had a close encounter with a German shepherd.

The Demise of Shorty Long

There was a Motown recording star named Frederick Earl "Shorty" Long from Birmingham, Alabama, who had a couple of hit records. I do not know how the singer received the nickname, but it seemed to fit his music performance. Sadly, Shorty Long the recording artist died in a swimming accident at Belle Isle in 1969.[87]

The nickname "Shorty Long" also seemed to fit a person I will remember as James Levans. Not because he could sing—he could not. Not because he could dance—he could not. He was given that name because he was obviously short in height with a heavy frame, but he claimed to be extra-long in the crotch area, ergo Shorty Long. He loved that nickname. And from the perspective of a young impressionable black male like me, Shorty Long had it all: a good-paying job in the auto factory, an apartment, a motorcycle, and a long green 1966 Cadillac convertible.

I stand corrected: Shorty Long had almost everything, but he did not have a girlfriend he could lavish with love and affection. As a person, Shorty Long was obnoxious and very uncouth. The first words out of his mouth in simple conversation always pertained to sex. His personality repelled both women and his associates. In reflection, Shorty Long had a lack of confidence in speaking to women with civility and decency, because his small talk seemed physical, offensive, and insulting. In addition, Shorty Long acted ignorant and cast aspersions that left his male friends embarrassed in front of females.

Nonetheless, the knuckleheads graduating from third degree to second degree tolerated Shorty Long's behavior because his apartment was used as a hangout. Often, Shorty Long overindulged in alcohol and other substances, but he could not stand cigarette smoke. He always picked up Eric Inkster because Eric attracted a lot of women, and he wanted Eric to fix him up with girls. Boyd Sloan and I were pretty close to Eric, so we were able to ride in Shorty Long's Caddy convertible too. I remember it was Boyd, Eric, and me who attended the first Monday Night Football in Detroit in 1970, the Detroit Lions versus the Chicago Bears.[88] Dick Gordon, with his Afro hair sticking out from under his helmet, scored a couple touchdowns, but the Lions prevailed 28 to 14. It was a great game, and it was crowded. We got tickets only by happenstance: we spotted Boyd's father in the ticket line and he purchased our tickets.

Shorty Long did not like sports, but he took us everywhere else in his Caddy: Dot and Etta's Shrimp Hut on Livernois Avenue, White Castle on Woodward Avenue, Esquire's on Dexter Avenue, up and down the east and west side of Detroit, and nearly everywhere else in the area. The Detroit freeways were our launching pad. We would run into celebrities like members of the Spinners, just out running errands, or the Originals, taking the kids out for a drive. In the process, I think Shorty Long broke every known traffic ordinance, but we looked cool!

It was a lot of fun touring the town with Shorty Long, but too often he cried wolf, like the boy in the story when there was no wolf. In other words, Shorty Long was prone to faking situations, as when he pretended to pass out after indulging in substance abuse. When it happened, the other members of the group would just let it go by not paying attention to him.

One night, Shorty Long passed out as usual from indulging. Most of the other guys under the influence left the apartment. Only Boyd and I, both under the influence, were left hanging out. We tried everything to get Shorty Long to stop playing or faking as if he had overdosed. After a good part of an hour, we even put him in a tub of cold water to shock him out of his fake trance. We quickly found that Shorty Long was not a light load to carry, but still he did not budge. At this point, a rational human being would have called for help, but this was Shorty Long, king of fake behavior. He did this kind of crap all the time. Boyd said "Forget him" and crashed on the couch. I went home.

The next morning, Boyd called and told me that he'd called emergency services a short time after I left. Boyd said Shorty Long did not make it; he died from an overdose.

I said, "What?"

He repeated himself, and I was in disbelief. How did this happen? Shorty Long had died from an overdose. Even though we were not close friends, I still could not believe it, but it was true.

Well, all the guys who had hung out at his house, rode in his car, and listened to his music were in shock, but no one was in a state of uncontrollable mourning. Shorty Long was gone, and there seemed to be more apathy than mourning. I learned something from the incident: a person has few true friends who really care about his health and well-being. It seemed even his blood relatives had their own agenda. Shorty Long's brother and cousin were fighting in the alley over who was going to get the motorcycle and Cadillac car. I do wish more could have been done to keep him alive.

THE LOST WEEKEND

Knuckleheads of various degrees lead risky lifestyle in Stupidville. Some of them survived, but others did not. I am thankful I am a fortunate one, I survived. Today, I think this state of mind hurts the family unit the most. A precious life is just passing by without paying dividends to the maker. However, back in the day, it was just being cool.

I recall almost every weekend, popular entertainers like Eddie Holman singing "Hey There Lonely Girl"[89] or George Clinton performing "Good Old Funky Music"[90] along with the Parliaments and Funkadelics would perform at United Automobile Worker Local 876 Union Hall. The group had undergone a metamorphosis: they no longer looked or performed like the Temptations. It was like somebody had left the basement door unlocked and a bunch of crazed musicians escaped. Once I spotted the outlandish and mostly diapered George Clinton from my barber's chair on the corner of Schoolcraft and Meyers Road in his distinct performance costume, fueling the curiosity of neighborhood kids and passing motorists. That scene was unexpected.

The hall was located on West Grand Boulevard near 12th Street, a block or two north of the Motown Museum and Swanson Funeral Home. The guys would put on fancy clothes, get together, and head on down to the union hall to dance and party. Generally, the social events and parties were BYOB (bring your own bottle). In the matter of alcohol, some of us carried in the very best in stock, like Chivas Regal, a distinguished Scotch whiskey for a person wanting to portray elegance while sacrificing a nice piece of their paycheck. Others did not care about image; they selected an alcoholic drink that fit their budget and lifestyle, inexpensive wines like Mad Dog 20/20 or Boone's Farm. My personal favorite has always been rum and coke.

The popular unknown pharmaceutical in capsule form was called Red Devils,[91] and if the truth be told, who knows what is in the delivery container when the item was purchased on the street from an unknown person? I surely did not know. But this dude I did not know gave me one for every five people I sent to him. For my effort, I spent the rest of the weekend at Eric Inkster's house under his bed, hidden away in a semi-comatose state. When I recovered, I was glad that I had been raised from the dead. When I arose and went home, my mother refused to let me in. This was most likely an eroding point in our mother and son relationship.

THE DISRESPECTING OF ALVIN TUCKER

I learned that knuckleheads who engaged in bad behavior, such as substance abuse, are always an inconvenience to others. Why is that? I think the reason is that people engaged in deviant bad behaviors like substance abuse tend to use other people's property as hangouts for their social deviance because they do not have their own, thus bringing other people down to the level of their stupidity. Remember Shorty Long?

My family was able to transition from the confines of the projects to owning our own home in a clean and safe neighborhood during the 1960s. My friend, Alvin Tucker, lived his entire life in the shadow of the Jeffries Projects. During that time, the Jeffries Projects declined in maintenance and became homestead to low-income families and criminal elements. Eric Inkster had long moved from the projects to the suburbs, but he and Alvin Tucker remained real close friends. Eric always seemed to share with Alvin anything that he had.

When the gang left our safer neighborhood miles away to invade Tucker's home to engage in deviant behavior while listening to the loud music of War,[92] the Isley Brothers,[93] and the Parliaments-Funkadelics,[94] we actually displaced Tucker's wife and baby from their apartment. Although Alvin participated, in reflection, we actually disrespected his home with social deviance and bad habits every time we came to hang out, but it was allowed. Alvin passed away as a young man a few years later. Regrettably, I do not know what happened to his wife and baby so I could apologize. I hope they did not become a negative statistic in the CDC database.

A STREET EDUCATION IS A RISKY LEARNING PROCESS

From my own life experience, the state of unemployment was a fork in the road. When one reaches this juncture, the person must adapt to the situation or die from it. In natural science, when a living organism is impacted by change in its environment, that organism has to adapt to the change or die from the change.[95] I was on the verge of dying from both idle and wasted time in the environment that I lived in. Time is a precious commodity we never get back.

The environment in which I lived in the 1970s was like being in the belly of the big fish that gulped down everything and everybody who dared run the streets of Detroit without a purpose, causing great suffering. I suffered the loss of property, the loss of family, and nearly the loss of my life at a young age. I was getting weary of it.

When a person is not sober, that person does not have a clue of what he or she is doing, and generally the first things lost are the things they worked hard for. Under the influence, I lent my Plymouth Barracuda to a first-degree knucklehead in Stupidville, for the lack of a better term. A few hours later, that same person and an associate were shot to death sitting in my car by another first degree knucklehead.

"Ahhh!" The clang of doorbell preceded a desperate lunge from the front stairway back onto the cement walk up. The visitor, scared and exhausted of strength from her free fall, is puzzled by the sight of the person opening the door. Is this a ghost or not? she wonders. If it is a ghost, how swiftly can she make it back across the street to the safety of her own quarters? If not, how did the person at the door come back to life, when the purpose of the visit was to report the death, being her, a good neighbor? In reality, death was reported at the door of another house this solemn evening.

This was my neighbor, Mrs. Lee, coming to my house to speak to my parents. I opened the door for her, but when she saw me alive, she thought a ghost stood before her and started into cardiac arrest. Why? It happened because she had come to the house to tell my parents that I was dead. It seems that the Detroit Police Department did not have a correct phone number for my parents' home, so they called another neighbor's house, who in turn passed the message along to Mrs. Lee.

It was obvious that I was not dead. However, when I answered the door, I might as well have been dead. My family suffered greatly in that instance. Later, I went to the salvage yard where the car had been towed and found my sporty orange Barracuda filled with bullet holes, blood, and brains. My car was gone. To make matters worse, the city of Detroit sent me, the person they thought to be deceased, a bill for emergency services rendered to me at the scene. This was unbelievable.

During the same dreadful time frame, I foolishly booted my wife, Jeanette, and my baby daughter, Jeanne, out of our apartment on Ewald Circle. A short time later, the apartment was lost to the same first-degree knucklehead in Stupidville who allegedly shot and killed the occupants of my car. This incident was a loss of personal property and personal dignity. Gone were my young wife and baby, my personal papers, my mementoes, my favorite music and my baseball glove. How can these insane actions be explained to family members, especially to your eldest daughter? I ended up in a street fight on Grand River and Mendota with the principal in this criminal affair and barely escaped with my life. I am not real sure, but sometime later, I learned through the Stupidville grapevine that the first-degree knucklehead was convicted of a crime and went to prison. This is the first time I've ever spoken of either of these incidents, and there is very little I can say about the whole affair, other than it was my fault and I apologize to Jeanne, Jeanette, and Mrs. Cottonlean Anthony who took my wife and daughter in. Both incidents have been a permanent blemish on my life.

TRAP PETERSON

I needed a car. My orange Plymouth Barracuda was gone forever. For transportation, I was either bumming rides or catching the bus. Sometime later, I was able to accumulate a few bucks to make a down payment on a 1968 Buick Electra from a used-car lot on Grand River Avenue and Birwood. I drove the car home and developed an attachment for that raggedy car. I nicknamed it "Trap Peterson" in salute to a utility baseball player for the San Francisco Giants named Cap Peterson.[96] Trap Peterson got me where I needed to go around town for a number of months.

After losing my apartment, I was back living at my parents' house when one night the car was taken out of the driveway after work. When I woke the next morning to find the car gone, I asked myself, who would want to steal Trap Peterson? Later, I received notice that the used-car lot had repossessed the car, claiming that I missed a payment, and they took me to court. What the heck? That notice was wrong. Luckily, I kept all of my receipts, and I showed up at court at the appointed date and time. My mother came with me.

When my name was called, I stood straight up and walked up to the judge, but no representative for the used-car lot stood up to be recognized. After a few moments, the judge dismissed the case, but I did not get the car back. It is my belief that the used-car company did have representation there in the courtroom that day. However, they probably did not think I would show up, so they did not make themselves known in open court.

I learned something from this incident: keep your receipts of purchases, and stand up for your legal rights. I also learned that there are millions of predators on the street all seeking to displace an unsuspecting person from his property, family, and dignity by any means necessary. As a result, I began to learn that I needed to be smarter in who I associated with and who I purchased goods and services from.

CLUB REHAB

Through contract negotiation, the automotive industry provided its workforce with first-class medical insurance. Some of the medical programs were abused—like five dollars for fake doctor's slip—and some of the medical benefits were not used—like programs that dealt with substance abuse. At a low period in my life, I chose to use my medical benefits to get my head straight from hanging out in Stupidville. I did not want to turn into a first-degree knucklehead, but once again, I was influenced by my buddy Eric Inkster. I went to rehabilitation at Birkland Hospital located on Detroit's west side for a week or so. My heart was in the right place, but it turns out that rehab was more fun than hanging out on the street. Every day there were comedic antics that usually appeared only in the movies.

On the first day, a beautiful young lady gave herself to me in the recreation-room bathroom. This only happened in the movies, or so I thought. She was looking to score, thinking that since I was a new fish in the aquarium I probably brought contraband with me. I remember the nurse came banging on the bathroom door to get us out.

Later, I remember sending out requests to the guys on the street for them to purchase contraband and bring it to the back of the hospital under the cover of darkness. They would find a string hanging outside a strategically selected open window. They would secure the contraband onto the hanging string, and then the package would be hoisted up through the open window to the second floor. Again, who really knows what substance was hoisted up on the string? These antics were not new, but it was the kind of crazy stuff you would only expect to see in a movie.

In this particular ward, there were generally three patients of the same gender assigned to a room. I remember making a midnight rendezvous with that same beautiful young lady one night in her room. I was a young man and did not mind taking risks to see a girl.

I waited patiently for the clock to move a little deeper into the night. I wanted to complete my mission and get back before bed check. When the time was right, I slowly eased out of my bed into the hallway. I avoided the big mirrors mounted in the hallway as best I could. I went into creep mode so that I could travel the shiny hallway undetected.

To the right of my room was the nurse's station situated at the front of the ward. At night, that was the only place where activities were above the quiet noise level. The rest of the patient rooms located to the left of my room were pretty quiet. I slinked down the hallway to the target room. The target bed was in the middle of that room. I slinked into the bed and announced "I am here!" I commenced to playing Casanova.

Things were going along pretty darn well until the nurse came in. She was conducting her bed check and was looking for me. This nurse was a beauty! She was light-skinned with long hair and cleavage. She escorted me back to my room and bed, where I did my best to convince her to share both a kiss and my bed with me. She refused. She told me not to leave the bed for any reason other than to go to the restroom. I reluctantly agreed.

I went back to sleep for a short time planning to return to my rendezvous. When I woke, I found that my front door had been booby-trapped. I could not get through the contraption without alerting the nurse's station. Man, I was pissed, and my mission that night was over. The next morning, my nocturnal activities were the talk of the ward.

DUMB STUFF JUST HAPPENS IN STUPIDVILLE

My parents, Reuben and Lydia, were born and raised in the agricultural South with great family values. They worked religiously to provide lodging, food, and a safe haven for their children. Those family values carried over as we were raised under the influence of the Baptist church and were taught on a daily basis the difference between right and wrong. My parents were not perfect; they were human beings and on occasion smoked, drank, and gambled in social moderation as previously mentioned. I never knew them to commit a crime against society or exhibit malice toward another person.

As a kid growing up, I felt that I was a good person. I did not harbor hate or malice in my heart. I also felt that I was a fortunate person because I had a roof over my head and food to eat. I never felt that I had to commit a crime to obtain something that belonged to someone else (girls do not count). I considered my friends to be normal young men who got into normal adolescent stuff that young men get into if left alone without mentorship.

Not everyone I knew or came in contact with was an angel. There were one or two guys in the group who were more daring than others who on occasion committed a crime—for whatever reason, they needed the item or just the sport of doing it. The guys I grew up with were most likely to be a victim of a first-degree knucklehead rather than *being* a first-degree knucklehead. There were consequences if things went wrong. My dad used to say, "Don't be in the wrong place at the wrong time, because then it is too late." As for me, I was very clumsy at taking something that did not belong to me (girls do not count).

I would consider my brother Glen to be a person who was a little more daring than me in the things of Stupidville. I remember my father took me, Glen, and a couple of friends, I think Clinton and Terry, to Kmart located on the corner of Plymouth Road and Southfield Freeway to pick up some miscellaneous items in the late 1960s. Dad wandered the store looking for whatever he came to get. I was not far behind, just looking. Glen, Clinton, and Terry were in another part of the store wandering—or so we thought.

A store representative approached my father and asked him to come to the office in the back of the store. My father, looking a bit puzzled, reluctantly said that he would. I went with him. As we walked along I looked about to see if I could see my brother and the other guys, but I did not spot them. So I continued on with my father.

I did not spot them because the three of them were already in the backroom under confinement. The store representative told my father that they were caught changing the price tags on items on the shelf. My father did not say much, he just asked what the store planned to do. The store representative told my father if they left the store immediately the store would not press charges. Dad did exactly that. I do not remember if we got what we came to the store to get, but we left in a hurry. The guys got dropped off somewhere and my father, Glen, and I went home.

Along the way home, Dad began his speech about stealing, hanging out with the wrong people, and getting into trouble. He cited the words of his father about getting into trouble that takes a lifetime to get out of. He said he was embarrassed, and that he would never go to the store with us dummies again. I still remember the incident because I think this was a strong indication that my brother Glen was greatly influenced by bad behavior.

In my days as a younger man hanging out in the street, the practice of stealing was called pulling a rip. I was the older brother and protector, but I was greatly influenced by my love for my brother, who in turn was greatly influenced by people who committed bold and daring acts. As per our personalities, if we were watching a movie, I liked the guy in the white hat and Glen liked the guy in the black hat.

There is always smoke and fire in a drug zone. I know because I wasted too much time there. One day, an unsavory merchant making his living selling drugs challenged his clientele to rip off his competitor, thus putting the competition out of business. I do not remember how this situation began, but some third-degree knuckleheads agreed to do the job, and it snowballed when somebody produced some pistols for the job. What's the big deal? It happens in the movies all the time!

For young men, it is difficult to back down from peer pressure, especially for young men of color. The next thing I knew, four or five guys were heading for the door of the competitor, and Glen was up front in the lead. The plan was to rush the door once it was opened.

There was a knock on the door, and the door slowly opened, but there was no rush. Two people were allowed inside the apartment. Oh my God, one of them was Glen. I told myself this was a bad situation, and I was really worried for my brother's life. A few minutes later, my brother and the other person came out without a scratch, and no criminal activity ensued. I was so happy that no harm came to my brother. I was so happy there was no progression from third- to second-degree knuckleheads. It was such a good day that I shot at a rat in the alley when we left the apartment building and missed.

I was as lucky as that rat as I continued my risky behavior in

Stupidville. Twice I was in apartments in Stupidville when a weapon discharged in my vicinity. The first time, a shotgun blast went over my head into the ceiling as I was walking out the door; being six foot three, I was very fortunate. The second time, the explosion of a small caliber shot hit my arm as I lay on a dirty couch in Stupidville. From these incidents, I learned if you are sitting or standing or knocking in the wrong place, the wrong thing is going to happen to you, and as my father and grandfather would say, "it would be too late."

The Big Four Strategy

In the 1970s, the Detroit police deployed four-man squads in plainclothes who drove the streets in black sedans as law enforcement and intimidation. The police employed a police decoy unit called STRESS (Stop the Robberies and Enjoy Safe Streets).[97] I used those terms in the same sentence because, during the course of apprehending bad guys, they would coerce naive males of any persuasion into their strategies. In my opinion, that is why the police have a difficult time in African-American neighborhoods. They ruin the lives of five good guys to get one bad guy. Ask Rick Wershe—aka "White Boy Rick."[98]

One day I was in Stupidville along with a group of mixed knuckleheads socializing and enjoying a mellow state. There were several unfamiliar faces in the crowd but nothing usual. There came a firm knock on the door. Slim was the person responsible for handling the door. Slim was no Samson; instead, he was a legally disabled person. His left arm was deformed, and he walked with a limp on the same side as his deformed arm. I remember that Slim went to the door, opened it, and then frantically tried to close the door as he screamed. The door was pushed in on Slim, and he was pushed aside like a rag doll. It was "the Big Four," and it was a raid. This was the wrong place to be at the wrong time, but it was too late.

Two black cops in plainclothes entered the apartment with their guns drawn, and they pushed all the occupants against the wall with their hands up and legs spread. They took what identification the people had on them and then began to search the apartment. They took select individuals into the different rooms to talk.

There was a third plainclothes cop standing near the door watching the group with his hand in his pocket; he was white. The cops handcuffed several residents of the apartment and then sat them down on the couch. Their focus shifted to the individual standing on the wall next to me. He was identified as a member of a family of criminals, which he boldly denied. They handcuffed him and took him to the police station along with my friends Clinton and Sammie Lee. They left me, my brother Glen, Slim the disabled doorman, and for the lack of a better term, two young ladies learning to be bad girls.

In the 1972 blaxploitation movie *Across 110th Street,*[99] the cops were in no mood for folly as they looked to capture three black men for murder. This was no time for levity if you wanted to live. I did my best to look stupid. Standing there with my hands up against the wall, I could hear Bobby Womack[100] singing the theme song from the movie. I would have been a fool to suddenly become cool with the Detroit cops.

This was one time that it was a good thing to wear glasses and have a dumb smile on my face. The deer-in-the-headlight expression kept Glen and me out of jail. On that day, the Big Four had specifically targeted one of the unfamiliar faces who happened to come from a family of felons. They took all of the advanced knuckleheads to jail and left dumb-looking me and my brother with the disabled doorman and the girls. At the time, my brother and I were so harmless we did not do anything interesting with the girls. In essence, my brother and I had no gold or game to make it with these girls. Sammie Lee told me later that the guy from the family of criminals thought I was laughing at him and vowed to kick my ass when he got out. For the record, I was not laughing at him. That is just the way I looked.

The Fake Brother

A person living or just hanging out in a high-crime area should always know who he is riding with, standing with, walking with, and talking with, because the person you think you know will experience a sudden case of amnesia when the cops show up. This is especially true if that same person has outstanding warrants. For those very reasons, Sammie Lee Ford always morphed into one of his brothers when he was questioned by the police. Generally, if that questioning was taking place in a high-crime area, guns were drawn and the police were a little more edgy in their questioning. Sometimes the identity switch worked for Sammie Lee, and other times it did not.

It worked one day on Mack Avenue near Interstate 75 in Detroit. The cops stopped my car Trap Peterson with guns drawn and told us to put our hands on the dashboard without delay. Then they asked us to exit the vehicle with our hands up. Once we were out, we had to stand with our hands on the vehicle and our feet spread apart. They searched the vehicle and found nothing. They checked identification and found nothing, but they extended our time together when Sammie Lee was found to have the identification of one of his brothers. The officers did not think the pictures matched, but soon after they let us go. I hopped in my car and drop everybody off and went home. I'd had enough fun in Stupidville for the day.

It's My Brother's Coat!

Another day, Chick Taylor, Sammie Lee Ford, and Murphy Brickgarden had been locked up for loitering and tossing a pistol out of the car in front of the Thompson's house on Birwood Street. Mrs. Thompson, the matron of the house, reported the action to a passing patrol car. The guys were then taken to jail in the 13th Precinct on Schafer between Grand River and Schoolcraft because they were not forthright in providing their true identities and they had outstanding warrants.

Later that same day in Stupidville, I was picked up at the skating rink on Greenfield Road for impersonating a street-cocktail salesman. For me, going big-time lasted five seconds. The police stopped me and patted themselves on the back, believing they'd caught public enemy number one. On my person there was a vial of lactose, a sugary white powder found in milk or dairy products typically used as a mix to stretch out the cocktail batch. Public enemy number one I certainly was not. I denied everything they accused me of, and like the dummy I was, I shouted just as any rat caught in a trap would, "This is my brother's coat!" Of course they did not believe my lame explanation, so they patted me down pretty thoroughly and put me in handcuffs to take me to jail at the 13th Precinct.

As I approached the back door in cuffs, my ears heard a familiar grunt and groan. It had to be Sammie Lee, one of the guys who had been busted earlier in the day on Birwood Street. It was—and he and the two other detainees were surprised to see me. It should not have been a surprise, because this is generally where everybody in Stupidville ends up.

The guys were locked in individual cells facing each other. I was patted down again pretty thoroughly and placed in the large cell called the bullpen. That day I had worn an orange gabardine shirt with deep pockets. The little merchandise I did have in my possession was wrapped in small aluminum packets and lay undetected in the deep pockets of my gabardine shirt. I knew I needed to rid myself of this stuff, so I opened the packets up and passed the contents around to the guys in the other cells. From the perspective of contraband, I made their day in the jailhouse a little easier, as the overlooked contraband was immediately consumed.

For me, that was a good thing, because later that evening I was transferred downtown to 1300 Beaubien Street. Again, the police thought they had a master criminal in their possession; they didn't know I was just another young black male with no criminal record and no identifiable goals. I was anxious to go home. However, my night in the big house was turning into a much greater life experience.

That day, I found out that people who are incarcerated for long periods of time adapt to their environment. They have assigned duties and responsibilities, and they perform them as if their assigned tasks were what they were meant to do all their lives. For instance, select inmates served meals and provided reading materials on wheeled carts with great responsibility.

Then there was the police lineup. The lineup is when a group of detained persons are assembled to allow a witness of an alleged crime to point out the perpetrator. Comedian Richard Pryor once said, "The lineup was fun, unless you got picked, then that was your ass!"[101] So I was asked to participate in a lineup and I did. This would be just another dumb thing to add to the pile if by chance I got picked for a crime I knew I did not commit.

Anyway, how could I refuse? So I appeared in the lineup, and yes, somebody in the lineup actually got picked for the rape of a white girl. Richard Pryor was right about the lineup; it was a lot of fun because I did not get picked. Meanwhile, the rest of the black inmates in the lineup were taken back to their cells by a trustee.

I think this particular trustee had been incarcerated for a long time. As we marched back, he provided bold theme music, as if this march back to the cell was part of a television show. Each time he closed the cell behind a person, he made a dramatic sound as the door closed until the very last person, who was me, as if this was his destiny or he was just passing time. Then there was the cinematic ending and grand bravado delivered in Sir William Walton's *Coronation March Crown Imperial.*[102] After that march, I knew it was time for me to go home, because jail was not my destiny. Early on Sunday morning I was released, with no evidence against me. I walked swiftly out of 1300 Beaubien a free black man heading for the bus stop vowing never to show my face in that place again. And in fact, I have never been back.

STAY OUT OF STUPIDVILLE AND GO TO WORK

When you become chronic in attendance, management has to take its own steps. I fell into the "under scrutiny" category after one day when my foreman, Gino, walked up to me on my forklift and told me that if I had one more unexcused absence, I would be gone. Well, I could not let that happen, especially since I was still living in my parents' house.

I began riding to work with a more dependable person, Eugene Walker. He had a family, and he had to work to take care of them. He influenced me enough that I started driving my own car and making it to work every day. After a year of no unexcused absences, I sought out Gino and asked him if he knew what day it was. He said that he did not know. I told him it was a year ago that he'd told me if I had another unexcused absence, I would be fired. We chuckled and shook hands. After that, I went another full year without an unexcused absence. Suddenly, I was becoming more dependable.

It was from this small victory that I gained confidence in getting away from the nonproductive activities going on down in Stupidville. A friend of mine, Bernice, told me that it was hard to stay away from the influence of bad habits. You know, she was right; it was very difficult to get away from a bad habit, but I had put my best foot forward in regaining my loss of direction. I started doing my best to stop trying to impress her on Thursday nights at the bar on Livernois Avenue after work. She was married and I was married, and that was a bad combination.

MARRIAGE OR MATRIMONY: A STRATEGIC ALLIANCE IN THE MIDST OF CHAOS

My oldest daughter, Jeanne, was born in July 1973 right in the middle of Hollywood's barrage of blaxploitation movies into the community. Jeanne loves football, making it possible to say that she grew from a seed planted during the time frame of the "Immaculate Reception" in the winter of 1972.[103] In my opinion, it stands as one of the greatest plays in any sport ever.

Blaxploitation movies helped the industry regain profits and employ black actors like Jim Brown or Pam Grier. Arguably, many of the movies manipulated the image of African-Americans. For instance, Jeanne's mother, Jeanette, looked and dressed like Pam Grier, the black actress who starred in several movies as the lead character Foxy Brown.[104] I was hooked, but again, I was also naive. Her choice of dress disguised her true age of fifteen or sixteen. Maybe she should have been preparing for high school, because I was five years older than she was and immature myself.

I missed Jeanne's birth because I was hanging out in Stupidville with my buddies. Early one morning, I had the feeling that something was going on with Jeanette, so I woke up and called her house. I was told that her mother, Cottonlean, had taken her to the hospital on Woodward Avenue a short time ago. I got in my car and drove to the hospital. I got to the hospital at 10:10 a.m. but I missed Jeanne's birth at 10:09.

Ironically, Jeanne's birth came a few months after the death of my grandmother, Roxie, the voice I heard when I was a baby. Later that summer, I was visiting Eric Inkster at his parents' house and we were talking in the backyard about my new daughter and becoming a father. Eric's father, Ted, was the father of a young daughter, Shawn, and he took exception to what he thought was bragging. He then posed this question to me: "How do you think the girl's parents feel?"

Mr. Inkster's remarks registered in my brain. I needed to do the right thing, so in September 1973 I decided to ask Jeanette to marry me. I did, and she said yes. I put on a shirt and tie and borrowed my brother's *Superfly* coat for real this time, and we drove downtown to the Wayne County Building to get married. Cottonlean met us there to serve as the witness, and then she went back to work at Children's Hospital. When we went into the Wayne County Building for the nuptial, we were the beautiful Pam Grier and the tall brother looking good straight out of a blaxploitation movie.

When we came out of the Wayne County Building as husband and wife, the future of our marriage was staring us in the face: my Plymouth Barracuda had a flat tire. A flat tire! What a great way to start a long and lasting marriage ... or a sign of the things to come. We were legally married for nearly eight years, but during that period of time we lived together as a married couple less than eight days. This situation was entirely my fault. I was a fourth-degree knucklehead floundering in the midst of chaos.

UNION STRIKE

A union strike is great until you miss that first regular paycheck! For a head of household like my father, a strike was a big deal. A union member had to walk the line to receive a small stipend from the union to make up for the loss of a regular paycheck.

In November 1976, a strike was called against the Chrysler Corporation's Sterling Heights stamping plant by the local union. The local newspaper reported that some two hundred dissenting members of the United Auto Workers Local 1264 refused to work minutes after an agreement was met between the union and Chrysler. Their claim was that there was not enough notice given to prevent the walkout.

I walked out like everyone else, but it was me who made the front page of the local newspaper. I posed for the camera with my shiny hair, sunglasses, my big sign, and a big smile heavily influence by blaxploitation movies as I headed for the parking lot toward my shining "Deuce and a Quarter"—most likely headed for Stupidville.

"HE'S BEEN SHOT!"

Earlier in the month of January 1978, I was fortunate to survive the trespassing situation mentioned earlier. I asked God for help and help was provided. At the time, I was angry at my friend Greene Cutlass for wanting to hang around a volatile situation, and I was angry at my brother Glen for influencing my behavior.

A few days later, all my anger toward my brother Glen became moot. My brother and best friend, Glen Alfred Davidson, had been shot on the streets of Detroit, Michigan. Glen died in the hospital over the weekend.

I came home from work about eleven-thirty p.m. and parked my car on the street. As I walked toward the house, the air around it looked and felt different. I had barely taken my key out of my pocket to open the door when my mother opened the door first.

My mother dressed in her nightclothes gave me an eerie feeling. She said my brother was at the hospital with a gunshot wound to the head, and he was not expected to live. I was devastated. I ran out to my car yelling, "I told him to stay away from those guys, I told him!" and drove to the hospital to see him.

Glen lay there in the hospital bed connected to different machines, with his swollen head bandaged over his once magnificent Afro mane and tubes sticking in and out of his body. I felt helpless and speechless. I stayed for a time, and then I went home in a somber mood.

My father, a staunch lover of the Western movie, had always said to watch out for road agents, a common term for bandits or bad guys. Well, there were plenty of those varmints lurching into Stupidville, and this time they shot and killed my brother.

All night and all day, I asked myself, how did this tragedy happen to my brother? The obvious answer was that my brother kept company with the wrong people. I had advised him to stay away from the wrong people. Who were the wrong people? I meant first-degree knuckleheads who knowingly committed crimes for a living and vicious acts of malice. I reminded myself of what my grandfather said and what my father reiterated: "You can get in a whole bunch of trouble hanging around the wrong people." Well, this was big-time trouble, and I personally had to get a grip.

I believe the road to my brother's demise started when he lost faith in God and cursed God after the loss of his first wife, Charlene, who was pregnant with twins at the time of her death in 1971. They had married and set up their household in my parents' basement. No one in my family knew that Charlene suffered from a blood affliction. There was no storybook ending as presented on television with perfection, or within the allocated sixty minutes. My brother was devastated. After that event, Glen became a different fellow and showed more malice toward others. He was hanging around individuals he would not normally hang around with other than in passing. It seems as soon as my brother got street smart, he got dead. When he and I were just dumb-looking fourth-degree knuckleheads with glasses, it seemed that we were never in harm's way. On Sunday, January 29, I felt my brother, lying in a hospital bed miles away, pass away through me that dismal afternoon while I was hanging out in Stupidville with my so-called friends.

I learned a lot about my friends in Stupidville during the 1970s, especially first few weeks of 1978. The biggest thing I learned was that I could have done without them. Now these so-called friends were egging me on to take revenge, just as in other street incidents as we grew from teens to men. I asked them, who should I take revenge on? There was a lot speculation but no proof. My so-called friends provided me with a small-caliber pistol, or what was called by the local media a "Saturday night special,"[105] to take to my brother's funeral at New Light Baptist Church with the intent of taking revenge by putting a cap in somebody—shooting somebody, as described in the urban lexicon. Of course, I was afraid, and I told myself this made no sense. Cap who?

Later, I went to comfort Glen's widow, Shirley. Our grief melted across the line of angst, pain, and vulnerability.

It did not really matter what the situation was with Glen, I had failed him. All my life, I had tried to protect him because I was the big brother. As young kids growing up in Cleveland, Ohio, I took a brick in the back for my brother. He was my responsibility. That night in 1978 had a great impact on my life, more than any other life event, and it was the most tragic year in my lifetime. My brother had a great influence over me in both good and bad times. I suspect that I will never get over his demise. I still miss my brother to this very day.

What I really learned in 1978 is that there is a God and he forgives both the most hideous and the most naive among us.

In addition, when I evaluated my status using Powell's man's life cycle I found that I came from a good home because my parents took care of my dependent needs in stages 1 through 4. But my stagnation became evident in my transition in stage 5 to 6, as my naivety of adolescence hindered my growth to adulthood. Although I had a good foundation, I had very little vision of what my path should be.

LEE IACOCCA AND THE CHRYSLER BAILOUT

I mentioned before that in the employee parking lots of Ford Motor Company you would find Ford products, in the employee parking lots of General Motors you would find General Motors products, and in the employee parking lots at Chrysler, you would find both Ford and General Motors products. The addition of the fuel crisis[106] took a toll on the company and its workers in the 1970s.

Lee Iacocca[107] took over leadership at Chrysler, and he used his personality and salesmanship to get a federal bailout[108] that helped the company out of its fiscal misery. As the face of the company, he was successful in presenting and meeting his goals and objectives in the public forum. As a result, the employee parking lots at Chrysler began to fill up with Chrysler products. However, the tradeoff was that he had to downsize the company organizational structure and employee ranks.

After nearly seven years at Chrysler, I was in the ranks of the unemployed again in 1979. This status was not good at all for this African-American male.

TIGER STADIUM: A PLACE OF SOLITUDE AND REFLECTION

When you listen beyond the catchy beat of Curtis Mayfield's "Freddie's Dead"[109] from the movie *Superfly*, the lyrics stress that a change of lifestyle was needed or else a person could end up dead way before their time like Freddie. But it was not my time to die.

After my brother's death, I had to find a place of solitude. I did my very best to remove myself from the crowd. Those knuckleheads were not going anywhere and to continue to hang out was leading to my own destruction. I slowly stopped engaging in bad habits and being in places that bad and disoriented people frequented. I sought out other diversions and professional counseling.

When you have issues to resolve, sometimes it's good to go back to square one. So I went back to my passion. I would go to Tiger Stadium and sit in the bleachers for the price of one dollar and think of other things to do in life, other than what I was doing. When things got bleak for the Detroit Tigers, Gates Brown,[110] the best pinch-hitter in the game, always came through in the bottom of the ninth with the bases loaded, two outs and two strikes.

"Talent develops in solitude, character develops in the stream of life," remarked Goethe.[111] I felt better just sitting alone in the bleachers at Tiger Stadium only a few short blocks from the remnants of my birth hospital. The quiet time allowed me to think about stuff. I made it through the chaos and nonsense with all my fingers and all my toes.

The 1970s were coming to a close. I was still struggling with the transition from Stage 5, adolescence, to Stage 6, adulthood. So I pondered the direction my life was going as well as renewing my passion for baseball. Lou Rawls, in his soulful 1966 hit song "Dead End Street,"[112] sang that he was tired of the dead-end street and that he wanted to get out into the world and learn something, and so was I. I started to see the world differently, so I took action to make a change.

MILESTONES AND KNUCKLEHEAD INCIDENTS

Knucklehead incidents:

- introduction of blaxploitation movies
- drug flood in Stupidville
- going postal
- unemployed
- flat tire/matrimony
- missed birth of first daughter
- lost personal property
- lost family
- lockup/lineup
- brother shot and killed
- gun in my hand

Milestones:

- introduction of blaxploitation movies
- blue-collar labor
- bought first car
- birth of first daughter
- Monday Night Football
- Tiger Stadium

Wayne with "good hair"

"Cool Breeze" Wayne with sister, Glenda

Three brothers and Dad celebrate Glen's wedding

"Deuce and a Quarter", lots of room and class but little gas

Key Events and Considerations (Macro Level) 1980–1990–2000

1980

- Industrialized global economic increase in wealth and production changes the social, economic, and general framework.[1]
- The framework of the Internet is under development.[2]
- The first space shuttle, *Columbia*, takes flight.[3]
- The discussion on global warming becomes public.[4]

1990

- The Soviet Union is dissolved.[5]
- Multiculturalism becomes more prevalent.[6]
- Alternative media sources blossom.[7]
- Dot-com wealth grows.[8]
- Hip-hop culture takes hold.[9]

2000

- Globalization increases.[10]
- The Internet explodes.[11]
- Global financial crisis erupts.[12]

Key Events and Considerations (Micro Level) 1980–1990–2000

1980

- Availability of television and television sets increase globally.[1]
- IBM personal computer (PC) is introduced.[2]
- The Berlin Wall falls and the Cold War ends.[3]
- The Persian Gulf War–Desert Storm/Desert Shield begin.[4]

1990

- Technology is constantly advancing.[5]

2000

- Attacks take place on September 11 (9/11).[6]
- The War on Terror–the War in Afghanistan (Iraq/Afghanistan) begins.[7]
- Barack Obama is elected President of the United States.[8]

CHAPTER 3

STATE OF REDEMPTION AND A MAN'S WORLD

"Ahhh!" The clang of bayonets preceded a desperate lunge into the icy waters below. The diver, scarred and exhausted of strength in free fall, knows if the flight is survived, then he could make it to the distant shore. Once ashore, he could seek cover among the terrain, mend his wounds, regain his strength, escape enemy lines, and return to his unit. Most importantly, this survivor can preserve the legacy of fellow United States soldiers and fight another day to protect the Fulda Gap.

THE FULDA GAP

The year is 1981, and I am a long, long way from the pine bleachers at Tiger Stadium. I am now a quartermaster soldier in a combat engineer battalion working in close proximity to a tank regiment and armored cavalry unit in the middle of the Cold War.[1] I can see the opposition through the pine trees across a divided border in Germany, and they look back at me.

During the Cold War, the Fulda Gap[2] was a strategic area where North Atlantic Treaty Organization (NATO)[3] soldiers stationed in West Germany trained each day to protect against an invasion from the Warsaw Pact[4] nations of eastern Europe led by the Soviet Union. The Fulda Gap was a geographical region of lower elevation between the then–East German border and the metropolitan city of Frankfurt in

West Germany, a corridor well-suited for invasion by large-scale armored forces.

Obviously, there were a multitude of scenarios for a Soviet invasion known only to others. The Fulda Gap scenario is the one I was directly aware of and the only one my chain of command was immediately concerned with and drilling into me. According to my commanders, the loss of a battle at the Fulda Gap meant the loss of Frankfurt. The loss of Frankfurt would destroy the economy of West Germany and start a chain reaction in the West. The loss of Frankfurt would also mean US reinforcements could not use the two large airfields designed to receive military assets when and if war broke out.

For the individual soldier assigned to the Western Allies after World War II, that meant standing guard duty on a full-time basis among the tall forest trees in cold weather with a finger on the trigger of a weapon. In addition, studying, identifying, and committing to memory the images and capabilities of Soviet tanks printed on the back of playing cards during hip-pocket training sessions. For the Cold War soldier, that particular deck of playing cards served as both recreation and a training tool. The table stakes in this East versus West card game was all the marbles in the world.

To deter invasion, Allied soldiers trained day and night in preparation for a major tank battle along the Fulda Gap. As a US soldier, I volunteered to be there in West Germany as part of the all-volunteer army[5] which led to twenty years of military service in comparison to less than one day in the military draft. In addition, sitting in a foxhole at the Fulda Gap was more honorable than poking about some else's dark garage.

MOVING ON FROM 1978

Why was I choosing this path in 1979? First, the death of my brother devastated my family a great deal. Secondly, I did not want the same thing to happen to me. In 1979, I'd been laid off again from the factory. I was tired of being unemployed, and most of all, I was tired of working in a factory, period. During my layoff, I drove a taxicab for a few days, but that too was not working for me. I needed more in my life than the tunnel view of the factory. I wanted a broader view of the world.

I remember the US Army marketing career opportunities in the media using two optimistic slogans that attracted my attention: *This is the Army* was the first slogan, and the second slogan was *Be All That You Can Be.*[6] One day I walked by a recruiting station on Woodward Avenue near Davison in Highland Park. I stopped to read the placard posted in the picture window that illustrated career opportunity, education bonuses, travel, and other material things obtainable upon the completion of training.

At the time, I knew very little about the army organizational structure, but from the placard I understood that the highest bonuses, up to $30,000, were tied to joining combat arms and combat support units. So if my immediate goal was to suddenly come into a large chunk of money, then these were the two areas I should look into for opportunity. Still, I did not have a clear vision; I just wanted to do what was necessary to get off the street and away from Stupidville.

A few days later, I was driving north on Meyers Avenue near Lyndon Road in my Buick when I spotted a person walking along the sidewalk who I had not seen in several years. The person was Arnett Brickgarden. I remember his brother Murphy was with him. Arnett and I had always been good friends and would sing the latest hit record and laugh at jokes. I asked him where he had been for so long, because I had not seen him around the neighborhood. He enthusiastically replied that he had joined the army, collected a few dollars, met some babes, and been stationed in Panama. I was surprised, because he was already a veteran of the US Navy.

Our conversation was short. Arnett appeared to be a happy camper. However, his recent experience in the military did not appear to manifest a change in his lifestyle, since he was still walking about the streets with his brother and living with his parents. We said our good-byes, and that was the last time I saw him. Sadly, I learned through a mutual friend that Arnett died in a street fight sometime later. This tragedy was not unusual; few individuals from my neighborhood did not return to the streets of Stupidville after serving a tour of duty in the military.

The Russians invaded Afghanistan in 1979.[7] The Soviet Union and the United States, engaged as Cold War adversaries since 1945, had stockpiled military arms and kept the world on high alert. Also during this period, an economic war emerged in the US domestic market between US automakers and Japanese imports. US dominance of the automotive industry in the worldwide market was no longer. Poor US product quality and the rise of fuel prices opened the door for foreign imports, with Japanese imports claiming a greater market share of the domestic economy.[8]

For people like me, US unskilled blue-collar labor, it was a time of economic uncertainty. I controlled very little of my economic circumstances, as Lee Iacocca wielded his mighty pen like a sword on national television.[9] It seemed that my fellow workers on the Ford assembly line of the early 1970s were accurate in their prognostications that their jobs would be gone if that camera picture was taken by the competition. The fact of the matter is the picture was taken and as a result, I had to make a change in my life or suffer the consequences of an at-risk lifestyle. Richard Pryor relates in one of his comedic skits that the judge gave him a choice of either going to jail for his offenses or going to the army. He quickly chose the army.[10]

When I flipped the television channel, there was the Soviet Union flexing its muscle in Afghanistan. I decided if I was going to die, then I wanted to die with guns blazing. I figured the United States was next on their list, so I might as well prepare myself for the showdown. Becoming a young warrior in defense of the nation for a year or two made more practical sense than becoming another young black male with the surname Davidson lying in the street for no reason at all. I took action.

OPPORTUNITY: THE MODERN VOLUNTEER ARMY

A very short time later, I went to the army recruiting station located on Grand River Avenue and Ward Street, not far from my parents' house. I met and talked with a recruiter, Sergeant Johnnie L. Brooks. He showed me a video recording and provided me with some pamphlets. I gave him some initial personnel data and disclosed my background to include any history of substance abuse for his review. I took the materials home to read. At some point, he scheduled me for a physical examination downtown at the new military facility. I went at the appointed time, and I learned later that I had passed the physical examination. The experience was much more pleasant than the one I recall almost ten years prior. The video recording the army recruiter provided made me very optimistic and gave me hope. I thought I could find opportunity in the army and subsequently retrain myself, as well as become a better person and citizen, if I volunteered to join.

A vivid interpretation of the time period can be found in the boredom of the two main characters portrayed by Bill Murray and Harold Ramis in the 1981 comedy film *Stripes*.[11] Murray plays John Winger, a slacker who drives a cab in the city of Louisville. The character suffers as a result of life-changing events when, in the span of a few hours, he quits his job, has his car repossessed, drops his pizza on the street, and gets dumped by his girlfriend.

Now severely down in the dumps, Winger comes to the realization that his life is a failure and he needs a new direction. Suddenly, at his lowest moment, there is a calling: a recruiting ad for the US Army playing on the television. Winger takes the recruiting ad as a great sign and decides that the army is just what he needs to get in shape and meet girls.

Ramis plays Russell Ziskey, Winger's best friend, who is also down in the dumps from his own troubles. Winger talks him into joining the army too. The pair quickly drive to the nearest recruiting office and are soon off together to basic training at an army installation. In their minds, they are now well on their way on their new journey and adventure.

I, too, was well on my journey and adventure. Sergeant Brooks informed me that I'd passed the physical examination and now it was time to talk about a legal contract. After a contract agreement, I would go back downtown at an appointed time to take my oath, sign on the dotted line, and be on my way. But first we had to discuss where I would go and what I would train to become.

Sergeant Brooks peered over his computer listing with bonus offerings, and then he said, "I got a job for you with a guaranteed bonus of $10,000, a 'Forty-Five Lima' Artillery Repairman." I figured he meant I would be carrying around tools trying to repair things. Immediately, memories came to mind of working with my father around the house or the car. It was not pleasant. My father had to work on stuff all the time and in all types of weather, the frigid cold or extreme heat, and then he would holler and scream at everybody to get the right tool or whatever. Subsequently, he and my mother would get into an argument. I would say to myself, *I hate this crap. I am a ballplayer, not a fix-it man.*

I told him I was not really interested in that choice. He also said the job was in Northern Germany, and that was another stunner. I had been to a foreign land before—across the bridge to Canada—but my mind was telling me that Germany was a lot further than I was looking for. At this point, I was getting turned off. I told Sergeant Brooks I had done blue-collar stuff all my life. I stated proudly that I had a high-school diploma, and I wanted an administrative job[12] where I could expand my educational benefits—something located a little closer to home, like California. At that time, my short-term plan was to be gone three years, see the world, and then return home in time to get a managerial position in the factory.

Sergeant Brooks heard me and acknowledged my comments. He looked back on his computer listing and then said, "Okay! There is an open position as a Seventy-Six Yankee Unit Supply Specialist. It is an administrative type position. There is no bonus; the only guarantee is that the position will be located in the United States." I told him that sounded closer to what I wanted to do. The negotiations were over, and I made my choice.

I felt pretty good. My first step toward a change in my lifestyle had been met. I was scheduled to go back downtown to take my oath and sign on the dotted line, and I did, at age twenty-eight—a career challenge many young people may have difficulty meeting in the twenty-first century.[13] I kept my initiative to myself, and I did not initially share my actions with my parents.

CLOSING THE BOOK ON STUPIDVILLE

It was now 1980, the first week of a brand new year, and hopefully a brand new me. I was now a "GI or government issue."[14] I did not have to report for duty for two more weeks. My goal was not to have buyer's remorse or change my mind, but I did have to wait for my unemployment checks. I was expecting a large sum of money from being laid off, and I could not just leave that money on the table, like in the dice game years ago. I needed money to give to my parents; I needed money to give to my estranged wife, Jeanette, to take care of our daughter, Jeanne; and I guess maybe I needed money for one last fling down in Stupidville. Within a few days, I received the money from my unemployment benefit, and I took care of my personal business. Shortly thereafter, I hit the dusty road out of town.

INITIATING CHANGE AT 0-DARK-30

The first change in my bleak routine came in my wakeup time: it changed to much earlier in the morning. "0-dark-30"[15] is what the army clock calls it when the alarm clock for duty goes off in the middle of the night. The alarm sets in motion physical activity, such as the movement of personnel and equipment preparing for a mission.

It was 0-dark-30 when I peeked through my parents' front window. It looked cold outside. I could see the headlights of the recruiter's car pulling up to the front of my parents' house. I picked up my stuff sitting in the corner that was packed, and I said good-bye to my father and my sister.

Then I heard my mother scream, "They don't want you!" as she turned her back, walking toward the kitchen. As usual, she exercised her opinion of the situation, most likely out of fear. But it really did not matter if they wanted me or not; I wanted them, and I was initiating the change in my life. So for the record, it was 0-dark-30 when I headed out the front door and down the steps in the cold morning to the recruiter's car.

When the recruiter and I arrived at the main induction center in downtown Detroit, the soldiers at the facility treated everyone with courtesy and respect. This atmosphere was quite different from my experience as a draftee ten years prior. As a recruit in the volunteer army, I returned the same courtesy and waited patiently in the locations I was directed to be. I was assigned to a group of individuals where I noticed that I was five to ten years older than many of the group members. However, several had prior military service.

Leaving Home at Age Twenty-Eight

My military orders directed me from Detroit, Michigan, to Fort Jackson, South Carolina, for the purpose of attending and completing basic military training. One of the prior military people was assigned the responsibility of leading the group and handling the transportation paperwork. Before this time, I had never been to South Carolina, only seen it on a map of the United States or the nightly news as another hot spot for the civil-rights movement. I was a little anxious. I was finally leaving my parents' home at the age of twenty-eight, and let it be known, this was also the day of my first-ever airplane ride.

I recall the winter of 1979–1980 in Detroit as being very cold with not much snowfall. But this January 23, 1980, was different. As I looked around, everything seemed clean and new—like snow, the neighborhood, the streets, the highway, and the airport. I walked onto the plane with some reservations, but I quickly made myself comfortable. I watched quietly as the pilot and crew worked to get the plane prepared for flight. Their every action was new to my eyes. Soon after the door was closed the stewardess gave directions over the loudspeaker. Suddenly there was quiet, and then the sound of a hitch, and finally the plane backed out of the gate. From those moments on, I guessed we were off toward our destination.

As the airplane headed forward onto the runway, I could see white snowflakes falling from the sky on this new day. On the inside of the sealed compartment, my body was reacting to the accelerating speed as the plane rolled down the runway. I truly was unprepared for the experience of liftoff and the thundering burst into flight toward the sky. The exhilarating takeoff then leveled off into a fantastic cruise. Now I just needed to sit back, relax, and enjoy the ride, and not worry about helping the pilot drive. *Oh yeah!*

Wednesday, January 23, 1980, had been a long and exciting day. How does one enjoy embarking on a new adventure and experiencing his first-ever ride in an airplane? With liquor, of course! When the stewardess came to me, I ordered a double rum and Coke and lit a cigarette. In those days, smoking was allowed during flights. Since this was my first flight, the buzz was good and needed.

During the flight, I got my very first look at military leadership. One of the guys placed in charge of the group because of prior service got a little impatient about his drink order. He was an African-American in his mid-twenties and a little rough-looking. He reminded me of a third-degree knucklehead seeking to graduate to second-degree knucklehead. The impatience led the young man to tug on the bottom of the airline stewardess's skirt to get her attention. I, too, was developing my critical thinking at his approach. I surmised the guy chose this action because of one of four things:

a. He thought he was in charge of more than the recruits.
b. He was already drunk.

c. He was stupid.
d. He thought it was his mother's skirt.

The answer was *c*. I learned later as a student, when taking a test and there is no clear answer, the test-taker should always pick *c*.

The stewardess was white and in her late twenties with dark hair. It was quite evident she did not appreciate the choice the guy made. The stewardess abruptly turned and gave him a scolding at thirty thousand feet that seemed to last an eternity in flight. On top of that embarrassment, I do not think he ever got his drink order. So the first lesson I learned in military leadership that day was the value of a strategic retreat.

The airplane landed in Atlanta, Georgia, as our first stop, and we took on more passengers, many of whom were also headed to Fort Jackson, South Carolina. An African-American girl from Atlanta sat next to me. She introduced herself, and I quickly nicknamed her Georgia Peach. She seemed very nice, and she, too, had joined the army because she wanted change in her life. She and I, and the rest of the recruits, were all smiles as we landed in Columbia, South Carolina. The army representatives were waiting at the airport to pick us up.

The airport in Columbia, South Carolina, is where real change in my life began. There were a number of people wearing brown wide-brim hats yelling, shouting, giving orders, and herding the new recruits into one large group. I wondered to myself, *Where did all these people come from at this hour of the night and why?* We were assembled as one group and told to be quiet, keep our mouths closed, and direct our heads and eyes to the front. A short time later, they marched the assembly of men and women of various cultures, nationalities, and walks of life looking for change and opportunity onto several buses parked outside the airport, and away we went into the night.

I can never forget the 23rd day of January 1980. This was my first day as a bird in the sky and my first night being herded about like cattle. This time it was too late to get cold feet.

BASIC TRAINING: TANK HILL

I had previously read that Fort Jackson was located within the city limits of Columbia, South Carolina. Fort Jackson is named after Andrew Jackson, the hero of the War of 1812 and seventh president of the United States. It is ironic that as commanding general in the War of 1812, Jackson used free men of African descent and Native Americans in the ranks of his army.[16] As president, Andrew Jackson led the fight for the Indian Removal Act[17] that pushed the Indians off their southeastern lands in the 1830s as the land and its resources became more valuable to a growing population.

When we arrived at the fort, we were taken to a set of administrative barracks. We were a mixture of men and women, so the first question by the cadre was whether you were male or female. When your name was called, it was male or female. Once it was confirmed that you were either a pink or a blue package, you were then assigned to a male or female platoon and instructed that wherever that group went *you* went, marching in cadence all the way. We ate dinner and were issued sheets, blankets, and pillows for our beds, and shortly thereafter turned in for the night. We were told to expect a long day when the sun came up the next morning. The sergeant was right: it seemed as soon as our heads hit the pillow, we were back up on our feet at 0-dark-30!

After showering and getting back into civilian clothes, we were told to muster outside into formation for the purpose of attendance and the march down to the chow hall, but not before squaring away our assigned personal areas. After eating chow, we marched back to the barracks and were then assigned to a platoon. From then on, we marched to eat, we marched to class, we marched to our assigned detail, we marched back to eat, we marched back to class, we marched back from our assigned detail, we marched back to eat, we marched to sleep. The in-between time was spent learning to wear and display the army uniform, including shining boots and brass. I was now learning to become a soldier.

Somewhere along the way, I was issued an army green uniform and a whole bunch of other stuff I knew nothing about except it was all one color: green. I was also issued a pair of BCGs.[18] For those unfamiliar with the term, it stands for Birth Control Glasses. This special eyewear served as a deterrent, because once the eyewear was placed properly on one's face, the opposite sex was automatically repelled and deterred.

As a matter of fact, at Fort Jackson change had already taken place so quickly in my life that I wished it would stop. I now marched everywhere, and there appeared to be no need for me to worry about the price of gasoline for my Buick. I did not have to worry about what to wear. I was issued a new set of clothes, army green, in a similar fashion as an automobile assembly line. All of this was hastily tucked in a duffel bag taking on the shape of rocket that was strapped onto my back.

My new concern was whether my back and feet would hold up under so much change. When we marched, we had to march with enthusiasm and to a verbal cadence. After three days of living and learning in the administrative barracks, we were marched onto the street and onto a long bus-like vehicle called a cattle car for a Sunday drive. Like cattle, we moved onto the vehicles quickly and prepared for transport to our new home. The moving vehicle was heading toward a large water tower that stood out as an imposing landmark overseeing Fort Jackson proper. The travel orders I carried stated Company C, 1st Battalion, 1st Brigade, Fort Jackson, located at a place called Tank Hill.

Tank Hill was the name of the training area for trainees. It was located on a slight hill filled with rows of old, white, wooden World War II barracks surrounded by red sand and pine trees. This place is where the real indoctrination process into the army got going. The cattle car pulled up to its designated spot. We got off at our new billets with enthusiasm. We were greeted by the cadre, who told us to stow our equipment, get chow, get a good night's sleep, and prepare for the next morning.

Again it was 0-dark-30, and it was chaotic. You could hear the sounds of cadence all over Tank Hill; it seemed to go on for miles. We marched to chow and back. But there was no getting back in our bunks, because it was cleanup time, and we were told when the next time to assemble would be. We had to be there and be square, whatever that meant.

The troops I was assigned to looked to be the next meal to be chewed up. They were just standing around like they were back on the block. If you recall, I had already had a taste of military leadership on the plane when our fearless leader decided to tug on the stewardess's dress. So I made my first attempt at military leadership. I strongly suggested to the rest of the troops that we get into a formation and stand at the position of parade rest before our drill sergeant got there. For some reason, the group listened to me. They quickly got into formation and stood at parade rest. We were there and we were square.

A short time later Sergeant First Class (SFC) Edwards and Staff Sergeant (SSG) Zachary or "Sergeant Z" walked up. They were dumbfounded. SFC Edwards said that they had been watching us for a few minutes and admitted that neither of them had ever seen a group of recruits stand quietly in a formation on the first training day. As a result, SFC Edwards said that he and SSG Zachary, as the assigned drill sergeants, would continue to watch to see how far the discipline we displayed this morning would last, because it would also influence how extreme their training tactics would be. SFC Edwards stated that at the first sign of backsliding, there would be hell to pay. Then he stood at attention and commanded, "Group, attention! About face! Forward march!"

We marched everywhere as a group, as one. When we did not march, we ran everywhere as a group. SFC Edwards told us we should be able to outrun him because he had suffered a leg wound in Vietnam and had a portion of his leg reconstructed. If we, as a group or individuals, got off track in our execution or appeared to be a little tired physically, SFC Edwards or SSG Zachary would reel us back in with on-the-spot calisthenics until either one of them got tired of looking at calisthenics. According to SFC Edwards, they were building us to do pushups and intensive activities.

As trainees, we were reminded by the drill sergeants that our status in life, on a scale of one to ten, was less than snail poop on the ground, and that their ultimate goal was to shape us collectively into soldiers with basic infantry skills. During the training cycle, we spent a lot of time in the classroom learning military discipline, leadership, physical fitness and sports, citizenship, and service. If we acted tired or unmotivated, we did pushups. The only free time we had was after-duty hours and Sunday.

On Sundays, the trainees would stand in line at the pay telephones to call home. I noticed that some of the folks could not handle being away from home for whatever reason. Again, I was a little older, so I really did not call home that often because I was seeking change in my life. I was where I needed to be.

I tried to be smart in utilizing my time by washing clothes and keeping my uniforms and personal area clean, because I did not want to do pushups. Then there were the first sergeant's work details around the mess hall: cleaning the grease trap and taking out trash; then police call and picking up cigarette butts in all types of weather; then supply room duties, driving, and picking up supplies; then guard duty. A poor job at any of these tasks resulted in pushups.

The drill sergeants generally addressed the individual trainee by name and rank if they knew it, or they might just address the person as Leroy if male or Suzie if female. When they were talking to the group at large, it could be plural, Leroys and Suzettes. As we progressed in our training, there was a guy from the west coast, Private Cali, who formed a doo-wop singing group filled with trainees. He and a couple of other guys serenaded our female drill instructor Sergeant Ruiz with a song from the phrase "She called him Leroy" in the mess hall one morning. She seemed to enjoy it. But the singing group still had to do pushups for being forward with Sergeant Ruiz.

Sergeant Ruiz was hot! She was a very nice-looking and shapely lady of Puerto Rican descent, and she deserved to be watched both coming and going. I remember one day my training unit was on the fire range. The cadre provided a number of demonstrations on how easy the M16 rifle was to handle and fire. When it was Sergeant Ruiz's turn, she put the weapon on her thigh and showed how easy it was to shoot off a few rounds. None of the Leroys could concentrate for the rest of the training day. Her sensuous demonstration greatly impacted those who, like me, had a very active imagination concerning the opposite sex.

I learned that I could not hit the side of a barn. Back home, I neither owned a weapon nor wanted one, since trouble always seemed to follow. Nonetheless, it always seemed that a small-caliber revolver would conveniently fall out of the pocket of a so-called friend down in Stupidville. Weapons Qualifications was a little scary because of rumors that always seemed to surface long before your group got to the firing range. It seemed that the previous group always provided the incoming one with a horrific story of how some crazed recruit took out either himself, his platoon, or the drill instructor with a weapon on automatic or a hand grenade, leaving a bloody trail on the range.

After a few days of training, I was doing well. I was becoming more disciplined, more mature, and more physically fit. A short time later, I became squad leader for the 4th squad and started developing my leadership skills. I think the scariest moment I had during basic training was meeting the brigade commander, a full bird colonel. Looking in his eyes as he shook my hand, I knew he had no reservations about sending me into a combat situation he perceived to be his destiny or moment in history. So I had better become a soldier fast to protect myself from the potential for mayhem.

Don't Turn on the Light!

I encountered one or two unusual things hanging out in Stupidville that I could have done without. Now that I was in the military, all of that crazy stuff was supposed to cease, right? No! I quickly found out that there were knuckleheads of various degrees in the military too.

There was one particular incident that happened during basic training that impacted the military careers of several young men and women. In addition, the event almost derailed my new start in life. Fortunately, I was too exhausted to get into mischief.

My training unit was comprised of men and women living in separate barracks. For most of the young men, the topic of sex was considered taboo—regulated by a strict training regiment, a confined area with strangers, and a commitment or promise to a wife or girlfriend back home. Nonetheless, when the Tank Hill sun went down over the nest, the lovebirds came out to coo.

In the nest there were also a few odd birds. One Tank Hill sundown, a young white male from San Francisco decided to show two young black males some of his San Francisco sexual hospitality. From this point on, I will identify the participants using a letter in the phonetic alphabet commonly used in military service, Private Alpha, Private Bravo, and Private Charlie.

It was noticeable that the military gear issued to Private Alpha never really fit in the manly fashion that was expected. It was noticeable that when he walked, his stride was more of a sway. In contrast, Privates Bravo and Charlie looked as if they were made for the army, as they were youthful and full of energy. The two trainees also had plenty of curiosity. As I recall, Private Bravo was from a city environment and Private Charlie was from a rural environment.

The incident in question began innocently enough after a long ten-mile road march. The whole unit was exhausted when we returned to the barracks. As I remember, Private Bravo and Private Charlie had been razing and baiting Private Alpha off and on for a few days prior. I asked them to tone it down. Then clear out of left field, Private Alpha offered his sexual hospitality to me in the open bay on the first floor.

Shocked, I quickly declined. Private Alpha had inferred that because I was twenty-eight years old I had the required experience to fill his flirtation. I assured him I did not and quickly told him "No, thank you!"

That overture seemed to incite Private Bravo and Private Charlie, who were lurking in the background, making them more anxious to get at Private Alpha than predators seeking prey. I sensed that, and I did what I thought was best to deter their thoughts. I told them with more military bravado, "Do not do talk about that crap in these barracks," and then I pointed to the woods. "Take that shit to the woods!" Although it was dark outside, it was my hope that this nonsense would cease and the barracks could get a good night's rest.

At that point, the barracks seemed to settle down for the night. I was squad leader for the 4th squad and bunked in the 3rd and 4th squad leader's room on the second floor. The room was separate from the open bay area, as was the 1st and 2nd squad leader room on the first floor. As I remember, when you entered the door of the squad leaders' room, the wall lockers stood along the left wall. There were at least two windows covered with army blankets that faced the wall opposite the door, and to the right were the squad leaders' beds, with the head of the bed against same wall as the door. The light switch was immediate to the door on the wall as you walked in. The door opened from outside to the inside to the left toward the wall lockers. My bed was the first bed to the right as you entered the room, and the 3rd squad leader's bed was against the right wall.

Incidentally, the 3rd squad leader had gone home on emergency leave and secured his government-issued linen in his wall locker. I had the room to myself this night, and I began preparing for the next duty day. I finished cleaning my field gear and checked to see if the fire guard was on duty. The duty of the fire guard is to walk about the barracks in two- to four-hour shifts to ensure the safety of the barracks as the trainees are asleep. After my check, it was time for my shower and then off to bed. Man, I was tired! The open bay lights on each floor were off, and I was the last one to shower.

I believe the shower room was an open bay with four or five showerheads to accommodate multiple users. I was in the shower room for about five minutes when Private Bravo came in to wash his private parts off. I was a little startled, and I asked him what the deal was. His response was that there was some heavy stuff going down.

I said "What!"

He said, "Yep, in your room!" Then he left as quickly as he showed up.

I repeated my "What!" and then quickly finished my shower.

I was more than surprised when the fire guard walked in and told me that there was a lot of activity in the squad leaders' room. Now I was getting a little worried. I left the shower room wearing a towel around my waist and headed to my room. I opened the door, and I could feel heat coming from the room. I reached to turn the light on when someone said in a sensual tone, "Don't turn on the light."

I walked toward the shadows, and the heat became more intense. Before I could get there the room lights went on. I turned my head toward the door and there were the 1st and 2nd squad leaders. They had come to pick up some snacks for the drill sergeant. Both of them were standing in the doorway with their mouths wide open. I turned my head back around to look, and there was Private Alpha stark naked on the 3rd squad leader's bed with Private Charlie next to a wet spot on the mattress. Then I turned my head to look down on the floor between the beds, and there were two more young black men, Private Delta and Private Echo, apparently waiting in line for service or just enjoying the show. My goodness—those two were in my original group from Detroit!

I had seen a lot of stuff in Stupidville, but I had never seen this. Believe me, after this incident, life in the barracks would never be the same. This was a serious offense. The 1st and 2nd squad leaders immediately ran out in the rain to report the incident to company headquarters. Meanwhile, I quickly found some clothes. Private Alpha, on the other hand, acted as if he was in no hurry to get dressed or anything else. I asked him to put something on, but he seemed to be lost in his own world. He did not return to his own bunk; instead, he stayed in the room.

Then the drill sergeant on duty, Sergeant Z, arrived at the barracks, and he was steaming. Sergeant Z stood at attention with raindrops dripping from his cap. He told the young man from San Francisco, with grinding teeth and in the lowest and firmest monotone voice I ever heard, to get all of his stuff, get out of his barracks, and report to company headquarters immediately as he was. In addition, all of the people with knowledge of the situation were directed to report to company headquarters immediately.

Man, this incident was unbelievable. I had been away from home less than a month, and I had already reached a critical point in my career. As the squad leader, I felt that I did my best to deter the incident at the outset by speaking plainly to all trainees. As a witness, I was responsible to give honest and truthful deposition as to what happened or face my own prosecution. To the best of my knowledge, I did just that. After being questioned by the company commander, I was excused and went to my assigned bunk for the night.

When I returned to the barracks, I watched Private Alpha move his gear to company headquarters in the rain. It rains often in South Carolina, especially at night. Wearing very little clothing, Private Alpha had to haul his military footlocker and personal items to the company headquarters in the rain, basically in one trip. I don't recall ever witnessing this kind of drama before, and I am glad it was over for me, or at least so I thought. But I learned sometimes you just got to let people carry their own load.

DON'T MESS UP OPPORTUNITY!

The next morning, I was the most popular person at breakfast. It seemed that everybody wanted to sit at my table to find out what had happened the previous night. It was very awkward. It was also too serious of an incident to laugh about in public without putting my own career and future in jeopardy in Stupidville. I learned that knuckleheads of all degrees come from all walks of life. I learned a lesson in integrity, humility, and leadership. In addition, what happens in the barracks stays in the barracks. I speak of this incident more than thirty years later because it almost cost me my opportunity, and it is pertinent to the theme of this text. I had already taken enough trips to Stupidville.

Private Alpha was now living, fully dressed, in the supply room in the headquarters company pending processing out of the army. Private Bravo and Charlie received disciplinary actions but were allowed to continue their military careers. For the rest of training, they were both less inquisitive about sex and more focused on completing their training. What was ironic is that both of those guys had been talking to two nice-looking girls, Private X-ray, a blond girl from Kansas City, and Private Yankee, the Georgia Peach in our coed unit. The two black males, Private Delta and Private Echo, who had been sitting in wait on the floor, had no disciplinary action taken against them.

During our final days of training, we had to learn to survive on the battlefield. It was night, and the sky was lit up with the sound and flash of pyrotechnics. We were paired in squads and given a mission that had to be carried out at all costs across a number of battlefield obstacles. Each member of the squad was assigned a job to do while carrying his or her own load. In my squad, there was a blond-haired female named Private Zulu. Yes, she was good-looking, but she was having problems carrying her load and it slowed the squad down. As I remember, I helped her carry her load and watched out for her, as she did not move as fast as the others. I don't recall if we completed our mission or not, but I do remember that carrying an extra load and watching out for the whereabouts of another trainee was a heavy burden on me and the rest of squad. So again, I learned sometimes you just got to let people carry their own load. No matter, how good she looked.

FORWARD MARCH!

Soon after, it was graduation day, and my unit marched onto the parade field at Fort Jackson after completing basic training. The ceremony was not like the graduation scene in the movie *Stripes*, where the guys stayed up all night to practice while their drill sergeant lay injured in the hospital. This ceremony was grand and full of military pomp. The army band played traditional marching songs as graduating units marched smartly in front of their friends and families. Their shining brass reflected the sun's rays and each sharply creased uniform cut through the breeze that flowed across the parade field.

At the command of dismiss, basic training was complete. The newly minted trainees broke ranks to hug and kiss their loved ones who had come in from the bleachers that sat along the parade field. I stood among the crowd alone. I did not invite anyone to the ceremony as my guest, but I felt good for the accomplishment, achievement, and recognition the day had brought me at age twenty-eight. The time spent hugging and patting people on the back was short, because the barracks had to be squared away prior to moving on.

I worked hard, and I did become a soldier. I completed basic military training, and I grew as a person. At the end of basic training, I received personal recognition with exceptional performance leadership awards that were completely unexpected. I realized I had acquired a different outlook in my life as I stepped onto the cattle car that transported me and my fellow trainees off Tank Hill to the next school down the road on Fort Jackson proper. I thought I was prepared for my next destination: Advanced Individual Training (AIT).

AIT: BUILDING SKILLS

The cattle cars stopped in front of brick billets on Fort Jackson. It is funny that this trip on the cattle car seemed less chaotic than any previous trip. Again, the drill sergeants took charge of basic-training graduates and reminded us that we were still the equivalent of worm poop in their eyes. My AIT drill sergeant was of Cuban descent with a heavy accent, and he agreed.

Just as in basic training, we were assigned to groups, and wherever the group went, you went marching all the way. We marched to eat, we marched to class, we marched to work, we marched back to eat, we marched back to class, we marched back to work, we marched back to eat, and finally we marched to sleep. At this point, I had forgotten about the price of a gallon of gas because I had not driven in two months. We marched with enthusiasm and to verbal cadence. We would mimic the drill sergeant and his heavy accent. I had grown into the next level of soldiering and learning a valuable administrative skill.

In this phase of training, we spent a lot of time in the classroom learning our Military Occupational Specialty (MOS), which was the job we expected to be assigned to and have expertise in. My designated area was quartermaster or unit supply. The training also continued the development of military discipline, leadership, physical fitness, citizenship, and service. During AIT, we had more free-time after-duty hours and weekends unless we were on the duty roster. But this army stuff was always in our heads, and we marched mimicking our drill sergeant everywhere we went.

Celebrity Soldier

For some reason, my drill sergeant selected me to participate in a soldier board. In preparing for the board, I had to enhance my knowledge of basic soldiering skills and compete against other soldiers representing their units in the battalion. I won the first competition that I participated in, and from that experience I earned a few perks. I did not have to participate in police call or guard duty, or be on the duty roster at all for about a week to ten days. I did have to study and become prepared for the next scheduled board that was to be held at the brigade level. I did well, but I did not win the competition.

I had enjoyed being a celebrity. My drill sergeant was not angry, but suddenly I was back on the police call, guard duty, and duty roster. It was also time for me to get back cracking in the academics of my MOS. I had to make up the classroom time I'd missed attending the soldier boards.

One of the MOS training requirements was a sling load of pallets of supplies for liftoff by a helicopter. The helicopter hovered above while soldiers made ready the load below. It was pretty cool training but very dangerous. Since I think in music, I was a bit leery of being under this hovering helicopter, so my mind was singing: "Sling load, sweet chariot, coming forth to carry me home!"

In 1980, Michael Jackson's first solo album, *Off the Wall*,[19] was a popular recording and absolute the monster jam. I woke up and I went to sleep with those songs in my ears. Being in such close quarters, you learned that each individual soldier had his own idiosyncrasies and personal reasons for being in the service. I remember one roommate was there because he was following the tradition of his father and grandfather in becoming an airborne paratrooper. When unit formation was called, the trainees would file outside the billets using the stairs. Not this guy: each day he would jump out of the second-floor window, practicing for entry into the airborne paratroops just as his father and grandfather had done before him.

The Military Police Have Lineups Too

There is truth to what my father said his father said to him: "Trouble is never far away." I initially thought that the military environment deterred bad behavior, because people had to respect authority or suffer the consequence. The incident in basic training showed how naive I was. I was unaware of all of the crap that was going on. I just was glad I did not get my nose stuck in it.

I remember one night at the dance club on Fort Jackson, the disc jockey stopped the music to announce the brutal assault of a young lady on post, and he asked for any witnesses to come forward and report what they saw to the military police. After the announcement, he put music back on with the same bravado, as if nothing had happened.

Then I remember one Monday morning at the work formation, the drill sergeant commanded all the black male soldiers in my formation to fall out of the regular unit formation into a separate formation further down in the parking lot. Once the black soldiers were assembled, the military police pulled up in a vehicle with a young white girl who was then escorted through the ranks of the black soldiers. This was not a military formation; this was actually a lineup. Remember, Richard Pryor said "the lineup was fun unless you got picked."[20] The young woman had been assaulted and raped over the weekend, and the formation of black soldiers was conducted so she could seek out her attacker. She did not find the person she was looking for in the lineup I stood in, and that was a good thing.

FOXY LADIES

I met a foxy young lady, Robin from Ohio, at the club during AIT. Ohio is the state my father moved the family from in 1965 because, in his opinion, the Republicans did not do things right there. Robin was white, and she had long beautiful red hair. She reminded me of the images of milk maidens often seen on milk cartons and advertising in the grocery store. She and I got pretty close during our time together on Fort Jackson. In courting Robin, my alpha-male traits began to manifest, because there was a lot of risk involved. I considered myself a little slow when it comes to women, and technically I was still married.

Robin was obligated to go to Fort Gordon, Georgia, to continue her training. One weekend in 1980, I took the bus from Columbia down to Augusta to visit her. I would be telling a lie if I said I was not a little nervous being on the streets of a Southern town with a pretty white girl, especially one who enjoyed being affectionate in public. When I got off at the Greyhound bus station in downtown Augusta, she hugged and kissed me, of course. It was nice, but I kept one eye out for people who might not like what they saw. What was I going to do? I did not have a clue.

I do not know if the white male cab driver was upset—I could not make out his face in the mirror—but I thought the white male clerk at the motel was a little miffed. On the other hand, I was probably paranoid after years of seeing hate on television and in public. In the South, interracial relationships seemed to always ignite violence. Robin and I had a nice time together, and later I returned to Fort Jackson on the Greyhound bus without incident.

Later during my visit, I ran into Private Bravo at the Post Exchange (PX). He told me of the punishment he and Private Charlie had received, that he regretted the whole incident, and that it had nearly ruined his career. We shook hands and went our separate ways. I moved on with my new career. I did not dwell on what happened, because I learned that "sometimes you just have to let people carry their own load."

As AIT wound down, I again found out that knuckleheads were just about everywhere in the world, and that more than a few came from St. Louis, Missouri. The Brickgarden brothers who I knew from Detroit were from there. They had been giving me crap about the Detroit Tigers versus the St. Louis Cardinals since the late 1960s. And then there were a couple of guys from my AIT unit, Private Spits and Private Crown, who were both from St. Louis.

I recall the weekend close to graduation when most trainees in the unit were given a two-day pass. The appropriate dress during the time of the pass was the Class A uniform. The weekend began as a beautiful day, and many of the trainees gravitated to the liquor store and onto the lake nearby to relax and unwind. For me, AIT was almost over, and I achieved another level of self-confidence. Then out of the blue, an incident transpired among the guys I was with that I still cannot understand to this day.

Private Spits and Private Crown were evidently toasted after a couple of swigs of alcohol beverages when they greeted three fellow soldiers and proceeded to curse at them. These friendly soldiers were white girls assigned to our training unit who were also enjoying the day on pass just as we were and with whom I wanted to socialize. For reasons unknown to me, Private Spits began a verbal barrage, with Private Crown providing backup support. They acted as if both of them were back on the streets of St. Louis. This was weird. The girls were puzzled, and I was puzzled at this missed opportunity.

To this day, I do not know what happened, other than the alcohol that was consumed having something to with it. It soon became a forgotten incident, because generally after graduating, AIT soldiers move on to their first duty station and may never see each other again in their military careers. Not so with Private Spits and me; we drew the same duty station, White Sands Missile Range, New Mexico. I had never been to New Mexico, but I hoped that they did not have liquor out there.

BACK TO THE CRIB—OOPS!

When I returned home to Detroit from Fort Jackson, I thought I was a quite different person from who I was when I'd left some three months earlier. I was a little taller in stature and brighter in brains. But I still had money in the bank from the unemployment checks I'd received before I left. I thought, *One more run down to Stupidville before reporting to my duty station ain't going to hurt anything*, and I succumbed to temptation. What I learned from that last trip to Stupidville was that the 1970s were over and I had survived, and I have been sober from Stupidville since May 1980.

Nonetheless, I had to get to New Mexico, and I was low on funds. I followed the direction on my military orders and contacted the closest military authority. I was instructed to report to the Detroit Arsenal to pick up a transportation ticket.

At the time, the Detroit Arsenal was where the army made armored tanks. It is located on Van Dyke Avenue in Warren, Michigan. Since 1972, I had worked at the Chrysler Sterling stamping plant just up the street. I had passed this place a million times on my way to work, but I had never been inside or even knew what was going on inside. I entered the Detroit Arsenal through the Van Dyke gate, went to the transportation office, and got my ticket. In my very best army lingo, I was "good to go"!

CROSSING THE THRESHOLD FOR A SECOND TIME

It was springtime and time to go. My mother insisted on driving me to the Detroit Metropolitan Airport. The grey spring day began to turn cooler. She walked me to the gate to see me off, and then she tried to slip me a few bucks. Since the Negro migration, it seemed a tradition for the host to extend every bit of hospitality to the guest, because the perception was that the road was long and unfriendly to people of color. But the person passing the cash was my mother, and at that point in my life I needed to make a clean break to independence.

I told my mother I loved her, but I did not accept the money, although I only had a couple of bucks in my pocket. I also gave her permission to sell my Buick Electra 225, and then I boarded the plane for my third flight as a free man of color at age twenty-eight. For the record, I severed my dependence on my parents' financial assistance on Wednesday, May 14, 1980. I have been independent ever since. As the plane headed down the runway toward a grey sky, I could see the rust of the automotive factories, Tiger Stadium, the Fox Theater, Mackenzie High School, Stupidville, and my family fade away as the plane made its way toward the clouds.

THE GREAT STATE OF TEXAS

A couple of hours later, the plane landed in Dallas, Texas, home of the Dallas Cowboys, America's football team and mine too. My image of Texas came from Westerns and J. R. Ewing.[21] But I never ever thought I would see the state for myself. This was a rest stop, so I got off the plane and wandered around the airport for an hour or so. For my first trip to Texas, I guess you could say that I felt the air to be a little different and a little cleaner, and obviously, it was certainly a lot sunnier. It felt warmer than the darker, more polluted sky surrounding industrial Detroit at the time.

From a tourist's point of view, it seemed that every person, place, or thing standing or moving about the airport terminal was stamped with the size and look of Texas. That distinctive look was really amplified in the people. Many of the men wore cowboy hats and boots, while the women wore a sexier version of Texas wear, looking lean and tough. This was an unbelievable experience, and now I could confirm that everything in Texas was big. It was time to reboard; I got back on the plane and headed to another Texas city, El Paso.

It was an unbelievable plane ride, looking down from the sky at the huge contrast of the Texas landscape. The terrain surrounding Dallas was green and pastoral, whereas the terrain heading toward El Paso was brown and black, rocky and mountainous and somewhat isolated. Marty Robbins's song "El Paso"[22] came to mind. My father had played that song on our record player when I was twelve years old.

When we landed in El Paso a couple of hours later, I stood there on the airport grounds in awe. I basked in the warmth of a beautiful sunny day surrounded by magnificent mountains with a desert breeze sweeping across my face. That was the moment that affirmed the decision I had made and the action I had taken was the right one for me. I felt my life changing for the better already. I had been given a second opportunity. I seized up the sword and hoisted it high.

THE VAST NEW MEXICO DESERT

I reported in at the military desk. I had to wait at the airport for more than two hours soaking up that beautiful sunshine on that fine day in May. My first duty station was in New Mexico, more than forty miles away from El Paso. When the driver finally arrived, I tossed my gear in the back of the van and we were off into the desert on a winding road along a magnificent mountain range. An hour or so later, we reached the main gate, manned by armed guards, where I was dropped off at the barracks of my new unit.

This place was far different from any other place I had been in my short army career. The first obvious thing was there were no troops in mass quantities marching from one place to another under the direction of drill sergeants calling cadence. The second most obvious thing was that there were no tall corporate or apartment buildings standing in rows like in northern cities. But there were mountains that stood taller than buildings and people leisurely walking about in short-sleeve shirts and tops.

I did my best to adjust to the environment. As a training requirement, I had the opportunity to rappel off one of the nearby mountains, but I came close to becoming a permanent part of the desert floor. I quickly found out that my legs were too long and uncontrollable to rappel for fun.

The size of the base was deceptive. Geographically, the post was a couple of square blocks, but the landmass covered nearly the entire state. In actuality, you could ride for days and still be on the army base. This part of the New Mexico desert was windy more often than blazing hot. Nonetheless, this was my new home, and I needed to adjust accordingly.

One of the perks on this base was that we could have four square meals a day. We were isolated, so the army had to take care of the soldiers and civilians who worked there. The main dining hall was near where I worked, but it was a much longer distance from my barracks. There was a television there, and you could eat and socialize with others.

I was perplexed. The regular army seemed to be more laid-back than the training base—or at least, that is what Private Spits told me. Yes, Private Spits had arrived a few days earlier from St. Louis. The last time I saw him was at Fort Jackson, when he verbally assaulted three white female soldiers. Private Spits gave me the layout and, lucky for me, his early arrival meant that he had already been assigned a room and roommate. That was a relief! Our barracks were coed and comprised of nurses and meteorologists, all enlisted personnel. And yes, there were drugs in the barracks. I stayed away.

ANOTHER ROLE MODEL NEAR DEATH ON THE STREET

I remember sitting in the main dining room one day in June 1980 when the television flashed breaking news. The reporter stated that actor and comedian Richard Pryor, under the influence of drugs, set himself on fire and ran down the street near his home in the Los Angeles area. He was then rushed to the hospital, where he was listed in critical condition after being badly burned.[23]

I sat there at the table with my mouth open. This was unbelievable. Another one of my heroes was in self-destruct mode—first Glen and now Richard. It is tough to learn that your heroes have flaws. Where there are drugs, there is pain and tragedy. Even in the desert, I remember the commanding general calling out the entire post to the parade ground in the heat among the dive-bombing dragonflies to address his son's involvement with illegal drugs. I had to once again get a grip and back away from my emotions and the chaotic situation as I did with my brother to move on. Thankfully, Richard Pryor lived to recover from that episode. It is a shame that social ills are brought to the attention of the public through the tragedy of a celebrity.[24]

LIFE ON THE DESERT FLOOR

I grew up in populated urban environments, but this place was isolated and sparse. It was the *Wonderful World of Disney* television show[25] that had introduced me to life in the desert growing up. But this was not on television; this was real. That made the indoctrination process of living and working in the desert very important. I quickly learned that the two most important things to know about living in the desert were to leave the snakes alone and leave the gold alone.

When it comes to desert life, be aware that rattlesnakes and other desert creatures live in the desert, and you do not want to casually walk around and step on a den of them. To paraphrase Richard Pryor, the creature, especially the rattlesnake, lives in the desert; *you* are the one visiting.[26]

I was on duty one weekend with a squad of soldiers who had to walk the desert floor to look for an individual with a medical condition who had wandered off into the desert alone. I remember we were playing basketball in the gym when we got the call to duty. We were required to suit up in the appropriate gear with communications equipment and drive out to the designated area to walk the hot desert looking for the person.

We walked in a spread formation to cover the distance. Suddenly out of the ground emerged a huge jackrabbit with long ears and large feet. We had unknowingly walked into his territory, and he made a hasty exit from his home. This chance meeting was totally unexpected, especially for soldiers who came from city environments. Despite being startled we continued to walk until we got the all-clear sign and returned to base.

As for the gold—there is gold in "them thar hills," but don't go out there looking for a gold mine. The legend goes that around 1937, a hunter, Milton Ernest "Doc" Ness, and his wife, Ova, found a cavern around Victorio Peak filled with gold bars. It is said that Doc would visit the cavern on occasion after that. Then sometime in the 1940s, the government took over the range and subsequently eliminated legal access to the area. The Ness family fought to regain access for years.[27] To this day, the whereabouts of the gold bars is unknown. But as tempting as it might be to retrieve them, it is illegal to possess gold bars. So leave the gold alone, and always remember that there are dangerous snakes in the desert.

The only practical way to get to the top of those mountains was to fly and be dropped in on a dangerous mountain range. Remember the operative phrase: *fly and be dropped in.* Up to this point, I had been adjusting to military life okay, but the recruiter forgot to tell this city boy that army life was very real and very interactive. At the base, the army fired live missiles into the desert that would sometimes set the desert terrain ablaze. To a city boy, firefighting meant that a local fire department brought gallons of water to put out the blaze. True in the city, but not in the desert. I learned that water in the desert was a highly valuable resource not to be wasted on such trivial stuff as a blazing fire.

In New Mexico, when there is fire in the mountains or on the desert floor, soldiers armed with picks and shovels are the alternative to tons of water. Soldiers with dumbfounded looks on their faces are loaded into helicopters and flown up to the top of mountains, where they jump out to contain and put out the blaze. This was not a sling-load exercise like back at Fort Jackson, but once you get the hang of the mission, the dumbfounded looks seem to go away.

Standing on top of a smoldering mountain, you can see forever across the vast desert terrain, much farther and wider than the squared view from the tenth floor of the Jefferies Projects. That is, until the rotor blades of the helicopter reignite the very flame you just worked so hard to put out, allowing the flames to rise and chase after you.

Celebrity Status: Too Fast a Track

From my perspective, life at the base was just what the doctor ordered. Although my military experience was fairly limited, there were more civilian personnel working there than the typical military population. The mission of the unit to which I was assigned was to study the weather. The duty day was basically nine to five, unless you had company duty. Soldiers had to train to meet annual soldier qualifications: physical fitness and weapons, for example.

I was fortunate enough to participate and win the Soldier of the Month[28] competition in September 1980. I was on-track to be successful. I was moving so fast that I got a promotion to the rank of Specialist Four—prematurely. The rank was pinned on my collar at the first formation of the day, but right after lunch the rank was rescinded. I was heartbroken, and yes I shed a few tears in my room, but I lived.

GI PARTIES AND ROMANCE

The barracks I lived in housed both males and females. There was always romance in the air and light tapping on the doors by visitors throughout the hours of the night. I had my fair share of romance, creeping up and down the hallways tapping on doors until they opened. In respect to having a social life, I remember that the unit sergeant major, a black veteran of the Vietnam War, provided a bit of mentorship about being such a long way from home. He said, "You got to do for yourself, because no one else will do it for you."

My roommate was Windrick Smith, a young black male from Florida. Smitty, as he was called, always walked and talked in the manner of his favorite entertainer, Elvis Presley. Our room was located on the second floor. We were roommates but did not hang out much, although he was good for a few laughs. I remember the unit had a "GI party" in the barracks because the higher headquarters commanding officer, General Emmett Paige,[29] was scheduled for an official visit the next day.

For those who do not know what a GI party is, I can tell you it is not what it sounds like. Generally, a party is a friendly social gathering where there is lively conversation, dancing, and liquid libation. A GI party is a social gathering where there is little lively conversation but plenty of choice words. There is no dancing but plenty of formations. And the intoxicating liquid is a combination of soap and water applied with plenty of elbow grease. A GI party is a favorite training activity designed by first sergeants to keep army personnel busy cleaning government equipment, especially those personnel in training status.

At our GI party, Smitty and I worked all night cleaning and shining our room and the assigned common areas, and we were exhausted. We had not yet had the opportunity to dress in the proper uniform, and it was only a few minutes before the general would arrive onsite. The unit leadership had to go out of their way to impress distinguished visitors because their careers were on the line, and it was part of the military protocol.

"Attention!" shouted the first sergeant as he stepped in our room in front of the female captain, who was African-American and very nice to look at. Then General Paige walked into the room. Smitty and I stood at attention and our eyes grew wide from surprise. General Paige was an African-American! We were given the command "At ease!" The general reached out to both of us with a slap of the hand and said in a moderate tone, "Hey, brother!" Smitty and I were still in shock over the good-looking captain, and then the two-star general gave us "five"!

The first sergeant, who was white, told the general where we were from and that we had the potential to be good soldiers. The general remarked, "Keep up the good work and learn to be good soldiers." Smitty and I responded with "Yes sir!" Then the group turned and headed out the door to the next room. This was too cool! We crashed onto our bunks and had a couple great laughs about how we loved the army life. I read years later that General Paige became part of the senior leadership in the Department of Defense.

Smitty did not play a lot of sports, but I was active and grateful. I participated in organizational sports programs, something I missed from the 1960s because I still possessed the desire and talent to play sports. My friend Leo Payne from Memphis, Tennessee, nicknamed me "Too Tall" because my height reminded him of Ed "Too Tall" Jones of the Dallas Cowboys.[30] Payne was a good teammate and a fun guy to be around because he loved to play sports and he loved the people who played them.

Back on the Field of Play

My unit had very competitive teams in flag football, basketball, and softball. The unit was king in the sport of softball, and each year our varsity team ended up as the post softball champions. The team was very talented and highly competitive in earning a spot. I earned my varsity spot on the second tryout. My defense was a little shaky at third base because of my erratic throwing arm, but my offense kept me in the lineup.

My statistics for the 1981 season were .481 batting average, seven home runs, and thirty-five runs batted in.

Man, I will never forget the last out of the 1981 season. We won the championship game, and we stormed the mound in celebration like it was the World Series. My dream had come true, and I felt great. I was a winner!

Earning Recognition and Privilege

I also really enjoyed the professional recognition and awards I received for my work in my MOS as supply technician. I worked for the unit property book officer, an army civilian, Mr. Ernest Utter, a Mexican-American who lived in nearby Las Cruces, New Mexico. It was an administrative position as I helped to maintain accountability for government property. I was learning a white-collar position rather than a blue-collar position, and I felt good about the learning process and my path forward.

Over the course of my first year in the army, I learned the military viewed certain things as a privilege. The right to serve as a member of the armed forces was considered a privilege, and with the privilege came select benefits: the privilege to shop at the PX, the post commissary, and medical care, to name the most obvious. I never paid attention to privilege until my parents visited me in New Mexico.

I took them on a tour of the post, and we stopped at the PX. My parents did not have the privilege to shop there. Any purchase they wanted to make was through me, because I was the authorized and responsible person. There was an awkward moment when my father asked in mixed company whether I had been to the cathouse or not. Other than that, my parents enjoyed the trip to the Southwest, although the trip was marred when they hit a deer on the way back to Detroit. At that time, my father had a late-model Buick sedan with a fancy custom grill. It seemed that a deer became attracted to it. Luckily, the horns did not puncture the radiator, because they might have been stuck in the hot desert. The rescue team would have had to be called out to retrieve them, and that would have been an experience for both of them.

Meeting with a Goddess

As a soldier, I was learning to become a more responsible person and citizen. Since I had been in the army for nearly a year, I was being introduced to different cultures I had only previously seen on television or read about in books. I met a beautiful young lady, Bertha Vásquez, a Mexican-American born in Juarez, Mexico, who worked in the office to which I was assigned. Bertha attended community college and worked as a civilian employee for the army in the summertime. She commuted into New Mexico from nearby El Paso. Soon after, we became very close and began to date. Some said we were the odd couple, because I stood six-foot-three and she stood five feet, but more than thirty years later we are still together.

On some weekends, she would return to the base to visit me. She would drive through the desert west from El Paso and back in a 1970s Ford Pinto. I must have been a great catch for her to do that. The challenge for me was my six-foot-three-inch frame and legs were too long to get in that car comfortably.

On occasion, we would drive west to Las Cruces, New Mexico, in her car. It was a challenge for that compact car with a four-cycle engine to make the climb over the rugged Organ Mountain range along the San Augustin Pass on US Route 70. But it was great fun being with her, so much so that I started to spend time visiting her at her home. Bertha comes from a large and very close traditional Mexican family. When I met her family, I was really being introduced to a different culture, custom, and food—especially jalapeño peppers. I believed God spoke to me about Bertha, and I did my best to be a gentleman. There were a few hiccups in getting to know the family as time progressed, but they seemed to enjoy me as our cultures collided. I am sure there is a Motown song that covers this cultural situation.

Bertha was supportive in our relationship, but at the same time she was concerned about her relationship with her family because I was married. After a while, I knew I wanted to take our relationship to another level. I formally separated from my wife, Jeanette, because it was time to seek a divorce.

By chance, I found an advertisement for a divorce lawyer in the post newspaper. I made an appointment to see him in his office in Las Cruces. I went to his office for my appointment but nearly walked out when I saw that the divorce lawyer was a quadriplegic. I did not know what to think. I did not think I was biased, but I needed a professional job done. Luckily, I stayed and explained my situation, and he moved promptly forward with my legal action. The final decree came in February 1981, when I was legally divorced with arrangements for child support and health care for my daughter, Jeanne, until her eighteenth birthday. Shortly thereafter, I asked Bertha to marry me, and she said yes. I confess that the gentleman was a great lawyer, because he got the job done with the help of his two beautiful legal assistants, both worthy of gracing the centerfold of any magazine.

MARRIAGE OR MATRIMONY: A STRATEGIC ALLIANCE IN THE VOLUNTEER ARMY

Bertha and I were married in June 1981 in El Paso, Texas, by the Justice of the Peace. It was a small wedding done in Mexican style involving her immediate family and a few people from work. My friend Leo Payne was my best man. My squad leader, SSG Berry, along with his family got me to the festivities on time. Yes, I was nervous, and I had more than a forty-mile drive through the desert to change my mind, but I did not. I think the conditions were much better the second time around; there was no flat tire or borrowed *Superfly* coat. We started our married life in a government-furnished house with government-furnished furniture on Lacrosse Street in the base housing area set against the vast New Mexico mountain range right outside our back door.

When Bertha and I married we made a commitment pertaining to obvious cultural issues. At the time, we did not marry with the blessing of the traditional Catholic church in El Paso. There was too much administrative baggage to overcome in too short a time. I did seek the permission of her father. When I went to ask for her hand in marriage, his biggest concern was not that I was African-American or divorced but that I was not Catholic. I promised him that our children would be raised in the Catholic faith.

During our courtship, I got transfer orders to Germany as a single soldier with MOS training at Fort Lee, Virginia. We agreed that we should stay together if I got transferred from New Mexico rather than her living at her parents' home while I was away. So I applied for a married accompanied tour for thirty-six months, adding eighteen months to my current contract. That was the best option. I was getting used to army life, and I had a new wife to take care of.

We also agreed that education was the key to our future, remembering that education was my original goal in joining the army. Since arriving in New Mexico, I had been contributing to the Army Education Fund, going to college at night and learning how to use the post library. In the 1980s, college education meant promotion. That banked money, although small, was now needed to put toward a new commitment, so I used my $750 savings to buy a wedding ring and finance the wedding, with $300 going to the ring and the remainder toward sponsoring the wedding party. Everything worked out and there was only one incident: the borrowed record player was stolen. To date, the reallocation of resources from my education fund to my marriage continues to pay dividends over and over.

HISTORIC FORT LEE, VIRGINIA

Fort Lee, Virginia, is the home of the Quartermaster Corps. As a quartermaster soldier, my goal at Fort Lee was to complete a primary quartermaster leadership course thirty days prior to leaving for Germany with my new bride. In the army, everything is subject to approval of a higher headquarters. If I was unsuccessful in passing the course, my request could be denied, whereas if I passed the course, there should not be a reason for my request to be denied. Subsequently, I passed the course and waited for approval of my request in concert with the army adage of "hurry up and wait!"

As I waited, I began learning more about the history of the United States. In my off-duty time, I took field trips to Washington, DC, and the surrounding areas of Fort Lee and Petersburg, Virginia. What was significant about these trips? I found out that the Commonwealth of Virginia is home to tons of American history. I only knew what I saw on the television or in history books; I did not know that those battlefields or historic sites still existed. Having the opportunity to visit the famous monuments and museums in Washington, DC, gives one a new perspective on America history.

My trip to Washington, DC, in 1981 was different from the trip with my parents to Aunt Rubye's Washington, DC, home in 1964. Although this was just a day trip, I told myself that there was a purpose for the visit, and for why the day was magnificent and memorable in my mind. I returned to my base in New Mexico a more knowledgeable, appreciative, and happy person because my request for accompanied travel had been approved. So in 1981, I could start a new phase of life with my new bride.

ACROSS THE POND TO DEUTSCHLAND

We departed El Paso at midday. The first stop on our journey to Germany was Charleston, South Carolina. We stayed overnight and enjoyed the Southern hospitality. I remember we ate breakfast at a nearby Waffle House and headed out to the airfield for our flight. At the airfield, there were a number of soldiers, wives, and children waiting for transportation to their destination.

We went through the required customs inspection and sat down until it was time to board the plane. We were both a little nervous when we got the call to board. The boarding took place outside on the tarmac using a wheeled ladder. The name painted on the rear of the plane was Flying Tigers. On the nose of the plane was the painted open mouth of a growling tiger. This flight would be the longest my wife and I had taken to date, but we looked at it as an adventure in our new life together.

The flight was interesting because we were able to listen to the military experiences of the other passengers and their families. The stories helped to ease our apprehension about the journey. We arrived at Rheine-Mainz Airfield in Frankfurt, West Germany, early the following morning on a clear but crisp fall day. We were no longer in the good old USA; we were now guests of the Federal Republic of Germany.

At the military airfield terminal, I sought assistance and direction in getting to my next duty station. My unit was contacted and told I had arrived with my spouse. Our next mode of transportation was a two- to three-hour bus ride. I was given bus tickets and transportation directions to my duty station, a place located twelve kilometers from the divided German border called Wildflecken Training Area.[31]

The bus was not scheduled to leave for several hours, so we found a place to sit and watch the sights. We would periodically walk around to get a glimpse of what was happening at the airfield. We did not want to drift too far away and get into trouble. I had noticed a funny thing in that a number of veteran soldiers were on the telephones trying to change their assignments. Some were lucky while others were not. We had an assignment, and I thought it best that since I was new, we should get on our designated bus when it pulled up and move on out to Wildflecken, wherever the heck the place was at.

The bus arrived at its scheduled time, and we hopped aboard with our bags to head toward our destination. The first thing we noticed was that while the buildings and activities in this new country were the same, the language was different, beginning with the signs on the bus. Although we were first timers, it seemed to us that we were taking the scenic route, driving through the great rolling countryside of green turning to brown in Germany, a place that experienced all four seasons.

This was a huge contrast to the mountain ranges and deserts of West Texas and New Mexico.

However, the familiar heavy smell in the air was not unfamiliar. We found out that the smell of cattle and cattle dung were the same all over the world. For Southwestern travelers, the smell can be an experience during the drive on Interstate 10 near the Texas and New Mexico border, where there are several cattle ranches. In the German countryside there are plenty of cattle, but their byproduct is used as fertilizer over miles of pasture and agricultural land.

ARRIVING AT WILDFLECKEN, AKA "WILD CHICKEN"

So my second army duty station was the Wildflecken Training Area in the Federal Republic of Germany, where our bus was met by SFC Donald G. Smith from Oklahoma, my new supervisor. To date, the two most famous residents of this army post, not counting me, were Elvis Presley[32] and Shaquille "Shaq" O'Neal, the basketball player.[33] A few years later, the youthful cast of the 1950s-set television sitcom *Happy Days* visited.

The municipality of Wildflecken and the army post sat in a picturesque nature park settled in the Rhön hills bordering Bavaria and Hesse. In World War II, Wildflecken served as a German prison camp that held captured Polish soldiers. The hillside camp was well hidden among the landscape of pine trees. When it was built, the German forces bent the tall pine trees backward with strong ties and rope and then proceeded to build the camp.

The story goes that the camp was discovered by the Allied Forces by accident, after days of searching. During the long and intensive search, one day an American soldier stopped to relieve himself when suddenly a tattered prisoner staggered up to him from out of nowhere and led him joyously to the camp's entrance. It seems that the prisoners had watched the attempted rescue for days and decided the Allies needed help in completing the mission.

The US Army took control of the camp and its surrounding area soon after the war ended in April 1945. The camp served as an assembly base for displaced persons and a training base for US forces. Wildflecken was an intense environment because the primary mission of military units stationed there was to guard and defend the Fulda Gap, the pathway through which the East Bloc could invade and possibly overtake the West through the use of large-scale armed forces.

I mentioned that Elvis Presley was probably considered the most famous soldier to train at Wildflecken, around 1960. I can recall being on temporary assignment to Fort Hood, Texas, in either 2001 or 2002 when I encountered an elderly veteran near the entrance of the Fort Hood Museum. He was visibly distraught about recent media reports by Elvis's former friends pertaining to his use of drugs and bad behavior while he was stationed in Germany.

The gentleman wore a cap that read either *Legion of Merit* or *Legion of Valor* across the front. In either case, when a guy with a hat like that is talking to you, it is best to listen. The gentleman stated that Elvis worked for him during that time period, and he never had any trouble with Elvis as a soldier. He continued to say that when he assigned Elvis Presley a task, that task was completed without incident. The man was really upset about the misconception, and some fifty years later there was no way he could set the record straight. I considered myself fortunate to have spoken with the gentleman.

During my assignment to Wildflecken, Shaquille "Shaq" O'Neal, the basketball player, attended high school there. Shaq's stepfather was a sergeant in the Armor Battalion located down the cobblestone hill from the unit I was assigned to. As I remember it, he also took constant ribbing from the senior noncommissioned officers (NCO) that I worked for in the Combat Engineer Battalion. Nonetheless, I believe he got the last laugh. When Shaq became a famous international personality, I would see his stepfather in Shaq's entourage living in the lap of luxury. My senior NCOs, I am afraid, each led rambunctious lives and may have well ended up in the old veteran's home.

I quickly learned that the army on duty at Wildflecken was quite different from the army I had left in the desert of New Mexico, beginning with the indoctrination process. It was mandatory for all new soldiers in Europe to attend week-long training in an indoctrination program called Headstart at the Army Education Center. The purpose was to provide the soldiers and their family members with a head start on learning the language and ways of German culture. Both my wife and I attended the class and enjoyed learning the aspects of German culture along with our own cultures which were different—African-American and Mexican-American.

Our class instructor was Fraulein Ute Dickerson, a pretty blond woman who walked with a limp. She was born in Germany in a place that suddenly became East Germany when the Berlin Wall went up. Later she escaped with several family members. She talked about how intense it was to grow up as a German under Soviet rule. She informed us that the Soviets blamed the East German population for the atrocities committed in World War II. They created great division and mistrust among the East German people. Under Soviet doctrine it was the responsibility of one East German person to inform on another East German person, no matter what the relationship: father–mother, sister–brother, or husband–wife.

For me, the most interesting part of the class was learning about Ute's escape from East Germany. She explained that she was in bed when her parents quietly scooped up their children and made their way to the border. The escape seemed to go well until it was her time to climb the fence toward freedom on the other side. That is when a shot rang out and struck her in the leg. It is unclear who in the escape party was left behind, but Ute made it. The exploit of her escape and the suppression of the East Germany population provided great insight into the things that transpire beyond one's own backyard or neighborhood, previously only seen in the movies or a history book.

ON THE ROCK, DON'T MISS TROOP MOVEMENT!

From the hardware and attitudes, this was no movie or history book; I was now a Cold War soldier. The armed forces stationed at Wildflecken were on constant alert and constantly training to meet the threat of potential invasion along the divided border or the "one-inch line" between the two Germanys. Here military protocol seemed to be more formal and the mood set by a hair-trigger. Even the formalities of military parades, like the payday formation held at 0-dark-30 at the post theatre were more solemn with less fanfare. There were no diving dragonflies and desert creatures. The concern when standing on the cobblestones of Wildflecken was the potential of diving fighter planes and armored tanks.

There was a clear understanding of roles and responsibilities in the military ranks. When the alarm went out, you really did not know if the alert was real or an exercise. Soldiers had to be where they were assigned or face the consequences. I recall my first unit alert; it happened quickly, and even though I had been on station for only a day or two, I was not excused. I did not have my personal equipment assembled, nor did I understand where my place of duty was located. I knew one thing: I needed to be somewhere, so rather than missing movement and being subjected to military discipline, I ran around in the company area with all of my equipment in my duffel bag and laundry bag until I found a truck to jump my butt on the back of. At this point, I understood that I was no longer in the calm of the New Mexico desert. I learned the first lesson of the Fulda Gap: don't miss troop movement.

After any military exercise, real or not, the maintenance of unit equipment is mandatory. The first major task I was given was to help another soldier who was responsible for the maintenance of a five-ton fuel truck change a tire on that truck. The tires were huge, and changing them was definitely not one of those soldier tasks specifically spelled out in my recruitment contract, nor was it one of my dreams come true. No real opportunity to complain now, because this environment was truly intense.

Begrudgingly, I learned to drive and maintain army equipment. I quickly found out that my legs were too long to drive jeeps. Doing maintenance on vehicles reminded me of my father desperately working on the family car so he could get to work the next day. Maintenance was priority one in the Fulda Gap, and working in the motor pool showed me how the army planned to go war the next day. I got through the motor-pool experience thanks to the mentorship I received from other soldiers.

JUST PLAY THE GAME!

My noncommissioned officer in charge (NOCIC), SFC Smith, told me to "just play the game!" I soon learned that he was right, and the more I understood what was transpiring around me, the better I was able to play. If you haven't noticed, I hated working in the unit motor pool, but guess what, the post education center sat right next to it. So after I played the game and did what they wanted done in the motor pool, I walked next door to the education center to do what I wanted to do. Remember the Strawberry Pie Rule? Do what they want you to do, and then do what you want to do.

I also stopped by the bank and picked up the countdown calendars. The calendars were a popular novelty item that showed the days of the year in countdown mode, beginning with Day 365 and ending with Day 1 and a wakeup. That way an anxious soldier could mark the days down until it was time to leave. My tour was thirty-six months, so I quickly picked up three of those calendars. I still have the original calendars posted on my basement wall.

Another company duty was to take a head count in the dining facility. I remember when the battalion commander, Lieutenant Colonel Daniel Christman, came into the dining facility and I thought he looked like George Washington. Later, I learned of George Washington's book of the colonial man and his conduct, and Christman fit the mode. As the taker of the head count and as part of military courtesy, I had to inform the entire building that the battalion commander was in the building by shouting out "Battalion Commander!" Then I took his money as payment for his meal. "Just play the game!" as SFC Smith said, because this was the guy whose butt was on the line as commander of the battalion. I learned later that Christman obtained the rank of general; amongst his prestigious assignments and credentials were superintendent of the US Military Academy at West Point and a law degree.

As a soldier with a thirst for learning, I found that many officers obtained their commissions from opportunities like formal military academies, reserve officer training, and officer candidate schools, to name a few. They were all different in terms of personal goals and backgrounds, but all were given the same authority in their military commission from the President of the United States, and they were all one step away from the unemployment line if they failed at their huge responsibilities.

ATTENTION TO ORDERS!

I was an enlisted man, and I worked in the S4 or supply section of the battalion. The S4 was responsible for the coordination of supplies and services needed by the battalion to operate, from food service to toiletries to vehicles to tires. The incoming S4 officer was Captain Ronald Russell, and he was from the South, either Mississippi or Louisiana. I remember he had a picture in his office of the final score of Ole Miss beating an arch rival.

It is my belief that Captain Russell was fiscally conservative when it came to spending money. However, his wife appeared to be high-maintenance when it came to expenditures. Mrs. Russell, a nice-looking young brunette, could have been cast as the persuasive Southern belle. She also worked at the post education center along with my wife, Bertha, and it was my hope that their friendship would not cause my wife to become high-maintenance too.

I thought Captain Russell to be an interesting fellow. He was not a very difficult person to work for compared to the stressful environment we operated in. He talked about living, growing, and working in the South and about the personal experience he had in operating a business. When he took over as commander of the headquarters company, he felt he had a smooth-running supply room. However, as his tour of duty was winding down, he confided in me that the supply room was no longer in good order. Captain Russell was right: the company supply room failed the brigade inspection.

The leadership training I was receiving as a soldier provided me with the confidence to take on challenges. My wife and I considered Captain Russell and his wife to be friends. So I asked permission from my new NCOIC, SFC Thompson, if I could lend a hand at the company supply room and help prepare it for a second inspection scheduled in the next thirty days. I was given a reluctant okay. Then my wife and I worked together as partners to get that room in better shape. I would go through the checklist and identify a problem area—in property accountability, inventory, or supporting document files. My wife had typing skills, so she would type up a new document that was prepared according to army regulations. We worked up to the very last minute the night before the second inspection. We did our best to set the assigned supply sergeant up for success.

Early the next morning, the supply room stood inspection, and things seemed to be going well. I was there only to provide assistance if needed. After the inspection, my NCOIC gave me the rest of the day off, so I went home to hit the hay. I took my clothes off and did just that. A short time later my phone rang, and I was told to report back to the headquarters company area on the double. I had been stationed in Germany long enough to know that when the phone rings, you must respond to the caller. I reported immediately, and I was escorted into the conference room where the brigade commander was being briefed on the results of the second inspection. There was a great compliment pertaining to the supply room. I was asked to stand. I heard the command "Attention to Orders!" and then I heard my name, the details of my accomplishment, and the presentation of the Army Achievement Award to me. It was an impact award, a fairly new service award that could be given on the spot by a commander as instant recognition of an outstanding accomplishment.

This recognition was really special because my wife and I worked together as a team on the project using our acquired skills to help someone else be successful. It was a great feeling and achievement. As a result, I earned a lot of respect as a quartermaster soldier around the battalion area.

After the ceremony, Captain Russell called me into his office. He thanked me personally and gave me a handful of German marks to take my wife to dinner as a thank you to both of us. His tour of duty was over, and he could hit the road without a blemish.

This is where that event got weird. I remember standing next to an executive officer who also achieved the rank of general some years later. He distinctly told Captain Skyking, the designated replacement for Captain Russell as the battalion S4 officer and the headquarters commander, to make sure the administrative paperwork for the impact award was processed properly. Well, somebody decided to save Uncle Sam a couple of bucks, since my three-year tour of duty ended in about five months and the impact award did double duty as my end-of-tour award. I was disappointed.

"Nigger": The Word Heard Around the World

Later in the afternoon after our all-night supply-room cleanup was the regular company formation. I was asked to stay so the results of the command inspection could be announced to the rest of the troops by the first sergeant. If you don't know, a troop formation belongs to the NCOIC, generally the first sergeant. That person turns over the formation to a higher-ranking person if the protocol calls for it. As requested, I stood in the doorway inside the building. The first sergeant, as usual, ended his huddle with the other senior NCOs who quickly moved to take their place in the formation outside the building.

First Sergeant Baldcrest, who was white, approached me with his right hand extended to shake mine as he patted my back with his left hand. Then in a nonchalant tone and seemingly nonthreatening manner, he called me a "good nigger" as he was making his way to the front of the formation to address the troops. I stood numb and in a state of shock. As many Richard Pryor and Redd Foxx recordings as I had listened to in my lifetime, I could not believe the words I just heard come out of the mouth of the first sergeant, the man in charge of the troops. It was like I had been thrown back a hundred years to the time of colored troops in the Civil War and their campaigns on the western plains when they had to endure the use of that word on a daily basis.

When my name was finally called to be recognized, I accepted the applause as gracefully as I could, but I was sad. I pondered the incident all evening at home, and it did dampen the thank-you dinner given to us by Captain Russell. Later in the evening, I came to the realization that the first sergeant was born an ignorant human being, lived as an ignorant human being, and would surely die an ignorant human being. That is when I learned that his ignorance in the use of the word *nigger* did not hurt as bad as when somebody with the same skin color as I directed that vile term at me.

FARM LIVING IS A NEW LIFE FOR ME

My wife Bertha and I lived on a small farm in the nearby town of Oberwiessbrunn[34] that sat in the beautiful Hesse/Bavarian border in a valley surrounded by green-patched rolling hills. The scenic background was beautiful and breathtaking. Sometimes my wife and I would sit on our second-floor balcony that overlooked the main street called Geigenstrasse and absorb the panoramic view of the countryside. There was a feeling of optimism in the vantage point. I was fortunate to find the place, because the availability of housing was a major issue for soldiers stationed in Germany who were accompanied by their families.

This is where I show off my listening skills. During my in-processing to the unit, I had overheard a soldier who worked at the housing office informing another soldier that he could no longer be eligible to maintain the apartment because his wife had left him. The apartment had to go back on the open listing for other eligible soldiers. I was eligible, I was on an accompanied tour with my wife, and I needed a place to live off-post.

I checked each day to see when the apartment would make the available housing list. The first day of availability, I rushed over at oh-dark-thirty to pick up the listing. Specialist Carlos Bulaza from the Philippines lived in the same town, so SFC Smith instructed him to drive me over to see the place. This is where I learned the cops are on duty everywhere in the world. As we approached the town, two German policemen or *Polizi* stood at the intersection with machine guns raised and ready. I do not know from whom or what but I'd learned in the German Headstart program not to mess with the *Polizi* at all. This was an intimidating scene, and there was no need for me to be concerned; as far as I knew, none of my old associates from Stupidville were living in Germany.

At our house, disco music—although dying on the music charts—was the center of our honeymoon household, wide-brim hats and high-heeled shoes and all. With the music playing, a great way to spend a lazy Sunday or *Sonntag* and at the same time maximize our limited budget was to sit and sightsee from our own perch. The perch was quaint, and the view was free. It was a beautiful sight when those shining Mercedes, sleek BMW, beautiful Volvo, and sassy Saab automobiles rolled out of the northern hills from Fulda right past our balcony on the Geigenstrasse through the town of Oberwiessbrunn and off toward the neighboring village to the south. Of course, the beautiful sight could be observed in reverse for the automobiles heading in a northerly direction.

The most astonishing thing about those cars, whether vintage or brand-new, was that the owner took pride in ownership. The autos were squeaky clean and free from rust. My wife loved the German-made BMW, but I had my eye on that Saab made in Sweden. It was sleek in its distinctive design. I enjoyed the quality and craftsmanship.

A DRIVER'S LICENSE IS AN EARNED COMMODITY

For the first few months of our tour, we did not own a car because we did not have recognized driver's licenses. I found out that they just don't give licenses away in Germany; you really have to *earn* a driver's license. It took me at least three tries to pass the driver examination. In the meantime, I had to hitchhike to work with some fellow soldiers: Specialist Bulaza and sometimes Command Sergeant Major Willy T. Seals. During this time, a GI hitcher had to be careful, because there were groups deemed to be terrorists, like the Baader-Meinhof gang, who looked to do harm against American soldiers.

Once I got my driver's license, I was able to buy a used automobile, a Ford sedan. I bought the car for a reasonable price from a female captain who was departing for home. This was another thing I learned about Germany during the time I lived there: you could not drive a raggedy car around town. The automobile had to be in good condition, roadworthy, safe, and rust-free, and that is the way I kept that car.

Remember I mentioned that I hated the motor pool? The first thing I found was a good mechanic. My mechanic, Herr Hess, owned an *autohaus* or repair shop in downtown Wildflecken. Herr Hess was a German national and looked as if he was the little brother of Frankenstein. He was somewhat tall in stature, with a Frankenstein-shaped hairstyle. He spoke in very proper, meticulous English and was always dressed in a clean white jacket. Moviemaker Mel Brooks could not have drawn the character of Herr Hess any more stereotyped in any one of his movies.

NAVIGATING THE GERMAN COUNTRYSIDE

When we were without a car and had to run errands, my wife and I would take a luxurious Mercedes or Audi taxicab to the post commissary located on the top of the next hill. My wife had to have hot peppers, and I had to have snacks. We looked like aristocrats as our well-mannered chauffeur provided us with the red-carpet treatment from our front door and upon our return with our bags of hot peppers and snacks. Sometimes we had to go long distances to obtain those hot peppers.

On Sunday afternoons, we would walk along the two-lane highway to the post movie theater about five miles away. Whenever we got too tired or got the nerve to throw out a thumb, a speedy but friendly passing vehicle would pull alongside and give us a neighborly lift to the front gate. One thing we did notice was how curious the German motorist could be. On occasion when we walked along the two-lane highway or on the cobblestones through town, motorists traveling at high rates of speed would stare back at the tall black man and short brown woman walking together. I do not recall any reported accidents. However, staring too long at anything could cause a traffic concern.

As we became more accustomed to the German lifestyle, I noticed that those magnificent automobiles only slowed for three things: the black ice that might become visible during the winter; the German police or *Polizi*, since the local people seemed to respect authority and the armament they carry; and livestock and farm animals on the road, which always had the right of way.

The motorist had to be alert and exercise caution in maneuvering all year round when approaching the huge backside of a German cow. The field of safe-driving vision became obscured by more than 50 percent the closer the car approached the moving herd.

The local herds were led to graze on the beautiful countryside and then back home again on the very same road, leaving behind dung residue. This was a potential hazard to be reckoned with. In addition, there was concern for the herdsmen themselves. A lot of the herdsmen were women, young and old, with their figures hidden under garments of sun-shielding scarves, patterned dresses, and heavy mud-stained goulashes. They would hold sticks that were used for leading or guiding the herd. Sometimes, responsibility for the herd lay with mere children. A cautious motorist had to wonder if they could handle the load.

The valley was like a scene on a postcard. During the height of winter, every structure and most moving objects wandering through this valley were totally covered in white. In the three other seasons, foliage surrounding the babbling brook changed from green to brown back to green again. The brook ran right through the congregation of grazing cattle, clacking chickens, and flocking geese. The heavy scent from these creatures, helped by a seasonal breeze, always made its way to my second-floor perch. I took every precaution, but to no avail. To the farming people of Oberwiessbrunn, it was a heavenly scent, because those animals were their lifeblood. Animal and man woke together, ate together, and prayed together.

THE CULTURE SHOCK

I confess the transition to rural living was a culture shock for me and my wife. We were both from metropolitan areas segmented by ethnic and industrial diversity. Automobile factories dominated the American way of living as people left farms to head for the factory. Those factories worked at great capacity to yield a product and to satisfy the public demand for a better life and economy.

The automobile was a success; nonetheless, there were many drawbacks. The sound of heavy machinery pounded the surrounding community all day and all night. The gray-black smoke from long stovepipes atop the factory roof blocked the sun from its duties. The foul stench of industrial waste crept up on our natural resources and choked them to their near demise. For this, thousands of Neapolitan-faced factory workers migrated from agricultural belts from across many lands to avoid toiling in God's good clean earth. The rows of tall corn they sought refuge from were replaced by tall buildings that housed the profits of industry. This was the industrial North that I knew.

My wife grew up in El Paso, Texas, which sits along the US–Mexico border. El Paso is a friendly international city that can bake an unsuspecting visitor in its desert oven. The mountain range, the arid desert, and the sun conspire year-round to provide opportunity for outside cookouts in the middle of January. The city is a major transportation point for the movement of goods and services passing through to Central America and back. The architecture of El Paso blends neatly into the desert contour. At night, the city lights are in full view from the New Mexico desert more than forty miles away. If a fire is raging on top of that vast mountain range, your imagination could roast zillions of marshmallows. Although the sun was warm, it could also be deceptive and disappear. No sun in the sky sent the desert temperature down fast to a chill.

THE SCHMIDT FAMILY: LANDLORDS

Our landlords in the town of Oberwiessbrunn were the Schmidt family. They were friendly, industrious, hardworking farmers. The husband and wife only spoke German and nodded to English, "Yah Yah!" Herr Schmidt was big, burly, and robust. He appeared to be at least sixty years of age and built for the daily rigors of the farm. His heavy coveralls, weather-beaten plain shirts, and body odor affirmed the fact that he worked from the crack of dawn to the evening shade. His big boots left muddy tracks wherever he walked, but Frau Schmidt was never far behind with the broom.

Frau Schmidt wore a faded red scarf that covered her tough skin and stringy hair. She was small in stature and moved about the property with a noticeable limp in her right leg. Her body was usually covered with sweaters, patterned cloth dresses, heavy stocking, and boots. She generally carried a stained carving knife, and her clothing was drenched with the smell of the farm and its livestock. She too nodded in response to English, "Yah Yah!"

Their daughter, Fraulein Schmidt, was around twenty years of age at the time. Despite having given birth to a son, she maintained a stunning figure. She worked a local job somewhere in the district and returned home to help with the chores. Occasionally, she would shed those coveralls and sunbathe below the big picture window alongside the balcony of our second-floor apartment. For me, those were the best days to watch cars go by on my porch, "Yah Yah!" Fraulein Schmidt spoke

English and served as the interpreter and never wore the same perfume her parents did.

The Schmidt family always seemed to be tending to the farm and livestock night and day. They worked in all weather—rain, sleet, or shine. The first chore of the day was feeding and milking the cows, and the rest of the work involved moving about the farm on the tractor. Frau Schmidt spent her day feeding chickens, collecting eggs, carving up food for both human and animal consumption, and tending to her grandson. The farm was quite prosperous because the flies were slow and fat, and easy targets for the flyswatter.

Impressed with their work ethic, I decided to lend a helping hand one sunny day. Yes, a Great Urban Warrior, six-foot-three, slim, trim, and looking like a gem. My government-issued uniform was sharply creased from shirt to trousers. The shine on my boots challenged the sun, and they could run me five miles in any direction, on roads where people with soft soles feared to tread.

Herr and Fraulein Schmidt were unloading sacks of grains from a wagon pulled by a tractor. They nonchalantly grabbed sacks onto their backs and carried them up to the storage area located above our second-floor apartment. I hadn't known that the landlord stored his farm yield above my head. I guess he could do what he wanted—it was his place. I told my wife, "I'll be back!" I took my shirt off to let my ego out and started to hum, "Hey, good looking, what you got cooking?"

I tossed my first sack on my back to tote upstairs. "Ahhh, my God!" I thought my back had been struck by an anvil. Carefully I regained my composure so that I could get the job done. I struggled up those four flights of stairs toward the storage room. My ego lay exhausted on the first staircase. My sharply creased uniform lost its edge on the second. My shining boots hid behind a cloud of dirt on the third. On the fourth staircase, my trembling hands dropped their burden and came together in a prayer of thanks. Then they came together again, but as a smack on my forehead. *Oh Lord, the wagon is not empty!*

It was too late to bow out of my goodwill gesture, especially since I could no longer bow. When it was over, I gingerly made my way to our apartment. A distance of only a few feet felt like a few miles. I sat on the living-room couch in my dulled uniform to rest my bruised ego. I knew this was going to be a long night, because I was too pooped to pop the cap off my favorite bottle of Asbach Brandy. Jimmie, my muscle-bound friend from the factory, would not have not been proud.

Shortly after my recovery, Bertha awoke and began to prepare for the day. I had gone to work. Our bathroom was typical European in style. The commode with a long flush chain sat next to the window. A shiny mirror hung over the bathroom sink. Along the full wall lay a wide oval-shaped bathtub with a handheld shower head.

Bertha had tied back her long beautiful black hair while she undressed, and then she jumped right into the shower … where she noticed that a small mouse had found its way into the bathtub. The bathtub was too wide for the mouse to escape up either side. That is when the hysteria began. Bertha grabbed a short, flimsy lace robe and ran through the apartment looking for help. I was gone. So she proceeded to run downstairs, half-dressed, to get the landlord.

Herr Schmidt sat on top of his tractor preparing to lift a load of hay into the hayloft. My wife now was in full view of the dairy cows contently chewing their cuds in their stall and the motorists in dream cars racing through town. Herr Schmidt was obviously startled by her appearance, and he just stared. He could not understand what made her upset because he spoke German and only nodded to English, "Yah Yah!"

My wife began to further complicate the situation by reverting to her native language—Spanish. She grabbed Herr Schmidt by his large dusty arm and feverishly pulled him by the coveralls toward the stairs. This was quite a task for a petite woman twenty-three years in age, with no shoes and one free hand.

Now Frau Schmidt peeked from the barn door toward the confusion. In her hand was not a German-American dictionary for interpretation but that ever-present stained carving knife. She followed the two excited people up the stairs as fast as her limp could take her. Herr Schmidt and my wife reached the bathroom door, where my wife pointed to the bathtub and the mouse as it skidded about in the tub.

Herr Schmidt begins his inspection of the area along the bathtub with a hardy chuckle. His finger found a small hole in the bathroom wall from the storage room where the sacks of grain were stored. Frau Schmidt arrived to assess the situation and quickly lowered her carving knife. She began to administer comfort to my wife.

Herr Schmidt must've been bewildered by the confusion created by one lost mouse and one foreign woman. After all, he worked around hairy creatures of all sizes all day long. He went down to the barn and returned with a long wooden stick and a dustpan. He boldly struck and exterminated the mouse and carried it away in the dustpan. He returned for a third time to repair the hole in the wall. The apartment was now safe and free from vermin, and the Schmidts returned to their chores.

I returned home later in the day to hear my wife share her story, and we laughed together. She had fully recovered from the ordeal. We sipped on a glass of Asbach and laughed again. She snuggled up to me and relaxed from her exciting day. I looked around our cozy apartment and laughed to myself. I didn't blame my wife for being upset. If I had been there when the mouse appeared, I would have been upset too. It would have been a lot more embarrassing for one of the US Army's finest to be running and screaming after Herr Schmidt because of a little mouse.

ARMY PERSONNEL AND THE LOCAL YOKELS

The army makes a home for a lot of wayward men who have different backgrounds and futures. I remember Captain Mike Skyking, who succeeded Captain Russell as both the battalion S4 officer and the headquarters commander. Skyking was an aviator by trade who was probably a fish out of water in an engineer outfit. Each organization has its own personality, and Skyking had to learn from on-the-job training. Generally, he would keep the heat off by showing a picture of himself as an aviator at a girlie bar in Montana or one of the Dakotas that had been published in one of the major girlie magazines. I remember he tried that on the brigade commander, who promptly told him to get that magazine out of his sight and to get some logistics charts up on his office wall.

Everybody missed home. Nobody missed home as much as single soldiers like the headquarters' heavy-equipment operators. For the purpose of demographics, they were primarily white soldiers, heavy drinkers, and heavy on rocking John Cougar Mellencamp's playful recording "Jack and Diane"[35] as loud as it could get from their barrack rooms, day and night. This, of course, was a nightmare for whatever soldier was on duty as in charge of quarters (CQ). Typically, the biggest concern for the CQ was staying awake, noise control, catching up on the latest girlie magazine, and making sure the coffeepot was on when the first sergeant got to the office.

The sport of drinking helped to relieve the pain of being away from home, and a lot of soldiers in all ranks appeared to be in pain. There were a number of places a drink could be found. On post, government-sealed alcohol could be obtained from the PX "Class VI" store using the government-issued ration card. A soldier could get a drink at the Rod and Gun Club or German guesthouse on post. Soldiers could take a trip to the nearby Kreuzberg Monastery to drink beer, or go downtown to a local establishment. A drink could be found almost everywhere, but there was a price to pay when it was overdone. Fourth time, "sometimes you just have to let people carry their own load."

I was on CQ duty one night when I went to pick up my dinner pizza from downtown Wildflecken. I walked in the door and found the drunk heavy-equipment guys engaged in a confrontation with a group of drunk German locals. Some yelled out, "Hey, the CQ is here to save us!" I immediately turned around and returned to my place of duty without my pizza, still hungry. *I'll let the military police save them* was my thought. Never try to outdrink the locals!

DON'T MAKE A FIELD PROBLEM A PROBLEM

As previously stated, there are a number of knuckleheads wearing army uniforms, especially during maneuvers or "field problems," as they were called. When soldiers do not follow directions, it could result in someone getting injured or killed. For example, my unit was setting up our perimeter in our assigned location, a heavily wooded area near Bad Hersfeld. During this time, perimeter guards were assigned by the first sergeant to provide protection. However, not everybody wearing service uniform was considered a crack soldier; many had cracked brains to pull the stunts they did to avoid duty.

During one particular field problem, there were two white soldiers, Private Mike and Private Hotel, assigned to guard the perimeter as instructed. The two soldiers did not properly man their post. They were caught heading back in the direction of the city of Fulda, some fifty-four kilometers south. There were several hours and manpower spent looking for these soldiers, and when they were found, these two knuckleheads claimed they were lost. They were lucky. The company commander took disciplinary action against them both that was equivalent to a misdemeanor.

A few days later, while still in the field, I experienced the coldest night ever bivouacked there in the frozen German forest. It looked exactly like a magnificent Christmas card. The night was clear as the stars illuminated the countryside covered with a fresh layer of snow. As a squad, we rotated pulling guard duty on the outside perimeter and maintaining the fire in the stove. Who would have thought the same two knuckleheads, Private Mike and Private Hotel, would ruin the serenity of this beautiful German Christmas card? This time they did not take care of their personal equipment, and when it came their time to stand guard duty their boots were frozen to the tree outside the tent. They were lucky again that they were not frostbitten.

Then there are some soldiers who make bad decisions and are not so lucky. During my tour, several black soldiers assigned to the ordnance company chose to engage in criminal behavior. They acquired explosive materials and allegedly wired up the company commander's office. Apparently, the material did not explode, and after a short investigation they were apprehended. It's fortunate that the materials did not go off, because it might have cost a number of innocent people their lives. This was not a misdemeanor—this was a criminal act. When the perpetrators were out-processing from active duty as soldiers and transitioning to a long stint in jail, they were in handcuffs and surrounded by military police. This was a scene I had seen too many times before, a couple brothers being escorted away in handcuffs. So don't be a knucklehead near the 1KM (1kilometer zone).[36]

BECOMING TECHNICALLY PROFICIENT

I was fortunate because my military career was progressing nicely. I was not influenced by the knuckleheads in the service as I had been influenced by the knuckleheads in my neighborhood back home. I did not share the same time and space. Instead, I was more interested in learning a profession. In Germany, I worked directly for the unit property book officer, Chief Warrant Officer James Warren, whose position was similar to Mr. Utter, the army civilian at my previous assignment in New Mexico.

Mr. Warren was a relatively young man, but he had been in the army a number of years before receiving a direct appointment to the rank of warrant officer. Both Mr. Warren and SFC Smith provided me with mentorship in becoming a better soldier and developing expertise in my MOS. Later, I was recommended by both men to a direct appointment to the rank of warrant officer. I submitted my paperwork and passed the Warrant Officer Board that was locally convened, but the Department of the Army denied the appointment, stating that I was not senior enough in my rank or the army for a direct appointment. Shortly after I received my results, Mr. Warren slipped into a coma a day or two before he was scheduled to return to the states after completing his tour in Germany.

SFC Smith called me about a year later to tell me that Mr. Warren had passed on.

While stationed at Wildflecken, I was recommended to attend the Noncommissioned Officer (NCO) Academy training at Baumholder under the 8th Division Mechanized. Attendance to the school in 1983 was of great benefit to me in developing and understanding leadership. This advanced training was designed to sharpen the skills of newly selected NCOs, and I became a little sharper. I would learn later that Major General Frederic E. Davison was the first African-American to command the 8th Division at Baumholder in 1972, and he went on to become president of Howard University.[37]

The course was very challenging. I remember there were several incidents during training that were significant in my leadership growth:

- A married female trainee who engaged in sexual activity with another trainee was terminated from the program; as I remember, the terminated female was picked up at the academy by another soldier, her husband.
- A loud, brash, newlywed African-American trainee turned to mush during his time as the leader because he missed his German bride.
- I had to make the call to move my unit from foxhole positions after our perimeter was perceived to be breeched by boars.

This was thirty days of tough duty, and I was glad to complete the school. After graduation, my beautiful wife's "loving arms were there to greet me," as soul singer Isaac Hayes[38] would moan. I missed her.

When I returned to my unit for duty, it was near the end of the fiscal year, and my new boss, Chief Warrant Officer Francisco Lourido, wanted me to spend the unit's allocated budget in a short period of time. This was my first real experience spending $1 million. So much of my effort was to coordinate supply actions with the civilians working the army supply system. The folks in the field tagged the dedicated civilian workforce as the "little old lady in tennis shoes" because of the speed or lack of speed for the requested item to be received by the unit in field. No matter, I found out that money is hard to come by but can be spent very fast. I soon learned, just like with the automobile factory back home, never submit any requisitions to the government on Monday or Friday, because nobody is there.

Suit Up, It's Baby Time!

My wife and I appreciated Specialist Carlos Bulaza and his wife, Neri, a very nice mature couple from the Philippines. They had been married for a few years and wanted to have a child, but it had not happened to date for whatever reason. I remember Bulaza as a very loyal husband who was dedicated to his wife. He frowned on womanizing, and he conveyed his philosophy concerning women to me with no hesitation: "Pick one, stick one!"

I followed his advice. My wife, Bertha became pregnant, and shortly before my tour was up in Germany, our daughter, Treasure, was born. My wife woke me during the early-morning hours to tell me that it was time to go to the hospital, and if we did not get there quickly the baby would be born in the bathroom. The hospital, in this case, was located in the German city of Fulda, about fifty kilometers north of our home in Oberwiessbrunn. We had everything prepared for a hospital stay.

I got my wife and our stuff into the car and then we headed to the hospital. Since there was little traffic, I made good time driving along the winding road toward the city. My wife seemed to be in good spirits. I talked to her along the way, and suddenly the hospital was in sight. Once we reached it, I found a parking spot as close as I could to the emergency-room door. I helped my wife out of the car, and I gathered up all of the belongings. I walked past her quickly so that I could open the door. I was almost to the door when she stopped walking because of a painful contraction. I went back to help her, and I held onto her until the contraction subsided. After the contraction, we were able to walk into the hospital, where the attendants put my wife into a wheelchair and started pushing her off to the delivery room.

I still had my wife's hospital stuff, so I looked around for the waiting room to go sit down. The nurse shouted in German, "*Nein!*" and motioned for me to follow her. She showed me where to place my wife's belongings, and she handed me a white hospital gown. She motioned for me to follow her again as we walked into the delivery room, where my wife was laying down on the hospital bed. The nurse informed me as best she could in her language and hands signals that I had a job to do helping my wife deliver this baby.

Quite frankly, I was not expecting to hold my wife's hand and help her with breathing. I thought my job was only to drive the car to get her here. But I was glad I was there to witness and to help in the birth. I had missed the birth of my oldest daughter, Jeanne. Now I was part of the miracle, witnessing a new life as it came into the world. The new life did not come without a price to my physical body; during the process, my wife did hit me and curse me for the pain she was experiencing, but somehow I survived her knockout punch.

COUNTDOWN CALENDAR

My three countdown calendars were coming to an end, which meant my tour would be over soon. Now, it was tough to prepare to leave. My wife and I had fallen in love with Germany. We went on bus trips all over Europe, including Switzerland and Spain. We visited memorable places like the Shrine of the Black Madonna at Montserrat,[39] Hacienda with a magnificent Sangria fountain near Barcelona, and the Palace of Versailles[40] in Paris, France. Not to mention a ton of places around Germany, such as the Neuschwanstein Castle[41] in the village of Hohenschwanhgau. The castle served as the inspiration for Walt Disney and the Disneyland Castle. We learned that holidays are especially appreciated when you are a long way from home in service to your country.

We liked German food, and we liked the atmosphere. We had just had a beautiful baby, and when the German currency was low in comparison to the US dollar, we purchased a brand-new Saab. I don't know if it was my love for the car or the attractive German saleswoman who enticed me to buy it. It was Captain Skyking who recommended the Saab dealer to me, which was located down in Schweinfurt. One Saturday, my wife and our new baby took a ride down to check out the car lot. I looked around, but I did not see the car or the color I liked. As I walked away, a flash of distinguished blue sitting under a billboard caught my eye. I walked over to see what it was, and I saw the color I liked. The saleswoman took me on a drive around the German streets with Bertha sitting in the backseat holding Treasure.

It was a great ride, and I don't think I was too influenced by the short skirt the saleswoman was wearing. Anyway, she said with good maintenance and care this car would last twenty years. She was right. I took care of that car for nearly twenty years, driving it all around North America, including Alaska. I passed it on to my father, who also admired it. The car was parked in front of our family home in Detroit one night when somebody drove into it and drove away without a note of apology or even an *excuse me*. Unbelievable!

It was summer of 1984, and I was getting closer and closer to finishing my tour and heading back to the states. The army was transforming and seeking to build up the warrant officer corps with younger and less-experienced soldiers. Recruiting teams were sent out all over the world to interview possible candidates. There would be no direct appointment, and the selected candidates would have to attend and pass a rigorous officer training school. I went to the interview in Frankfurt, but a short time later I receive a letter of rejection. I was rejected from becoming a warrant officer for the second time.

The consolation was, it was time to go home to the states. However, at this time in both my life and career, I had options. From a recruiting standpoint, I was considered a highly qualified and desirable recruit, so I could select my next duty station. I chose Fort Huachuca, Arizona.

Return to the City of Champions, a Champion

In the fall of 1984, I returned home to Detroit from Germany on leave with my new family. This was my first trip back to Detroit since 1980. I introduced my wife, Bertha, our new daughter, Treasure, and my new set of wheels to the African-American side of the family prior to us heading to Fort Huachuca, my new duty station.

I was just in time to witness the Detroit Tigers beat the Kansas City Royals, 1–0, to win the American League pennant at Tiger Stadium on October 5, 1984. Milt Wilcox pitched a gem with relief from Willie Hernandez to seal the deal. Manager Sparky Anderson so loved his ball club all the way to the World Series that he anointed their championship with the phrase, "Bless you Boys!"[42]

My friend Chili picked up three tickets for himself, me, and Bertha—reminiscent of 1968 when Chili, Miranda, and I sat in the right-field stands. This time we three sat in the upper deck in left field. When the game ended, the celebration scene was much more controlled than the full-blown chaotic pennant-clinching game of the 1968 season against the New York Yankees. This time, the celebration inside the stadium was limited to the players on the playing field and appreciative fans in the stands. In contrast, the celebration in the streets was very destructive and violent, and was depicted clearly on the front pages of newspapers across the country.

The Detroit Tigers went on to capture the World Series against the San Diego Padres. I watched it all unfold in front of my color television set in Fort Huachuca. I cannot argue, 1984 was truly a great year. I had a new daughter, a new car, and my favorite baseball team was the newly crowned champion. This was wonderful. It was only five short years earlier that I had sat out in the stadium bleachers dismayed and looking for a change in my life.

Before we left for Arizona, I took Bertha in our new Saab around Detroit to show her my old stomping grounds. The place was really starting to change, and not for the better. I was not looking for anybody in particular, but I drove up Griggs Street and Sammie Lee Ford happened to be home. He came outside, and I introduced him to my wife. Sammie Lee responded with a "Hey, baby!" I told myself, *Some things never change*. That was not a correct greeting to extend to a person you were meeting for the first time, especially your friend's wife. So before we could catch up about the rest of the guys, I told Sammie Lee "*auf Wiedersehen*," German for good-bye. I put my car in reverse, and that was the last time I saw Sammie Lee Ford.

FORT HUACHUCA, ARIZONA: THE REAL WEST

My third tour of duty began in 1984 at Fort Huachuca, Arizona,[43] in the desert with the Huachuca Mountains as a backdrop, a place that got extremely hot during the year. This was truly the Old West. It was a fantastic dream come true. I'd watched cowboy movies all my life. The drive west from Detroit was magnificent, and we visited tourist sites and attractions that we had only been able to see on television. Of course we stopped in El Paso for a few days to introduce Treasure to her Mexican-American family members.

Then we headed out to Fort Huachuca, a four- to five-hour drive west. There were signs of the Old West everywhere along the desert road of Interstate 10 in both New Mexico and Arizona. After you cross the Arizona border, the signs read, "Do not drive through dust storms" and "Keep lights on." I had previously witnessed heavy winds in New Mexico, but not a desert dust storm. I continued on the interstate in Eastern Arizona, and I noticed swirling dust brewing up on the desert floor to my right. The dust appeared to subside, rise again, and subside—and then suddenly it rose and crossed over onto the highway at an alarming pace. I reduced my speed considerably, almost to crawl. The dust storm was over as quickly as it had started. I turned around to see if my wife and daughter were all right. There they sat, Bertha half asleep in her seatbelt with Treasure secured in her arms. (In those days, car seats for children were not yet mandatory. Bertha hand-carried Treasure to Arizona all the way from Germany.) The only damage was the sandy residue left on my beautiful admiral blue Saab 900S.

This was another great opportunity for expanding my cultural learning. I discovered the stone architecture of Cochise Stronghold,[44] where the Apache tribe retreated when chased by army soldiers. When you approach the rock formation as a tourist, the first question is, of course, how were the Apache able to escape so quickly up this mountain with an angle so straight up? This was much different from the television shows I watched growing up as a boy.

Then there was the town of Tombstone, where Wyatt Earp, Doc Holliday, and the Clanton Gang walked to their destiny at the OK Corral in 1881.[45] The first thing you notice is that everything looks so small in real life versus the silver screen, in movies like *My Darling Clementine* starring Henry Fonda and Victor Mature.[46] Later I learned from a city official that the town of Tombstone is still divided over the legend of Wyatt Earp to this very day.

In reflection, I wish I had spent more time visiting around the state of Arizona, but since we were so close to California, I took my wife and daughter there on several occasions instead. Driving through the Arizona desert was magnificent, but sometimes the heat was unbearable. When Treasure was two, she found the asphalt in Yuma, Arizona, to be the hottest place on earth when she leaped out of the car onto the asphalt and sprang back in again in one fluid motion. I was glad she wasn't barefoot, because there was warm asphalt residue on the bottom of her shoes. Better that than a permanent imprint on the bottom of her feet.

I had to get to California because I had seen it on television all of my life. It was at Disneyland that I realized a simple concept: the Disneyland Theory. I do understand that there are many sophisticated, scholarly, and academic thoughts on the premise of success that I don't wish to encroach upon. But in my interpretation, the Disneyland Theory finds its foundation in the achievement of personal dreams or aspirations. A question is asked: How would your offspring know about Disneyland (the people, places, or things they could become or do) unless you, the parent, tell them of Disneyland and take them to Disneyland (have or had personal dreams to be pursued or magnificent quests to be aspired to). Without such action on the part of the parent, how do the children begin to seek? I think the first family trip to Disneyland in 1985 helped shape the life of my daughter, Treasure, who has since made a number of astonishing achievements as a student, a professional, and a person. She adapted to the "it can happen to me" atmosphere and themes associated with Disneyland as the place where dreams come true.

Nonetheless, what little I saw of Arizona was great. In nearby Tucson, my new family and I visited the movie lot Old Tucson[47] during the comedic production of *The Three Amigos*[48] with actors Martin Short, Steve Martin, and Chevy Chase around 1985. The Old Tucson movie lot was the production home of many famous Western movies and movie stars, including John Wayne and Frank Sinatra. I love movies; the 1965 movie *100 Rifles*[49] starring Jim Brown, Raquel Welch, and Burt Reynolds is a vivid example of the movie West and its contrast in inhabitants. I was greatly influenced by Jim Brown's role as a hero and the presence of an African-American male in the desert, remembering that as a young boy, I had met him a year or two before the movie was made.

The Buffalo Soldier

As I adapted to living in Arizona in 1984, I think my most important discovery was that of the Buffalo Soldiers[50] and their great unpublicized contribution to American history. When I was growing up, traditional American schoolbooks featured very little detail of the heroic story of the Buffalo Soldier. I recall reading one line in my history book that identified the Buffalo Soldier as a person, place, or thing, but the book did not give recognition to the Buffalo Soldiers for their role in the opening of the West for settlement. In the cinema, a Negro actor, Woody Strode,[51] a world-class athlete as well as a football teammate of Jackie Robinson and Kenny Washington, always portrayed the lone figure in military uniform in big production movies and television. For years, it made me curious as to why he was there. Now I surmised that he represented the Buffalo Soldier on-screen.

Fort Huachuca was home of the Buffalo Soldiers, and the US Army of the 1980s and 1990s was being educated about the existence and history of the Buffalo Soldiers under the leadership of General Colin Powell.[52] The Buffalo Soldiers were Negro volunteers assigned to peacetime duty as US troops in the Western plains of the United States. Buffalo Soldiers fought both Chiricahua and Apache Indians in the west after the Civil War ended. The consensus is that the name "Buffalo Soldiers" was given to them by the Indians of the Great Plains because their coarse hair was like that of the buffalo.[53]

Buffalo Soldiers served under white officers; one of those officers was General John Wynn "Black Jack" Davidson as a lieutenant colonel leading the troops in opening the West for settlement. Later, General John "Black Jack" Pershing was a company grade officer in the 10th Cavalry Regiment at Fort Huachuca, a unit composed of primarily Negro soldiers serving in the Southwest before World War I. Both men had the nickname "Black Jack" bestowed on them by the media of the day because they commanded Negro soldiers.[54]

The 25th Infantry Regiment took over Fort Huachuca in 1933, and sometime later the 92nd and 93rd Infantry Divisions trained there in preparation for World War II.[55] The area surrounding Fort Huachuca is desert floor that is naturally desolate and barren. At least two of my maternal relatives were stationed at Fort Huachuca at different times, 1941 and 1951. One day, the three of us sat and reminisced about Fort Huachuca during the times we each served; how long it took us to get home on leave to Bolivar in Hardeman County, Tennessee; and the mode of transportation taken to get there.

My uncle said that in 1941, it took him about ten days to get to Bolivar on a combination of trains, buses, and hitchhiking. My cousin said that in 1951, it took him about seven days to get to Bolivar through a combination of trains, buses, and hitchhiking. Both said as black soldiers they had to be aware of the people around them, because Negroes in military uniform were despised in many communities. I told them that in 1996, it was just a matter of putting gas in my car and hitting the road, and I could make it to Bolivar in less than two days. I also told them that the communities were just learning about the exploits and achievement of the Buffalo Soldier.

I enjoyed life in the Arizona sun and its wide-open spaces. The sun and openness gave a feeling of optimism. I spent a lot of hours completing army correspondence courses under the rays. During the winter months, I would be in my backyard grilling meat while my parents were dealing with the cold winter snow back in Michigan. It was fun driving on a moonlit Interstate 10 into Tucson some sixty miles away to take my Saab to the dealer for maintenance, or to check out baseball spring training, or in response to an alert that former Beatle Paul McCarthy was in town. It did not help that my favorite comedian, Richard Pryor, did not exactly tell the true about the African-American population of Arizona in one of his funniest movie sketches.[56] On the contrary, there was a sizeable African-American community in Arizona that was not sitting in an Arizona jail. Many of them were very successful and had strong ties to the community as descendants of the Buffalo Soldiers.

TECHNOLOGY AND THE US POST OFFICE

At Fort Huachuca, I was assigned to a communications unit comprised of senior army personnel. I operated a specialized tool room used by trained personnel assigned to install sophisticated mainframe and computer systems around the world using fiber optics.[57] Fiber optics allowed cheaper bandwidth for long-distance communication. I was a responsible person learning to be a better soldier in understanding the army's way, but I did not foresee fiber optics changing the world of telecommunications—another missed opportunity. At the same time, I also was learning to become a better father, because I had two daughters to set the example for.

In addition, I gained the confidence to become a better student. While stationed in Wildflecken, I was enrolled in the service members' Opportunity Network System Associate and Bachelor's Degrees for the Army (SOCAD)[58] program at the post education center. SOCAD facilitated the requirements between my selected degree program and academic residency. My wife was employed at the education center as a clerk and maintained the academic records. I recall that every time I escaped from the motor pool, I would stop by to say hello to her, and I would see the special tag attached to my folder. Although other soldiers were enrolled in the program, I could spot my personal file folder among alphabetic records a mile away. There were three things in that building I loved: my wife, the SOCAD program, and the post library.

I attended classes each semester and earned a Certificate of Completion of thirty hours from Central Texas College in 1983. I was very proud. Subsequently, I completed enough hours to earn an associate degree. There was no opportunity to have a formal graduation prior to leaving for the states, so I filled out the paperwork to have the diploma forwarded to me at my new duty station, Fort Huachuca.

One day I received notice from the post office that I had a package to pick up. The notice did not identify who the sender was. The next day I went to the post office located on Fort Huachuca, which was quiet with very little traffic. I provided the postal clerk, an African-American male, with the notice that I received in the mail. He took the notice and went to retrieve the package in the back of the post office. In a few moments, he returned with a package and had me sign for it. I took the package from him and opened it up. There inside the postal wrap was a document binder, and inside that document binder was a diploma for an associate degree from Central Texas College with the name "Wayne Rudolph Davidson" inscribed on it. I was ecstatic and almost passed out on the floor of the post office.

I showed the postal clerk my new status and shook his hand emphatically. Then I headed off to Cochise College to continue my studies. For me, two soulful songs, the Winstons' "Color Him Father"[59] and Clarence Carter's "Patches"[60] grooved the reality of the need for education in order for a working-class guy like me to compete in this tough world. I remembered that my own father was raised on a farm with limited education; any advanced education was a walk down a country road thirteen miles down and thirteen miles back.

COCHISE COLLEGE AND THE SPACE SHUTTLE DISASTER

When I got settled at Fort Huachuca, I resumed my academic studies and perusing of the post library. I attended classes at Cochise College on the army post and on the college campus. Most of the time, I would be in my duty uniform and the only African-American. I enjoyed the campus because it gave me the opportunity to interact with traditional students and teachers. I was always learning something new.

One day in my American history class, I learned that the Mexican population is derived from the Spanish and Native Americans. My spouse is a Mexican-American, and I did not know that two cultures formed a third culture. I was enrolled in high-school Spanish for three years but did not really know my spouse's cultural background. Maybe I had not been in school before. This revelation encouraged me to be more attentive in the learning process.

Dr. Donald Dewig stated that when World War II began, he had missed getting to the assigned location of his US Army commission at the appropriate date and time. As a result of being tardy, he began serving the government in the newly established atomic program and subsequently moved to the National Aeronautics and Space Administration (NASA)[61] program, where he worked as a senior-level manager for more than forty years. Now, recently retired from NASA, he was beginning a new career as an instructor at Cochise College. He was there to share his knowledge and expertise on the topic of special issues in management.

A day in that class I particularly remember was January 28, 1986. The class began as usual with the professor clearing his throat to get started and the students yawning from their typical boredom. Suddenly a shaken school administrator appeared and asked Dr. Dewig if she could speak to the class for a moment. He acknowledged her presence and allowed her to speak. She then stepped forward and announced that "the *Challenger* blew up!" She thanked Dr. Dewig and continued her journey to notify the other classrooms.

Challenger was the name of one of the space shuttles in the NASA fleet. Early reports indicated that it had blown up seventy-three seconds from the launchpad into its space mission.[62] New technology had given birth to the twenty-four-hour news channel, which was becoming a popular mass-media tool. It showed the incident continuously throughout the day. This was a special mission because there was an elementary-school teacher, Christa McAuliffe, on board as a member of the crew. Her parents and family were in the grandstand, and her students back at her school were watching the liftoff too.

Of course, we students were in shock. The shaken administrator had gone as quickly as she'd come. It seemed the only person cool and calm during the announcement was the professor. As mentioned, Dr. Dewig had retired as a senior manager in the space-shuttle program. He spoke from his experience without expression in addressing the solemn news. "We in the space program always knew there were risks. When you put men and women on a giant candlestick and light it, something is going to happen. We have been very lucky because over the years, we expected more casualties."

What did I learn from his class? First, I learned to have more control of my own bearing in the face of disaster as displayed by Dr. Dewig. Secondly, from the standpoint of academics, I learned the following from Dr. Dewig of the 1980s heading into the 1990s:

- Computers turn leaders into clerks over time.
- The manager of the 1990s hoards the computers so much that he neglects training his subordinates.
- Personal computers (PCs) have had an impact on society and business, overexposing the organizational computer hobbyist,

most likely to the person appointed as manager, who probably also owned a home PC.

- Homes without PCs more than likely belong to worker bees, providing the worker bee with little or no experience with PCs, either at home or on the job.

As a result of his expertise, Dr. Dewig provided the following quotes:

- "Once management takes off his tie to physically help the worker complete the assigned task, then there is no management."
- "I believe we minimize accidents because managers provide management and technician provided technical expertise."
- "There is a need for balance. Managers must evenly utilize their management and automation skills on the job. Enhance the skills of the assigned worker. If that does not happen, then when disaster strikes the manager is unprepared, not the worker."

I would say these observations and comments made in the mid-1980s would conflict with the "do more with less" philosophy and technology boom that are the tenets of the 21st-century marketplace.

THIRD TIME'S A CHARM

Since joining the army, my continuing education helped me to build confidence in my ability to learn and comprehend new knowledge that bolstered my career. One duty day, I was walking about on Fort Huachuca and a voice came into my head telling me to take my warrant-officer application over to military personnel. I was given the name of Mr. Ramos as the administrative person to see. I was to do this that very day.

For the past three years, I had been carrying completed copies of the required documents, even though I had been turned down twice. Mr. Ramos looked over what I had, and then he helped me prepare a new set of documents for signature through my current unit to the Department of the Army. That meant I needed the support and signature of my chain of command.

The first meeting was with my section supervisor, Chief Warrant Officer Kelly Bolton. This was not a problem, because Mr. Bolton had previously given me exceptional marks on annual ratings. He said that the onus was now on him to convince the battalion commander, Lieutenant Colonel Charles Glave, that I was worthy of this opportunity. After Mr. Bolton spoke with the commander, an appointment was scheduled for me to meet with him. I arrived at the appointed time in my dress green uniform and extend the utmost military courtesy. We talked about my military career to date and the opportunity I had before me to become a member of the warrant-officer corps.

Then we talked about my encounter with substance abuse as a younger man and a civilian. I told him that those days were long gone, and I would greatly appreciate this opportunity to serve. He said that according to Chief Bolton, my work ethic was superb, and I deserved the opportunity. He reminded me that becoming an officer representing the United States involved integrity, and then he signed his name on the dotted line. I stood up, thanked him, rendered a military salute, and made a facing movement out the door. I continued on with my warrant officer packet in hand over to Mr. Ramos's office for further processing as quickly as I could.

A few long weeks later, I received a letter from the Department of the Army addressed to "SSG Wayne R. Davidson" that read, "I congratulate you on your selection to attend the United States Army Warrant Officer Candidate Course (WOCC)," along with official instructions for reporting for training. Unbelievable! I had been accepted as a warrant-officer candidate. When I'd first reached in my mailbox, I was afraid I would be turned down for a third time. But no, I persevered, and the third time was the charm. When I opened the letter and read its contents, I was flabbergasted. I started hugging my wife and daughter, because this acceptance letter represented a new phase in my life. My patience, endurance, and hard work had paid off. I saw Chief Warrant

Officer Bolton a few months later and then-Colonel Glave a few years later, and I thanked them both for the opportunity and the confidence each had in me.

The first sergeant, upon hearing the news, had one last detail for me as an enlisted man: to participate in a military parade. Many times when I marched in a parade, because of my height, I was assigned to the base position in the front rank. Basically, I had no other choice as an enlisted man because my duties were assigned by the first sergeant, and I was obligated to assemble in the formation until given orders to dismiss. I went where the formation went and did what the formation did. Metaphorically, this status was like being stuck in the neighborhood with no viable options.

From this experience, I learned that I have more latitude as an individual than as a member of a group. I can do more to help the group as an independent than I ever could as a captive member of a group.[63]

After being selected to another career path, I noticed the difference in the way people treated me. Once I obtained the rank of warrant officer, I operated under a different set of rules. I was an individual, and I saw the world through a different lens. Metaphorically, I had options, and I enjoyed my newfound status. I found that I could help my family and others more as an individual than as a member of a formation. In my academic work, I expanded on this topic.

Aberdeen Proving Ground: Run, Run, Run, and Glow

I got the news that there was another soldier on Fort Huachuca who had been selected as a warrant-officer candidate (WOC). His name was Russ Jones. I learned that he lived just around the corner from me on Fort Huachuca. We were ecstatic, and we got together to map out our new careers. We were both scheduled to attend the basic course at Aberdeen Proving Grounds (APG) in Maryland before continuing on to complete our certification at Fort Lee, Virginia. Our journey was to begin in the heat of the summer.

We flew into Baltimore, Maryland, and by chance we picked up another candidate, Kim Li, a female of Philippine descent. At first, Russ and I thought she was a local girl trying to pick up two cowboys from the Old West at the airport. Russ and I laughed and made the presumption that Baltimore was a "mighty friendly town." However, it turned out that Kim only wanted to share the expense of transportation to Aberdeen. The reference to "mighty friendly town" is an ongoing joke between us three.

We found lodging and prepared to report for duty the next day. We were proactive, and that was a good thing. We found out ahead of time what uniform to wear, what the requirements were, and what to expect when we reported in for duty the next day. At APG, the goal was to earn certification in basic leadership and soldiering skills as a WOC. The course was designed to be Spartan in style: very formal, very physical, and much discipline. Our preplanning saved us a lot of grief when we reported in at the front desk the next day, but no matter, as WOCs, we were looked upon as lower than snail poop in the eyes of the cadre.

Our tactical (TAC) officer was Chief Warrant Officer 3 Grier. I believe he was of German or Austrian descent, and he spoke with an accent. He was also a marathon runner, and he ran my platoon from one side of APG to the other side from the first day of training to the last. At the time, APG dealt with a lot of chemicals as part of the arsenal, so if you've ever met me and I looked like I was glowing, now you know why.

Personally, I am glad he ran us all over town, because the activity kept us busy. Once again, this was training mode. The candidates were in close quarters in every aspect: we ate together, slept together, and went everywhere together as a unit. The atmosphere was very challenging both physical and mentally. It was designed to help develop leadership attributes, and if you did not meet the challenge of the day, you ended up with a whole lot of demerits.

As I remember, on the first training day, demerits were pinned on candidates like Christmas-tree bulbs. As for myself, I remember getting over nine hundred demerits during the first week in training.

At that point in time, the only way to remove the demerits was on work detail. The work detail could be a variation of many tasks that required physical labor. My first weekend on APG, I had to dig ditches and move boulders to work off my demerits to a manageable level. I discovered that Chesapeake Bay is home to some very hungry mosquitoes.

I was glad when the weekend was over. That Monday morning, the TAC officer stood in front of the assembled formation and asked if anyone had a calculator. I had been in the service going on six years at this point in my career. The first thing a soldier learns in the army is to never volunteer for anything. However, this day for some strange reason, my hand went up, and I said, "Sir, I do!" Evidently, my leadership attributes were developing, because I never got another demerit after that day. I became the person responsible for counting up the demerits. As my administrative duties increased, my demerits decreased.

As the course continued, I kept myself mentally and physically prepared and learned to be a better teammate. I learned more about myself as I kept myself amused by singing and laughing through the stress. Sometimes the other candidates joined in when we were assigned tasks that needed to be completed for inspection. In this environment, I learned how to work under stress, and I learned how others worked under stress. I did not want to go postal as I had years ago when I worked at the mailroom. I became a better person and a better soldier. When I graduated, I was happy that I made it through the first hurdle.

Roaches and Historic Fort Lee, Virginia

This was the second time I was at Fort Lee on temporary duty status, training as a student. At Fort Lee, the goal was to complete the academic requirements, earn certification, and be pinned as a warrant officer in the Quartermaster Corps. I was doing my best to be successful, because becoming a warrant officer was serious business. Just as it was for six weeks in the basic course in Maryland, we were again in close quarters in every aspect. We ate together, slept together, and went everywhere together as a unit, with slightly less intensity. The popular song of the day was a spoof song named "Roaches" sung by Bobby Jimmy and the Critters.[64] When I woke at 0-dark-30 for the duty day, that song played on the radio as my alarm. It went, "How did roaches get started?" The lines of the song and the perceived voice of a roach brought a smile to my face in the wake of another challenging day.

Like it or not, each member was responsible for the actions of his or her fellow classmates. I learned more about integrity and responsibility when I had to report my classmate who violated a class rule to the TAC officer. That same classmate later put the whole class in jeopardy by not reporting for duty. I did my best to be a good candidate and not jeopardize the careers of my classmates.

I began to learn more about the inner workings of the army as a career through mentorship from senior leaders. I remember when a senior leader in the Warrant Officer Corps, Chief Warrant Officer Hess, came to visit us at Fort Lee. He provided guidance learned from both his professional and personal experience in hopes of prolonging our new careers. It was significant to me when he told us to join organizations that would benefit our careers, write down a financial plan, and work with financial institutions that had our careers in my mind, such as the United Services Automobile Association (USAA).[65]

Mr. Hess was candid in his discourse concerning the progress of our careers. He stated that we should remember for the first two years of our warrant-officer service that we were considered just "Christmas help" until we successfully passed the requirements of evaluation at the end of two years. If we did not successfully meet the requirements, we would revert to our former rank or be mustered out of the army. He also told us to do our best to adapt to our new positions as warrant officers and that it would take about two years for that adjustment period to end. I have heeded those words as a foundation to my personal and professional growth to this day.

STAFF RIDE AND FOOT STOMPING

Although our class was expected to fulfill our academic certification, we still had to learn the historical aspects of the army. To fulfill historical requirements, our class went on staff rides. Generally, on a staff ride, a group of soldiers would visit a historical site in order to learn firsthand about the events that made the place significant. One of the staff rides my class went on was to the Petersburg Battlefield located in nearby Petersburg.

Usually these trips were boring, and I was still trying to process my recently acquired knowledge pertaining to the Buffalo Soldier. Well, it is obvious from previous chapters that I know more about Negro soldiers now, but that day I gained three significant bits of new information to process. First, there were many Negro soldiers in the Union army formed as the United States Colored Troops (USCT).[66] Traditional history books only spoke of a few insignificant numbers, seemingly always represented in movies by actor Woody Strode.

Second, I learned that the Battle of the Crater[67] featured hundreds of Negro soldiers trained to lead a Union engagement into a great battle. However, the politics of the day proved more important than the lives of a prepared military unit. The military leadership was concerned about the political ramifications of a unit of Negro soldiers engaging and ultimately beating Confederate soldiers on the battlefield. The wrong decision could put political lives and causes in jeopardy.

The West Virginia soldiers, who were miners by trade, dug a crater for Union troops to spring on the enemy. Along the Union line, several units of colored soldiers trained for battle against the Confederate soldiers. The white troops who had previously engaged in battle and skirmishes were now exhausted. But politics dictated that the exhausted white soldiers lead the way. A battlefield catastrophe ensued, and the blame was placed on the inexperience of the colored troops, not the decision-making of the military leadership.

The third thing I learned was that there were colored soldiers serving in Confederate uniforms in defense of the South.[68] As of this writing, I am still processing this bit of information. I am interested in this topic without judgment.

As graduation day neared, I invited my parents to the ceremony to be held at the Quartermaster Headquarters in Fort Lee in the fall of 1986. The ceremonial tradition is that the ranking officer and a person selected by the candidate do the honor of pinning on the new rank on the officer. My wife and daughter did not attend the ceremony, because they were still at Fort Huachuca. I asked my mother to do the honors of pinning on the new rank. The official ceremony was to be videotaped for posterity.

From the time I joined the service, my parents had taken to the road to visit me wherever I was stationed. My mother's stepsister lived in Washington, DC, approximately a hundred miles to the north of Fort Lee. Just like so many others living in 1986, my mother's stepsister faced economic challenges. That did not deter my parents from visiting her or staying overnight at her house, as African-Americans generally had to do since the Negro migration began. For people of color, travel was especially expensive, both monetarily and morally. As a houseguest on this particular trip, my father recalled lying in bed and watching king-sized roaches scurrying about during the night.

This was a big day for me. I was proud of my recognition, and my parents were very proud too. My mother was dressed very nicely, as she always is. The commanding general was in position as each candidate and family member executed the pinning. My name was soon called, and I escorted my mother up onto the stage for the ceremony. I stood in position, and my mother and the general executed the pinning. As I escorted my mother from the stage, the general was making small talk with my mother and looking at her awkwardly. This was not unusual, because my mother was always talking to the person in charge about something.

The ceremony ended after a group picture was taken. I was a free man and a new warrant officer heading to Alaska for my first duty assignment. Less than an hour after the ceremony, I hopped into my parents' car, and we drove over to my billet to drop me off. My mother felt a little uncomfortable sitting in the front seat of the car, and there seemed to be a lot of motion going, on but the source was not readily identified. Then my mother spotted a roach and calmly pushed it away from her.

From experience, when you have seen one roach, that generally means there are others crawling around, but the question becomes "where?" Jokingly, my mother said that she hoped that one roach did not ride all the way down to Fort Lee from her sister's house in Washington, DC. Suddenly she spotted another roach on the front seat and then another. Now she begins calling on the Lord, "Lord, lookie there!"

Now, my mother was dressed in a very nice outfit, and she decided to get something out of the matching fancy purse she had worn onstage at the ceremony. When she opened the clasp on the purse, a rush of roaches came running out. Those roaches were running everywhere—in the car, on my mother, on my father, on me. We jumped out of the car and started stomping everything in sight, like we were on some sort of dance show. This was unbelievable. Where did all these roaches come from? My dad and I continued to stomp and laugh at the same time. Finally, the roaches were either free running the countryside or stomped into the sidewalk. That day, I learned that it took a lot of energy to track down and kill millions of roaches in an open space.

My mother surmised that the roaches must have climbed into her purse at her sister's house, reproduced, and hatched themselves. It was hilarious. I was glad the roaches did not break out during the ceremony, because that would have been an embarrassment to my military career forever. However, later when we viewed the videotape, it is funny that the general looked at my mother awkwardly. He may have spotted a roach or two during the ceremony. I was glad to leave my parents, those rambling roaches, and the roach song behind and head for Alaska. I was hoping it was too cold for roaches in Alaska.

WAY UP NORTH: FORT WAINWRIGHT, ALASKA

After the roach incident, I hurried back home to Arizona to pick up my wife and my daughter for our move north to Fort Wainwright, Alaska, near the Arctic Circle, for my fourth tour of duty. The map showed that Fort Wainwright was adjacent to Fairbanks, Alaska. I was anxious to get there, because Wayland Baptist University, located at the Fort Wainwright Education Center and post library, had accepted me as a student in a bachelor program. The letter addressed to "Mr. Wayne R. Davidson" read, "We are please to inform you that you have been accepted to Wayland Baptist University." Unbelievable—for a knucklehead who graduated high school as student number 451 out of 534, I was now an individual in a four-year college program.

The plan was to catch a flight from Seattle, Washington, to Fairbanks, Alaska. It was wintertime when we began our drive up to Seattle from Fort Huachuca. I decided to employ the Disneyland Theory as we made this trip a vacation of opportunity. Along the way, we stopped to visit San Diego, Los Angeles, and San Francisco, and to see whatever sights we had never ever thought we would ever get to see except on television. We also stopped for a few days in Chico, California, not far from San Francisco, to visit with a married couple we knew as friends when we previously lived in Germany.

At the time we arrived in the Chico area, the weather was beautiful and autumn-like. Notably, the University of California at Chico had been recently named the top party school by a national adult magazine. It was also a nice visit with friends, as we made our first ever trip into the city of San Francisco. However, as the old adage goes, "all good things must come to an end," and so too did our visit and the good weather. The local radio station reported that there was a winter storm watch for Northern California for the next day, which was our travel day.

We got up early to continue on our journey toward Alaska, but again the radio reported an impending storm that could hamper our drive to Seattle. There was a strong chance that Interstate 5 would be under a blanket of snow. The closer we got toward the California-Oregon border, the more snow we began to encounter. When we reached Shasta National Forest,[69] located above Redding, California, we were suddenly in a monster snowstorm. I was not expecting this situation.

The state police stationed at the base of the interstate highway awaited official word to close the road through the park. The sign on the side of the interstate read in bold lettering, "Vehicles must have chains to proceed." By chance, I had purchased tire chains in Germany with my car, but I'd never had to use them or even wanted to. The time had now come; the snow falling outside my car window was accumulating steadily around my wheelbase. I was a little worried for my wife and daughter, because I did not plan on having this much forced fun in a snowstorm on the trip. Luckily, there was a guy on the side of the road taking advantage of the weather conditions and economic opportunity by helping motorists put tire chains on their vehicles for a fee. I was glad to pay the twenty dollars.

That day, my Saab may have been the last car to cross into the park on Interstate 5. I do not recall the distance or travel time, but it was treacherous driving along the ridge of the mountain roads in the park. I knew from the map that northern California was different from southern California in terms of weather conditions, but I was clearly unaware of this national park and its terrain. Bertha and Treasure sat in the backseat clutching one another while I did my best imitation of John Wayne[70] setting his submarine on a collision course, boldly telling his crew to hold on tight. I drove slowly and quietly up the mountain road, although the weather got worse during our climb. It was difficult to visualize my surroundings because of the falling snow. Sometime during the drive down the mountain road into a valley, the weather conditions got much better; it seemed almost autumn-like. As the weather got better, so did my breathing.

When we had made it down the mountain, I saw a place off of Interstate 5 to stop for a rest and fill up with gasoline before continuing on the journey. I always enjoy speaking to local people, so I said, "Wow, that snowstorm was not too bad, I wonder what all the fuss was about?"

The female clerk queried, "Which way are you headed?" I told her north, and she replied, "Sir, you still have one big mountain to go, you just crossed the first one."

I said, "Oh, my God!" and headed back outside to secure the car and prepare for the next climb—evidently, the big one.

The clerk said the second mountain ridge was a lot more roller-coaster-like, a lot more treacherous with the falling snow, and a greater distance than the first ridge. She also said to be careful!

My wife and daughter sat in the backseat again clutching one another while I again did my best imitation of John Wayne in the submarine on a collision course, telling his crew to hold on tight a second time. And again, I drove slowly and quietly, with focus, until we started on our descent from the high country rolling past the Klamath River across the California–Oregon border. We survived the roller-coaster ride with all of our fingers and all of our toes. It was later that I learned of the topographical design and elevation of Trinity Mountain and the Mount Shasta national forest region.

We arrived in Seattle later that night, and the weather was much more pleasant. We were exhausted, but after a good night's rest, it was time to visit the Space Needle and other landmarks around town. The following day, I turned the Saab in to the port authority for shipment to Alaska. Our hotel was located near the airport, so we watched airplanes come and go for a day from the picture window of our hotel room.

Then it was our turn to fly off on our Alaskan adventure via Alaska Airlines. The route we took from Seattle provided us with a majestic view of the vast mountain range that lined the Pacific Coast of North America. From our altitude, it was like enjoying a magnificent movie as we sipped our favorite beverage. A few hours later, we landed in Fairbanks, Alaska, in the Land of the Midnight Sun.[71] The first to greet us was the giant brown bear with sharp claws encased in glass that sat in the lobby of the airport.

THE HUNT AND FISH BRIGADE

My military orders sent me to Fort Wainwright, Alaska. The current brigade was to transform into a new, larger footprint as divisions go, but lighter in the type of equipment assigned to a large military organization. As I understood it, the previous unit was nicknamed the Hunt and Fish Brigade because soldiers trained vigorously in the winter months and hunted and fished vigorously the rest of the year. I had only been on Fort Wainwright a few days, and without argument the landscape of Alaska was truly magnificent.

To survive in Alaska as a citizen or soldier, you must be properly attired. So the army issue of clothing fills up two shopping carts: boots, outer garments, insulated garments, undergarments, gloves, and caps. These provisions are designed to allow a soldier to participate in physical training and field training during extreme conditions, including skiing. I quickly learned that I lacked any Alpine attributes: my legs were too long to ski.

The city of Fairbanks and Fort Wainwright are located in the interior of Alaska, a few cold miles from the Arctic Circle. So I had to take an early-morning flight down from Fairbanks to Anchorage with my field gear to pick up my car from the port. The flight time is short, and the mountaintops are magnificent. One commercial airline operating in Alaska gives you Häagen-Dazs ice cream once you are in flight.

The distance between the two cities is approximately three hundred miles. It was a requirement for military personnel in Alaska to first have a safety briefing and to take survival gear along when picking up personal property, such as an automobile, from Anchorage. This was because the drive back through Denali Park to Fairbanks, especially in the winter, could be dangerous because of the potential for severe weather conditions that changed quickly. Denali Park[72] is the home of Mount McKinley, the tallest mountain in North America, which is 240 miles north of Anchorage and 120 miles south of Fairbanks. I hoped I would not need that gear, because this would be the first time I drove on an Alaskan road. Just my luck, there had been a steady snowfall.

A senior warrant officer, Cliff Myers, met me at the Anchorage airport and took me to the port to pick up my car. This was also my first time ever being in Anchorage, and I found out quickly that the snow-covered roads were slippery. The port was located down near the docks of Cook Inlet. Mr. Myers drove a small truck with a standard transmission and was familiar with the area, so we found the pickup location at the airport.

Once we arrived at the pickup point, I inspected and signed for my Saab, and I was ready to go. I was supposed to drive close behind Mr. Myers, following him to the office on Fort Richardson because I did not know my way around the area. But in the light falling snow and with the slippery road, the plan quickly changed. Mr. Myers in his truck with the standard transmission overtook the slippery hill on his way through the stop sign. I was not far behind, and suddenly there was another small truck with a standard transmission approaching from the left. I hit my brakes and barely stopped in time, but I still clipped the right rear fender of the truck. The driver jumped out to check for damage to the vehicle. I also got out of my car to check for damage, but it appeared to be minimal on both my car and the truck. The other driver signaled no harm no foul, hopped back into his truck, and headed down the slippery street. I was glad no one was hurt and that there was only a little damage to the vehicles, but I was a still shaken. What a way to start my tour in Alaska! An accident five minutes after getting my car off the boat. I hoped the rest of the tour would be better.

I had lost sight of Mr. Myers, but after a short while, I was able to find Fort Richardson and subsequently my boss's office. I stayed a while at the office to get acquainted with the folks. However, I had to hit the road north to Fairbanks while the weather was still fair.

MY FIRST MOOSE

I soon learned about the uniqueness of driving the Alaska Highway,[73] a two-lane road that cuts through the wilderness. A driver in Alaska must be alert at all times because of the rugged terrain and uneven road surfaces, and depending on the season, the volume of other travelers in case of emergency. It is also important to remember that weather conditions in Alaska are subject to change for the worse within minutes.

The highway between Fairbanks and Anchorage sits below a magnificent mountain range, and on this day the terrain had a significant blanket of snow. I got a glimpse of the Alaska Railroad out in the distance. I soon found that this would be the longest three hundred miles of my life.

The road is not constructed in a straight line. For instance, the distance between Fort Huachuca, Arizona, to El Paso, Texas, on Interstate 10 is approximately three hundred miles. That trip can be completed in about four hours at speeds hovering between 80 and 100 mph if the cops do not stop you along the way. The Alaskan terrain did not allow for the Alaska Highway to be constructed in that sort of straight pathway. In fact, the road goes everywhere but straight. There is a curve here and a curve there, up the hill and down the hill. Traveling at speeds between 80 and 100 mph would not be a good idea.

Then there is the added feature on the Alaska Highway that all conscientious drivers should always be aware of and look out for, which is the wildlife. After several hours of driving north toward Fairbanks, I noticed in the distance that a tree and its limbs were shaking off on the right side of the road ahead. I was curious as to what could be making the tree shake. It was a clear day, and there was no noticeable wind. The closer I got, the better I could see this giant dark figure shaking the tree. I started to slow down but kept my foot hovered over the gas pedal. There he was: the biggest animal I had ever seen that was not in a cage, a moose, shaking the tree for food. I was amazed. That moose was enormous, with four huge legs. This was unbelievable—I just saw my first moose!

ALASKAN SOUL BROTHER

As I drove down the road, I continued to look at the moose through my rearview mirror. The construction of the road was a wonder, and I thought about the resources and ingenuity it took to build in a land that is called the "Last Frontier." In my indoctrination, I learned that the road was built by the United States military in World War II to support the defense against a Japanese threat of invasion, and that many of those who built highway were Negro soldiers who worked in conjunction with white soldiers during the war. I also learned that even in the last frontier of Alaska, detached from the continental United States, those Negro troops faced issues of racism and discrimination. Like the heroics of the Buffalo Soldiers, this information was not noted in any history book that I had ever seen before. At this point, I would bet not many people from Detroit even knew that black people lived in Alaska.

The next few hours were quiet as I got closer to Fairbanks. I made it through Denali National Park for the first time, and the vast landscape was covered with majestic mountains, pure green forests, and birds of prey on patrol. It was the vastness of the land that provided the feeling of optimism. After I passed through the park, I spotted a roadhouse or two off the highway and several sparse communities. I was in the vicinity of one of these communities when, off in the distance to the left, I spotted what I thought to be a familiar sight. But no, this was not another moose shaking a tree for its leaves, although I had been looking for more moose since spotting my first one south of Denali Park a few hours earlier. This being was two-legged and walked with a distinct urban flair.

This was unbelievable! Up to this point in my trip, I thought I was the only black person this far north in Alaska. I was wrong, and the soul brother strutting alongside the road was proof that I was not alone. My father uses the terms *soul brother* or *soul sister* when he is out of his element and looks about for people who look like him. I was out of my element, so the term popped into my head.

Suddenly, I felt a little more at ease, and also hilarious as I yelled out, "Thanks, Lord! I am not the only black person in Alaska. Thanks, Lord!" The next thing I knew, I could see the outline of a large community in the distance, and it seemed I had made it back home to Fairbanks without incident—but with a revelation.

Over the following weeks, I learned that there was a significant community of African-Americans living in the town of Fairbanks, Alaska. Some were descendants of former military personnel; others had found their way north from the "Lower 48"—what Alaskans call the forty-eight states on the continental United States. Ironically, my barber was black and from Detroit, Michigan. He said that he left Detroit right after the civil disturbance in 1967. He was tired of the crappy social and economic circumstances, so he just got on a bus with his barber supplies and headed north to Fairbanks, where he had been ever since.

ALASKA: A UNIQUE PLACE TO LIVE AND ESCAPE TO

Formally the property of Russia, the territory of Alaska became a possession of the United States in the nineteenth century. Fort Wainwright is a small military post that first belonged to the army air corps as a defensive measure before World War II. After serving as an air-force asset for a number of years, Fort Wainwright once again became an army installation. A few buildings still standing had Russian markings on them. Soldiers stationed in Alaska have been on standby to serve in both war and peacetime. Over the years, the post had transitioned from a single outpost to a vibrant community.

When we first arrived in Fairbanks, we lived in a small apartment complex within the city limits. The housing area on Fort Wainwright underwent new construction, and when it was completed, I was assigned one of the newly constructed quarters. Unbelievable: my first brand-new house, courtesy of Uncle Sam!

My family and I were starting to like this place, and over the next five years we found Alaska to be a place of many unique sights and sounds: the Northern Lights; twenty-four hours of darkness; twenty-four hours of light; the Alaskan Pipeline, a short distance from my house; dodging the Alaskan state bird, the giant mosquito; automobiles with electric heater plugs; automobiles left running in parking lots while the shopper shops inside the store; the ability to purchase firearms on post; moose routinely walking about in the housing area; bears walking casually out from the woods, and then people stopping their cars thinking bears were cute and cuddly suddenly getting too close; volcanic rain; camping; and tons of winter activities at Alaska Land, a local park. I guess the most unusual sight was coming home and seeing an animal carcass drying out in the neighbor's garage.

We soon found that the only escape from the extreme cold was to plan a vacation to Hawaii during December and January. That trip to Hawaii was too much fun in the sun. My daughter Jeanne was nearly lost at sea asleep on a raft, and my speedy daughter Treasure got lost after jumping into the hotel elevator without her parents.

THE CHRISTIAN BIBLE IN A NEW LIGHT

I am grateful that Wayland Baptist University provided this African-American male with a great educational opportunity. I was one of the few who participated at the time, and I completed a four-year degree at the Fort Wainwright campus. In addition, I learned to read the Bible as a requirement of my curriculum studies. I remember quipping that my mother would be happy.

My instructor informed the class that he was a born-again Christian and that Jesus Christ was his savior. This was said with sincerity, without the injection of entertainment or bleak prognostication, as had been my previous experience with the church. I soon learned that it was okay to make written notes in the Bible text and the support materials just as any student could do in any other class, meaning the Bible in front of me was not just a display item. We had to read the entire Bible and sign an honesty note that we'd completed the requirement. As a result, I rose to another level in my Christian walk.

The timing for this class could not have been better. I believe that having the opportunity to read the Old Testament, the New Testament, and the support materials as an academic student was of great benefit to my changing lifestyle. For years, I'd heard others say how difficult the Bible was to read and understand. I, too, found it challenging at first—but at the same time, I became more in tune with what was actually written in the Bible. As a result, I learned that the Bible text had been misquoted on a number of occasions in both private and public forums.

A few years later, I found Pastor Frederick K. C. Price of Crenshaw Christian Center, who provided me with a spiritual understanding as I learned the Bible through his teaching technique. This objective, focused, and progressive discourse helped me to grow as a person, academically and spiritually. I got much more value out of reading and studying on my own than listening to ranting and raving from the pulpit about the social conditions of the masses.

My Thank-You Gift and the Local Pulpit

After my graduation from Wayland Baptist University, I took my family to visit my parents' home in Detroit in June 1991. During our four years in Alaska, we had added two new members to our family: Lydia and Lynette, both of whom I plan to speak about later in the text. We had a very nice celebration and family gathering at my mother's house. As a token of our gratitude and appreciation, I presented my mother with my cap and gown as a gift for the role she played in getting me into Highland Park College back in 1969. I was proud of the accomplishment. I had traveled through difficult times, and I was learning that knowledge and the ability to adapt to change were key elements in personal growth and the growth of the family unit.

In honor of our visit, my extended family members living in the

Detroit area were invited to my parents' house for a feast of barbeque ribs, chicken, and a host of other goodies in the summer sun. In the black community, that invitation is always extended as well to the family minister, who in turn blesses the event with a prayer. During each visit to Detroit, my mother had always invited my wife (a Catholic), my girls (raised Catholic), and me (no denomination) to attend her church. As a matter of courtesy, I reluctantly accepted the invitation this trip and took my family to New Light Baptist Church for Sunday service.

We went into the sanctuary and found seats on the left side facing the pulpit. My mother sat in her usual spot with the choir in back of the pulpit. The pastor provided his message of salvation to the people with the expected thunder and lightning. Salvation is a topic taught quite often in the black community. I had attended this church for many years, but now I considered myself a guest, and since that early time my understanding of the Bible and its teachings had evolved from the single topic of salvation.

At some point in the service, guests were asked to stand and be recognized. My family and I stood, and my mother got the credit for us being there. We sat back down in anticipation of the minister's message. The next thing I knew, the pastor lit up his fire and brimstone using *me* as an object lesson in his message. He looked in my direction and said that "just because you have a piece of paper stating your level of education, it does not mean you can forget the Lord" or something to that effect.

I was in shock and stunned, and I asked myself, *Why is this knucklehead on my case?* I did not come here to be made a public spectacle. I thought if anything, he should state that my accomplishments as a soldier and a student should be emulated by others festering in the social and economically challenged black community. He did not retract his fire or make that suggestion. When I left the premises, I was upset with the pastor. I hoped the next time I visited my mother's house, that minister was not invited to "break bread" with us, as my father would say.

From that incident in June 1991, I understood that reading the Bible page by page had helped me grow in Christian knowledge. Salvation is a very simple process: acknowledge the Resurrection and Jesus Christ as your personal savior, done deal! I became aware that many church leaders have an agenda to maintain the status quo of their congregations through the ignition of emotions. I prefer to listen to progressive presentations that supplement my reading of the Bible and instruct the worshipper to learn how to fish for themselves. I no longer go to church for the floor show.

Back to Alaskan Opportunity

After the visit was over, I packed my family up and headed back to Alaska through Chicago. However, we missed our connecting flight in Chicago. So we sat around the Windy City for a few hours and felt the electricity of Michael Jordan and the Chicago Bulls engaged in the first set of their three-peat National Basketball Association championships.

At this point, I had been in the army for eleven years and had adapted to the lifestyle. I was proud of my accomplishments and the tapping of my potential. After completing my studies at Wayland Baptist, I was accepted at the University of Alaska-Fairbanks (UAF). The student body was predominately Native Alaskan; there were very few African-Americans that I encountered. As a career move, I decided to work toward an accounting degree at UAF in the hope that I might have opportunities as a professional later. I researched and learned that the army had an education program that would allow me to become a fulltime student at a college or university for twelve to eighteen months. As quickly as possible, I made a formal request through the warrant-officer branch to complete my accounting degree, but the request was not approved. Master Warrant 4 Davis informed me by formal letter that there was no authorization or billet for a warrant officer to attend civilian school, and as a result, I did not get the opportunity to complete my degree program at UAF with the support of the US Army. Yes, I was a little perturbed at the decision.

Since joining the army, I was learning to do better at keeping my eyes and ears open for opportunity. If I had listened to one of my accounting professors in the very early 1990s, that denial from my branch would have been a moot point. One day in class the professor provided this prognostication: if you want to be rich, invest a few bucks on technology, in particular, flat-screen monitors. That was a homework assignment I should have completed, because over the past twenty years, if you look around, flat-screen monitors have become prevalent everywhere in the home and place of business.

NATIVE ALASKAN HERITAGE

Living in Alaska and attending UAF expanded my knowledge of the Native Alaskan culture. Around campus, the many aspects of Native Alaskan heritage were on display almost everywhere. In the classroom, I enjoyed listening to Native Alaskan students tell stories about their culture and lifestyle. They talked about their own Native Alaskan Olympics games,[74] like the "swing kick," where the participant kicks at a suspended ball at various heights, and the "ear pull," where two opponents pull in a tug-of-war fashion on a string firmly attached to their ear structure.

They talked about life in the fish camps and living off the land. Their heritage taught them to respectfully use every part of the animals hunted for sustenance, clothing, and lodging. Subsequently, unusable waste material would be stacked out on the frozen Bering Sea and consumed back into the thawed water when the season changed to warmer temperatures. I learned that an unsuccessful hunt for game made the hunter and his family inadequate. I also learned that the heritage handed down to them by their forefathers was greatly restricted by government legislation. For some reason, I could relate to their social plight, but at this point I did not know why.

The weather on campus was very cold on some days when I attended school, but I was not deterred. I enjoyed UAF and the knowledge I gained through my classes, and there was only one time that I felt really awkward. It happened on or about March 5, 1991. I was sitting in my logic class when someone asked the instructor about the situation concerning a fellow named Rodney King.[75] It seemed the entire classroom turned to look at me, and I did not know why. I thought to myself, *Who in the hell is Rodney King?*

As the discussion progressed, I learned that a black man named Rodney King had been beaten in Los Angeles the previous night, and the entire incident had been videotaped and aired on television. I think the class thought I was the local Jesse Jackson and wanted me to provide commentary. Since I restarted my academic career in 1980, many times I was the only African-American in attendance. From my point of view, I did not know Rodney King from Albert King or BB King, so what did I have to say? Nothing! It has been my lifelong experience that black males have always been subjected to harsh treatment, and it sounded to me that this was just another harsh day in the life of a black male. I had already experienced that predicament. However, once I viewed the tape, I was stunned and I understood that harsh treatment of black males had gone to a new level.

ALASKA: BE AWARE OF THE ENVIRONMENT

In Alaska, awareness of the environment was a survival requirement. The lack of knowledge could make you a casualty. Soldiers are always vulnerable and had to be on constant vigil while making good decisions in conducting soldier business. I was especially wary of encountering a bear during physical training. As I ran along the trail, my eyes were always looking for a seemingly cuddly bear of any type with sharp teeth, large claws, and good closing speed on a hiker or runner. Once while I was on an official visit to Fort Richardson in Anchorage, a black bear came wandering out of the woodland area between two military locations onto the road. Bear gawkers started piling up along the thoroughfare, stating, "He's so cute!" We remembered that we had passed a pedestrian walking on the roadway. We had to turn our vehicle around to pick the guy up before he reached the spot and became a quick snack for the bear.

It is and always has been my belief that black males have to be aware of their environment; if not, something bad always happens. I learned a lot of hard lessons along the way because of immaturity and inattentiveness to things around me. One absolutely cold Sunday morning, my inattention to my environment caused me to nearly freeze to death in the parking lot of the Fort Wainwright service station.

It was about seven thirty a.m. I had gotten off duty from the night before, and I noticed that the front passenger tire on my six-year-old Saab was low and needed air. I was able to drive to the service station on post with the sound of the tire thumping along the frozen way. I thought to myself, *This is not good*, but I had to make a choice in surviving the cold. I could either walk home or wait for the store to open up. For the average person in distress in those days, a cell phone was not an option.

I calculated that the distance to my house was a little over a mile in a straight line across Ladd Field and about three miles walking around the airfield. Historically, the weather on Fort Wainwright ranges from sixty-five degrees below zero in the winter to ninety degrees above zero in the summer. This was not summer, and believe me, it was too cold to walk anywhere. The post service station generally opened around nine a.m. on weekdays, but this was a cold and wintry Sunday morning. The establishment on post did not open until after ten a.m., and the air pump was stored inside the warm shop, not outside in the winter cold. So it was obvious I had to wait for the store to open.

I thought to myself again, *This is not good.* I checked to see what survival gear I had already stored in my car that would help me stay warm. I found enough covering to keep some cold off of me, and then I checked to see how much fuel was in the car. The gauge showed that I had a little more than a quarter of a tank of gasoline. I needed enough fuel to run the car heater for almost two and a half hours. My plan was to run the car heater and keep warm. I thought I had a good plan, but the winter cold on the outside of my car was more intense than my car heater on the inside.

In the past, when in trouble with one of my previously owned cars, I would talk to the car on a personal level about it being low on fuel, the alternator belt is okay and not broken, and any other mechanical problem, including being low on air pressure. It seemed that today was another good time to start a conversation with my car about the fuel situation. In addition, I was able to fine-tune my skills of prayer during this troubled time. I prayed continuously for the door of the service station to open, and it did: promptly at eleven a.m. My ordeal was over, and I found that prayer works—and to keep gas in the car along with warmer clothing, especially if you live in Alaska. I put air in the tire and headed home a short distance away. I made it through the ordeal with all my frozen fingers and all my frozen toes.

THE PERILS OF SERVICE

Alaskan weather conditions can be both dangerous and humorous, especially if you serve the public. I remember an incident during Fort Wainwright renovations where the plan was to reduce an old building located on the airfield to rubble with a series of precision explosions. The event was big news and broadcast on local television. During the broadcast, the wind direction changed, causing sparks to jump from the building designated for destruction to the building next to it. That building caught fire and also went up in smoke. Luckily, no one was hurt by the catastrophe, but that building housed the equipment used by the smoke jumpers. The smoke jumpers were an elite fire-control team that traveled around the world providing assistance to others in managing raging fires. This time it was the smoke jumpers who needed assistance, because their rescue and safety equipment had gone up in smoke. I am sure they could find humor in the incident years later.

Tragedy anywhere is unforgettable. Alaska is a beautiful land, but as cited, that's only when the weather conditions aren't treacherous. During the winter months, there are a number of training exercises going on all over Alaska. One particular training exercise was called "Brim Frost." I remember a winter day in 1989 where a thick ice fog covered Fort Wainwright, and visibility was barely two feet in front of your face.

It was the end of the duty day, and I was heading home from my warehouse office. As previously stated, I lived in the new commercial housing area on the other side of the airfield across the Chena River on the River Road Bridge, which was about three miles and a very short drive under the right conditions. As I approached the small bridge, I felt a low-flying airplane pass over the roof of my automobile, and I was startled.

I continued home cautiously and parked my car before going inside the house. I was telling my wife about the low-flying plane when the phone rang and I answered it. The person on the other end stated that this call was a general alert and to report immediately to the main building in cold-weather gear. I hung up the phone and complied with the order.

Once I got to the building to report for duty I noticed that there were a number of field-grade officers in the staging area with looks of concern on their faces. What I found out was that three Canadian aircraft had tried to navigate a landing onto Ladd Field, but the landing was aborted because of poor visibility. One of the aircraft had crashed in the vicinity of the airfield, and the two other planes were directed to Fairbanks International Airport. This was a serious incident, but visibility was so poor that the commander could not risk sending soldiers and equipment out to provide assistance without putting those soldiers' safety in jeopardy. For several hours, soldiers remained on standby, but the order came to return to quarters. This was a frustrating set of circumstances, because the soldiers were anxious to help fellow soldiers.

Over the next few days, the weather became much clearer. The wreckage at the crash site was in plain view across the banks of the Chena River. The plane lay against a row of power lines with the nose down, not far from the golf course. After an investigation, the Aviation Safety Network reported that the Lockheed CC-130E Hercules had landed three hundred to six hundred feet short of the runway at night in minus-forty-six-degree temperatures, and as a result, there were nine fatalities among the eighteen occupants. It was a solemn occasion as the clearer sky showed the crash victims were just moments away from fellow soldiers willing to help with emergency equipment.[76] This tragedy can never be forgotten.

The Army Must Like Me

I did not grow up in the army, like many other soldiers. I did, however, mature in the army. I learned and trained according to the big picture as presented by army leadership. I was near completion of my two-year probation period—or "Christmas help," as Chief Warrant Officer Hess put it—and was becoming more comfortable in my development as a warrant officer.

In 1988, I found out the army must really like me. Instead of promoting me to chief warrant officer 2, my orders stated that I was promoted to first lieutenant.[77] That really messed my pay up for two long months. The previous year, 1987, I'd received a letter addressing me as captain and inviting me to Advanced Civil School because it seemed I had the potential as an instructor at West Point in the Department of Mathematics.[78] Truly that was in error; it is my father who is busy figuring numbers out in my family.

General Schwarzkopf Comes to Town

Prior to the beginning of the Gulf War, General Norman Schwarzkopf[79] made a visit to Alaska for the purpose of instructing an officer professional development (OPD) class to officers of the 6th Infantry Division (Light) at both Fort Richardson and Fort Wainwright. Some years prior, Schwarzkopf and the division commander, Major General Fields, had been stationed together in Alaska.

Fort Richardson was the general's first stop that morning because the command flag was located there. Later in the morning, the two generals flew up to Fort Wainwright for a midday session with the officers stationed on Fort Wainwright at the post theater. At the time, I was the lowest ranking officer stationed on Fort Wainwright, so I did not know what to expect. I was a little intimidated, and I didn't want to be in the way of the military commanders and their staff. It was obvious these career military men were both anxious and nervous about the general's visit.

The auditorium, full of military commanders in the rank of full-bird colonel and below, were given updates on General Schwarzkopf's whereabouts and the time of his expected arrival. As the general got closer, those in the auditorium were asked to take seats for his arrival. In basic training, recruits learning to be soldiers are instructed to fill up the front rows, to get close to your buddy without leaving an empty seat, and to do this quickly and quietly. That is not what happened that day among those career officers.

I was surprised to see these officers lollygagging around like recruits. Suddenly from the rear of the theater a loud command voice ordered the auditorium to attention and blasted them with profanity concerning their lack of professionalism in filling up seats in a timely manner. For the purpose of this story and my inability to remember his name, the command came from Colonel X, promotable to brigade general and rumored to be a protégé of General Colin Powell. When given the command of execution, the officers and gentlemen scurried to the seats like little kids caught with a hand in the cookie jar. As the low man on the totem pole, I was astonished by their behavior—including that of the general officer who chastised them. I remember Colonel X because my wife and I had met him at a social function. My wife was pregnant at the time, and he made a comment that she appreciated.

Shortly thereafter, General Norman Schwarzkopf appeared on the stage. He talked about his role as the US central commander (CENTCOM) and provided a command briefing on a world map indicating the roles the United States Army played in the world, and how the army would respond to threats to the security of US interests around the world. I was amazed at the level of detail the general provided.

Honestly, I felt like I was clued into the situation room of the Pentagon. Ironically, some weeks later, the Iraqi army marched into Kuwait and the military went into action, just as it had been described on the general's big board. His presentation was mind-blowing.

I learned two things that day: first, plans can work when they are written out in great detail, and second, the people who execute those plans can be knuckleheads too, no matter how much brass or rank they have on their collars.

SUIT UP AND PLAY THE GAME!

One morning, shortly after I arrived at my office, I received a phone call from a female officer at the Department of the Army. She told me I was on orders for the Middle East, and I was to report to the medical facility as soon as possible for a physical examination. I was stunned—as anybody would be during this time—so I stopped by my house first to tell my wife what was going on. She was a little sad, but we hugged and I reported to the medical facility.

I arrived at the front desk of the medical facility to report in as ordered. About the same time I got there, the same female officer from the Department of the Army called to rescind the previous order. It turned out that my military specialty by regulation was no longer interchangeable with the military specialty that was needed. I did not debate the issue; I quickly executed a facing movement out the front door.

GLAMOROUS MOVIE STARS AND THE ART OF SMOKING

I quit smoking in 1989. I did not consider myself a heavy smoker, and the practice of smoking had lost its luster for me. I remember long ago when Sammie Lee Ford told the guys as we waited at the public bus stop heading for school on a cold wintry day that smoking a cigarette would keep us warm. That big fat lie Sammie Lee told lasted about twenty years for me.

I quit smoking because I did not want to pass on secondhand smoke to my family. In the 1980s, the issue of secondhand smoke had become a medical concern through public awareness. I did not smoke like a chimney, but I smoked enough that it was probably annoying to those around me. My excuse was that I was a student, and smoking and drinking were part of my study process as I did my homework during the evening hours.

In my process of quitting smoking, I started by smoking less and less each day. Then I accelerated the process when I enrolled in a smoking cessation program at the Fort Wainwright hospital. The class was small, but it provided graphic detail of the ramifications of continuing to smoke.

There was a white lady in her sixties in my class who was wrinkled from head to toe. Her skin, height, and bone structure had been adversely impacted by smoking. She had grown up during the 1930s and 1940s when smoking was the rage in movies and magazines. She stated that she smoked because all of the movie stars smoked and she wanted to be just like them. Many of those same movie stars died at very young ages because of their habit.

I completed the class, and I have not smoked since. In reality, smoking is probably the most difficult habit to break. The practice of smoking has both physical and social ramifications.

When I quit smoking, besides getting my sense of smell and taste back, I noticed that I no longer engaged in social conversations that lasted for hours. In reflection, smoking crossed social boundaries and brought people together for a social hour. In the world of smoking, smokers always offered to share a cigarette when asked. "Hey, buddy, you gotta cigarette?" Then the reply, "Sure Mack, here you are!"

In a military organization, the lowest ranking soldier, Private Jones, could have a smoking relationship with the military person at the top, General So-and-So. During these informal connections, there could be plenty of influence-peddling, second-guessing, bad-mouthing, or bias toward others that made it difficult for appointed managers in the organization to perform their assigned duties and responsibilities. It was difficult to make personnel change if the soldier or civilian had a smoking relationship with the chain of command. No matter, twenty years of smoking was long enough for me.

HOMESICK FOR BASKETBALL'S BAD BOYS

One nice thing about living in Alaska is the time zone. Alaska Standard Time (AST) is four hours earlier than Eastern Standard Time (EST) and, as a result, a national sporting event would come on earlier in the day. For instance, if the national televised game started at one p.m. EST, then it would be nine a.m. AST. So when the Detroit Pistons formed their powerhouse championship basketball team nicknamed "The Bad Boys,"[80] I could roll out of bed just before nine a.m. to watch the game. The game generally ended around noon with another Pistons victory. After they won the championship series, I sipped champagne and danced in the street with my six-year-old daughter, Treasure, and then I had the rest of day to do other stuff as the June Solstice approached.

I was so into the victorious Detroit Pistons that I bought my wife a brand-new Jeep Cherokee four-wheel drive right off of the showroom floor. Jeep was now a Chrysler product, and at the time it was marketed as the official car of the National Basketball Association (NBA).[81] I was so inept at driving a four-wheel-drive vehicle that I slid off into a ditch during my drive home from the car dealer. A few weeks later, after taking directions from Treasure, I ended up driving into another ditch. It was another four-wheel drive vehicle with a winch that pulled me out. I learned that people who live in Alaska and endure the artic climate are generally friendly and helpful. Subsequently, I got better driving a four-wheel-drive vehicle because that Jeep had a long family drive to make of more than fourteen years. Then more than a decade after the Jeep Cherokee was donated to a Michigan charity in 2002, it pulled up beside me at a stoplight with a set of four giant off-road tires and a new family inside. I could tell it was my former vehicle by familiar markings; the worn out paint that no longer covered its body and the Alaskan dealership sticker on the rear hatch door.

HEADING BACK TO THE LOWER 48 WITH TWO BUNDLES OF JOY

My tour was up. I had served five years as a chief warrant officer in the 6th Infantry Division (L), and despite living in the cold weather of Alaska, I had adapted and almost never returned to the "Lower 48." But official orders made the division go away and the Hunt and Fish Brigade returned. I requested reassignment to Fort Huachuca and got it. Although I never turned into an outdoorsman, there were still a lot of unique Alaskan activities I was going to miss: the longest day, June 21; the longest night, December 22; the stories that sportsmen told about fishing and hunting in the Alaskan waters and wilderness; and the tragedies I wished would have never happened, like the Canadian air crash and the Exxon Valdez oil spill.[82]

We had also reached a point in my tour where the adventurous climate in Alaska fit nicely as the remedy for couples having trouble bearing children. The weather almost guarantees that you and your spouse will take out more children from Alaska than you originally brought in. I am a witness! The birth of my two youngest daughters happened in Alaska under the Northern Lights.

My daughter Lydia was almost born premature but still three weeks before her projected due date. The last two months of the pregnancy were difficult for Bertha because she had to stay off her feet. I think that time of rest created a special bond between mother and daughter.

My daughter Lynette was also in a hurry to get to the party—she came three weeks before her projected due date. Lynette must have had a watch on; she was popping out of the womb before the doctor was properly dressed and ready for the delivery. I remember the doctor yelling out, "Hold it, Hold it!" as she tried to keep pace with Lynette's speedy exit. It's the same attitude with which Lynette has approached her life goals and objectives: "Let's get it done now!" Someone has to slow her down.

Lynette's birth was recorded on videotape, and each year on her birthday the family brings out the videotape to play for all to see and remember. During the viewing, Bertha's family, both young and old, will sit down with popcorn and enjoy watching the tape over and over again, just as if they were in a theater. In contrast, my family, a God-fearing, churchgoing, "nothing left but the shouting" people, found it very hard to sit and witness God's greatest miracle unfold on the screen. I do not understand the contrast or why it is difficult for my family to watch.

Anyway, these two additional dependents help to beef up my check from the Alaskan Permanent Fund, the annual stipend received by Alaskan citizens as a result of the interest payments on the oil reserves. At the time I lived there, an eligible Alaskan citizen with ten legal dependents would typically receive $1,000 per eligible dependent. However, when you move away from Alaska, the money does not follow you. I miss the Alaskan Permanent Fund.

As a family, we had grown from three to five members—one male and four females. When we'd arrived five years before as a family of three, there was snow on the ground. As we prepared to leave as a family of five, there was snow on the ground. I had driven the Saab to the port authority in Anchorage for shipment to Southern California, a week or two earlier. So we loaded up the Jeep Cherokee with bags of provisions, babies, and warm clothes and then drove off from Fort Wainwright onto the Alaska Highway.

DAY 1: PUMP UP BOB SEGER

On the first leg of our journey along Alaska Route 2, we passed the Santa Claus House in North Pole, Alaska,[83] for the last time as we headed south to the "Lower 48." Detroiter Bob Seger and his Silver Bullet Band's *Nine Tonight*[84] began to spin in the cassette deck for the first of a zillion times played on this journey. The complementary tracks "Against the Wind"[85] and "Fire Lake"[86] were especially appropriate when we drove through extreme weather conditions or wilderness areas.

My daughter Treasure rode with me in the front seat while Bertha sat in the middle of the backseat with the two babies, Lydia and Lynette, secured in their car seats. The radio reported stormy conditions, so we had to outrun the forecast of a winter storm on our tail. Our destination was Haines, Alaska, where we were scheduled to board an Alaskan ferry in two and a half days' time bound for Washington State.

I was armed with a travel book called *The Milepost*[87] that provided information on the location of lodging and fuel along the Alaska Highway. In Alaska, you can never leave home without knowing where to obtain essential services, especially if you're traveling with small children. The nightfall comes pretty fast in the wintertime, so the first night of travel on the road we spent at the Border City Lodge. The lodge was a rustic cabin located out in the darkness of the Alaskan frontier. Only the Northern Lights, the snow-covered landscape, and a bright neon sign pinpointed its location a few miles short of the Canadian border. We quickly unloaded what was absolutely needed for the cold night. Just baby milk and toiletries—we all slept in our clothes.

DAY 2: CARIBOU WITH SHARP ANTLERS

The next morning, we got up at 0-dark-30 prepared to continue our drive to Haines Junction in the Yukon Territory. It was Day 2 of our journey. I checked out the car and Bertha checked out the babies. The northern sky was illuminated with stars, but it was still dark. I pulled slowly onto the highway and then drove about a mile before I had to make an emergency stop. The countryside, white with snow, was suddenly filled with the sound of snorting, the patter of hoofs, and sharp antlers.

Out of nowhere, a sizeable herd of caribou had crossed the road, and I was right in the middle of them. I told myself not to startle the herd, because a wayward antler could puncture a tire, a window, or my radiator. Then we would be stuck on top of the world in the wilderness. My patience paid off. The herd passed by us by without incident, and we slowly motored off toward the US-Canadian border crossing over into the Yukon Territory.

As we cross the border, the morning light unveiled the vast mountain range surrounding our Jeep. We could have filmed a commercial for Chrysler: "Jeep, official car of the NBA, in the wilderness of the Yukon Territory." I quickly understood that when driving in the wilderness, the driver, the occupants, and the automobile must be in right standing with God. There is nobody out there but you and God, and if you don't have faith in Him, you could be stuck and never be found. My goal was to enjoy the majestic scenery, keep my family safe, and make it to Haines Junction in the Yukon Territory before nightfall.

We did make it to Haines Junction after a glorious day of driving through God's country. For the weary traveler, there was lodging and plenty of food and fuel. We stayed at a motor inn and had dinner. The local population, indigenous people to Canada, informed us that there was news on the radio of a snowstorm approaching. The plan was to retire for the evening and then get up early to beat the storm heading toward Haines Junction. Once again, I checked out the car, Bertha checked out the babies, and we all hit the sack.

DAY 3: THE VALLEY OF THE EAGLES

The next morning, the snow did begin to fall, but not enough to delay our departure. This was Day 3 of our journey. We were back on the Alaska Highway, heading south through the Yukon Territory to British Columbia, the US-Canadian border, and the Alaskan port city of Haines. As we crossed back over the border, we suddenly found ourselves and the car gliding in the middle of a James Bond spy movie. Pure white snow covered the road, river, and landscape of the Chilkat Valley.[88] Once your eyes adjust to this wonderful postcard, they're distracted by flying objects in the sky. When your eyes come into focus, the flying objects are quickly identified as eagles—hundreds of them perched in trees and hundreds of them soaring in the sky. The Valley of Eagles was an unexpected sight for a family of five driving the Alaska Highway heading toward the ferry dock in Haines a few more miles down the road. The ride through this majestic valley was almost better than Disneyland.

Haines is located in Southeast Alaska on a body of water called the Portage Cove. "The end of the trail" is the interpretation of the original Indian name for Haines, and the name appropriate for the nearly three full days of driving through God's country with my wife and small daughters. We all agreed it was nice to be off of the wilderness trail and into a town with people.

We found the Alaska State Ferry terminal and then stowed the Jeep Cherokee along with our belongings. It would be evening before the ferry embarked from the dock on the next leg of our trip, a three-day voyage on the Pacific Ocean to the "Lower 48." Although the snow-covered mountains could still be seen in the distance, Haines is closer to sea level, so the weather conditions were more temperate, with drizzling rain instead of the extreme cold of interior Alaska. We found it nice and leisurely to walk around this historic town without fear of freezing to death.

Our debarkation point was Bellingham, Washington. To this point in my life, I had never traveled more than an hour or two on a seafaring vessel. I had ridden the Detroit River and Lake Lucerne in Switzerland on local ferries but never on a seafaring vessel that was scheduled to land at a different debarkation point days after the one we left.

The Ferry, Seasickness, and the Motorcycle Dudes

As I remember, the ferry took the inside passage as the traveling lane. A state ferry is not the same as a cruise ship. The typical cruise ship used the outside passage as the traveling lane and had numerous amenities for passenger enjoyment. A state ferry is equipped with an observation deck and vehicle deck and is limited in customer amenities. That is because it serves more as a shuttle or taxi service in between the Alaskan chain of islands. It appeared that many of the passengers were local Alaskans and academic groups.

The view from the observation deck was perfect for spotting whales and other ocean life swimming across our bow. We visited Skagway, Sitka, and Ketchikan, all located on the inside passage, which gave us an opportunity to reflect on our memories of the state of Alaska and its vast cultural heritage.

The state ferry had a small store with a limited inventory and operating hours. It had cafeteria-style offerings with limited dining choices, and a cocktail lounge with premium prices. As a result, it was recommended that travelers bring their own snacks, books, games, and toiletries as required. Most notably, if traveling as a family, like my family of five, it was best to reserve a cabin for sleeping and privacy. If you did not have a cabin, the alternative was deck passages, where there was no privacy and sleeping was done on lounge chairs or on the deck itself. Getting a cabin was a good choice so that my wife and children could have privacy. For a family of five, sleeping out on a deck passage would have been a bad choice.

It is the bad and bold who choose to sleep out on the deck passage. On this voyage, there were at least three motorcycle dudes spread out on deck passage, and because they looked a little rough from the rugged road, they had the deck passage all to themselves. The guys were laying in the lounge chairs asleep when the ferry debarked from Haines for two whole days until we hit rough seas at the Pacific Rim. Then the motorcycles dudes jumped up and went to the bow of the ship, held their arms high, and screamed as each wall of waves clashed against the bow of the ship. I watched them for a while, shook my head, and returned to the cabin with my wife and girls. All four were spread on the bed in one big pile of seasick woman. I was also overcome by the waves and added my body to the pile, changing its gender. Later, when we reached calmer waters, I went up on the deck passage to find that the motorcycle dudes had also returned calmly to their lounge chairs and had passed out until the next event.

Now that the water was calmer, the whole family went back up to the observation deck. The closer we got to Bellingham, Washington, the happier we felt about getting off the boat. We had survived five years in Alaska, the last frontier, and we had brought with us a ton of golden memories. We had lived in a new house, bought a new car, launched new careers, achieved a higher level of education, and had two new babies, and soon we would be on vacation in the Pacific Northwest. But first, we wanted to get off of this boat.

HEAD OFF THE BOAT AND HEAD DOWN THE ROAD

When we arrived in Bellingham to debark from the vessel, it was morning. Bellingham was about an hour's drive north of Seattle. The goal was to drive to our lodging in the Seattle area, rest for a short period, and then go sightseeing for the day, all to the accompaniment of Bob Seger and the Silver Bullet Band. Once we rested, we drove around town and stopped to visit the Space Needle, Fort Lewis, and Mount Olympus.

A day or so later, we headed south through Oregon looking for the Pacific Coast Highway, strategically bypassing the Mount Shasta region. We went onward through the Giant Forest and Napa Valley before traveling over the Golden Gate Bridge into San Francisco for a few days of sightseeing. In a small dark San Francisco alleyway, I learned where the secrets of life are typed and printed out and then neatly placed in Chinese fortune cookies, a process not unlike an automobile assembly line. When we'd first visited Fisherman's Wharf on our way up to Alaska in 1986, there was little wildlife making a home so far inland, but after San Francisco experienced the devastating Loma Pieta Earthquake[89] in 1989, the sea lion population had made Pier 39 its home more days out of the year.

A few days later, we were in Southern California visiting the tourist sites we had missed before. My sister lived in Fullerton near Disneyland,

and since it was the holiday season, my parents were also there. We were in luck and attended the inaugural opening of Toontown at Disneyland. That day may have been a celebrity day at the park, because Michael Jackson, the King of Pop, was there with a fair haired young friend enjoying the sights, sounds, and rides.

We also rode the monorail around the park just for fun. As we approached the Disneyland Hotel, I noticed that the man seated directly across from me was Dr. Jerry Buss,[90] owner of the Los Angeles Lakers basketball team. He appeared to be with his family. By happenstance, only a few weeks before in November 1991, his star player, Earvin "Magic" Johnson,[91] had announced to the world that he was HIV positive and retired immediately from the game of basketball. Out of respect, I thought it to be cruel and callous for me to query Dr. Buss on that subject. I was having too much fun with my family at the park and hopefully he was too.

A few days later, we loaded up the Jeep Cherokee, popped Bob Seger and the Silver Bullet Band back in the compact-disc player, and drove down to San Diego. We went sightseeing and enjoyed the San Diego Zoo, where my daughter Treasure got up close and personal with a killer whale. Then we hit the road to El Paso, Texas, to visit Bertha's family for a few days. We then drove back to Tucson, dropped the Jeep Cherokee in the airplane parking lot, and took a plane back to Southern California so that I could pick up my Saab from the docks in Compton. We returned to my sister's house in Fullerton for a few more days of sightseeing around Southern California before heading out to my next duty station, Fort Huachuca, Arizona. I learned that fun can be exhausting and expensive.

Fort Huachuca, Back Home with the Buffalo Soldier

This was my second tour of duty at Fort Huachuca, home of the Buffalo Soldier. I had been gone for five years. I was excited to return, not just for the assignment itself, but because I had been accepted into a master's program at Western International University, located on post. The letter addressed to "Mr. Wayne R. Davidson" read, "We are please to inform you that you have been accepted to Western International University ..." This was unbelievable! I had to pinch myself, because acceptance in a graduate program is something I never thought I would receive.

During this time, Fort Huachuca was a great place to be. There was greater media attention to the heritage of the Buffalo Soldier at Fort Huachuca and other places located in the Old West under the tenure of General Colin Powell. I became very informed of the Buffalo Soldiers and also embraced their service.

This Is the Mission

In my second tour at Fort Huachuca, I served as the property-book officer for a sophisticated communications brigade in the United States Army. In reflecting on the past twelve years, I was very proud of my own service. To date, joining the army was the best career decision I had ever made, and becoming a warrant officer was undoubtedly the second best. However, my second tour was probably the most challenging because the unit to which I was assigned had just returned from the Gulf War, and property accountability was in chaos. Then, more than six months later, two warrant officers who were senior to me arrived in the brigade, and they both wanted the position I had at the brigade level instead of the battalion level. I thought the issues were petty, and after a while I submitted my resignation.

I considered that my time so far in the army was gravy, so after consulting my wife I took my stand—right, wrong, or indifferent. It is not that easy for a commissioned warrant officer to resign from the service unless all service obligations have been met, and still the resignation packet must go through the brigade commander for approval. As a result, I had to have a formal audience with Colonel Downey, the brigade commander.

I dressed in my Class A uniform as a military courtesy and then reported to Colonel Downey's office at the appointed time. We talked about my resignation and the benefit of taking it back. We also talked about his career and the challenges he faced in obtaining his rank and position. In summary, he told me that in the army you have to "play the game." When my ears heard that phrase, I thought to myself, *Whoa, where did I hear that phrase before?*

The colonel continued on to state, "When that two-star-general across the street calls me to say, 'Colonel, this is the mission!' it is not a matter of liking or dislike, I am obligated."

My response to him was "Yes sir!" Why? Because I had to play the game. That speech was similar to the speech SFC Smith once gave me in Germany a few short years before, when he said, "Play the game!"

As Colonel Downey paused, I thought to myself that the Buffalo Soldier faced tougher hardship than this episode I was facing now. Reluctantly, I agreed to see my career through and take back my resignation. Some fifteen years later, I saw Colonel Downey again at a logistics conference at which I had the opportunity to sing the national anthem. He was retired and working as a contractor. I thanked him for the opportunity to reconsider my position and continue on with my career.

At the time of my tour at Fort Huachuca, the Gulf War—Desert Storm/Desert Shield—was formally over. Then there was the peace mission to Somalia.[92] From a logistics standpoint, there was always a contingency force to provide support, as needed. If I did not know this before, I knew it now that the commander in the field has great power and gets anything he or she deems necessary to complete the mission. To be successful, the soldier in the field must have basic needs met, or there is very little good a soldier can do for another, especially if the unit consists of male and females.

ACCOUNTING FOR EQUIPMENT AND OUTFITTING SOLDIERS

I recall a lot of sundry or incidental items being sent to Somalia for the purpose of making sure female soldiers had personal items that maintained their quality of life. I also recall that regular army laundry and bath units were unavailable for whatever reason. I believe it was because of the lack of electricity and harshness of the water in country. So the unit sent brand new commercial washers in order to make clean laundry available to the soldiers. There would be no Maytag repairman[93] if and when the washing machine broke. So I imagine the washers went into the ocean to shore up the shoreline. There were no dryers, so clothes had to be hung out in the sun where they were subject to pilfering by the local Somalis.

Speaking of clothes, my greatest headache as the accountable officer of army property was outfitting units and individuals with the proper desert uniform for field duty. Why? At the time, there were very few desert uniforms in large quantities in various sizes available in the army supply system. The aftermath of Desert Storm and Desert Shield were high-profile military contingency actions. A unit commander with troops heading to a war zone in a desert environment had to not only feel good but also look good for both the public and media attention. As an accountable officer, I remembered to "play the game," because no matter what, the mission goes on. On occasion, I felt like I was dealing uniforms out of the trunk of a car like back in the old neighborhood.

There was an instance I remember where I needed to acquire a desert uniform for a young African-American male who was at least six foot six and 275 pounds. My soldiers did everything possible to requisition those items from the army supply system in a timely manner. It took weeks for those items to come into my warehouse, but they finally did. Strangely, I had not seen that soldier in the brigade area for some time, and then one day I saw him and asked him where he had been and informed him that his uniform was in. The soldier told me that he had already been to the desert and returned dressed in what he was issued in basic training. I did not ask any more questions. I played the game. I understood the mission goes on regardless of the absence of a proper uniform or anything else that can only be seen as a slight obstacle.

MY DIVIDEND

To this point, I had faithfully provided combat service support as a military member since 1980. While playing the game, I sought solace in expanding my knowledge base. I headed to the Fort Huachuca Education Center and brand-new post library to begin my graduate program at Western International University. I moved along each semester at the appropriate pace. Again, in many of my classes I was the only African-American. Then, suddenly, as I was nearing the finish line of my program, federal budget cuts slashed army funding for soldier education programs.

"What the f—? Over?" I was upset because when I joined the service, my option had been either a monetary bonus or education, and I chose education. It was thirteen years before I really knew that I was in the army, because I was going to school each night. Lucky thirteen. As my knowledge base expanded, I learned that my ancestors had to go through the back door to get an education. I call the route I took to the schoolhouse the side door, because I wanted my offspring to be able to go through the front door for their education. To date, my offspring have entered the front door of the University of Michigan, St. Andrews in Scotland, the Actor's Studio at Pace University, Central Michigan University, Michigan State University, Walsh College, and Rochester College—and exited with diploma in hand. With these results, I found the mutuality of the Strawberry Pie Rule to work when it is considered and applied, making me a proud papa!

With the change in financial policy, I was finally tired of playing the game, but I had rent to pay and small children to feed. I had come too far to quit, and I could not just be sitting around like in my factory days. I was too close to the light. One of the things I learned was that one of the benefits of education was that it enables a person to brainstorm options. I pulled out my own credit card and paid for my remaining classes. It was expensive, but it was my best option.

When I did that, I also severed my dependence on the army to further finance my education. My choice to continue under my own funding provided me with control. That attribute made me feel pretty independent, because I did not have to ask permission of anyone other than my wife. I believe this new independence began to show in the quality of my graduate work.

As a graduate student, I learned that I needed to look at the issue from a different perspective than my socialization process as an African-American male and independent of my fellow students and army officers who selected topics germane to their assigned units. I wanted to learn about owning and operating a business, and I did just that to complete my program in 1993.

The topic of my master's thesis was a case study of the United Services Automobile Association (USAA).[94] Today it remains unpublished, but it serves as personal accomplishment and a confidence builder in my much-improved process of critical thinking. In addition, the topic expanded my knowledge base immensely in financial management. USAA is the same company Chief Warrant Officer Hess invited my WOC class to join previously in 1986. I discovered that, as a financial institution, USAA was innovative. It was one of the first companies to promote going paperless, and at the time, USAA served only a select clientele: military officers.

I researched USAA in great detail with their assistance and then I worked long and hard to complete the document. My professor and academic mentor, Dr. W. R. Wheeler, PhD, stated that I had a passing grade and the content of my case study was off the charts. However, he suggested that I do a little more work in editing my thesis. At the time I thought it was too late to re-edit my paper. It was a screaming hot summer in Arizona, and I had just earned an MBA. I was pooped.

I chose not to re-edit, but I did send an unsolicited copy to the USAA just for the heck of it. Early in the 1990s, the financial market spiked in growth. In that regard, USAA had a select customer base, so in my case study I did my best to identify that this was a great opportunity for the USAA to expand its customer base.

Sometime later, USAA did respond to my submission. No, I was not offered an executive position or a sizeable payment, which I would have gladly taken. I did, however, receive a complimentary letter in 1993 from an executive manager, William T. Flynn, pertaining to my efforts. The letter called it a "top-notch document ... but at this time USAA must maintain the status quo."

The paper and the response from USAA at the very least proved to me that I had developed the confidence and academic skill to select and professionally write about a timely and strategic topic beyond my neighborhood view. I give credit to Wendy Bishop, a teacher at UAF, for her mentorship in writing. In developing my case study, I learned to research objective literary databases as resources, and my critical-thinking attributes became more enhanced and fine-tuned.

A few years later, in 1997, USAA did expand the demographics of its customer base. After a second inquiry, Mr. Flynn again replied that customer expansion was always a long-term company goal and the timing of implementing that goal was right. Today, USAA is featured in prime-time commercials illustrating its history with the military and military families. I like to think that as a graduate student I helped make it happen.

With that response from USAA, I had reached a high point in my academic life. I now understood that I needed more than just academic theory in the real world of business, I needed practical experience too. By chance, I was hired to conduct an independent audit for a nonprofit organization located on Fort Huachuca. I learned quickly how an audit of fiscal assets should be conducted. As a result, I learned that I did possess technical skill and provided value and service to the business opportunity. Notably, I did not know how to set my own compensation for the skill I possessed. Nonetheless, I was paid a handsome fee, and as a result, I wanted more work so I could make more handsome fees.

MY WHITE-COLLAR LEARNING CURVE

I was hired by H & R Block as an independent-contractor tax preparer to prepare personal income taxes. At the Sierra Vista location, I learned how a business owner operates in providing a service to the public. The independent franchise owner had concerns about keeping his business competitive in the 1990s. This was significant, because that time period saw the introduction of personal computers and specialty software in the home. The concern was that technology could impact his business operations and customer base.

In previous years, the franchisee had done well in servicing the Sierra Vista and Fort Huachuca area. The business was number-one in sales for its size the first year I worked there as a tax preparer. The primary reason was probably because of location. The franchisee had a commercial office on the military post. Besides the convenience to the soldiers, the franchise offered a popular financial product that provided a short turnaround time if the taxpayer received any refunds from the government. The financial product was actually a high-interest loan for qualified individuals.

The following year was different. Sales were down because the legalities of the speedy refund program came into question. Many franchisees were unable to secure a business office on a military post. Economically, the independent franchisee lost thousands of dollars because it no longer had the authority to operate at its prime location.

I learned that the profession of taxation was big business and that it directly impacted the coffers of the government, specialty associations, and the citizenry. I learned that the subject-matter experts on a particular topic influenced elected officials' positions or votes. In this case, the tax industry influenced the legislators with the draft framework of potential legislation. This happens because members of Congress generally lack professional expertise but have positions of authority. Later, they attach their names as sponsors to the bill which may become law.

Lastly, I learned individuals have different tax situations. For example, there could be a set of twins standing in front of the tax preparer with no obvious distinction. But when the twins come in at tax time to prepare and complete tax forms, the chances are great that each has a different tax situation. I learned in tax preparation that one size most likely does not fit all.

After tax season ended, I enrolled in real-estate school. I completed the course materials, but I did not complete the course requirements to obtain my real-estate license. Nevertheless, I became more informed in the process of buying and selling commercial and private property. As with the tax association, I also understood that the real-estate association had great influence over formal legislation.

Additionally, I realized that in both professions, the key element of success was the quality of people who owned, operated, and associated with the public. From that observation, I understood that I needed to become more involved with people. So I began attending local meetings of the Kiwanis Club in Sierra Vista, Arizona, to learn about the community and the people who served it.

I went to my first meeting with little understanding of what the organization's mission was or even what they did. The people in attendance were the people I generally faced from across a business counter—the school principal and teacher, the bank president and teller, the local business owner, and the elected or appointed government official—and yes, they were all white. I introduced myself as a soldier stationed at Fort Huachuca, and it was obvious that I was African-American. They welcomed me with open arms, and after several meetings, I joined and participated.

One service to the community the Kiwanis Club provided was keeping the highways clean. Which was funny, because I remembered police call or picking up trash as one of the very first things new soldiers are tasked to do as recruits. This is crazy—now here I am volunteering to do the same with the service club? What had I learned? I learned that a lot more people tossed trash on the side of the road than picked trash up from the side of the road.

As the volunteers walked along the side of the highway, drivers passing would blow their horns. This activity was dangerous because of speeding automobiles, and we often had to take quick refuge in the desert bush. As a result of the experience, I learned to appreciate what service clubs do for the community. No longer do I throw trash out of my car window; I keep it in the car until I find a trash receptacle.

In my learning process, I also became more involved in professional organizations in the fields associated with me earning my living. As a member of the army for the past twelve years, my profession was military logistics, so I became a member of the Society of Logistics Engineers (SOLE). I participated as a member, and then I became an elected leader for my local chapter. This is where my leadership attributes and management skills grew to another level as the responsible officer of a small professional group comprised of a number of active duty and former soldiers, sailors, and airmen, including a retired one-star general, a full bird colonel, and their families.

Self-Employment

I think the added responsibility helped me become more professional in my thought process, which also increased my personal interest in doing other things, such as becoming self-employed. I was still in the army and earning a comfortable living, but at this point in my life, I had a lot of desire to own my own business, although had no idea what that business would be. I came from a blue-collar family that lacked any perspective on owning and operating a business. As with many African-American families, my parents were primarily consumers and typically were concerned about the price of food items in their budget. I had little business experience or knowledge other than selling my services as physical labor doing chores, working in my uncle's Fuller Brush shop or as an independent contractor.

There was a "Start Your Own Business" seminar advertised on television that was to be held in nearby Tucson. I took a one-day leave from my duty assignment and drove to Tucson to attend the seminar at an area hotel. There may have even been a Kurt Russell and Goldie Hawn sighting in the Tucson area announced over the radio that day. As I recall, the host company of the seminars was from Utah. There were several business opportunities offered by the seminar presenters for what they called a low, low price. I jumped at the chance. I whipped out my credit card and chose two offerings: excess inventory management and telecommunications, at the low, low price that was happening that day and that day only according to them.

On that day, I committed material resources to becoming a small-business owner. At the moment I made my payment to the presenters, small-business ownership was no longer a pipe dream. It was a reality. I wanted to have all of the personal advantages of being a small-business owner: personal independence, job satisfaction, and greater income. All through my blue-collar life, people in business were always referred to as "them" by my family and friends and looked upon with a jaundiced eye. Now when I spoke of my aspirations and inspiration, I was viewed as standing among "them." This jaundiced eye is also why I later chose to research African-American self-employment in my academic study. So let's get started.

After reading the startup kits, I chose to focus my attention on the telecommunications kit. This actually involved the leasing of a telephone line commonly known at the time as a 900 service line. During the 1980s and 1990s, 900 telephone service lines were owned and operated by businesses for the purpose of providing customer information to the public for a fee. At some point, practical usage of 900 numbers as a customer-service application died as the Internet exploded. Additionally, the inference of a 900 number was that the product or service was seedy. Although I had no previous experience in operating and owning a business, I was a businessman, full speed ahead. What I did not know at the time was that I buying the back end of a horse. The 900 number was already being made obsolete by new technology.

The sales pitch had made it sound so easy. Now I had to put my education to work. I had to utilize my own creativity while developing my business acumen to activate my service line and keep it running. I spent countless hours creating a detailed business plan, something I should have done first. I pushed on anyway. I researched my market, I designed my product and service, I obtained legal trademarks, I tried to obtain funding, and most of all, I acted as if I was in business and that I was successful.

Bertha shared my vision and became my partner in this venture despite holding a full-time job and being a mother to three young children. This undertaking toward self-employment did not divide us; if anything, it strengthened our relationship. We still conversed about our home life and family goals, but our conversation expanded to a much broader scope, including how we could make our business successful. Our family benefited from both our successes and our failures, because we worked well together as a unit.

I was a businessman, and I was looking for a business opportunity. During the 1990s, Native American business opportunities exploded with formal recognition of their sovereignty in the passage of the Indian Gaming Regulatory Act of 1988.[95] Prior to legislation, for example, Native American gaming was a mom-and-pop operation. Then almost overnight, multimillion-dollar casinos went up on Indian reservations around the country under the management of professional corporate teams. Casinos located on Native American lands became a source of income and economic redevelopment for recognized members of participating tribes.

My research indicated that the gaming industry itself, which includes all games of chance, if consolidated as a whole would be considered among the top three corporations in sales in the world. Unlike other games of chance, the game of bingo is operated by both charities and private organizations and considered to be an acceptable vice, similar to the belief that drinking a small amount of alcohol is okay for medicinal purposes. The barriers to entry into the bingo segment seemed less fortified than other forms of gambling. Therefore, my company mission statement was to provide a viable service to the gaming industry—in particular, the bingo parlor.

I was still in the army, so I had to balance my business activities with the shenanigans of Sadaam Hussein in Iraq and the humanitarian mission in Somalia. Nonetheless, during my off-duty time, I traveled around the country to research and learn how Indian gaming and other bingo halls operated. On occasion, I would sit down to play in a bingo hall and win a couple of bucks. I was amazed by my research, and I found that millions of people from all walks of life played the game of bingo, not just little old ladies. Most importantly, I discovered that the typical person who played bingo on a regular basis was territorial, superstitious, and cranky as he or she carved out a comfort zone at the bingo hall.

The diehard bingo player set up a playing area with all types of artifacts, including pictures of beloved family members and friends. These individuals believed that such items would bring them good luck. Woe unto the person who distracted a bingo player from hearing the bingo caller clearly for whatever reason. Distraction in a bingo parlor already filled with cigarette smoke would fan the flames of the perturbed mob, and subsequently the fiery raft would be dispersed back at the distracter.

The commercial service I decided to provide to the industry was that of an audio publisher, using my 900 telephone line to broadcast activities and advertisements associated with the game of bingo. My audio publication was launched as *Bingo 900.* I wrote stories about bingo players as characters and then prepared the script for production on my service line. As previously stated, prior to the Internet explosion, 900 telephone service lines provided customer information to the public for a fee. My stories were designed to operate in the same fashion to provide useful information and humor to the millions of bingo players and associates anytime of the day for a fee.

My wife and I conducted a marketing campaign to identify bingo halls and their locations. Our research revealed that thousands of bingo halls were located all over the United States and Canada. Once we located the bingo halls, we tried to identify their common needs, and then we bulk-mailed marketing materials to the database. We soon found out that bulk mail can be expensive, as were other aspects of small-business ownership, and ready capital was needed for everything.

I gained more confidence in taking risks—so much so that I thought I would take my creation to the big time as an exhibitor in the International Gaming Trade Show held in Las Vegas in 1994, Milwaukee in 1995, and Las Vegas again in 1996. The first lesson I learned was that I was the only African-American exhibitor; the second was that although my creativity was sky-high, my available budget in comparison to any competitor was extremely low. The Las Vegas trade show was the largest and most expensive showplace I had ever seen. It cost money to purchase booth space, it cost money to fill the booth space with furniture, and if you could not carry your product to your acquired space in a small box or briefcase, then it cost money to have the trade union move it for you from point A to point B.

In my first year as an exhibitor, the theme of the Las Vegas International Gaming Trade Show was the introduction of technology and the communications application dubbed the Internet to all aspects of business ventures. The Internet revolutionized the way business operated by leaps and bounds, and it extended the hours of operations to twenty-four.

Although my audio-newsletter product was creative and humorous and had the potential to add value to the marketplace, in reality, the Internet rendered my delivery system—the telecommunication 900 service line—obsolete. This lesson was very expensive, but I learned that timing is a critical component in making business decisions.

The Internet also had an impact on the potential of my business opportunity on selling of excess inventory management. Successful websites like Overstock.com sprang up at the dawn of the new technology. I felt myself sink further into the depths of the marketplace. I felt like I was drowning; I had no business relationships other than that of a consumer.

I had no mentorship and no commercial funding. If this was baseball, I was out of my league.

These endeavors cost me time and money, but they did not cause me embarrassment. I was a person with a blue-collar background seeking fortune. I was disappointed and my wife was disappointed by our business collapse. However, I was not disappointed by the learning experience, because I gained real-life knowledge pertaining to the concept of business ventures and their required resources.

So as I sat there in the toilet of the Las Vegas Convention Center wiping away my tears, I decided to make the best of a no-profit situation, remembering what SFC Smith told me years before in Germany: "Play the game!" That's just what I did—I just played the game. I returned to my booth in beautiful Las Vegas, and I acted if I was the most successful person in Nevada. I greeted fashionable people from all points around the globe, and I learned to schmooze with them. I got my picture taken in my expensive booth and then, when the hall closed down at night, I went to my room and drank expensive rum and Coke as I watched the Las Vegas lights from my hotel room. I was fortunate I was still alive and ready to head back to my family—but not before I commemorated my experience in a poem titled "Bells and Whistles":

> They came from parts well-known, with names not made
> to pronounce,
> each name was short and long.
> They came from parts well-known, to look for bells and
> whistles that go
> clink, clank, bong.
> Men with pointy shoes and ladies of vision in pointed
> shirts,
> their bags all laced with golden trim, snatched from each
> lighted perch.
> Arm in arm, brief to brief, entangled with corporate lace.

They prance each lane and touch each pane, but not my
unshimmery base.
Hot lights flashing, long legged nylons sashing,
mystic eyes and that magnificent hairdo,
prune noses arched high, gold eagles stay straight,
my stand in full view.
Like the beggar on a cluttered and unlit street,
a cubicle of pale.
Ye weary traveler journeys the globe with fortune to
make, to see, to hear, to touch,
No bells, no whistles … no sale!
O, the dream lay trampled there, under the pointed
shoes and bags of golden trim,
the eye goes dim to hold the tear,
Yet, the chin stands up, the chest expands,
And the mind shouts "*Next year!*"

After Las Vegas, I returned quietly to my duties as the property book officer. My job was to maintain accountability of army equipment. Many soldiers returning from the Middle East suffered from stress. In all honesty, it was also hard on military personnel who did not deploy to the combat zone.

MANAGING STRESS

I battled the stress of my military responsibilities and building a business by engaging in Shuri-Ryu Karate along with my wife and my daughter Treasure. Our *sensei* or teacher was Lee Ann Freeman. No, I did not achieve a competitive level, but I think the practice of karate helped me develop my patience and improve my mental focus, as well as engaging me in a family activity. I believe it was the meditation that helped me keep my stress level down during difficult times. In addition, the development of physical and mental focus increased my leadership attributes. I bring up this subject because human behavior was beginning to cost the army money, for there were many negative images in the technology-driven media.

I remember traveling to Fort Gordon, Georgia, on a temporary-duty assignment to visit a unit newly assigned to the brigade. The unit had only just rotated from Iraq, but shortly thereafter, it had been tasked to support a peace mission in Somalia. Evidently, the stress of deployment was too much to bear for someone. A suspicious fire after duty hours destroyed the unit's equipment that was stowed and secured in the motor pool and scheduled for deployment that very day. This catastrophic event was a pencil-pusher's worse nightmare. To date, I have not heard that the culprit was ever apprehended, but the army lost both human and material resources that day.

James Brown and DNA

Sometimes the army is not so bad. In the military, soldiers travel on official business or temporary duty regularly. In 1993 or 1994, I was on temporary duty to Fort Gordon, Georgia, from Fort Huachuca, Arizona. Augusta, Georgia, is the primary airport used when visiting Fort Gordon, and Augusta is also the home of James Brown, the hardest working man in show business.

When I arrived in Augusta, thinking out loud, I told my fellow soldiers how it would be too great to meet James Brown while we were here. I remember this trip distinctly because the unit we planned to visit was an army reserve unit from a Southern state training at Fort Gordon. The unit bivouac site was near a small lake that attracted snakes. You could see and hear the snakes flopping down the hill toward the water, but it never caused a flap with the unit. I thought the unit was very cohesive and apparently unafraid of snakes.

The unit was waiting to meet the commander of the major army command, Major General X, who I knew as Colonel X when I was stationed in Alaska. I befriended the first sergeant of the unit on site while I was there. The first sergeant was an African-American, and he was surprised when I told him the commander of the major army command was a person of color. The unit had a long storied history of white officers, and he was sure that they did not know that General X was a person of color. The first sergeant was anxious for the general to show up; he desperately wanted to see the looks on the faces of his unit commander and staff officers. I thought the training event was successful, and as I was leaving, the commander was entering the training area. I chuckled because I believe the first sergeant got to see his Southern unit officers scurrying about under the command of a general officer of African descent.

On the return trip from Fort Gordon to the airport in Augusta, my traveling party noticed a long white limousine sitting in front of the airport. I wondered out loud, in jest, if it was James Brown's car. I checked in at the desk for my flight and then decided to stop by the restroom before boarding the flight. When I got there, I encountered a large African-American man who seemed to be guarding the door for some reason. Politely, I said to him, "Excuse me, sir," and proceeded in through the door. Suddenly, the hardest working man in show business, James Brown, came out of the stall dressed in a white suit. My eyes opened wide, and I grabbed and shook his hand with excitement and without thinking. I stuttered, "M-m-m-mister Brown!"

Retrieving his hand, he replied, "How you doing, Brother!" and continued over to the sink to wash his hands before strutting out of the bathroom on his way. I wondered, *How many movers and shakers in the world has his hand shaken?* Then I regained my composure and understood that I did need to wash my hands as a matter of hygiene.

As a result of this experience, I learned that heroes are people too. And if you give the hero room to breathe when he is taking care of bodily functions, the whole experience is much nicer and cleaner. I returned to Augusta on many occasions after that. I never got the opportunity to run into James Brown again, but many of the airport housekeepers had grown up living with James Brown in their community. I would ask about him, and they would keep me updated. One gentleman told me that you could gauge the success of the trip when James Brown returned from the road. If the trip was successful, he would pass out twenty or thirty dollars to individuals in the work crews as he walked through the airport. If the trip was not good, there weren't any tips passed out when he walked through. James Brown has since passed, but he is still a hero because he gave black people a sense of pride in their heritage through his performance and songs.

Not Everybody Is Going to Cross the Jordan River

Speaking of pride, on my flight home, I had the pleasure of sitting next to an African-American female who had earned an engineering degree from the University of Michigan. I applauded her achievement and inquired about her journey to a most prestigious university. She was proud of her accomplishment but said the journey was long, and she felt lonely at times because she was the only African-American and sometimes the only female in many of her classes.

At this point, I could only remember stories from the Bible—the Old Testament books of Numbers and Joshua—when only a select few were given the opportunity to cross over the Jordan River. You had a chance to cross over. Your talent and potential qualified you for the academic endeavor; not everybody is qualified. By completing the program, you left tracks for others to follow and emulate.

We parted when the plane landed. I was glad I had the talk with her, especially since one of my daughters attended the same university some ten years later.

Wait! I'm Black: African-American PhD Program

Without a doubt, education allows a person to have career options. My businesses had not brought me immediate success, so I altered my career plan toward becoming a college professor. I had already earned a graduate degree going to night school using the side door to get in the schoolhouse. In 1994, I discovered there was an opportunity for me, an African-American, to enter the field of education. A consulting firm, KPMG Peat Marwick, in association with the National Consortium for Educational Access, Inc. (NCEA) Fellowship, declared its mission to be putting more African-American professors with doctoral degrees in the classroom through a program named "the PhD Project."[96]

For me, this was a front-door opportunity. I submitted my application to four participating universities as instructed: Harvard, Virginia Polytechnic Institute and State University, Rensselaer Polytechnic Institute, and University of South Florida. Not long after, I learned that I had been turned down by each school. As I read the non-acceptance letter, I was in shock, because I thought this program was to help qualified African-Americans become college professors. I asked myself, am I not qualified? When I read further, I found out the reason for denial was that I did not score high enough on the Graduate Management Admission Test (GMAT), a standardized test.

Traditionally, places of higher learning have used standardized tests[97] as the discriminating factor in the admission process. Therefore, in the lowest common denominator, standardized testing is simply a contest, and to date, I had not done well in contests. Arguably, standardized testing has been a barrier or exclusion mechanism to the minority experience for a lot of years and worst of all has snuffed out many dreams and aspirations. Nevertheless, I did not stop trying, because you cannot win if you don't play. I studied and tried to improve my score, but I still lost the contest.

A few years later, while I was stationed at Fort Leonard Wood, Missouri, Nova Southeastern University's doctoral program also turned me down. At this point, I was disheartened and frustrated with rejection in my career, both in academics and business. There is an old adage that infers that fruit does not fall far from the tree. In the matter of standardized testing, my young daughters broke that model and did well enough to be accepted through the front door of major universities. How? My wife and I got them the academic tools they needed to be successful in the undertaking, as we learned from our failures. For their achievement, my wife and I are extremely proud, and we applaud them. As it turned out, I earned my doctorate a few years later, and I keep those letters of rejection[98] as a reminder to keep pushing past roadblocks and obstacles.

SURVIVING REJECTION

Rejection is frustrating, but I have learned to deal with it. However, my frustration escalated when the heated driver's seat in my ten-year-old Saab automobile had an electrical short on the way back from Tucson. It was a warm day as usual, and I was driving south down Highway 90 back to Fort Huachuca. I was about to make a right turn into the Buffalo Soldier gate when suddenly I discovered my pants were on fire and jumped out of the car. To the other drivers, I must have been a sight to see, hopping around trying to put out the fire in my car seat and my backside. Later, I surmised that the fire was an accident caused by me leaving the car sunroof open over a period of time, allowing moisture from rain to combine with the sun's harsh rays.

Anyway, I survived rejection and the fire. A promotion to chief warrant officer three and a pay hike helped to soothe my superficial burns. As mentioned earlier, the army was changing, and federal budget cuts were taking their toll on military programs and personnel. I remember Greely Hall on Fort Huachuca was once considered a fortress surrounded by an army of armed police. Now it took only one soldier on staff duty to guard the area. I had that duty one evening, and I remember walking around the great hall in my stocking feet with munchies in my hand looking at the portraits of the former commanders and general officers, including General Emmett Paige, hanging on the marble wall. Then I retired to the waiting room in the general's office to watch the mediocre Detroit Lions trounce the Super Bowl-bound Dallas Cowboys 20–17 in overtime on Monday Night Football in September

1994.[99] I screamed with joy, but nobody heard me in this fortress. I dug the Cowboys, but a Lions victory is always good for the city.

FORT LEONARD WOOD OR FORT LOST-IN-THE-WOODS

It was time to leave the desert sun. My sixth tour of duty was at Fort Leonard Wood, Missouri, working with the Fifth Army headquartered in Texas. There are many who call this post Fort Lost-in-the-Woods. Similar to my first unit at Fort Huachuca, the soldiers assigned to my new unit were all senior army personnel. The unit had a simple mission, and that was to build one army from the regular army, reserve component, and National Guard units. Prior to my assignment, I really did not understand that there was more than one army in the United States. Figuratively, yes, there is, because each command is organized and budgeted differently; literally, no, there is not, because each command is obligated to one authority, the President of the United States. It seemed that during the Gulf War, some unit practices in readiness and training conflicted with the "one army" concept, so the job of my new organization, the Fifth Army, was to right the ship.

My job as a military advisor and logistician was to facilitate the "one army" concept using skill levels and techniques equivalent to those used by a management consultant. I had no command authority. My job was to inform and advise the unit of the authorized regulations and requirements. I recalled that there are those who believe that much of the destruction during the Detroit riots in 1967 was caused by army reserve and National Guard troops called in to enforce the law.[100]

The unit had a fleet of government automobiles for the purpose of traveling to military units in an assigned region. My assignment at Fort Leonard Wood was to drive around the Ozarks backwoods of Missouri and Arkansas providing logistical assistance. Historically, both states have been known to have communities with strong opinions about the United States government and its citizens and non-citizens. For safety's sake, it was the S2 or intelligence section of our unit that was responsible for keeping us apprised of the situation around the world and the countryside. Somehow I knew my knowledge base was about to expand again. My trip to the army reserve center in St. Louis, Missouri was the day the federal building in Oklahoma City, Oklahoma was bombed.[101]

NOTORIOUS OZARK HISTORY AND GEOGRAPHY

Springfield, Missouri, is the site of a notorious lynching on Easter weekend in 1906 of three black men held on suspicion of murder and assault.[102] A poignant poem of social injustice by a Jewish schoolteacher from the Bronx provided the basis for the Billie Holiday song about the lynching of black males in the South titled "Strange Fruit."[103] About the time I arrived in the area, in 1995, the city of Springfield extended an open apology for the 1906 lynching. However, a reoccurrence happened in downtown Springfield in the fall of 2002 when a young black male was found hanged from a communications tower thirty feet in the air a few blocks from the 1906 incident.[104]

Ironically, southwestern Missouri is also the birthplace of the African-American inventor George Washington Carver.[105] There are also local alerts when favorite son Brad Pitt, the actor, is in town. Additionally, Fort Smith, Arkansas,[106] is the place where Negro soldiers served under Isaac Parker, the hanging judge of the Old West. These previously unknown facts made the Ozarks a place of discovery, good and bad.

Once you get on the road, the first thing you must learn when driving the backwoods, besides navigation, is to find out where the blue-haired people eat. Why? Because blue-haired people are senior citizens with fixed incomes, and the places they eat have value and a full menu of home cooking. Few blue-haired people spend money at fast-food places on themselves—maybe for their grandchildren, but not for themselves. These dining locales were generally provided through word of mouth.

The next important thing to know was geography. Why? You could very well end up on a rural secondary road going nowhere but the wrong way. Then there is the weather. Missouri has a lot of secondary curvy sloped roads in rural areas. You do not want to be on a curvy sloped rural road when water builds up from a downpour. If this happens to you, your automobile will probably need swimming trunks and to know the backstroke, because there is little room to maneuver on rural roads.

Around the Arkansas Bend and Political Confabs

In Arkansas, there are a lot of round-the-bends or curves on hilly roads. My first week of travel, I was informed by the S2 section to be careful, because in Arkansas there is always heavy traffic of trucks pulling heavy loads. The previous week, a truck carrying construction equipment came round the bend too fast and lost its load in the oncoming lane, killing the driver of another car. And lastly, be aware if a political group (Democrats, Republicans, Black Panthers, Boy Scouts, Girls Scouts, Ku Klux Klan …) is meeting in a town you are traveling through so you can avoid contact. This was the equivalent of a "be safe" speech given before I left the house as a young man of African descent.

Back in Mizzou

Then there was the New Madrid fault located in the bootheel of Missouri. It sits in silence, maybe waiting to uncover another murder like that of the 1811–1812 earthquake when two blood relatives of Thomas Jefferson and Meriwether Lewis murdered a slave for sport as the quake began.[107] The mighty Mississippi River was also poised to cause trouble.

During this tour of duty, I learned a lot about the potential for disaster and how the military command and its logistics infrastructure and material resources are trained to handle the particular situation. When I returned to Michigan in 2000, I had the opportunity to train at the National Fire Academy in Maryland not far from the Gettysburg Battlefield in Pennsylvania and work for Federal Emergency Management Agency

(FEMA) for a short time. Although the flooding of New Orleans was a tragic event, there are material resources standing by and ready to help the people in distress. However, the best opportunity to minimize the fallout from disaster is that we all have a feasible plan and then act on it with speed and urgency when the time comes.

Typically, people without means and resources stay in place, believing they have no other options, whereas people with means and resources head for high ground. It's just like when the plague hit Europe—the nobility headed for safety at higher ground.

SELF-IMPROVEMENT ON THE ROAD AND MORE SPILLED MILK

As mentioned, I grew up in the city, but my parents were both born and raised on farms. Additionally, many of the people I worked with in the auto factories came from rural communities. During my tour at Fort Leonard Wood, I met a great many interesting people who lived in rural communities and learned about their lifestyles.

I remember one meeting in particular. I had driven for hours to Arkansas from Fort Leonard Wood. I finally arrived at the unit location and the unit representative, an NCO, was very receptive. Shortly after we sat down to talk, the NCO received a phone call. When he hung up he was a little shaken, and he said he had to leave for home because his cow was sick and needed immediate attention. The standard operating procedure did not address this as a potential situation, but the common-sense test said to let the representative leave and take care of his home and property. So in this particular case, the well-being of a cow had priority over the affairs of the Department of the Army.

In this assignment, I was on the road nearly every week and earned the Army Driver's Badge for safety at the end of my three-year tour. The formal recognition was nice, but the real benefit came with how I spent my time during those long and winding drives. Basically, I stopped listening to music in the car that fed my boogie. Instead, I began listening to self-improvement audiocassette tapes that fed my mind. For miles and miles heading to and from my destination, I listened to self-improvement tapes, how-to tapes, and the Bible.

My success mentor and a world-renowned speaker, the late Mr. Zig Ziglar,[108] called this learning discipline "Automobile University" and stated that listening to audiocassette tapes in volume is the equivalent of academic hours spent in a college classroom. Listening to self-improvement tapes on different topics shortened my learning curve and increased my comprehension in a number of educational disciplines. Prior to listening to audiocassette tapes, I spent a lot of time at thrift shops picking up used paperbacks books on many diverse topics. Now I had the words on tape.

I was greatly influenced by Claude Bristol's *The Magic of Believing*,[109] in paperback and audiocassette tape. The narrative focused on putting our desire into action to achieve great success by activating the attributes we were born with and having confidence enough to believe in them. This text brought great revelation to a person who had fallen into an environment of "I can't." A second text helped fulfill an academic promise to read the King James Bible in its entirety. I did just that with the voice of narrator Christopher Marshall[110] providing a majestic narrative.

Over the past thirteen years, I became aware that the learning process rewards learners with opportunities. For instance, finishing high school allowed me to leave the factory floor and join the military during a time of economic downturn. By entering military service, I was able to earn a graduate degree some thirteen years later, an opportunity that would have never presented itself while I worked on the factory floor. In building up a positive learning attitude and meeting my required military studies and obligations, I was able to build a higher standard of living for my family.

In 1995, I was obligated to attend the Warrant Officer Advance Course (WOAC) at Fort Lee, Virginia. Many of my classmates from the basic course completed in 1986 were in attendance, and it was grand to see that most all of them were doing well in their careers. Their success made me work harder. I was among the honor graduates, but this time I did not invite any family members or roaches to the ceremony.

Because of my educational achievement, class standing, and seeking out of opportunities, I became the first warrant officer selected to attend the Logistics Executive Development Course (LEDC). This was a prestigious academic course in logistics that lasted nearly six months at the Army Logistics Management College at Fort Lee, Virginia.

I submitted my paperwork shortly after my Quartermaster Branch Manager, Chief Warrant Officer 4 Rufus Montgomery, came to speak to the warrant officers at the advanced class. He informed the class of the opportunity, and I took the appropriate action. After my return to Fort Leonard Wood a few weeks later, Chief Warrant Officer 4 Montgomery called to inform me that I had been selected to attend LEDC. The Department of the Army would foot the bill for my attendance. All I needed to do was to get the permission of my unit commander to attend.

The Midwest gets a fair amount of rain that helps to keep farmland fertile for growth. My learning opportunity was rained on by my chain of command, and my opportunity drowned. My commander and my supervisor did not give permission for me to attend the course at the time. Their decision stated that I was needed in the unit, and I accepted that. At the time, the understanding was that once my tour was up some eighteen to twenty-four months later, I would be free to attend. I may have sounded a little selfish with the decision. I was honored to be selected, but I believed a great career opportunity was lost and that this was another case of spilled milk. Frankly, I was very disappointed and angry. I shall continue on the subject later in this segment.

TEACHING OTHERS

So with that disappointment, I settled in at my duty assignment at Fort Leonard Wood. Not long after, I saw a small article in the local newspaper seeking college instructors. I thought this article to be of interest, especially since I had earned my graduate degree about two years prior. I became inspired to teach and felt pretty confident in my ability to do a good job, so I responded to the article. A few weeks later,

I was interviewed and got the position as an instructor in the discipline of business management at Central Texas College at the Truman Education Center on post.

After years of entering school through the side door as a nontraditional student and adult learner, I was now in front of the classroom as the instructor and adult learner at Central Texas College, my old alma mater. I did a good enough job to teach there on a regular basis. Not long after, I was hired to teach by several other colleges located at the Truman Education Center. This could have been because the pool of qualified and interested candidates was limited by location. It did not matter to me, a person of African descent, because I was working and had access to the post library.

Doing extra duty is what I had done over the past fifteen years. After I performed my duties and responsibilities as a soldier during regular duty hours, I had spent my other waking hours as an adult learner. Now I was doing the same as a college instructor. The majority of the students in the class were nontraditional students, as I had been. They worked low-paying jobs, raised families, and sought other economic opportunities. I could relate to their plight because their path was similar to the one I had taken from the factory floor. Upon reflection, the only way I could have made a better way for myself and my family, other than hitting the lottery, was to do exactly what these students were doing. So I worked hard to prepare myself to teach. Many of my classes were rewarding. I learned something about the topic, and in turn the students learned something about the topic.

JOHNNY B. BUSINESSMAN

Many students enrolled in business management courses for the purpose of learning how to better operate their businesses. For instance, Johnny B. Hutchins, one of my students, was a taxidermist. He was an African-American and a former drill sergeant who retired from military service at Fort Leonard Wood and remained in the area with his family as a single parent. Although the job market in the area was not great, the cost of living was low.

During his off-duty time, Johnny had learned the art of taxidermy. Taxidermy is a painstaking process in which an animal that had been hunted for food or sport is brought back to life for public display. For years, it was rumored that the area surrounding Fort Leonard Wood was unfriendly and off limits to African-Americans. Johnny said that he was advised "not to go out the back gate" of Fort Leonard Wood into the rural community. He said he did not listen; if he had listened to the warning, he would never have learned the skills of taxidermy to earn a living.

Johnny had artistic skills, and he had mounted displays in select shops around the state of Missouri. Johnny was informed by fellow taxidermists located in the St. Louis area that there was no need for them to create their own work because of the high quality and low price of his work. They could easily earn a very comfortable living buying and selling his work. Johnny became a college student so that he could better price and market his work. As an instructor, I did my best to help him operate his business better.

EVERYBODY WANTS AN "A"

For every student with a defined purpose, there were a number of others without a defined purpose. In the classroom, I soon learned that it is not the academic material that stagnates the learning process; in my opinion, it is the attitude and personal dedication of the student that either moves or impedes the learning process. I also learned that adult learners all want the highest grade, A-plus, even if they did not do A-plus work because it was they who wrote out the check to the school that paid the instructor's salary.

On a number of occasions, school policy did not facilitate the learning process when dealing with adult learners. On a traditional college campus, students are required to fulfill prerequisites to enroll in a class, and sometimes classes are filled on the very first day. On a satellite campus, the rush to enroll is not so great. Periodically, in order to fill up a classroom, the satellite campus would allow students without the proper prerequisites to register and take a class. This policy placed an additional burden on the instructor.

I learned this the hard way one semester. The class was about financial management, which involved understanding the markets, investing, and staying connected with the *Wall Street Journal*. I grew up in a blue-collar house and we lived week to week, paycheck to paycheck, no investments and very little savings. As a student I had passed the class, but now I was the teacher. It was a small class with a diverse student enrollment, including two African-American females who did not have the prerequisite to take the class. They struggled and I struggled. I had extra sessions at the library, and it still did not work. As a result, I was fired by the local administrator—not just because the females complained but because of the input of a white male student/enlisted man who routinely failed to come to class but had the ear of the female administrator. I did not find fault in the administrator's action if I did not do a good job, but I did find fault in the student's back-door maneuver. How did he know about the class? He was never there.

There was another incident that put me in hot water, and it was another example of student absenteeism. The wife of a soldier deployed overseas was a student in my class. For whatever reason, she never showed up for class, and when she did she was full of excuses. At the time, I wondered why with so much going on in her life she had even considered attending school. I wondered even more when an NCO assigned to my own organization stood up for her to give her a passing grade. How did he become her advocate? The NCO was not even a student of mine. I thought his energy was better served on the job looking after his own troops. From those encounters, I learned that adult learners can cause storms over their grades, tuition, and attendance.

TORNADO ALLEY

Speaking of storms, Fort Leonard Wood is located in the vicinity of tornado alley, crossing Kansas, Missouri, and Oklahoma. I recall one pleasant evening when I was teaching a class in one of the adjacent wooden buildings when suddenly the area emergency sirens went off. Just that quick, the weather took a turn for the worse with really strong winds.

The first obligation is the safety of the students. Some students were familiar with the sirens and quickly headed for a safe haven away from school grounds. Others did not move as quickly, so the remaining students and I found safety in the basement of the building where students and teachers from other classrooms soon joined us. There was one teacher who had experience with the weather conditions and had a radio. He stated that we were preparing for the sound of a railroad train coming through. We monitored the radio until we got the all-clear sign from the broadcast. The train sound did not come through our building. I don't recall any deaths, but there was plenty of property damage, including brand-new boats and trailers lying in shambles along Interstate 44 between Fort Leonard Wood, Lebanon, and Springfield.

Although the storm provided a certain degree of excitement, I quickly gathered my belongings and headed home. I lived on the army post, so my ride home was only a few minutes. I took the same scenic route that I took to the post education center each day, only my return route that day was not so scenic. The storm had knocked down many trees, and there were power outages in many places in the post housing area. I drove through the debris and made the left-hand turn toward my house. As I approached my house, I noticed that it did not show any signs of stress from the storm.

I parked my car in my driveway and headed to the front door. I opened my front door with my key, and to my amazement there was a party going on in my house. My wife and three daughters were doing whatever girls do. Music was playing, the lights were on, and there were snacks everywhere. It was quite evident that they did not know that the weather had caused all types of destruction all around them. They did not have a clue about what was going on outside the house. Nevertheless, I was truly grateful that they enjoyed themselves during the distress period and were not injured in any way.

LEARNING FROM THE EXPERIENCE OF OTHERS

At Fort Leonard Wood, I learned another interesting story about Negro history from an African-American World War II veteran. The story pertained to the creation of the army education center and how the education center became a fixture on military posts. Fort Leonard Wood had a beautiful physical-fitness center that included an outdoor track. I would spend a lot of time there during physical training. An African-American gentleman with a white beard in an athletic track suit and carrying a walking cane circled the track every day as part of his regiment. I do not have his name among my notes, but he was well known in the community. When I saw him, I would spend a few minutes talking to him. In turn, he would tell me about how army life was when he served and the dogwood trees that he enjoyed.

One day, we were discussing education when he informed me that the original mission of the army learning center was to help Negro soldiers learn to read and write. At the time, many of the Negro soldiers came from places where they had little or no formal education. These soldiers had to be able to communicate in order to perform their duties, so the army command established a place where illiterate Negro soldiers could acquire basic reading, writing, and math skills so they could perform their duties. The gentleman stated that he was part of the administrative process that trained the illiterate Negro soldiers because he was literate.

He stated that this administrative action was met with great resistance because it was perceived by the larger white army that the Negro soldiers were getting a benefit that was not available to white soldiers. According to the gentleman, there was a great debate among the army command, and the end result was to shut the learning center down completely. However, the gentleman stated that cooler heads prevailed and educational opportunity was provided to all service members. As a result, the army education center has been the headquarters for soldiers seeking educational and career opportunities, of which I am a witness!

LEARNING FROM THE LOCAL COMMUNITY

The army education center provided me with a chance to meet some of the local people. As far as I knew, I was the only African-American male instructor at the Truman Education Center. One of my white teaching colleagues invited me to have lunch at the Lions Club in Houston, Missouri. The rural community is located about twenty minutes out the back gate of Fort Leonard Wood.

With the social and economic growth taking place at Fort Leonard Wood, the gentleman thought I might be a good fit in helping the rural community adjust to the changing times. Since I had previous experience with the Kiwanis service club, I decided to accept the invitation. I drove out the back gate onto the rural highway just as my former student Johnny Hutchins did, heading for my destination. I arrived at the meeting place and everyone was cordial as I sat down to have lunch with the membership. It was a very pleasant affair.

The essence of a service club's charter is to provide service to the community. On this particular day, a family in distress stood in front of the presiding service club leaders seeking financial help as a result of criminal activity with the family that involved sexual assault, incest, and child abuse. I was seated as a guest near the head table.

As I dined, I was in shock over the telling of this family's plight. Despite the hideousness of the crime, to my knowledge, the details of the incident had not been plastered all over the front page of the newspaper. The members of the community seemed to be handling this social problem well. That day reinforced what I later cited in my academic work, which is that local media act as the gatekeeper or controller of the headlines. Arguably, if your community has a lot of positive press, that may indicate that the community leadership has leverage within the media. On the other hand, if the local community leadership is bombarded with negative press, that probably means your community does not control any workings of the press.

"IT'S A MAN'S WORLD"

Mr. James Brown gives testimony in his 1966 hit song "It's is a Man's, Man's Man's World"[111] that a man is supposed "to be strong for a woman and a girl." In the man's life cycle, I had finally made the successful transition to stage 5, adulthood. My vision had grown immensely. I turned myself into an alpha male[112] as I went out to get the things I needed to survive and the things I wanted for my life. That is what I learned to do and be in this period of redemption. The army was paying dividends—not the bonus they offered but getting me out of my neighborhood to a new environment of learning. Under the concept of the 3Ts, I first developed a *talent*, and the *timing* of my new talent grew in value. which then enabled me to *take part in new opportunities and advancement*. My service to the country provided me with foundational training and opportunity to grow in this man's world at a higher level. I was becoming a better man, husband, and father for taking action.

MILESTONES AND KNUCKLEHEAD INCIDENTS

Knucklehead incidents:

- military lineup
- sexual conduct of three soldiers
- race relations in the South
- drunken soldiers/white female soldiers
- backsliding after completing army training
- the "N" word
- rejection entry to the warrant officer program twice

- my mother and roaches at graduation ceremony
- nearly frozen in car in Alaska
- airplane accident
- Rodney King.
- resignation from the US Army
- rejection from the African-American PhD program

Milestones:

- joined volunteer army.
- left home at age twenty-eight
- first airplane ride at age twenty-eight
- completed both phases of army training
- received leadership awards
- won soldier-of-the-period award
- severed dependency on parents
- traveled to Southwest United States
- won soldier-of-the-period award again
- met black general officer
- played sports again
- accepted into New Mexico State University.
- learning the duty of a soldier and military specialty
- met future wife
- divorced and remarried
- accepted into Central Texas College.
- completed advance army training, sent to Germany with spouse
- learning the duty of a soldier and military specialty is continuous
- earned a service award
- applied for warrant officer candidate program
- build marital foundation
- birth of second daughter in Germany
- purchased a brand-new Saab 900S
- return to US from overseas
- Detroit Tigers 1984 championship season

- stationed at Fort Huachuca, Arizona; introduced to Buffalo Soldiers
- earned associates degree from Central Texas College
- learned object lesson from Space Shuttle *Challenger* disaster
- accepted as a warrant officer candidate
- discovered Civil War Negro soldiers, Union and Confederate
- completed candidate training and promoted to Warrant Officer 1
- stationed at Fort Wainwright, Alaska
- spotted first moose in Alaska on drive south of Denali Park
- spotted first Alaskan soul brother north of Denali Park
- accepted into Wayland Baptist University
- obtained academic understanding of the Christian Bible
- quit smoking
- promotion to Chief Warrant Officer 2
- General Schwarzkopf visit to Alaska
- Detroit Pistons basketball champions, 1989 and1990
- purchased Jeep Cherokee, the official car of the NBA
- birth of third and fourth daughter in Alaska
- earned four-year degree from Wayland Baptist University
- accepted in master's program, Western International University
- drove from Alaska back to Fort Huachuca, Arizona
- General Colin Powell's celebration of the Buffalo Soldier
- earned master's degree from Western International University
- master's thesis on United Services Automobile Association (USAA)
- engaged in white-collar opportunities: H & R Block, real estate
- engaged in professional and community organizations
- engaged in self-employment, gaming industry
- promotion to Chief Warrant Officer 3
- met entertainer James Brown on TDY trip
- moved to Fort Leonard Wood, Missouri
- became a college instructor at Central Texas College
- engaged in Automobile University/self-improvement on the road

- joined Toastmasters International
- joined the National Speakers Association
- First warrant officer selected to attend Logistics Executive Development Course (LEDC)

Tank Hill on Fort Jackson; the road to change

PVT Wayne Davidson, Squad leader at Fort Jackson

PFC Wayne Davidson, Soldier of the Month, New Mexico

Bertha Davidson, Southwestern sweetheart

SPC Wayne Davidson enjoying the leisure life in barracks

The Wedding Party; bride, groom and best man

New wife and new backyard in the mountainous desert

Tranquil view to the south from German farmhouse balcony

Tranquil view across the street from German farmhouse balcony

Tranquil view to the north from German farmhouse balcony

Winter walk along the German countryside

My brand new automobile: DA SAAB

CHAPTER 4

State of Connectivity and Personal Development

"Ahhh!" The question was tossed out to the masses from the board in front of the classroom. The question was not complex and deserved a simple response. The answer was known, but the response time was slow. The student had been reserved in speech since the days of the assassination of President Kennedy. The venture of learning had not always been friendly to the potential of this young man's bright mind. The young man pondered, "Should I answer or should I not? If I answer, my classmates will think me to be a 'smartass brother.' If I just sit and say nothing, I will meet the expectations of my peer group." In reality, why did I need to talk? Nobody listened anyway.

The Art of Communication and Its Source Connection

The major asked me one duty day, "Mr. Davidson, do we have *connectivity*? I have to communicate with higher headquarters to get my orders and complete my mission." In relative contrast, my father stated that he was not a public speaker and had little desire to take the lead even in submitting a prayer. This attitude derived most likely from his limited formal education and being ticked that my mother, serving as his surrogate, constantly prodded him to participate.

The ability to communicate and express thought is an essential part of the leadership development process.[1] Aside from imaginary television characters, such as Uncle Martin in *My Favorite Martian*,[2] I think few in the human community have the ability to literally read the minds of other people. The general fact is, when there is no communication between parties, there is little opportunity to generate or convey thoughts and ideas.

The protagonist in many stories in books and on screen and stage is perceived to be bold, hearty, and full of communication attributes in one form or another. Attributes of communication have been most likely passed on to me through the image of public figures or formal training rather than the genes of my biological father. This is not a criticism; remember his claim of not being a public speaker, most likely fostered by his limited educational opportunities. The ability to communicate is a key component of an alpha male.[3]

THE LEARNING EXPERIENCE

Somewhere I heard, "Join Toastmasters and learn to communicate better!" I also heard that successful people practice, practice, and practice their craft. Making practice a habit was challenging for me, because at times it was difficult to find a designated place to practice and people with the same interest. Surprisingly, there are many people who don't recognize self-improvement as a necessity and spend quality time criticizing those who do. Someone informed me about Toastmasters International meetings held at the Fort Leonard Wood education center. There is that place again: education center. So I went.

I learned that Toastmasters International[4] was a communications club where members and guests practiced oratory skills while building leadership skills. During this period, I was instructing college students, and I wanted to learn how to be a better communicator—as well as associate with others working to enhance their careers and aspirations. I also learned that Toastmasters International had a large following in the Filipino population.

I needed a nurturing environment, and the Fort Leonard Wood

chapter of the Toastmasters was that place. The chapter members were men and women taking charge of their personal growth and careers by participating in the roles and responsibilities of the chapter—first as an elected leader, helping the chapter to conduct orderly meetings, and second as a participating speaker, either extemporaneously or in a prepared speech. I served as a chapter leader and worked hard to fulfill the certification requirements and earn certification as a speaker. I was the chapter's only African-American member.

Thanks to Toastmasters, both my confidence in speaking and my listening skills were enhanced—so much so that I wanted to go to the next level in communications and possibly earn my living as a speaker. I soon learned of the National Speakers Association (NSA),[5] headquartered in Phoenix, Arizona, home to many of the speakers I had been listening to over the past few years. Zig Ziglar, Og Mandino, Les Brown, and Brian Tracy all mentored me on making my life successful through my audiocassette player in the same intense manner as I listened and laughed to Richard Pryor tapes and popular music.

It was Les Brown[6] who told me that I should live out my dream and people would come out of the woodwork to help me when I got good at whatever it might be. It was Zig Ziglar[7] who told me I was a winner and encouraged me to establish my goals and write them down as reinforcement. Zig Ziglar also suggested that I understand the difference between empathy and sympathy, especially if I was attempting to help others. Cassette tapes were a practical learning tool in surpassing those goals. Not to forget that Zig Ziglar alerted me to the understanding that all of us seeks acknowledgement of our human existence.

It was Og Mandino[8] who introduced me to the concept of persistence and conserving resources in the art of selling both product and myself using a biblical setting. It was Brian Tracy[9] who introduced me to building greater confidence in developing a winning sales philosophy. But Rita Davenport[10] was most likely the first NSA member speaker I ever heard. I recall her stories to be family oriented and filled with homespun humor. She also talked about learning the piano with her children from a professional teacher. The activity brought them together and built analytic skills in the participants. I went out into the Missouri backwoods and bought a piano to emulate the learning relationship with my own children. I could see their interest in learning begin to increase. Later I had the opportunity to shake her hand at an NSA national event.

The learning experience is supplemented at the local chapter. At the Michigan chapter I currently participate in, Pam Wyess acts as the program director under the tutelage of Leslie Charles, Marilynn Semonick, and Mary Jane Mapes. But the seeds of learning opportunity were planted at the St. Louis and Carolina chapters that really got me energized. I perceived these messages and styles to be grounded in the foundational texts of the New Thought Movement.[11] As a mechanism, I found this philosophy helped to ignite my endeavors and put them into action, instead of daydreams or wishes, as I proceeded down the road.

LISTENING: A KEY COMPONENT OF COMMUNICATION AND THE ROAD TRIP

I began commuting to the NSA chapter in St. Louis whenever a meeting or seminar was scheduled. Sometime later, I learned there was a major convention to be held in Anaheim, California, and I wanted to attend. So in 1996, I decided to drive my family in our Jeep to Southern California on a budget.

The plan was for my family to spend their days at Disneyland enjoying the rides while I spent my days next door at the Anaheim Marriott attending the NSA convention. To save on lodging, we would sleep at my sister Glenda's house in Fullerton; after all, it was not far from Disneyland. I explained to Glenda what my mission was and asked her not to cook or do anything special for us. Of course, she did not listen; she went ahead and cooked dinner, another example of the fruit not falling far from the "Momma" tree. Remember, as a child, all information in my family was disseminated through my mother. Surprisingly, my mother once admitted to me during a casual conversation that she was not a good listener.

Protect the Ear Gate: What You Hear Is What You Get

I was hooked on becoming a member of NSA. Why? I wanted to be a better communicator and earn a better living. As an adjunct college instructor, I found out that I was eligible for national membership, so when I returned home I applied and was accepted in 1996. I have maintained a learning relationship ever since. I found out there were a number of African-Americans members at the national level. This trip was a spur-of-the-moment action and designed to be economical, and from it I experienced immense professional growth.

Before we returned to Missouri, I was able to stop in the Los Angeles area and visit the Crenshaw Christian Center campus, home of my spiritual leader, Dr. Frederick K. C. Price. From my home office, I watched Pastor Price on television in conjunction with studying my Bible from an academic perspective. My formal study at Wayland Baptist University opened my mind anew to Bible knowledge. Dr. Price provided my belief system with a broader and more progressive foundation than what I had learned as a youngster in the traditional Negro Baptist church.

That a person is greatly influenced by what he or she hears through the "ear gate" is probably the most significant message I've received to date from Dr. Price's teaching on the topic of self-esteem. It seeded the development of my own "If/Then" Rule: *If* you hear that you are a bum continually, *then* you will probably believe yourself to be a bum. *If* you hear that you are a king continually, *then* you will probably believe yourself to be a king. I believe this understanding is foundational in building self-esteem.

I drove onto campus and went into the bookstore to buy reading materials. As I walked around, the feel of the place was different, and the people seemed different and very representative of Pastor Price's doctrine. Pastor Price's ministry is nondenominational, and I found that to be most rewarding in the learning process. Arguably, denominations tend to get in the way of the spiritual process or turn it into a street argument: my church is better than your church.

That argument never made sense to me, although my children were raised in the Catholic faith to fulfill my promise to my father-in-law when I asked him for my wife's hand in marriage. I believe there is one God Almighty, and I am saved through his son, Jesus. I have since learned that the one God has many names as given by many cultures. At the Fort Leonard Wood chapel, I assisted with the Sunday school program for Catholic youth. As a result, I became acutely aware of the differences in denominational practice between the Catholic and the Baptist church, to include the secular literature. My mind was open, and I learned something about Catholicism.

Tell People Where You Have Been or They'll Think You Were In Jail

For more than thirty years, I served as an army professional. I acquired technical and professional skills that have great value. My warrant officer evaluations and training opportunities, along with civilian evaluations and training opportunities, support that assertion. As a result, I surmised that I was not just a dog-faced soldier in the army, and because of that I needed to be proud of my accomplishments. The army has served as my mentor.

I mentioned my reservations on this subject during my initial meeting with Mr. Tony Reusing, my mentor at NSA. I told him that I did not really want people to know that I was in the military. Tony replied, "If you don't tell people where you have been the last twenty years, then they will think that you have been somewhere else, like jail." That would have been easy assumption for people to make, since I am an African-American male, and African-American males have a high rate of incarceration.[12] Additionally, many who have been incarcerated find it difficult to economically melt back into the mainstream for various reasons.[13] I learned from that bit of mentoring to be a little more proud of my military and civilian service and use it to my advantage.

John H. Johnson, the publisher, explained that the goal of a mentor is to provide mentees with news they can use in their quest. *If* you do not have a mentor readily available, *then* seek and select a mentor who is available on radio, television, or recorded material.[14] Aside from my army life, I did not have a mentor readily available, so I found mentorship in recorded material. I found out listening to people outside of my family circle helped to expand my knowledge base, change my attitude, and broaden my outlook on life.

Throughout my time at Fort Leonard Wood, I continued to be involved in self-improvement. I continued to attend professional training sessions and learning opportunities in the St. Louis Area to seek certification, mentorship, and fellowship. I found that it was not unusual for me to be the lone African-American person at any of the training sessions or group events I attended.

Listening and Learning from People in the Know

Also in 1996, I became a member of the St Louis Chapter of the Institute of Management Consultants (IMC).[15] I recall one particular IMC training session hosted by an experienced senior consultant who during the course of instruction remembered one of his early assignments. He had worked with Mr. Berry Gordy[16] of Motown Corporation, a company whose performers I grew up singing and dancing along with on the streets of Detroit and Cleveland—in some cases, living in the same neighborhood they lived in. The consultant recalled that the first time he ever saw a million dollars in cash was in the late 1960s when Berry Gordy, also a shrewd African-American businessman, was in the process of purchasing a building outright as part of his recording operation. As a young consultant, he stated that he was flabbergasted at the sight of so much money packed neatly in a single suitcase.

I too would have been flabbergasted, because over the course of my life as a Detroiter, I passed that particular building a zillion times. With Motown's move to California and the economic decline of the city, the building stood as a skeleton and an eyesore for years until it was brought down to make way for a parking lot a few years back. Now through the winds of development, the parking lot is part of major rebuilding effort for downtown Detroit.[17]

That same year I was able to attend the IMC National Convention in Reno, Nevada. It was another learning experience, and that reminded me of the Las Vegas Convention I'd attended a few years before to promote my telecommunication service. Besides the many people renewing relationships, the primary topic at the convention was the explosion of the Internet and the potential marriage of technology and retail sales. There was a professional camaraderie and sharing among peers and a call for more African-American members.

I was fortunate to sit in at a roundtable discussion led by a distinguished gentleman highly regarded and recognized as the guru of retail sales. This was my very first national meeting, and I did not know any of them personally or professionally, so I sat quietly and listened to the conversation and discourse. Again, this was 1996, and the gentlemen engaged in a discussion centered on the question of what needs to happen with technology growth before the Internet could impact retail sales as a viable marketplace for the future.

If I remember correctly, the consensus was another instance of the "If/Then Rule," where *if* customers did not feel safe engaging in online transactions with their hard-earned money, *then* selling products and services using Internet technology would be short-lived. That question has been answered some fifteen-plus years later with the exchange of $78.1 billion in the third quarter of 2014—great bling and a sign of approval.[18] The Internet has overwhelmingly changed the retail marketplace and the way consumers spend their money, and because of that there are fewer shoppers in traditional stores. *If* you are reading this manuscript in its final construction, *then* chances are great that it was purchased through the Internet.

COMMUNICATION CONNECT OPPORTUNITY EVERYWHERE

As a lifelong learner, I considered the opportunity to sit among this leadership group to be significant and appreciated in my career progression. Historically, the information I got about the world tended to be secondhand, and never from practicing creditable source. This key discourse took place at a professional level on a technological and commercial telecommunication application that changed social economics around the world. As with Euro Disney, flat-screen monitors in Alaska, paperless at USAA, animated movies and the Internet introduction in Las Vegas, and economic growth opportunities surrounding the military business communities, I had no connectivity. I also had no vision or concept of my role in acting on change or the resources to react with an immediate response. I could only store this information in my mental file cabinet. I was totally unprepared to react to the forecast of future or changing times. I saw the big picture, but my face was not in it just as many others from my demographic background.

I did learn from my experience that the management consultant who works from the outside of the organization on contract tends to have more success than the management consultant who works on the inside of the organization as an employee. Why? To me, it is the bureaucracy of the organizational structure, easily amplified by the biblical adages found in the book of Matthew 13:57, Mark 6:4, and John 4:44, where Jesus informs that "a prophet is not a prophet in his own home."

FRUITFUL GIVING

Another person I met in Reno was a young African-American female consultant, Ms. Kim Patton, from Alabama. Kim had been in the consulting field for some time and recently earned her doctoral degree. She was at the national convention to receive her professional certification award as a consultant. Although our conversations during the three-day convention were intermittent, they were full of substance.

One of the topics we talked about in particular was "tithing" and our financial responsibility relative to the Old Testament book Malachi 3:8–10. As a result of our fruitful conversation, the young lady promised to send me some reading materials, and soon after the promised material arrived. The author of the material was Dr. Frederick K. C. Price of the Crenshaw Christian Center in Los Angeles, California.

To this point, I had seen Dr. Price on television but had never read anything he'd written. I delved into the reading materials and then, as Dr. Price suggested, I checked it in the Bible. I also refreshed myself with my study materials from Wayland Baptist University and materials I obtained from assisting with the Catholic Sunday school on Fort Leonard Wood. What I learned from those few days at the national convention changed my financial, family, and spiritual life for the better.

What is curious to me is that this topic is always answered with denial or abstained from among family and friends. It seems that the act of giving can cause great debate. I surmised from the debates that the hard part in tithing is actually letting fruit leave the hand without worrying about its whereabouts.

ANCESTRY JOURNAL

Now that my financial, family, and spiritual life were on an optimistic path, I looked to increase my knowledge of my ancestral heritage. I had always been inquisitive about family roots. In the mid-1990s, I learned that a distant cousin, Katie Bennett, had written a book titled *Soaking the Yule Log*[19] that documented much of my maternal family of Bolivar, Tennessee, in Hardeman County. I had not met her at this point, but the family was abuzz because as a result of her research, there was a rumor that Lionel Richie, former lead vocalist for a Motown group the

Commodores, was a member of my maternal family. Then, just as the buzz came, it went, for whatever reason. Nonetheless, I was still interested in knowing who I was.

Since my maternal family was well documented, I started to collect bits of information pertaining to my paternal family members and events that happened during their lifetimes. Katie spoke to me about her joyful journey and how the book finally came together. As a result of her mentorship, I have followed her path. That conversation was the genesis of this trilogy.

My first stop was the census records, and I encountered a few African-Americans searching for their roots along the way. I found the best sources of data were the public library and the Mormon Church. So I would drive to Rolla, Missouri, to the Church of Latter Day Saints to look at microfiche containing census data. I learned that the Mormon Church had a special interest in the caretaking of census records. As I progressed and my level of understanding grew, I went on down to the St. Louis library to look at books containing census data. I gathered bits and piece of data, information, and oral history at every opportunity. All of the acquired knowledge—good, bad or indifferent—became the basis for this text and my other academic works.

As I fine-tuned my research skills, one of most intriguing interviews in the St. Louis area was with Sadie Rogers, the daughter of Maggie Cheshier and George Polk. Maggie Cheshier was a sister of my maternal grandfather, Wade Cheshier. I was fortunate to speak with her; she was well into her eighties and very personable in providing me with added insight on my maternal family. She and her husband, Frederick Rogers, a former grocer, welcomed me into their home in St. Louis. The interview went very well, but I was a little worried when Mr. Rogers, well into his nineties, had to walk the dog. The dog was a feisty terrier that barked throughout my visit. I sat calmly on the couch with a smile on the outside, but on the inside I was praying that Mr. Rogers had enough physical strength to hold the leash. From this social encounter, I also found that prayer works.

PAPA'S GOTTA BRAND NEW SET OF WHEELS

I had a lot of stuff going on during this time. My family of five was maturing in both age and size. I thought it would be nice to have a recreational vehicle with greater capacity, where four girls and a guy could have enough room to be comfortable. I had received a notice in the mail that the car dealership in Rolla, Missouri, was having a bank sale. Rolla is located about twenty miles east of Fort Leonard Wood off Interstate 44.

I drove there early one Saturday morning alone just to browse the lot when I spotted a white Plymouth van. The van was equipped with comfortable seats and a radio and television; that would be just right for the girls. I checked the vehicle out and thought the price was right and the size was right. This was my new vehicle.

Cell phones weren't everywhere back then; I had to hop back into my own vehicle and head home to speak with my wife about the van. This was during the summer, and my parents were visiting from Detroit, so I decided to bring the whole family to check out the vehicle. Why did I do that? It is typical when parents visit the home of offspring that chaos is part of the package, and this visit was no different. On this particular trip to Missouri, my parents made a wrong exit on Interstate 44 prior to arriving at my house, and that incident became the basis of bickering between them during their entire visit.

My wife and I were in agreement that the vehicle was what our family of five needed. My parents, on the other hand, did not like the vehicle at all. They found fault with everything. They said it was too small, they did not like this, and they did not like that. The vehicles on the lot they liked did not fit my family profile or particular need. Their fancy was a vehicle that would take them to church on Sunday and turn heads.

I was a little perturbed, but my parents' opinion was of no consequence. The decision belonged to me and my wife. So I hopped everybody back in the car and drove them all back to the house. A few minutes later, I jumped back into the car, returned to the lot, and purchased the van.

I needed a practical solution, not a Sunday-go-to-meeting one. A few weeks later, I took my family of five, plus one nephew, to Disney World in Florida in the brand new minivan, and we had a great time. That minivan served my family for ten years. There are times when you have to do what is right for your immediate family's needs without the input or approval of your extended family.

Be Professional: Promises Are Made to Be Broken

It was now the end of my tour at Fort Leonard Wood. Sometime during the middle of my tour, the major command underwent reorganization. This experience provided me with my greatest opportunity as a scholar to witness organizational change and the impact it has on the workforce. Although previously I saw great organizational change in the automobile factory, that experience was as a survivor, not a scholar.

To soldiers, reorganization meant their family's stability was no longer. It was a very stressful time for many of the soldiers, who were now concerned about where they were headed. Some had just arrived with families in tow. I had been on station for twenty-four months, and it was nearly my time to leave. I was cool, calm, and collected. I was informed by my branch manager that I was heading to Belgium for an assignment at the Supreme Headquarters Allied Powers Europe or SHAPE HQ.[20] Believe me, I was ready to go!

Sometime later, I was told that the manager who offered me that assignment had suddenly retired to take a job offer at Disneyland with a high-ranking buddy from the Gulf War, or so the rumor goes. That career move left me in limbo, because the new career manager did not know me from Adam. The new guy came into the position with a new agenda and a new attitude that did not help my position at all. Later, he informed me that I was not the candidate selected for the assignment in Belgium. First of all, I did not know it was a contest—as you know, I don't do well in contests. So the new guy looked all over Korea for a job for me, but because of downsizing Korea was closed.

Then there was the matter of my attendance at LEDC, pending from two years prior. I resubmitted my request through my command structure, as the same two field-grade officers were in place. However, the financial conditions for attending class had changed. The class was no longer paid for at the Department of the Army level; payment would have to be made by the major command, Fifth Army. As a result, my application was denied, and the opportunity for career progression fell by the wayside ... but not for the two field-grade officers, because they moved on to new cushy jobs while the distraught soldiers left behind awaited their disposition, with me now tossed among them. My wariness of people in positions of military authority increased.

At this point, I had been denied the position in Europe and the opportunity to go to school. I was still proud of my service record and achievements, but I was not happy. I was mentoring others, as a teacher and soldier, to be successful. My latest achievement was obtaining 281 points out of 300 possible on the army physical-fitness test,[21] the highest I had scored since being in military service. I had always been fit throughout, but I learned to visualize and see myself at the finish line, a technique I learned from my association with professional groups. I also recalled my lowest point total, scored during a readiness test in Alaska. I was disappointed at the failure then, and I am still disappointed about the incident now, but I keep striving to do and to be better.

I pondered resigning again, but I first sought legal counsel from the post lawyer. He put things in perspective using quantitative figures, comparing on paper leaving the service now versus finishing at twenty years, which was in approximately three years. From our discussion, I clearly understood that money talks. I sucked up my pride once again and moved out to complete my twenty years of service to be eligible for a pension. In the interim, I continued to seek learning opportunities in professional seminars and the field of education. The philosophy of lifelong learning continued to help my development as a person as well as the development of my family members. I learned not to make rash decisions born from emotions.

As One Decrease, the Other Increases

Up to this point, Bertha and I had been married about fifteen years and had three young girls. She had previously earned an associate's degree from El Paso Community College, where she was the first female in her Mexican-American family of ten siblings to complete high school, and then the first sibling to earn a college degree. She, too, has been a lifelong learner while supporting my career decisions and the learning experiences I had.

When we arrived at Fort Leonard Wood, Bertha enrolled at Columbia College to complete a four-year degree. Later, she started her own business in direct sales as a consultant for Mary Kay, an organization that promoted diversity, enthusiasm, and self-esteem in its product line. It was this opportunity that helped her develop business attributes that had been dormant. These newly found attributes enhanced her decision-making process in making career choices. Her confidence grew, and she was determined to get on a faster track of promotion into mid-level management as a Department of the Army (DA) civilian. Upon earning a four-year degree and developing her leadership attributes, Bertha became eligible and was accepted as a candidate for entry in the DA Logistics Intern program. She trained for two years around the country, in some cases training classes as if she were an active-duty soldier.

As a family unit, we looked at this selection as a payoff for previous achievement, opportunity for career progression, and family growth. When we informed my mother of this good fortune, as usual she looked upon it with skepticism, but it was not her decision to make. My wife and I made a family decision, and I took on the challenging role of Mr. Mom and a retiring soldier.

Fort Jackson: the Farewell Tour

Almost twenty years earlier, I had escaped from Stupidville and embarked on a journey as a twenty-eight-year-old recruit at Fort Jackson, South

Carolina. I had come full circle in my view of the world I lived in. Now I looked about the post to see a lot of newly constructed buildings that had cropped up among a few familiar sights, like the lake and water tower. I also heard a few familiar sounds, like the inflexed voice of a person in a drill-sergeant hat motivating recruits and soldiers to get from point A to point Z in a hurry. I was back on familiar ground for my seventh and final tour of duty, but in a different capacity. There was one nuance: I was also "Mr. Mom" to my three daughters, Treasure, Lydia, and Lynette. This status cut into my library time, but I made do with what I had. As Mr. Mom, my goal was to hand those kids back to their real mother in the same condition in which they were handed to me.

Bertha was at Fort Lee, Virginia, a few hours away beginning her training opportunity as an intern with DA. It was her time to shine in a career that also started out twenty years earlier as a college student on the local level. After twenty years of following my career around Europe, Alaska, the Ozarks, and the Southwest United States, she deserved the opportunity to work toward her own aspirations. No problem.

As Mr. Mom, I did the best job I could in order for my wife to be successful. My older daughter, Treasure, helped me greatly with her two younger sisters, Lydia and Lynette. Many people do not know that military families are very fortunate. Fort Jackson, like other military bases, provided soldiers and their families with all types of recreational opportunities and facilities. Believe me, my girls took full advantage of South Carolina's warm weather and the swimming pool located across the street from our quarters. Then on the weekend, we would jump into the van and drive a few hours north to visit my wife at Fort Lee.

The one true challenge I had as Mr. Mom was combing hair after the girls spent hours at the pool. On occasion, my office associate, Alma Gadson, would lend a hand with girl maintenance. Alma was also known for her home-cooked breakfast that she served at our office. I was fortunate my chain of command was generous in maintaining a family-friendly environment as I wandered through my Mr. Mom status and my off-duty projects. The only real issue I had in performing my primary duty as a warrant officer was getting ample manpower and support from the sergeant in charge.

Fort Jackson is located in the Bible belt, so the sergeant in charge was always playing gospel music and holding church services in his office. The only thing missing was the collection plate. I soon found out it is very difficult to get regular army work done when you are dealing with somebody in the spirit.

The only other problem that I recall was another distracting visit by my parents. As previously cited, my mother had a tendency to cause chaos. Not understanding life on a military base, she thought my daughters had too much freedom and fun. She decided to call my wife at school to report on an issue she thought was her business. My wife's response was that she could not do anything about it and that she trusted me to do the right thing in any case. Then my mother told my wife not to tell me that she called, but Bertha told me anyway. I did not call my mother out on this issue, but clearly the woman had a lack of understanding about me and my military life. This was one instance of why my wife and daughters had a poor relationship with my mother.

As mentioned, Fort Jackson was different the second time around for me. During my first four months of military service, I was in a training status with little or no time to enjoy Fort Jackson and the surrounding area. My new unit assignment was similar to the mission of my previous organization: to train the reserve component to become one with the regular army. In between my tours, I learned that many of the scenes from Danny DeVito's movie *Renaissance Man*[22] were filmed on Fort Jackson, and some of the soldiers I worked with supported the movie production. My office was in view of the post headquarters building, a prominent fixture in the movie. Cuts in the federal budget were evident when the post flag came down during "Reveille." There were two soldiers pulling a detail that could have used a few more good men.

When I arrived at Fort Jackson, the first thing I did to continue my education was find a local Toastmasters club. The club I located held its meetings at Midland Community College. The membership was comprised of local residents who had lived in the Columbia area for a number of years. I was the only African-American member. It was astonishing. There was one longtime resident who remembered my mentor, Zig Ziglar, as a young man when he sold cookware in and around the city. As a lifelong learner, I did my best to serve and participate in the club's proceedings as I continued my commitment to be better.

LEARNING THE ART OF PERFORMANCE

At this point in time, my goal was to build my speaking career and earn a living at it. I found the closest NSA chapter in nearby Charlotte, North Carolina, and attended the meetings. This chapter was home to several high-profile members. As mentioned, the membership roles at NSA are primarily made of people who speak for a living and are successful at their craft. There are many suggestions, recommendations, and mentorships available at NSA meetings. But in reality, the listener has to be selective, because it could involve a significant investment or commitment.

One suggestion I got at an NSA meeting was to take acting classes for the purpose of improving stage presence and abilities. One evening, I saw an advertisement for acting classes to be held in Columbia's theater district. I enrolled in a class and, along with several others, learned about the stage as a platform and stage acting as a craft. I was the only African-American student. On the first night I saw, for the very first time, how actors prepared themselves for a formal audition in the theater below. It was a musical production, so I gathered enough confidence to audition myself. The accompanist handed me some sheet music, and I sang the song. Afterward, the director thanked me for coming and quickly dismissed me, but I had gained a ton of professional experience in a professional process and setting.

I continued in the acting class for two semesters, learning Shakespeare and other traditional themes of the theater. In addition, I began to read more about the craft of acting and the people who earned their living acting. As a result, I improved my platform mechanics, and my confidence level greatly improved. Unbeknownst to me, the military had a history of providing service men and women the opportunity and resources to engage in activities of their personal choice while serving Uncle Sam. For instance, I learned that when actor Gene Wilder served in the military, he was stationed in New Jersey. On the weekends, he would take the train into New York City and study acting before returning in time for the next duty day.

One day I was reading the local paper again and there was an acting scholarship available to African-American men and women at the Trustus Theater, a local African-American theater. I applied, and soon after I learned that I had earned an acting scholarship along with about twenty other African-American men and women. It was unbelievable. I earned a scholarship!

The curriculum had a narrow focus on drama found in many African-American works. During a reading of Lorraine Hansberry's *Raisin in the Sun*,[23] I quickly found out that I smiled too broadly for the main character, Walter Lee Younger, a man on an economic mission once portrayed by the legendary Sidney Poitier. The director, Greg Leevy, said I was the happiest person he had ever seen play the part of an angry black male in a domestic tragedy. What he did not know was that it was this same dumb smile that had kept me of out of jail all these years.

At the end of the course there was a recital. My partner Reginald Harvey and I were to perform an exhibit or sketch titled "Symbiosis," a scene from *The Colored Museum*[24] written by George C. Wolfe. The character I played was the Old Dude and my partner played the Kid. In the sketch, a man is confronted by his childhood self while trying to throw those years away. There is great personal conflict between the present and the past. I learned that throwing away the past for an African-American male might be a bad move, especially if there is positive history. Trustus Theater was a great experience. I learned that my strength was in my voice and musical theater, not the darkness of drama.

As a result of the musical audition, I began to formally work on my voice. I could always sing but never found an inspired audience among my family or friends. There was no freedom of expression in my childhood home. I used to practice in the basement of my parents' home, but my mother was always annoyed, and she would say that she was trying to take a nap.

I looked in the directory and found the Carolina Music Academy nearby, and I enrolled. My first vocal coach was a male opera singer named Marc Rattray. He helped me reclaim my gift, and "The Twelfth of Never"[25] became my "drop dead" audition song. Some weeks later, I learned from the local newspaper that an audition for an African-American male singer was being held for a musical production titled *Five Guys Named Moe*[26] at the Workshop Theatre, featuring the early rhythm-and-blues music of Louis Jordan. I knew the name Louis Jordan but not the range of his contribution to music. I marked the date on my calendar and began to prepare myself to perform my audition song.

On the day of the audition, I was in Virginia visiting my wife with our children. I promised myself that I would make it back for the audition, and I practiced all the way back driving south on Interstate 95. I dropped my children off at home and took my refreshed gift and newly acquired skills to audition for a musical play. I performed the song, thanked the folks for the opportunity, and went home. As I walked in the door, my phone was ringing. On the other end the musical director told me, first, that I got the part, and second, the rehearsal times. This was unbelievable!

My character was Four-Eyed Moe, who sang alongside five other characters: No Moe, Big Moe, Little Bitty Moe, Get Moe, and the dreamer No Max. This was another great theater opportunity and experience. I saw myself singing but I forgot to see myself dancing. I was clearly the newbie in the ensemble, the one with the two left feet, but I helped the show to be a success.

From the experience, I learned that the other cast members and production crew depend on you as an actor to be there and ready to go. We received good reviews, and they added several performances. I also learned from the experience that if the media did not write something bad about you, then you did okay. What I learned provided me with the foundation to assist my daughter, Treasure, in her formal audition to enter the Actor's Studio at Pace University in New York in 2006. The audition was held behind a sheer net, but I like to think Al Pacino, Harvey Keitel, and Ellen Burstyn—the resident leadership that year—were sitting down in front.

A few weeks after the play ended, my office associate Alma asked me to sing "Always and Forever"[27] at her wedding. I practiced and performed the song as she asked. It went very well because the musicians gravitated to my song, and we finished it really nice. I did not try to mimic the unique sound of the original presentation, but I did add my own twist at the end. A young lady standing along the wall said I could sing for her anytime. I smiled and thanked her, because I felt good enough at this point that I could incorporate vocals into my speaking career. I could always carry a tune in a bucket. I went out and got mentoring to improve my confidence level. I have been working harder to be better ever since.

I'M OUTTA HERE: THE NEW MILLENNIUM

The certificate reads, "To all who shall see these presents, greeting: This is to certify that Wayne Rudolph Davidson, Chief Warrant Officer, Regular Army having served faithfully and honorably was retired from the United States Army, 1 February 2000." After twenty years and one day of military service, it was time to transition from the service in late 1999. I feel the term *transition* is more appropriate than the term *retirement*, because transition has the sound of change to it while retirement has the sound of termination. The army observed when able-bodied and vibrant soldiers retired after years of being responsible for people and equipment that they go home only to sit on the porch, and they drop dead soon after because of a new dedication to inactivity. So at the time of my transition, the army philosophy used the operative term *transition* rather than the traditional term *retirement*.

It was the year 2000, and at this point I did not regret having joined the volunteer army twenty years before. I felt fortunate I had all my fingers and all my toes. From all of my assignments, I learned that all types of people depend on the military to provide all kinds of basic services in their service to the nation. I was truly grateful for having an opportunity to honorably serve those people and at the same time turn my life around. I learned that the army is a starting point for change.[28] Bobby, my younger brother died in 1996 from unknown circumstances in Southeast Texas where he sought out his aspiration of being a songwriter. Instead he was found lifeless in the Gulf of Mexico. Bobby loved playing soldier as we grew up as kids but he was unable to transform that same affection of soldiering into a real life career or experience. Still, I believe that Bobby was the real soldier in my family and he would have been proud of my achievements.

The journey was unbelievable. I spent the 1980s learning basic military doctrine and becoming a more disciplined person. In the 1990s, I developed professional attributes that helped me believe in "I will" versus "I ain't." As a result, I went from being an unemployed autoworker living and working in a dark tunnel to positions of responsibility and authority as a member of the US Army in strategic places around the world. I went from earning a subpar high-school diploma to earning a graduate degree with honors.

THE "I AM" BOOK

To possess knowledge and have the ability to understand its meaning spawned the birth of a familiar maxim "Know Thyself," introduced by the Greek philosopher Plato.[29] In my journey, that maxim had proven true. I began to learn more about who I was as an individual. I understood that I had more to offer to the community than when I knew nothing about myself as an individual. In many of my professional associations, I was able to use personal assessment tools that allowed me to record my attribute measurements and develop self-knowledge.

Standardized testing[30] has a negative connotation and consequence on the minority community, but there are other assessment tools like the army entrance exam, select army training courses, the Myers-Briggs Assessment, and learning mechanisms, such as, Automobile University. There are also abstract personal assessment tools: an astrological study, a tool of prediction used as far back as Biblical times to mark the coming of the Christ as in the New Testament Book of Matthew 2:1; graphology studies, a handwriting analysis; a numerology study, an analysis of letters and numbers associated with my name and birthday; and learning and understanding the definition or meaning of my Christian name. Out of all of these, I think the Bible was my most influential personal assessment tool. By simply reading it, I no longer had a secondhand understanding of what was written there.

I recall that I did well on the army entrance exam in 1979, and as a result I was able to go into a career field I had chosen. At the time, I had no way of knowing whether my score was high, low, or they were just feeding me a yarn. But the result helped me get the job I wanted at the time, and then it helped me meet the basic criteria to enter into the warrant officer training program. If the score was not what it was, higher or lower, my career options would have been different. The result of each assessment influenced me to create my own "I AM" book for the purpose of building on the attributes I possessed and influence my offspring and others. At this point in time, twenty years later, I had evolved into a more knowledgeable and pluralistic person who was leaving the army for new career opportunities that I was better prepared to seek.

Unlike my arrival in 1980, my departure from Fort Jackson was met with little fanfare. I attended no formal parade. I had my honorable discharge in hand and an American flag that still hangs in my basement as a gift for service. One regret I have is that I left during my year of promotion eligibility to Chief Warrant Officer 4. But it was my wife's time to shine.

I returned to the Detroit area in the new millennium a different fellow than the one who left in 1980. I had a new investment in the country. I had a new family, a new home, a new lifestyle, and a new belief system.

I'd learned from my military experience that the world operates on the principles of "If/Then," meaning *if* I got off of my butt, *then* I could make things happen. It should be noted that in the new millennium, the military life is a road less traveled by African-American males.[31]

BACKSLIDING

I was looking for career opportunities as a white-collar worker. After all, I had credentials, education, and experience in different professional disciplines. My mother, on the other hand, was badgering me to call the Chrysler Corporation to get my old job back on the assembly line after twenty years, because as a union member I left in good standing. I was sure I'd broken free of my mother's influence on May 14, 1980, but I acquiesced to her request—and how quickly I regretted that decision made out of respect.

I first called the plant's administrative office, and then the union office across the street. Both telephone calls made me really angry, because I could have done without their laughter and sarcastic explanation that I had been gone too long and that the automotive world had changed. What my mother did not take time to find out is that I had my own plan. I needed to recover from this backsliding and get back to it.

Again, in the book of Matthew 13:57, Mark 6:4, and John 4:44, Jesus walked his ministry about the countryside while healing and giving people hope. When he returned to his hometown, he received little respect or acknowledgement. As a result, Jesus said, "A prophet is not a prophet in his own home." I can relate to the words of Jesus. I had gone away from home for twenty years and achieved good success. With my experience I hoped to return to give people a little hope and inspiration, but I instead received little respect or acknowledgement. When I spoke of my experience, the reaction was only a distinct stare from the offspring of friends and family. They were still reaching for hope. At some point, hope must be turned into action. Sir Francis Bacon once said, "Hope makes a good breakfast but hope makes a *poor* dinner."[32]

HOME OWNERSHIP

I returned to Michigan because my wife was able to swap assignment locations with a classmate who wanted to go to New Jersey. As a result of serving in the military, I became a homeowner in September 1999, an achievement I once thought unachievable. When I left Detroit in 1980, the framework of redlining and housing discrimination[33] was still prevalent in the city. Historically, I would have been ineligible to secure a home loan from a local lender to buy or lease a home in the neighborhood if I wanted to live somewhere other than a declining minority community. Twenty years later, I was back with my own materiel resources and a personal map.

My wife and I worked as a team in this effort, as we had done many times before. Since our first day of marriage, we had worked on the premise that "man shall cleave or join unto his wife," as cited in the book of Genesis 2:24. I got one bit of advice from my office associate, Alma Gadson. I asked her if it would be better for me to just pick a house for a woman or let the woman pick the house. She informed me that most women would not be happy living in a house they did not choose. I found that to be good advice.

Earlier in the year, I had moved my wife into an apartment, and she went about the business of searching for a house she liked that was near where she worked. Our primary goal was to find a place that had a good school system for our children. Again without knowing our goals and objectives, my mother provided unsolicited assistance by contacting a real-estate agent of her own choosing for a house in the area of her own choosing. I made the assumption that my mother was afraid that we might buy a home in the suburbs surrounded by hate groups. It was her nature to be fearful; after reading the newspaper or seeing the news on the television, her reaction to the situation was always "Lookie there!" However, she did not realize that the intercity also had hate groups in high-crime areas. I empathized and continued on my quest to find a house for my family of *our* own choosing.

What my mother did not know was that we had sufficient funding to live where we wanted to live, and we had a plan. My friend, Chili Carlson, and his family assisted me with employment. If you recall, my wife and I had graciously declined my mother's unsolicited assistance on several occasions, as when we purchased the minivan while living in Missouri. We did the same here.

FEAR FACTOR

My mother's fear of the suburbs carried over to my father. That was surprising, since my father had worked in the suburbs for so many years. I asked him to cut my grass on occasion for a quick buck, and one day while cutting the grass, he thought he recognized the flag on display at a neighbor's house as a Confederate flag. He reported what he thought he saw directly to my mother who, no doubt, informed her church members in her daily chats.

Remember, my father grew up in the segregated South and had limited educational opportunity. It turns out Dad was mistaken in his observation. The flag on display was actually a British flag. I live in a neighborhood that has many observances because it is comprised of people from many countries. That absence of knowledge will surely destroy people, as described in the Old Testament Book of Hosea 4:6, is relevant here.

ROLL CALL

At this point, I think it is appropriate to have a roll call of the people I knew growing up in Detroit and the status of the city in the year 2000. Since my departure in 1980, the city had lost much of its economic tax base and much of its population.[34] In general, the city streets and roads were in terrible condition. Neighborhoods were being abandoned, and the once well-manicured homes were dilapidated, with foliage growing into stalks that hid the stalkers, man and beast. I loved the city of Detroit, but the state of the city conflicted with my family goals, objectives, and safety. It is a shame, but many long-suffering Detroiters of African descent would probably categorize me as an "outsider" who was not living in the city during the hard times. I beg to differ. It is clear those people are focused on their hard times, not on the hard times I endured. That is why I share my story.

If we took a drive, for instance, on upper Griggs Streets, the guys I'd grown up with since the mid-1960s were all gone to parts unknown or dead. Nicky Ford, a navy veteran, lay in a stupor in the midst of rubble that once was the family's manicured home. His father, a city bus driver who was long gone, had cared for his palace with enormous pride in the 1960s and 1970s during his pit stops from his city route. It was a palace no longer; both the house and the favorite son had fallen from grace and were clinging together in a pile of a dilapidated frames and weather-beaten building materials.

Next door, the former home of Eric Inkster was now occupied by Larry Ford (no relation to Nicky Ford), the older brother of Sammie Lee Ford, one of the brothers Sammie Lee used as an alias when he was stopped by the police. In the few moments I spoke with him, he informed that Sammie Lee and Eric were somewhere in the South, and Eric's brother Will had been run over by a car and suffered major damaged to one of his legs. That bit of information left Eric and his brother Will Inkster unaccounted for.

Across the street in the same block, the former home of Sammie Lee Ford had new occupants. Next door, "Little C" Rice, nephew of a local politician, was long gone, a victim of street crime in the 1980s, I heard. By chance, I encountered the mother and sisters of Clinton Delray up the street, and they were doing fine, but Clinton had died in the 1990s without a lavish funeral, unbeknown to his boyhood friends. Turning south and driving down and then across the Jefferies Freeway onto lower Griggs Street, rumor had it that Terry Grittle was unaccounted for and a motorcycle accident had put Ben Grittle in a wheelchair. However, the younger brother was heard to be announcing local sports on television.

Around the street on lower Birwood, Pops Greer was unaccounted for. Back across the Jefferies Freeway on upper Birwood, Boyd Sloan was long gone, I was told, a victim of violent street crime who lay dead in the street and morgue for days without identification. A few houses up the street is where the Brickgarden brothers once lived. I am told Arnett, the person who informed me about the volunteer army, was killed in a street fight, and his brother, Murphy, was unaccounted for. A drive back down across the Jefferies Freeway on Pinehurst, I recalled my own brothers, Glen and Bobby, also long gone as a result of violent deaths on the streets. It appears that only Chili and Chick, who were brothers-in-laws, were still around and moving forward raising families in Detroit's shaky economy.

Maybe the most demoralizing drive was to the corners of Michigan and Trumbull. The place where I'd found much needed solitude and sanctuary, Tiger Stadium, stood as an empty palace. It was a victim of apathy, and it was maddening to watch its slow death of deterioration and aborted demolition for over a decade.[35] My heroes, the Detroit Tigers, were now playing baseball at a wonderful place called Comerica Park.[36] This magnificent ballpark is located a short walk away from the black fertile soil that was once the home of Detroit's black community, Paradise Valley and Hastings Street. There is a historic plaque in the vicinity that serves as a remembrance.

GREEN-COLLAR JOB

I was truly grateful for my life experience over the past twenty years, and I thought it would be good for me to return some part of that back to the community. I decided I would seek teaching opportunities in the Detroit Public Schools (DPS). So I went down to the DPS main building to submit an application. By chance, I saw a couple of soldiers in military uniform, so I made an abrupt stop. I introduced myself and told them

I had just transitioned from military service and how grateful I was for the opportunity, and I wished the same for their careers. Before I could swiftly move on, the sergeant major in response gave me a quick overview of the DPS JROTC[37] program. Then he invited me to interview with the commandant for a position at one of the schools. I suddenly remembered that I, too, had taken JROTC at Mackenzie High for a semester or two in the 1960s. I also remembered I quit because I never got a uniform.

I thought this might be an interesting opportunity to give back. As cadre, I would continue to wear the uniform I was used to wearing. JROTC could be an extension of my army career. I gained a new perspective as I learned that the mission of JROTC was to help cadets develop good citizenship, patriotism, and key leadership attributes, such as self-reliance and discipline, as part of the school curriculum that enhances community growth. I didn't get that the first time around. I learned JROTC is not a mandatory school program and is not accepted in every community for various reasons, I'd guess mostly political.

I took the reading materials from the sergeant major and told him I would read them and give him a call with my decision. He asked where I lived, and I responded, "Sterling Heights." I was a little insulted when he then said, "Sterling Whites!" In two seconds, this representative of the Detroit Public Schools insulted me and my community. It was quite evident that he knew nothing of either one of us.

Sterling Heights had consistently been voted a safe city. It had a diverse culture, including me as a one of its newest residents. It had a strong economic tax base that employed thousands of people with diverse backgrounds, including me as a former automotive employee at a local factory in the 1970s. It did make me wonder about the health of the JROTC program, because the sergeant major made a negative comment so abruptly and presumptuously.

I still thought it was a good economic opportunity, so I went home and discussed the position with my wife. We had been successful in inspiring our own children to take advantage of academics and student life. I accepted the position with the assumption that I could help the child of somebody else do the same. The pay was equivalent to my full military salary, so I had no squabble over money.

INTERNATIONAL STUDENT BODY

I was assigned to Chadsey High School, a school I was familiar with from years past but which was now located in a high-crime district. Notably, Chadsey High was one of the only schools in DPS that did not have a majority of black students; instead the school had a large mix of foreign-born students. I drove over to Chadsey to meet with Master Sergeant (MSG) Kerns, the person I was to replace. I soon discovered that Chadsey High, like many urban schools in the Detroit metropolitan area, had metal detectors.

I first met with MSG Kerns, and then I interviewed with the school principal, who wished me success. On the first day, I noticed how the students, especially black students, flocked around MSG Kerns, a white male. He had taught JROTC at Chadsey for years and accumulated experience and wisdom with the assistance of SFC Anderson, a black male.

MSG Kerns said that he was glad I was there and then conveyed his accumulated wisdom on me. First, he stated that most of the children attending Chadsey came from low-income families or single-parent homes. There were one or two legends still living and working in this international neighborhood. The Kronk Gym[38] was located nearby, home of world-championship trainer Emanuel Steward[39] and world-champion boxer Thomas "The Hit Man" Hearns.[40]

MSG Kerns stated that there was a great need for black males to mentor black children, especially black males. In his opinion, the absence of the black male as a father figure created a mentorship gap with black children. Therefore, little respect was shown to older black males. MSG Kerns continued on and said the potential for a life of crime and underachievement was high among the low-income black-student population.

I concurred that he was right on target with his assessment. That is why I believe a place like redesigned version of Paradise Valley/ Hastings Street would provide a cultural training ground in commerce and community for learning alternatives to poverty and bad behavior. It could help boost the self-esteem of the African-American male population and reverse the popularity of the practice of wearing a pair of trousers below the waist line in public known as sagging.[41] A popular fashion statement among youth and repairmen.

MSG Kerns also had his finger on the pulse of Hispanic students. He explained that from his experience, young men and women of Spanish heritage sexually matured very early and, as a result, started families at an early age. Thus, the completion of the formal education process becomes secondary because an immediate means of income is needed in the form of military or low-paying jobs. From my perspective, for Hispanic students in comparison to African-Americans, Mexicantown in Southwest Detroit provided a training ground for alternative skills to relieve the pressure of long-term poverty and bad behavior.

Then MSG Kerns explained that girls from Muslim families left home for school in their traditional dress and changed into regular street clothes in abandoned houses along the way to school. They did this so they could fit in with their classmates and not be gawked at in the classroom. Once the school day ended, the reverse would happen, and they would change back to traditional outfits as they headed home. In my observation, I saw that many Muslim students had options for continuing their education. Many of their family members owned and operated local businesses, so education was secondary. I also learned that many of the Muslim girls were already promised or committed as a wife to someone, and that any particular day could be their last day as a high-school student.

THE COMFORT ZONE

In befriending the student body, MSG Kerns and SFC Anderson allowed students to use the JROTC office as a refuge from their personal problems. This was because many of the students were at-risk children and had no refuge at home, and some had no home at all. The Detroit of old was a place where employment opportunities were great and income levels high, but the downward spiral in the local economy had been devastating for current Detroiters. The Detroit News reported in 2014 and 2015, in several articles written by Karen Bouffard, that more children lived in poverty in Detroit than anywhere else in the United States.[42]

This extension of goodwill to the students was made with the understanding to all that the next day of class was not promised to them. The school administration and other teachers approved and encouraged this sanctuary because when the students with problems went to the JROTC office, they could teach students in their classroom the lesson for the day. This was both a good and a bad practice. The students had a sanctuary, but on the other hand, the JROTC curriculum could never be taught as a full benefit.

LACK OF CITIZENSHIP KNOWLEDGE

I found MSG Kerns' candor and experience at Chadsey High School to be genuine and insightful. It contributed to my knowledge base and growing perplexity. At my first school assembly, there was a tall African-American kid who did not stand for the national anthem. Instead of standing as requested, he chose to drape himself across a row of auditorium chairs. I promptly asked him to stand and he did so, slowly and reluctantly. He did not appear to be a threat, but he lacked a capacity for heritage and the learning environment. From this teacher-student encounter, I felt that this particular young man had little knowledge of his own citizenship, and obviously, no knowledge of the price others before him paid to obtain the promise of citizenship. During my school years, the preamble and the national anthem were practiced daily.

The incident made me feel kind of odd, because over the past twenty years I had encountered few African-American kids who acted in such a manner. The typical African-American children I had encountered were the sons and daughters of military personnel and were generally well-disciplined. Knowledge of the flag and what the flag symbolized, as well as how to behave at formal ceremonies, were practiced with pride as part of their lifestyle or regimen as students in the Department of Defense school system.

Lack of Investment in Parent-Teacher Conferences

I also found that Chadsey had difficulty getting parents to come to parent-teacher conferences, for whatever reason. The school administration tried very hard to get the parents or legal guardians to attend, but attendance was very weak. In contrast, schools in the district my children attended did not have a problem with parental participation. The conference was marketed as a community event with games and prizes, and in many cases, the whole family showed up. It was not unusual to see the mayor of the city sitting patiently in line to talk to the teachers of his own children.

Another concern in suburban versus urban schools was the grading system. A student who received an A grade in an urban school had really achieved a grade of C in the suburban school in an equivalent class. Many times in urban schools there were fewer resources and less time allocated to programmed class materials because of the family situations of the student body.

At a conference I attended at Chadsey one evening, I recall one African-American parent, a single mom, pleading with her son to do better in class. The young man had a grade-point average that was less than 2.0. He seemed like a very nice young man, but he was wearing $300 athletic shoes. His shoe money was higher than his grade-point average. The solution seemed simple: stop buying the young man expensive footwear and invest in a tutor, but of course, there is peer pressure, a school problem of its own. The schools in the suburbs had teenage identity issues also, but maybe the difference was that two parents participated in the academic process, and their professions and income levels allowed them flexibility to participate in school events and activities.

Heroes and Their Toys

MSG Kerns had mentored a lot of students over the years, and some had become successful in their chosen field. On occasion, those former students returned to Chadsey to visit. One such person was a young African-American male who was a career football player. The young man had gone on to attend the University of Colorado, where he made a famous last-minute, game-winning catch against the University of Michigan on a "Hail Mary" pass play from the quarterback in 1994.[43] He later turned professional and played in the National Football League.

With success come expensive toys, of course. His Hummer was parked outside the school with a few local buddies in it. Kerns probably should have made a proper introduction, since I was standing next to him, but these were his kids.

Student Investment

I thought extending common courtesy to all instructors was a personal attribute that successful people needed to display, especially on school grounds, so that any student in the vicinity could emulate it, and most especially in front of African-American males like the student who had sprawled across a row of auditorium chairs during the national anthem. But Kerns had already given me his opinion that the absence of a black male in the lives of black children had led to little respect shown to older black males as role models.

For many low-income students, professional sport is the way out of the neighborhood. A number of heroes found their success at the nearby Kronk Gym. Then there was the young man of perhaps Eastern European extraction who came to school with a broken nose from boxing. The young man said he could not go directly to the hospital because his father had to work. If the father missed work, the paycheck would be short that week. It was at least a week to ten days after the injury when the young man was finally seen by a doctor. In this type of situation, the JROTC staff was limited in what we could do. We just tried to keep a close watch on the student.

I remember that several male Hispanic students quit school during the middle of the semester to enroll in a professional wrestling program. I do not remember their names, but their aspiration was to be a part of the mega wrestling scene. There were also the Middle Eastern males who parked their cars on school grounds and illegally entered and exited the school through the JROTC room. Just like a cat caught eating the family pet parakeet, when confronted they would act as if they did not understand the language or what was going on. The Middle Eastern males were always asking, "Were you in the war and did you kill anybody?" I thought that was a topic best avoided.

The leader of this group thought he was physically fit, so I challenged him to a footrace while I was dressed in my Class B uniform. I had thirty years on him, and I still see him eating my dust. Of course, after a few feet, he conveniently pulled up lame. My point in this challenge was to show the younger person that I was fit and not a pushover, and I wanted to help him become a better student. This incident happened well before September 11, 2001, and since that day relationships between the US and Middle Eastern people have been strained.

Suburban Student Body

Student problems were not reserved for inner-city schools. Doing my best imitation of Sidney Poitier in *To Sir with Love*,[44] I also worked as a substitute teacher in my suburban district on occasion and had to referee a catfight during lunch between two white females apparently from the glamorous cast of the popular television show *Dynasty*.[45] I also had access to the teacher's lounge and often listened to what teachers had to say about their students. One teacher told a story of a female student informing the female teacher on what private part on her body her latest piecing was located.

I will tell you, I was a little shocked at how the other half lived. I thought this happened only on television. Nonetheless, I observed that the biggest environmental difference between the school systems was that the suburbs had paid security guards posted in security vehicles while the city had armed police with metal detectors and chained doors.

TAX DOLLARS

For the most part, my job in the military was accounting for military equipment. There is a great concern among government employees about being singled out pertaining to the safekeeping of government property versus the improprieties of waste, fraud, and abuse. At Chadsey, I quickly learned that taxpayer dollars were being wasted because of the lack of care and accountability for school property. I was sorry to see that uniforms and equipment from various sports were just tossed into a big pile in a room and not cared for in a manner that allowed the next group of students to use them.

Maybe that was just a bad day, but in comparison, at the school my daughters attended, the sports uniforms and equipment were neatly stacked and accounted for and ready for the next group. In the New Testament, Luke 19:11–27 infers the need to take care of the little things in order to prepare ourselves for taking care of the larger things.

THE PERK AND THE JERK OF JROTC ANNUAL BALL

At the end of the school year, the JROTC program hosted an annual military ball for the students in the DPS program at the local armory. The JROTC student could bring a guest of the opposite sex, because there was formal dining and appropriate ballroom dancing. As this was a military ball, military courtesy was expected. The JROTC schools also participated in a drill and ceremony competition.

The military ball was intended to provide the JROTC students with a fun evening and life experience to remember their contribution to a successful program. I attended the event as a member of the program cadre, and I thought the JROTC program was a fitting way for growing teens to have choices in their lives. I wished I had taken advantage of my opportunity as a student.

JROTC provided scholarships for students going to colleges and universities that parents might not have had a budget for. Nonetheless, the future of a child did not matter to one irate African-American parent who came to pick up his daughter and her date from the ball with a bad attitude and a loud mouth. It was in the second week of June 2000, and the basketball championship series was on television. The parent was extremely angry that he had to extract himself from his television set to pick up his daughter, because he was missing "Shaq, Kobe, and the Lakers" on the basketball court. It was quite evident he did not see this event as an opportunity for his daughter to excel. Instead, he was very vocal and vulgar on the premises. The daughter must have been embarrassed, because I was.

CADRE TRAINING

Later that same month, I got the opportunity to expand my knowledge of JROTC and its mission to teach citizenship at historic Fort Monroe, Virginia. I learned that Fort Monroe was the United States Army cadre barracks of Confederate General Robert E. Lee. It was also the place of incarceration for Jefferson Davis, the president of the Confederacy. Historically, the Lee family has been prominent in the growth and wealth of the colonial United States, including Kentucky. The surname, Davis is a Sept member of Clan Davidson.[46]

In August 2000, I left the JROTC program for a permanent position with the United States Army civilian workforce. Shortly thereafter, I read of the wide sweep of allegations brought against many people in authority at the DPS, including the release of the Chadsey principal. Notably, she came from a prominent African-American family, but she was relieved of her duties because of allegations of the misuse of DPS funds and equipment. It was a terrible thing to read, because it provided the students with just another negative image of a person of color.

As a soldier, I look on my time at Chadsey as a great opportunity to be associated with the next generation. As a performer, I learned about a music workshop hosted by jazz master Dr. Harold McKinney[47] from a musician and former Chadsey student. The workshop was held each week at the Detroit SerNgeti ballroom on Woodward Avenue. I was very appreciative of the information, and I went down and introduced myself to him. At the time, Dr. McKinney was recovering from major surgery, and the workshop was his way of giving back to the community. I began attending the workshop, and Dr. McKinney helped my voice and confidence go to another level.

I also worked with a voice coach at Marygrove College named Kim Streby. Kim was an opera vocalist and taught from an opera background. We worked well together. In celebration of Detroit's 300th birthday in June 2001, Kim and I put together a musical show at Marygrove College in conjunction with the many other events scheduled around the city. Unfortunately, we did not attract a huge crowd, but we gave a wonderful performance. My family helped me put on the show, and I was pumped. I knew I was on my way up the ladder.

A few weeks earlier, I'd tried to get Dr. McKinney to participate in the show, but with no luck. He, too, was working to host a showcase at the SerNgeti, which he expected his students to participate in. I was one of those students, but I did not have the opportunity to prepare myself to perform between my eight-hour job and my own show. I attended the showcase at SerNgeti, and I remember Dr. McKinney telling the crowd that there was another talent in the room that day who should have been on the stage but wasn't. I assume he was speaking of me because he was looking in my direction when he spoke.

After our show ended at Marygrove College, I could not wait to see Dr. McKinney at the next practice session and give him the good news. I gathered up my family for the drive home. I was ecstatic as I drove north on Livernois Avenue toward 8 Mile Road. As I passed the famous Baker's Keyboard Lounge located on the right-hand side of the street, I noticed a billboard that read "Rest in Peace, Jazz Master, Harold McKinney." This was unbelievable. I read that Dr. McKinney had slipped into a coma and died the previous day. He was gone, and perhaps my career as a vocalist was too. But I kept my aspirations and developed a live radio jazz recording at the Jazz Café at Music Hall hosted by Judy Adams[48] and a music video titled, "Rah! Rah! Detroit!/ Michigan Morn."[49]

The US Government: They Were Hiring That Day

You may recall from the first volume of this three-part series that in 1619, the first group of enslaved Africans to enter Jamestown harbor[50] actually became the first minorities or civil servants working for the provisional government, although the duties were surely limited in responsibility, pay, and freedom. In the 1970s, formal legislation opened job opportunities for minority employment. Government service has been a safe haven for African-American employment since the 1960s.[51]

There is a crazy scene in Keenen Ivory Wayans's 1988 movie spoof *I'm Gonna Git You Sucka*[52] where the young hero is seeking militant assistance from the community. He goes directly to the Black Power leader, as portrayed by actor Clarence T. Williams III, whose character has surely changed from a powerful radical with command over thousands to a homebody now married to Jan of *The Brady Bunch*.[53] When asked about his new lifestyle, he explains that one day he led thousands of angry brothers and sisters marching with arms to overturn the government for keeping his people poor, frustrated, and downtrodden. However, the march ended without a shot being fired. The black militant leader was asked, "How was that the case?" His response was that by chance the government was hiring that day, and all of the angry brothers and sisters were no longer angry. They all got hired.

During the summer of 2000, I rejoined the ranks of the government. A job opportunity opened up for me at the Detroit Arsenal, a logistics organization under the Department of Defense. As it happened, I had also been offered jobs by the US Post Office and the Federal Emergency Management Agency. However, I thought the Department of Defense offered a better opportunity for full-time employment and career progression.

My paternal cousin Doris Davidson McClain Porter had been a government employee in Detroit since the 1950s, prior to civil-rights legislation. During the 1970s, when the government recruited the African-American population from college campuses, she mentored many of the young African-American men and women who came to work there. She, too, came north from Rocky Hill, Kentucky, during the Negro migration.

Doris remembered growing up in the late 1940s and early 1950s on Detroit's eastside with members of Berry Gordy's family. The Gordy family was prominent and industrious because they owned and operated a construction business in the black community. Berry Gordy Jr. later founded the Motown Record Corporation. Recently, she mentioned that several of the Gordy siblings also worked at the Detroit Arsenal at one time or another during the 1950s.

For me, government work represented a good opportunity to have steady employment using the professional expertise I had acquired from the military and still work toward my aspirations. I was now working logistics as a civilian at the Arsenal of Democracy, home of the "little old lady in tennis shoes," the term that field soldiers use to describe the expeditiousness of the logistics support structure. I could support my family in the manner to which we were accustomed.

WAY UP HIGH

In early July 2001, I represented the Michigan Chapter of the NSA at the national convention in Dallas, Texas. I was a bit nervous, of course. On the plane, I spotted a prominent female chapter member who owned and operated a booking agency. She was also heading to the convention with her lovely daughter. She elected to let her daughter ride in first class while she rode in coach. I knew her only slightly from the chapter meetings, but I had begun to learn that marketing your skills every chance you get is part of being successful.

The plane had taken off and then leveled off above 30,000 feet. I practiced my drop-dead song and mustered enough nerve to go back to the rear of the cabin to sing for her, even though the flight attendants had just begun to serve. I had to treat this awkward opportunity as an audition. I saw myself singing, so I got down on one knee in the middle of the aisle and sang "The Twelfth of Never." The people in the vicinity seemed to enjoy my performance.

When we arrived in Dallas, we shared public transportation to our separate lodging, and I serenaded the ladies as we rode along. It was a great opportunity to perform, and what I learned was that I can carry a note even at 30,000 feet. In reality, I did much better with my serenade in the sky than I did representing the chapter at the convention.

AUDITION

Since August 2000, I had performed the national anthem at a number of formal ceremonies held on the Detroit Arsenal. If you do not know it, I will tell you that "The Star-Spangled Banner"[54] is the only song that if a word or line is missed, everybody in the room knows it. There have been many beautiful renditions by the likes of Robert Merrill, Marvin Gaye, Whitney Houston, and a long list of others. On the other hand, there is another notorious list of those who did not meet the patriotic challenge of performing the national anthem, including Carl Lewis and Roseanne Barr.[55]

Sometime in late July 2001, I learned that the Philadelphia Eagles were holding auditions at their training camp for participants to sing the national anthem for the upcoming football season. Fresh off my grand performance at 30,000 feet, I loaded my family into the van, and we headed off to Pennsylvania for the audition on Saturday, August 4, 2001. We arrived early in the morning, but still there were a lot of people waiting for their opportunity. After my audition was over, we decided to continue on to New York City to spend the weekend there. It was only a couple of hours away and my family was all for it, so away we went.

New York City: An Unforgettable Weekend

This would be the first time I had visited New York City since 1964 with my Aunt Rubye, her husband James, and my brother Glen. It was a beautiful summer day. As we got closer to the city, I did not want to get lost, so I used the driving directions I'd mapped out. What the map did not tell me was that the traffic heading toward the Holland Tunnel would be bumper to bumper, and we would have to sit for about an hour looking at cars. Slowly we made our way through the tunnel, and yes, we got lost. I made a quick right turn, and there I was in the shadow of a maze of tall buildings.

I drove around these buildings for a number of minutes before I realized I was in the Wall Street district and the shadow cast over us belonged to the Twin Towers of the World Trade Center.[56] I saw Battery Park on a street sign, and I followed the directions on the sign. The sign took me to Pier 17, a place in Lower Manhattan off the riverfront where we found hundreds of tourists shopping, dining, and enjoying the day. I found a parking spot, and we spent the evening scouring the area until we went to our lodging. The next day, the weather was even warmer and more wonderful, so we spent hours walking the Manhattan streets and taking in more New York sights. In Central Park, we watched an organized league baseball game with teams that appeared to be composed of policemen and firefighters. Baseball is my passion, and I wish I'd have had the opportunity to play with them that day.

This short weekend trip produced a lot of great memories that will live in our minds forever. We took off for home early that Monday morning, August 6, 2001. Daybreak was coming over the island of Manhattan as we came out of the Holland Tunnel and headed down on the Interstate in New Jersey. It was a magnificent view as the sun's rays bounced off all the buildings in the concrete jungle. As in all of our family journeys, the girls were all asleep: my wife slumbered in the front and my daughters were crashed out in the back. I was awake and alone, sitting behind the wheel making good time down the highway on this early morn. I kept looking back at the Twin Towers standing tall in the morning sunlight. I promised myself that I would return to visit New York City again in the near future and be once again in the shade of the Twin Towers.

New York City: An Unforgettable Day

It was Tuesday, September 11, 2001.[57] A little more than a month had passed since the wonderful trip to New York City that my family still reminisces about. I was on duty at my computer terminal thinking about my next performance opportunity when a fellow worker's cell phone rang. It was the fellow's wife informing him of a breaking news story pertaining to a plane flying into one of the Twin Towers. He responded, "You're kidding me!"

I thought nothing of his private conversation, just thought of how I was just there under the shadow of the Twin Towers not so long ago. *The towers are okay*, I figured. *It must be the weather.* I thought it would not be too unusual, because I had read an article where a small plane accidentally flew into the Empire State Building in the 1940s as a result of bad weather.[58] I said to myself, *The weather was probably bad.*

Then the floodgates opened. The people on duty where I was located began to connect to news outlets via their computer, television, or calls from home. We were aghast. A few minutes later, the same worker's cell phone rang again; it was his wife. He answered and then shouted out, "You're shittin' me!" His wife had reported that a second plane had flown into the second tower. This was unbelievable.

The dazed people in my office were now glued to television and computer screens. A few minutes later, the shadow of the Twin Towers was no longer, and the federal workforce stood in astonishment. That wonderful weekend in New York City became permanently etched in memory, but now we were at war with an unknown enemy. I cannot help but wonder how many of the police officers and firemen who played baseball that day in Central Park were lost a few weeks later in the Twin Towers. Shortly after, the local workforce was asked to quickly but quietly return to their homes until further notice.

LEARNING TO BUILD A FINANCIAL PLAN

Over the years, I learned that successful organizations and family units understand their finances. After I left a successful career in the military, I returned home hoping to help my family members, mother, father, sister, and in-laws have an easier life using the knowledge I'd acquired. I was rebuked. I quickly found that it did not matter what I'd learned; their way of doing or believing was the status quo, especially in matters of finance. My input conflicted with the way personal business had been conducted in my parents' household for years, pouring more cement into the foundation of the Bible passage from the New Testament, Matthew 13:57, Mark 6:4, and John 4:44, "A prophet is not a prophet in his own home." In my mother's house, it seemed that the person down the street or around the corner had more knowledge or more talent than any member of her household. Perhaps it was fear of success; no matter, it was very disappointing.

I also mentioned that my academic standing in high school provided me with limiting credentials to become anything except a lifelong blue-collar laborer. Over the course of twenty years, I greatly improved my educational status, knowledge base, and credentials in several professional disciplines. From the standpoint of a husband and a son, I was under the impression that the purpose of education was to improve the quality of life for the family unit. In training to become a financial planner, I studied and worked long hours to obtain my state license and work with a local financial company. I sought to make my family's life easier by learning the real rules of the financial game and not just hearsay, speculation or envy.

I recall inviting my financial trainer to my parents' house for the purpose of training me as part of obtaining my license and informing my parents of a path to financial freedom. What a disappointing day! I was hurt by my mother's apathy toward my developing skill as a financial planner. As my training was taking place, my mother read the paper and drank her morning coffee instead of being attentive. My father was attentive, but his limited education and lack of authority got in the way.

I discovered that this apathetic attitude is prevalent throughout my ethnic community. As I conveyed in my academic work, there are a select few persons in positions of perceived authority that are given the full attention of an ethnic audience. This observation makes a person wonder: why does the black community send children off to schools of higher learning to acquire skills and information that are met with great resistance in the home and community when the children return with knowledge and ideas applicable for change? When you have the tools, the days of protests marches are over.

Nevertheless, I used what I learned as a financial planner to bring knowledge to the lives of my wife and daughters that placed them on successful economic paths. In reflection, I would guess that my mother was too embarrassed to talk about the family finances she'd taken charge of, and my father simply lacked the knowledge. This observation proved to be true some ten years later when my mother passed away suddenly, leaving my father with many unanswered questions pertaining to family finances, including my mother's final resting place. Sadly, the remembrance of a wonderful life became a financial nightmare and debt creator for those remaining among the living.

THE GROWTH PROCESS: THE STUDENT BECOMES A DOCTOR

Opportunity does knock twice. I worked for years to overcome my high-school academics. During my military career, I was able to upgrade my academic and professional credentials, illustrating my potential to move into the white-collar field. At that point, I thought my formal learning career was over. Sometime later, in 2002, I was sitting at my computer terminal engaged in my assigned duties in support of the national defense when there was news I could use sent in an e-mail message.

The e-mail announced the planned visit to the Detroit Arsenal by representatives from the University of Phoenix (UOP).[59] The visit was to discuss educational programs at both the bachelor and graduate level. I continued reading through the message and found that one of the programs available at UOP was a doctoral program in the discipline of management. I felt good about the overview of the program in the message, and I thought this notice to be an unbelievable second opportunity.

The day of the seminar, I was right there in attendance. I listened to the University of Phoenix representative as she spoke about the educational offerings. I was ready to be accepted into the program and to get started. I mentioned several times that I never seemed to win contests of any sort. Well, at the end of the presentation, I won the door prize: a University of Phoenix book bag that I still have and use daily.

Winning the door prize was an omen that things were looking up. I submitted all of the required paperwork, including my essay on leadership. I chose to discuss why the mayor of Detroit at the time, Kwame Kilpatrick, should not wear an earring while performing his elected duties. (Sadly, the former mayor is now serving a lengthy sentence in federal prison for public corruption.[60]) A few short weeks later, the mailman came with a letter from the university. The letter, addressed to "Mr. Wayne R. Davidson," read, "We are pleased to inform you that you have been accepted to the University of Phoenix." Unbelievable! I was accepted into the doctoral program. It was only eight years earlier I'd applied to five doctoral programs seeking qualified African-Americans candidates and been rejected by each. But I played the game! I waited patiently, and now I was accepted into a bona fide doctoral program.

However, I was now in uncharted waters. One slip and I could drown. The first academic requirement was a letter of thanks to the person or "unsung hero" the student thought was most influential in helping him get to this point. I wrote my letter to SFC Donald G. Smith—the person who encouraged me to "play the game"—but the letter was undeliverable. I have not seen or spoken to SFC Smith since the 1980s. I still have the letter to deliver if I ever locate him.

I immediately went to work on learning the course materials as I also learned to become a better student. This was an online environment, and the library materials were at my fingertips. Many of my classmates were professional people with incomes and material resources that varied between great and small. In comparison, my income was small, and I needed to budget both my time and money. I turned down a fast-track promotion to maintain focus on the new challenge of program.

I quickly found that doctoral work was no walk in the park, from the reading to the writing and the arithmetic. One morning while in the city of Phoenix for my residency class, I took a trip over to Camelback Mountain[61] and started my way up. It was a tough climb up the mountain, but I made it far enough to where I could survey the topographical terrain forever. During my climb, I also saw that there was opportunity as far as my eyes could see. So when I climbed down and headed off to class, I knew I had to make up for any shortage of material resources by increasing my physical attributes. What I tried to do better than anyone else was to be observant and be a better listener. I believed the use of these attributes would help me become a better student and classmate.

BLOWING A MENTAL TIRE

I remembered from my master's program that Dr. Wheeler once informed me that doctoral students can blow out a "mental tire" very easily because of the stiff academic requirements, especially in the field of science and mathematics. He continued to explain that on occasion, doctoral students have assaulted and killed their professors and then subsequently committed suicide, primarily because the rejection of their work caused a mental blowout. This was astonishing to me, but not long after Dr. Wheeler's comments several incidents involving serious altercations in student–professor relations at the doctoral level were broadcast over the news.

Yes, I found the stress level to be high. But I think the discipline I learned in my military career and karate kept me on an even keel until my final exams. That discipline was needed in 2004. I thought I was going to lose it when one of my exams did not pass muster. I could feel my mental tire wobble. I questioned why I was in the program. I did not know anything; my father did not talk and my mother did not listen, a great combination for not knowing anything. The air in the mental tire was escaping fast.

I thought I had let my family down and placed them in great debt. My classmate from Mexico gave me a special-edition bottle of tequila that he and his family had planned to celebrate with so I could drown my sorrow. I had driven to Phoenix from Detroit alone, and I had grand plans to celebrate in Las Vegas upon completion of my exams. Instead, I went to Las Vegas driving through a vast desert with the saddest and longest look on my face. My vision was blurred. Along the way, I passed through the Grand Canyon, the Hoover Dam, and Lake Mead, but at each landmark my anxiety and regret went even higher. I seriously thought I should become part of one of the three monuments. Once I reached Las Vegas, there was no celebration. I stayed out of the bright lights in a local hotel overnight trying to figure it out.

I did not talk to my parents. I had talked to my wife several times during this time period, but I think the phone call that helped me the most was when I spoke to my friend Frank Garcia, a member of the Motown Hall of Fame, as I drove through the desert. Frank had health problems and was recovering. He provided me with mentorship on what a good person I was and how I was an inspiration to him during his recovery period. From our conversation, I felt better, and I found that I had the right stuff. I just needed to get moving to fulfill the requirement. My anxiety started to go down, and the "If/Then" Rule began to kick in. *If* I get off my ass, *then* I can get some help.

The next morning, I headed back to Phoenix seeking help. This time as I passed along Lake Mead, the Hoover Dam, and the Grand Canyon, the view from the desert road was not as gloomy and I did not want to be part of the monuments. When I arrived back at Phoenix, all of the other students had left, but I felt the environment to be better. I did speak with a professor for a few minutes, and he provided me with encouragement.

I sat in my room to formulate a plan of action, and then I put that plan into motion to complete the requirement. In all honesty, my biggest fear at the time was being unsuccessful with my requirement for a second time. However, a second shot of encouragement from my classmates helped me overcome that fear. A few weeks later, I learned that my examination passed muster, and now I could move on with the program full speed ahead. The seal on the premium bottle of tequila remains unbroken to date.

I felt good, but my program challenges were not over yet. I still had to complete my dissertation. In perspective, the research topic of a dissertation should be based on an interest. For instance, if the writer had the power to change the world, what topic would the writer bring to the world's attention and why? I had an opportunity to live in different places around the world and observe their lifestyles. The local people owned homes and businesses that provided economic foundations to their communities, and I had an interest in knowing why.

MY ACADEMIC TOPIC: HOW I WOULD CHANGE THE WORLD

My first significant ponder in how I would change the world through academics happened on a sightseeing trip to Texas and the San Antonio waterfront in the mid-1990s. I was walking along among the crowd when I saw an industrious African-American boy between the ages of seven and ten standing along the side of the thoroughfare selling candy. I was impressed by the boy's initiative, but I was concerned that he was not dressed for the part of salesman. His attire reflected great poverty rather than success. I do not recall making a purchase that day, but a picture of him is still vivid in my mind. Why? Because I wanted to help the young man and others who looked like him to succeed, but I could not that particular day.

In Spike Lee's 1989 movie of social consciousness, *Do the Right Thing,*[62] there is a scene where three black dudes are sitting on the corner having an eyeball contest with the police. Slowly, the police move on, and as that confrontation decreases, another one increases. One of the staring men notices that the Korean business across the street is thriving in a black neighborhood and angrily addresses the question of why there aren't any black businesses in a black neighborhood. I, too, often wondered why black businesses did not operate in the neighborhood where I grew up.

Additionally, I found that there was very little knowledge in other ethnic communities about the existence or history of African-American businesses as owners and operators versus their status as consumers. This lack of knowledge first came to me from a fellow Toastmaster, who was Jewish. He told me that he applauded my topic, and then roughly told me that the Jewish community has struggles too. Many Jewish people have come to this country with nothing only to end up building great economic foundations that helped their community thrive, and he thought black people should be able to do that too!

What I learned from the few minutes we spent together was that both he and I had no prior knowledge of African-American business. Later,

I interviewed for a position with a high-ranking government official who was responsible for encouraging small-business owners from all classes to compete for government contracts. She stated with candor that there were less than a few black-owned businesses in the open marketplace competing for government contracts, especially in the fields of science and technology. This interview took place after I formally completed my academic work. But, in my mind, the topic of African-American businesses could change the world, beginning with the United States government.

I began my research with the history of African-American businesses and their business philosophy in the Detroit metropolitan area. I discovered that to access and assess the pulse of the African-American business community, I would need to join a professional group: the Booker T. Washington Business Association.[63] Through research, I found this organization had been of service to the community since the days of Hastings Street and Paradise Valley as far back as the 1920s.

At two separate association gatherings, I had the opportunity to sit and speak with Mr. Edgar Brazelton.[64] Mr. Brazelton was a longtime florist who had been an advocate of African-American business for many years. The gentleman represented and led the cause of African-American businesses at the state legislature, and I was inspired by his historical knowledge. Sadly, shortly before I started the project, Mr. Brazelton passed on.

I pressed on with my quest because it had real value because of merchants like Mr. Brazelton. I was met with stiff resistance in getting started and a lot more resistance during my data-collection phase. From my initial perspective, I quickly found that black business owners are basically a closed group. I tried not to take it personally, because the resistance I encountered could be because they had to protect their business interests from those who did not want them to be successful. I had already learned that none of this academic stuff was easy.

I had few volunteers, but I interviewed select members who owned and operated businesses because I was able to get some welcome assistance from a longtime member who was a retired lawyer, Sharon Bernard, Esq. Without her help, the project would have never been completed. I learned a great deal from the experience. I found that there are a small number of successful African-Americans business owners, but that number was going to remain small because not everyone was prepared to invest the time and resources necessary to be successful. My data collection truly expanded my knowledge base. It netted me the written history of black business and the oral history of local African-American business owners.

I often attended meetings, but I felt it was more of a social experience than a learning experience. I soon learned that black business does play a large role in the community. The late Don Barden, CEO of the association, introduced the Rev. Jesse L. Jackson to a small audience, of which I was part. Before that day, I had never been in the presence of Rev. Jackson.

I was there speaking to a state official, a black female, about why African-American males have a difficult time in school and beyond. Ironically, Rev. Jackson began his oratory about the same topic and spoke about the plight of African-American males. His oratory was eloquent, poignant, and succinct, and he left the meeting with a sizeable contribution from the business community for his social cause that would be ultimately doubled by the late Mr. Barden. I left the meeting with the same topic but without any generous gifts. Today, I still recall the experience of his voice ringing in my ears, and I have a clearer of understanding of the real world—celebrity status brings lots of gifts.

No matter; all through this academic process, it was the power of prayer that got me through without blowing a mental tire and provided me with the required resources. When I needed mentorship, I prayed and it came. When I needed material resources, I prayed and they came. I prayed without ceasing, and the desired outcome was a completed academic work entitled *Manufacturing African American Self-Employment in the Detroit Metropolitan Area*.

THE DISNEYLAND THEORY: DETROIT TIGERS FANTASY CAMP

"God, I love baseball!" professed Roy Hobbs, the character portrayed by Robert Redford in the 1984 movie *The Natural*,[65] and so do I. When speaking of dreams, my dream of playing baseball was rekindled. Throughout my army career, I played softball on several organized teams. The play was competitive. I also encouraged and coached my daughters. Remember, they earned their letterman sports jackets.

After the season ended in 2002, my reward from the team I coached was a gift card to a local restaurant. It turned out the establishment was frequented by a local rap artist named Eminem, who sat a few tables away with five to seven people. His presence at the table and the large luxury SUV in the parking lot did cause a slight commotion among the staff and guests. A short time later, I saw him perform on television during a prestigious musical event. I guess dining with famous people is just one of the perks of coaching at any level.

In 2003, I had the opportunity of a lifetime to participate in the Detroit Tigers Fantasy Camp[66] in Lakeland, Florida. I loved it so much that I attended for six straight years and then returned after a four year hiatus. The camp is sponsored by the Detroit Tigers organization and is open to baseball fans, especially fans of the Detroit ball club. The camp director and founder, Jerry Lewis, is a fantastic person and has a knack for catering to the wants and needs of each person. I remember him giving me two premium tickets to a Detroit Tigers game where my wife sat in the stands on one side of home plate and I sat on the other. His co-founder was Jim Price, a former Detroit Tiger player turned radio announcer, who I called "Mr. Wow." Jim was kind enough to stop by my workplace and visit with me and several of my co-workers to talk baseball one afternoon when he was in the area. I felt the personal treatment was equivalent to being courted by a college or professional team and the tickets sealed the deal. Wow!

THE ROOKIE RIDE TO TIGERTOWN

The rookie luncheon is traditionally held at Comerica Park on the second Friday in January, and that's where the fantasy-camp experience begins. At the luncheon, rookies, veterans, and their friends and families can rub elbows with former major leaguers and share their experience of the training facility in Florida. The following Sunday, after a flight to Tampa, Florida, the troupe of players both old and young scoop up their gear from the airport baggage claim and head out the door to the transportation lot for the bus ride to Lakeland about an hour east on Interstate 4. Many of the veterans had rental cars, while rookies like me rode the bus. I quietly sat down to take in the sights on a beautiful January day in the Sunshine State. Our driver was a senior citizen who was familiar with the Florida roads, and sooner than expected we were in front of the motel, the winter home of the Detroit Tigers. I got my luggage and then went to my room, where I met my roommate, a Tiger fan from Canada.

After formal introduction of players and campers at the sponsoring hotel, I found myself back on the bus heading toward Joker Marchant Stadium. The ride over was a bit tricky, but our driver maneuvered the bus well along the narrow roadway. Then he suddenly made a right turn that I will never forget, as the sign on the side of the road read "Tigertown." I had waited a million years to see that sign and these pearly gates. The next week turned into pure heaven.

In this heaven, the campers use the same facilities at Tigertown that members of the major-league club use. The feeling is that the fantasy club members really open up the baseball season for the Detroit Tigers for the coming year. The campers test out the locker room, the ball fields, the bars, and the girls (just kidding!) before the major-league players get there. Strangely, I have been mistaken for a former Detroit Tiger when I am at camp, which is an extra boost to my ego. Perhaps it is because of my demeanor, but there is an adage in career management of *fake it until you make it.*

Despite the disparity in skill level, the camp becomes a team-building opportunity both on and off the baseball diamond. The environment of the professional athlete and the lifelong fan melts encouragement and comradery into a union. As a result, an appreciation and awareness of social issues is gained as campers open their wallets to charity.

THE BIG-LEAGUE LOCKER ROOM

It was fantastic that the fantasy-club members had the opportunity to sit and converse with their heroes from days gone by. There were members of both the 1968 and 1984 Detroit Tigers championship teams, and other players who gave their best to bring a championship to the city. These former heroes would tell their story and then coach the campers in the baseball fundamentals to improve their game. Over the years, the names on the back of jerseys included Kaline, Horton, Lolich, Brown, Hiller, Warden, Wert, Price and Harwell then there was Brookens, Trammell, Whitaker, Tracewski, Kuntz, Grubb, Allen, Billingham, Wilcox, Petry, Evans, Bair and more, Tanana, Terrell, Kemp, Palmer, Rozema, Leach, Thompson, Monroe, Maroth, Cuyler, Jones, Zumaya, Blessitt, and Wood. I respect each former Detroit Tiger for contributing to my personal growth. Therefore, I call each one I come in contact with "Coach," no matter his celebrity status, because I am there ready to receive the knowledge that they impart from their own personal or professional experience.

I would have to say without a doubt that the greatest thing in the world is to walk into a major-league locker room and wander around. The next thing would be to stop and stand in front of a locker with your last name etched on the top of it. The grandest of all is to reach into the same locker and touch a major-league baseball uniform with your last name, "Davidson," embroidered on the back over your favorite number. It is beyond belief.

Another fantastic feeling is to have your photo taken by a professional photographer that is then placed on a major-league baseball card that you can autograph and give to folks to admire and as a form of communication. To date, there is only one person who did not admire the personal experience—my supervisor at the time, which is probably why I rejected his mentorship. (I should have followed Zig Ziglar's philosophy, which in summary was to only share personal goals that you want to give up instead of goals that move you to another level of success. People have a bad habit of shooting down activities that make you different from them.) Finally, it is simply wonderful to see your name on a major-league contract, even though the salary was only one cent. It was well earned. The life of a fantasy leaguer is magnificent!

When I attended my first camp in 2003, it was the thirty-fifth celebration of the 1968 championship team. If you recall, I was at that pennant-clinching game against the New York Yankees, and I was one of the crazy fans who ran onto the field sliding into bases and ripping up grass. Remember, that film is on display at the National Baseball Hall of Fame in Cooperstown and it plays continuously, so I am technically in the National Baseball Hall of Fame. Somewhere in that film I am chasing after Al Kaline crossing home plate and then sliding into second base among thousands of people.

Now, thirty-five years later, many of my heroes from that game are in regular attendance at the camp: Willie Horton, Gates Brown, Mickey Lolich, and of course, Tiger great Al Kaline. Each player takes a few moments to reflect on his own life and how the game of baseball provided him with the opportunity to earn a living and live his passion. I learn something new every time I go.

I learned recently that I lived around Willie Horton for years without knowing it. In the 1950s, Willie grew up in the Jeffries Projects and attended Poe Elementary School.[67] I, too, lived in the Jeffries Projects for about two years in the late 1950s before moving to Cleveland, Ohio. After school ended for the summer in June 1959, in the same time frame, Willie hit a mammoth home run to right field at Tiger Stadium as a sixteen-year-old teenager.[68] I also attended Poe Elementary School. As a kid of six or seven years old, I probably saw Willie Horton every day heading off to a baseball field toward his destiny. Willie Horton is now honored by decree of the Michigan legislature. Every October 18 is decreed "Willie Horton Day in Michigan and his baseball image captured in a bronze statue that sits beyond the outfield grass of Comerica Park in Detroit. During his playing days, Willie Horton was the neighbor of soul singers Marvin Gaye and Aretha Franklin in Northwest Detroit, a few miles from my parents' home.[69]

Now it was 2003, and the roles were reversed. It is the camper with the opportunity to be the hero and the former Detroit Tiger the fan. For eight straight days, my fellow campers and I hit the baseball diamond. We swung the bats hard, made the plays in the field, and, yes, we were dog-tired. After losing our first game, my team picked up the pace and went on to win the first week's championship game. We were coached by Milt Wilcox and Gates Brown, and once again there was one big mess of folks hugging each other at second base. It was great, but I learned that becoming a champion at any endeavor does not come easy. It takes a plan, a little talent, a lot of desire, and a lot of luck.

I remember coming to the plate in one game with the bases loaded and then striking out in front of my heroes. I was embarrassed and a little dejected because I had just let my team down. On the other hand, baseball is a strange game, and it is generally played with a full nine-inning approach. For instance, take my coach Milt Wilcox, a former major-league pitcher who came within one out of pitching a perfect game. That one hit stepped between Milt and baseball immortality. For a baseball pitcher, a perfect game means that the minimum twenty-seven batters come to the plate and each batter is retired by the pitcher. After the hit, Milt may have lost the opportunity for baseball greatness, but he was still a hero in the midst of adversity. He gathered himself and maintained his composure to get the last out to preserve a Tiger team victory.

Later in 1984, Milt Wilcox and Willie Hernandez pitched the Detroit Tigers into the 1984 World Series. I was there. One sad note that first year at camp in 2003 is that the campers stood on the baseball diamond awaiting the pass-over of the Space Shuttle *Columbia*, but we soon got word that the shuttle had blew up in flight to Cape Canaveral, Florida.[70]

"LINE DRIVE DOWN THE THIRD-BASE LINE, FAIR BALL!"

I did my best to maintain my composure. In the very next inning, I came up again with the bases loaded. I put my focus on the pitch and then I smoked a line drive past the third baseman down the left-field line that cleared the bases. Now I had a big foot on second base and a big smile on my face. I was the hero for the moment, and I was ecstatic.

After our half of the inning was over, I trotted over to the water fountain to get a drink of water. Suddenly, a hand reached out to me, another hand patted my back, and a familiar voice cheered, "Way to go, Big Guy!" It was Al Kaline congratulating me on my big hit. I remember jumping out of the right-field stands at Tiger Stadium in 1968 and running to congratulate him when he crossed the plate with the winning run, but he had long gone into the dugout by the time I got there. Now thirty-five years later, Al Kaline was congratulating *me*. Although this baseball camp was clearly a fantasy, my statistics for the 2003 fantasy-camp season were a dream. I had a .430 batting average and got a number of accolades from my coaches, Gates Brown and Milt Wilcox, for being a good teammate and player. Over the course of a week, each camper is enthusiastically recognized for participation, no matter the skill level or physical limitations, with priceless mementoes. I finally earned my letterman sports jacket, and I wear it all the time. I also learned that Gates Brown for years only lived a few short miles from my parents' home.

In 2011, I had the opportunity to appear in the opening shot of the Detroit Tigers weekly program on the Fox Detroit television channel.[71] Jennifer Wagner, my work associate, was able to slow down the footage frame by frame, providing me with a powerful sequence of my flawed pitching motion. There are few African-American campers, but I completed my tenth year of participating, and I entered the camp's Hall of Fame in 2015. So let it be known there are many ways to make it to the big leagues. I got there through fantasy camp. Opportunity does come twice.

The Star-Spangled Banner

Working for a government agency, I have on occasion volunteered or been asked to sing the national anthem at formal ceremonies. I am thankful for the opportunity, so I do the best job I can with what I got. When I began attending the fantasy camp in Lakeland, Florida, each year, I would perform the national anthem at the celebrity game at Joker Marchant Stadium. In reality, I wanted to be the first ever to sing the national anthem and then immediately come up to the plate after the words "play ball" and hit a home run over the left-field fence. Once I was introduced as a camper, I would peel off from the other campers and head for the back of home plate to await my introduction as the singer of the national anthem. I would use those few minutes during the player introduction to prepare myself to sing.

At the celebrity game, there is a nice crowd of a hundred people or more, and I thought I did a good job each year. However, one year the performance did not go so well after my coach, broadcaster and former Detroit Tiger Rod Allen, called me out of my trance to ask a question about some team business. I answered the question but I lost my silent preparation time. I started the first two lines and forgot the third. Luckily, I turned and saw broadcaster Jim Price and Peggy Thompson, an executive for the Detroit Tigers, singing in key, and as a result I was able to recover and finish up nicely. When I left the field, I told Jerry Lewis that I'd had an equipment malfunction, like Justin Timberlake and Janet Jackson's wardrobe malfunction at Super Bowl XXXVIII in 2004.[72] Coach Rod Allen redeemed himself with some fine hitting tips in 2015.

On Sunday, May 22, 2005, I had the opportunity to sing the national anthem at Comerica Park in Detroit. The game featured the

Detroit Tigers against the Arizona Diamondbacks.[73] This had to be destiny, because I got the call on Friday night and the next day my good neighbor gave me four first-class infield box tickets right behind home plate. I was able to take my wife and two of my daughters. Les Brown was right: if you are good at something, people with resources come right out of the woodwork to help.

There were 23,124 fans in attendance, and yes, I was nervous. I was met by the club representative, Eric Bayless, who chuckled when I provided him with my introduction. In reflection, it was a little bit over the top. With that out of the way, we walked under the stadium stands down in what I call the "Aretha Franklin Room" or the celebrity room to practice before I went out onto the field. Yes, I was still nervous, but I was prepared.

The weather was beautiful leading up to game time, but suddenly the sky opened up with a downpour of rain just minutes before I was supposed to begin. The rain caused the game to be delayed three hours and fourteen minutes. How do you like that? My big chance, and it was literally raining on my parade. What should I do, forget about it and just go home? I spotted Detroit Tigers president and general manager Dave Dombrowski pacing about. I knew I had to be patient and professional. If I packed up my voice and left, I would never get a chance to sing for the Detroit Tigers again. So I waited the three hours and fourteen minutes, and I went out there onto the field and gave them the best performance I could give. Afterward, I had a number of autograph-seekers as I sat in my comfortable seat.

I saw myself being successful in my performance, and I was. This was ironic, because more than twenty-five years ago, I was sitting in the bleachers of Tiger Stadium in solitude and despair. But today, as baseball's Bob Uecker would sum it up, "I am in the front row," a 180-degree turnaround from sitting in the bleachers in despair to singing to the crowd at home plate with great pride. In addition, when attending a game, I have two options: I can roam about the outfield area where the statues of the Detroit Tigers immortals to include Al Kaline and Willie

Horton reside, or I can sit up in the club with the championship trophies, because after a long journey I discovered I was a champion too!

The camp is life-changing. After my first year, I had a LASIK (laser-assisted in situ keratomileusis)[74] procedure on my eyes with the thought of improving my hitting. Well, my batting average stayed the same, but my self-esteem went up. My nearsightedness was corrected, and it felt like I could see a mile away without glasses. Despite the bantering of the game, I learned that baseball culture is an optimism community. If a particular goal is not reached today, the belief system understands there is a tomorrow.

Proud Parents

I was proud of my performance and grateful for the opportunity. Nonetheless, the proudest moment in my Detroit Tigers history was in 2006 when my daughter Treasure worked as a temporary hire during the Tigers' drive toward the playoffs. Representing the ball club during the baseball playoffs, she stood on the outfield grass with the color guard during the rendering of the flag ceremony that included a military jet flyover. My wife and I were very proud and teary-eyed because it seemed that Treasure's many years as a military brat and the discipline of school band showed. She stood tall and straight in front of 40,000 fans in the stands and the worldwide audience.

Since her birth, Treasure has always been aggressive in obtaining her goals. I recall the time I went to pick her up from a high-school dance at a school with a predominately white student body. After the dance, she rushed out from the school, jumped in the back of my car, and proclaimed that next year she was going to be elected Homecoming Queen. I looked in my rearview mirror and became a little afraid. She looked possessed, like something right out of the movie *The Exorcist.*[75] The only thing missing was her head spinning around.

As I said, Treasure is not shy about working toward her goals, and this goal was no different. Treasure worked and worked all year on her campaign to make that happen, but sadly she fell short. Instead of being elected Homecoming Queen, Treasure was elected Homecoming Princess, which was also quite an achievement given the demographics of the student body.

SHHH! THE SOUND OF SILENCE

I grew up in the shadow of people who were able to display their great talents in their field of endeavor. They often went on to earn a comfortable living and world acclaim using their gift with the encouragement of their family support structure. For example, the foundation of Ben Wallace's successful career as a professional basketball player with a championship ring was the investment his family support structure made in developing his dreams and aspirations.[76] In contrast, personal dreams and aspirations in my family ran second to obtaining and maintaining a job. The purpose of a job was to earn a few pennies and keep a person out of jail. As a result, whatever talents I possessed as an individual person at the time were not recognized or unknown to the family structure. Most of the time, my siblings and I were quickly silenced with a "Shhh!" from my mother when we made the attempt to practice an undertaking. Why? I think because the euphoria of the church is where my mother spent her time, and she had a pessimistic view of the world. She loved that old-time religion, but it was always somebody else who was blessed.

I think it was that same narrow view that made her fearful in day-to-day life rather than understanding that Genesis 5:2 states that everyone was blessed by God. I learned that squashing one's ability to express himself generated very few ideas and or talents. Remember the message of Matthew 25:14–30, the parable of the talents: "If you don't use your gifts, you lose your gifts."

I remember my mother once stated that my siblings and I did not have talent. I was shaken by that assertion, because as I matured I learned that the protected environment did not allow us to develop whatever talent we possessed. My mother was a kindhearted person who

I believe was shaped both by the fear of fear and the fear of success. I think her fear of fear was developed from real events in her life. I believe my mother had a fear of success among members of her own family because it meant change in the family unit that she did not control; it seemed all right for the people down the street to have this or have that, but not us. Despite the constrained atmosphere, I feel good about my achievements and providing an environment for my offspring that is open to expression, growth, and development. From this contrast in environment, I learned that talent, training, and taking the opportunity—the 3Ts—are important in expression.

DEACON SO-AND-SO

I believe life is good and that life is also too short; therefore, I believe life should be lived. That is why I have always tried to share my experiences of good fortune and misfortune with friends and family who cared to listen. I enjoy mementos that can be put on display to show achievement and experience, or just serve as a conversation piece. I believed the mementos, no matter how quaint, are priceless because of the experience itself.

As I said before, my parents have always hosted warm gatherings at the family home on Pinehurst Street to celebrate special occasions. My mother was an exceptional cook, and my father kept the landscape manicured. My mother always extended an invitation to the church leadership to feast at her house because the church is what her world was about. On this particular occasion, Deacon So-and-So was invited. I give him that name because I did not know him from the man in the moon.

When the table was set with food, the deacon was asked to give the blessing and then, of course, fill his "grill." Later, when the deacon prepared to depart, my mother handed him a photo of me enjoying myself as a Detroit Tiger down in Lakeland, Florida. The picture showed me dressed in my grey Tigers uniform standing in a baseball position in front of a mural of the Detroit Tigers from a championship year that was long past. That photo was a great memory for me.

Deacon So-and-So adjusted his full stomach to look down at the picture, shrugged, and then said, "The Tigers are a prejudice organization!" The first thing that popped in my head from this snide comment was that here is another out-of-control church boy who thinks he has the authority to smash other people's dreams and aspirations in the name of the Lord. Instead of taking the high road and just saying "That's nice" and then going on his merry way, Deacon So-and-So chose to take the low road and imply, "That's bad!" From my perspective, this was another example of suspect leadership emanating from the African-American church.

An invitation had been extended to dine at a family gathering as a guest, to say grace; enjoy whatever was put in front of you, be it vittles or a photo; compliment the host for a wonderful time; and then go home in peace. Instead, he believed his position gave him the authority to act like a bull in a china shop, knocking over personal things because he was too ignorant to know or understand the value of a memento. It took me fifty years to obtain my dream of wearing a Detroit Tigers uniform, to play and sing on a Detroit Tigers' baseball field, all of which was slandered in less than five seconds. This same Deacon So-and-So presided over my Aunt Wadean's funeral a short time after. I hope she is able to rest in peace, because I did not.

This reminded me of a few years prior when a guest pastor slammed me at his church after I had earned a four-year degree and then gave my cap and gown as a gift of appreciation to my mother. What was his purpose? I was perplexed. I should have received a pat on the back for my achievement, not a kick on the butt.

In reflection, it was my mother's choice to show Deacon So-and-So the picture, because it was, of course, her house. But I did not come to her house to be made a public spectacle of or be on trial. If anything, Deacon So-and-So or even Pastor So-and-So should have recognized my accomplishments as a soldier, a student, and a person to be emulated by others in the social and economically challenged community. From my experience, I learned that many congregations invest too much of their own fragile hope in the questionable human attributes of church officials. Sir Francis Bacon's quote is once again of consequence: "Hope makes a good breakfast but hope makes a *poor* dinner."[77] I think church congregations should understand that these appointed persons are just flesh and bone with their own demons to combat and may stand as barriers to freedom.

Just like military officers, I am leery of men of the cloth because a few of them have too many hidden agendas involving misbehavior from the pulpit or parade stand. While I appreciate their service to the community, a person of any authority does a disservice to all if he does not respect the aspirations or accomplishments of others. I think many times church leadership keeps the congregation in a state of discombobulation.

We are individuals, despite efforts to clump people in general together as a collective group or culture. This was a topic I discussed in my academic work.[78] I learned from my H & R Block experience that we taxpayers may look like twins, but we all have different tax liabilities, and relative in this case, we all have different dreams and aspirations.

KNOWLEDGE AND GOAL SETTING

I recall during a training session that Bill Gove, another NSA professional mentor, talked about how black female singers like Aretha Franklin, Whitney Houston, and Billie Holiday resonate a haunting wounded sound that illustrates the pain and suffering in their storied songs. Bill has long passed on, but when I went to shake his hand that day, he thought I was a pastor of a church. He was mistaken, but by no means was I upset; as a matter of fact, my mother would have probably enjoyed hearing that comment, since ministers are held in such high regard in the black community. On another occasion during one of Dr. Harold McKinney's music workshops, Dr. McKinney asked me how I planned to use my voice and about my ministry goals. I responded by telling him that I was not a minister.

In my academic work, I explored the relationship of black males and ministry. I found that the religious ministry has been the path of least resistance for black males into leadership,[79] so much so that the field may be oversaturated. This misperception of my personal motivation and goals provided me with greater insight into the selection of my own leadership topic, African-American self-employment.[80]

It was never my goal to be a minister of the cloth, although I have tried to help people as best I could. In essence, when you are in the process of helping people get better, do better, and be better, then in reality your activities really constitute a ministry. In my particular case, the foundation of my ministry is to help people be successful in the legal endeavor of their own choosing.

It is my belief that each person possesses a God-given gift through His blessing, as cited in Genesis 5:2. I believe the person must nurture the gift through education. I learned that a person can go to school and intend to learn the subject matter, but if the person does not have a dream or aspiration for that acquired knowledge, learning will seem like hard work. I discovered that it was the journey that enriched me, and what I learned on the journey must be passed on to others. How would I do that? I learned that I could teach better and pass it on when I was empathetic to a situation or circumstance as opposed to sympathetic. At a minimum, I think the learning process requires two active elements: interaction and reciprocation.

Over the years, that is what I surmised from my professional associations and endeavors. I learned to set goals. I learned to set my sights on my own personal topic. I learned to write thoughts down on paper. I learned to select mentors. I learned to listen to my mentors, and as a result, I started winning small victories, one at a time. I was then able to measure where I came from and where I was going. All of these learning attributes carried over to my renewed spiritual belief and acquisition of ancestral knowledge to help develop my leadership attributes. I then passed on what I learned in professional associations to my interested family members. Note I specify *interested* family members.

I found that I could reach my goal a day at a time; taking one action a day would get me there. An accomplishment a day builds commitment. I also found that I would only share my aspiration, goal, or plan with people who had a place in my big picture or my dreams, never randomly. Personal aspiration, goals, or plans are subject to being shot down by a general crowd, as the crowd places doubt on your big picture or dreams. My beautiful daughters provide this example; all are outstanding scholars with an exceptional knack for academics, but I learned through a third party they chose not to be exceptional scholars just to have friends at school. To me, the choice was poorly made, not only from the view of my pocketbook but because my daughters did not realize that there were friends to be made at the exceptional level.

I learned that there are leadership attributes that can be learned through simply activities, such as ballroom dancing[81] at Arthur Murray Studio.[82] When my wife and I enrolled, I soon learned that the man and woman each have a role on the ballroom floor. If the woman is not guided correctly across the dance floor by the man, as the lead, the result can be disastrous. On the other hand, if the male exhibits the appropriate dance techniques and coordination in leading the woman, the woman can be led with grace across the ballroom floor. This practical activity provides another vivid example that leadership attributes can be developed through knowledge.

Booker T. Washington informed that lack of knowledge comes with cost, for its absence and development of personal knowledge enhance one's ability to create.[83] Again in the book of Hosea 4:6, God said, "My people are lost without the lack of knowledge." This statement told me directly that without knowledge, education, and learning experience, I am doomed to be a prisoner of my environment. On the other hand, plug in the "If/Then" Rule here, for *if* I acquire some form of knowledge, *then* I have a greater chance to become free and not a prisoner of my environment.

KUMON KIDS VERSUS KARTOON KIDS

My daughter Lydia is a smart girl and did very well in her formal schooling. She did lack confidence in tackling analytic subjects in mathematics and science. She had to work harder than the rest, so we decided to get her extra tutoring help in preparing for standardized tests. We tried several tutoring centers, then we came upon the Kumon Learning Center.[84] Lydia was still apprehensive and self-conscious, because in this particular center she was a junior in high school and appeared to be the only African-American student. The student body was of an international flavor and starting at the lowest formal school grade all the way up to college preparatory classes.

On any given Saturday morning, the Kumon Learning Center was full of international kids with their parents doing homework and getting additional practice in math and science and preparing their skills at high levels for the corporate world. In addition, Kumon shared success stories and the achievements of students who had grown up in the program.[85]

In Chapter 1, there was a discussion on how the wonder of television has been a pacifier to the American viewing audience.[86] Saturday morning has been a great contributor to the pacification since the 1950s.[87] It was estimated that the viewing audience was at its peak of 20 million views throughout the 1970s and 1980s until federal intervention in the 1990s reduced the product availability, which then led to a reduced viewing audience.[88] The viewing audience was subjected to animated and concocted behavior that in turn greatly influenced human behavior. One research study found that the average child could be found in front of the television screen for 1,680 minutes per week and 1,500 hours annually. In addition, 70 percent of daycare centers used televisions in their facilities, where that same child might spend an entire day. The research indicated that quality interaction between parent and child were calculated at 3.5 minutes per week.[89]

This is significant, because many African-American families are dysfunctional according to the CDC,[90] and many African-Americans spend a lot of time in front of the television set. Demographic research indicates that African-Americans watch the most television, as much as seven hours each day in comparison to the Asian population average of three hours. The national average is five hours each day.[91] Notably, DVRs and electronic game console usage is also high. However, white families' use of the DVR is greater; at least 40 percent of white families own DVR, a machine that can be programmed for desired usage.[92] As a result of high usage of electronics, African-American viewing habits are commercially tracked,[93] arguably nullifying the buying power and voting power of the group and devaluing the personal freedom in decision-making power. I confess television shortened my learning curve with visual programming of information and data that I may have overlooked in a book. Nonetheless, research also shows that black millennials are watching less television than baby boomers.[94] That maybe a good sign for the future and the culture, allocating more time for reading, writing, and meditation.

The Wonder of Science: Deoxyribonucleic Acid (DNA)

I must state that besides the knowledge of Jesus Christ as my Lord and Savior, my next best bit of knowledge is that I discovered my ancestral roots and where my ancestral seed came from. Although my search began with my surname, as chronicled in the first book of this trilogy, it is through DNA tests that I found my ancestral homes, for which I am truly grateful. As previously cited, in 2006, I submitted a tissue sample for the purpose of DNA testing through a commercial organization named African Ancestry. The DNA test results connected me to my ancestral roots, the Ashanti culture of Ghana on my paternal side and Native American heritage on my maternal side.[95]

I will speak of both these findings in the third book of the trilogy, with a focus on identifying the social norms, customs, and ways of life experienced in ancestral heritages and comparing them to my life experience as an African-American male in Western civilization.

In discovering this science, I learned that DNA testing is an important piece of the ancestral puzzle. Although accurate recordkeeping was an accepted practice in genealogy until the wonderment of science, arguably there was no validation of true members of the family tree. Now it doesn't matter. For instance, a member of a family tree can be connected through DNA and not be of any influence on the life of other members of the tree. An example is a blood-related parent who has little or no involvement in the growth of an offspring. A male who donated sperm or a surrogate mother provide two distinct instances or circumstances where this might be true.

On the other hand, a member of a family tree may not be connected as a result of DNA yet provide great influence on select members of the family tree. A stepfather, a teacher, or a friend mentoring the growth of a young person come to mind. For heroes who serve our community, the adage of "the apple doesn't fall far from the tree" is of great benefit to us all.[96]

My DNA indicates that my paternal seed's journey began in Ghana and germinated in Virginia, North Carolina, and Barren County, Kentucky, and then Detroit, Michigan. The name "Barren County" may sound as if it has a negative connotation, but I personally gained more pride in my heritage. I embrace the gifts and talents passed on to me by those who came before me in whatever capacity.

THE BIG C AND THE "IF/THEN" RULE

"Mr. Davidson, the biopsy showed that you have cancer, but it is in the early stage. I want you understand you do have feasible options: you can choose to do nothing about the condition, you may be all right; you may choose to have radiation, but the process application is generally irreversible if there is a change in the diagnosis; or you can have surgery to remove the cancer, and there are several surgical procedures to choose from. Please take a week to talk about it with your family and then come back later with a decision."

In my travels, I learned that life is made up of personal choices that are never easy. In this time of great stress, I did learn from the medical staff one other thing about my peer group, the African-American male. It was conveyed to me during one of my visits that African-American males shy away from medical treatment most often because of the lack of medical insurance and the imposition on their manhood. I suspect the lack of medical treatment would cause CDC statistics pertaining to African-American males to spike upward.

In pondering my options with my wife, we decided the first two did not seem to be correct choices. We decided I should have the surgery, and subsequently, all indications more than six years later are that I beat the adversary. Although I beat the cancer, the human body is just not the same once any type of incision cuts into it and God's portrait of perfection is altered.

In addition, surgery takes a toll on family members, who also suffer through the fear and anxiety. Because of scarring, I did have additional procedures done for the purpose of my quality of life. I was grateful for my clean bill of health, but on occasion the Angry Black Man syndrome slowly creeps into my reflection of this life-changing event.

I did miss my daughter Lydia's high school graduation program in June 2008, but I ensured that she had a grand party. My recovery period was just in time for my own graduation a few weeks later from the University of Phoenix doctoral program. I had tears in my eyes because I had beaten a lot of odds to stand on that stage as an academic scholar. My brother Glen, sometime called "the professor" by our buddies, would have been proud.

CHANGE CAME WHEN

History has shown that there will undoubtedly continue to be periodic hard times in the economy wherever people live. Undoubtedly there will always be those who will overcome the circumstances. My brothers Glen and Bobby did not. For me recently, the downsizing of military personnel and furlough days for government employees have reminded me of the uncertainly of being an unemployed blue-collar factory worker. The unemployment situation was okay until you got that first short paycheck or no paycheck at all. Unemployment makes it easy for chaos to creep into a person's lifestyle and turn it upside down as well succumbing to the "po, Poe, poor" syndrome that is part of my family belief system. To wit, a ton of energy and resources are needed to overcome the situation and subsequently get life back on track. At this point in my life, I certainly do not want to backslide in my professional career.

I learned that the attribute of desire is an essential element in the process of change. It was my desire to be a better person, and that motivated my first step toward turning my life around. The most important person in the change process is the individual standing at the fork in the road. In Luke 4:23, Jesus said to the undecided, "Physician heal yourself!" Also applicable is when the family of Dr. Martin Luther King stated that the masses should not expect another leader like their father to make change for them. It is the individual who must commit to the process.[97] Eddie Rickenbacker, the famous aviator, provides a six-word formula for success: "Think things through then follow through."[98] I think the financial rebirth of Detroit, Michigan, is an example of the healing process as individuals are stepping up.[99]

In his book *Change or Die*, Alan Deutschman poses a question to the individual standing at a fork in the road of life.[100] Making the assumption that all people have been anatomically engineered with great potential for a long life, the question posed is, what would you do if you were given options to change your life, hopefully for the better, or continue your life as is and die from the consequences? I chose changing my life for the better because that was the only way I could honor my fallen brothers and help others. Still, few African-American males in their choices select a confirmed change for the better, as reflected in periodic CDC statistics.

During a recent fantasy-camp trip, I met a young African-American female working as a food-service worker who informed me that her husband lost his dream of playing professional baseball. Her young husband was drafted to play baseball right out of high school and possessed a skill set that could bring glory. However, the young man suffered a devastating injury in the minor leagues that ended his career and aspirations. Instead of taking to the streets, the young man adapted to the change in his life and took a blue-collar job in the municipality so that he could take care of family.

Deutschman suggests that there are three keys to change:

1. *Relate* (new hope)—Move away from negative associations and finding new associations that are inspiring and provide hope.
2. *Repeat* (new skills)—Emulate these new associations by practicing their training and master the newly acquired habits and skills.
3. *Reframe* (new thinking)—Discover and experience new points of view make an assessment of current lifestyle.

For me, change came when I left the old neighborhood for military service. I found new hope in my new association. Consequently, on that journey I encountered better people, or at least it seemed so. I began to emulate military leaders, public servants, and professionals more and more and street-corner knuckleheads less and less, and as a result I gained new skills. I made a holistic assessment of my attributes in comparison to my past lifestyle, and my thought process became new. I made a choice to change to a new lifestyle rather than die in the old lifestyle.

I consider myself fortunate that the trait of malice never took root in my basic personality and view of life. I was a full-fledged member of Stage 5, adulthood, the cycle of life. I took it upon myself to broaden my learning and knowledge base and put my attributes on display. Remember, it was Mr. Les Brown who informed me that when you make a commitment toward success, the right people will come out of the woodwork to help you with the task at hand. If you recall throughout my exposition, there were a number of people who stepped forward to help me expand my vision, to include the decision by a former friend not to pull the trigger. Mr. Brown was right. I have a number of achievements that I am most proud of that came with the help of others. This has been my journey as an African American male and it has extraordinary.

MILESTONES AND KNUCKLEHEAD INCIDENTS

Knucklehead incidents:

- parents and white Plymouth Voyager
- LEDC missed for a second time
- SHAPE HQ assignment lost
- neighborhood roll call
- September 11, 2001
- the big "C"—cancer

Milestones:

- learned of family genealogy (maternal)
- completed Toastmasters International program
- trained with NSA St. Louis
- visited Crenshaw Christian Center in Los Angeles, California
- trained with Institute of Management Consultants
- trained with Society of Logistics Engineers
- spouse completed four-year degree at Columbia College
- spouse learned direct sales
- spouse entered DA Intern program
- move to Fort Jackson, South Carolina
- trained with NSA Carolinas
- joined local acting studio, Columbia, South Carolina
- acting scholarship to Trustus Theater, Columbia, South Carolina
- voice lessons, Carolina Academy, Columbia, South Carolina
- earned singing role in local production of *Five Guys Named Moe*
- honorably discharged after twenty years of military service
- purchased first home in suburb of Detroit

- green-collar job teaching Junior Reserve Officers Corps (JROTC)
- trained voice with Dr. Harold McKinney, jazz legend
- trained with NSA Michigan
- employed by US Army, TACOM
- accepted in doctoral program, University of Phoenix
- Detroit Tigers fantasy camp
- performed national anthem at Comerica Park May 2005
- received DNA results
- completed doctoral program and dissertation
- honorably transitioned after fifteen years of civil service

Warrant Officer Davidson

Zig Ziglar providing mentorship

Les Brown providing mentorship

Singing up storm as Four Eyed Moe

Entrepreneur at world class convention in Las Vegas

The Van

Motown induction of Frank Garcia

National Anthem

Detroit Arsenal Idol

Mr. and Mrs. Wayne Davidson

A great combination: graduation and baseball

EPILOGUE: STATE OF REORIENTATION FOLLOWING A DEVASTATING BLOW

"I did not like taking history class in school because it never showed black people in a positive light!" exclaimed Maudie Baker, a Detroiter and mother of this author's lifelong friend, Chili Carlson.

In contrast to Mrs. Baker's claim, Sir Winston Churchill, renowned statesman and world leader in the twentieth century, believed that we as a society must understand our historical past in order to be prepared for the future.[1] It is most likely that Mrs. Baker and Winston Churchill had different learning experiences. One of the goals of this text was to increase the knowledge base positively on the African-American experience, past and present.

I, too, had a different learning experience. It was most difficult as I recovered from the discombobulating blow struck at my mouth by my female classmate, Wendy, as recalled in the preface of this text. I remember I was delusional and making threats for a brief period of time, but as I started to regain my senses and composure my thinking became clearer. The most positive action I took in the sequence of events was to exit the bus and go home quickly and quietly. By the way, Wendy had a brother who was on the fast track toward becoming a first-degree knucklehead.

When I got to the safe confines of my home some five blocks away from the bus stop, I asked myself the following questions: How did this happen? How do I get my life back on track? I concluded that I had to reorient myself to who, what, and where I was currently. Once I understood the dynamics of the track, maybe I could understand how this incident happened and the factors that led to it. I did not want a similar incident to happen again!

In the first part of this trilogy, I learned the dynamics of my tracks, beginning with my surname and its alignment with Western civilization or the "big picture." I discovered this system evolved into a distinct social order composed of four categories of man, whose roles and responsibilities became more defined as Western civilization progressed, leaving a historical footprint:[2]

1. Those who *ruled* over the land, specifically the king, the absolute authority
2. Those who *defended* the land, specifically the feudal lords, the long arm of the absolute authority
3. Those who *prayed* for the land, specifically the church, the religious arm of the absolute authority
4. Those who *worked* the land, specifically the peasants, the masses who had little authority over anything in their daily lives

But for many African-Americans there is still a disparity or disconnection with the big picture, as Mrs. Baker's comment attests. Statistically, most identify with the fourth social order, the masses who worked the land, to include my family of African descent.

In my growth process, many of the audio, video, and print media sources that influenced my life on the urban streets are no longer prevalent, but they are worshipped in the hall of fame of their genre. But there is also a need for a strong cultural voice to be informed about contributions by unexpected sources. This is a paradox, yet the Nixon administration is a contributing factor to leveling the socioeconomic playing field with the establishment of the minority business institution and self-rule of Native Americans.[3] Richard Nixon is often portrayed as a comedic joke among the uninformed masses. I learned the aforementioned from a prominent African-American statesman and businessman and the latter from a popular black comedian. With that in mind, I later learned from a popular movie[4] that Nixon's economic initiatives to the black business community were actually a political counter to the powerful stance and social initiatives taken by the Black Panther organization.

No matter, this underrepresentation in the American dream shows there was a need to examine this discombobulated state inferred by Bill O'Reilly. The social order below uses the same descriptive/comparative model previously outlined. The difference is that the blanks are filled in at a macro and realistic level from the perspective of an African-American male born in the post-World War II era during the time of the social-change agents or baby boomers:

1. Those who *ruled* over the land, or government authorities—A black president was elected in 2008. Despite being of African descent, the new president should not be considered a savior for the social ills of the black community, which represents 13 percent of the total population.[5] He has a legal obligation to represent all American citizens. In addition, elected officials do have a shelf life. Political change can be difficult when one person holds a political position for decades;[6] at some point, that person and the legacy become a barrier to change in an evolving world.
2. Those who *defended* the land, or military personnel and the industrial base—There are great benefits and challenges in serving in the military or a government agency. For the African-American population, government service has become a great place to start a career. Maybe that is the reason some people look at government with contempt. Unofficial employment figures indicate that the ratio of black soldiers is 18 percent to 75 percent of white soldiers.[7] The ratio of black federal employees is 18 percent to 66 percent of white federal employees.[8] Realistically, many minorities have difficulty obtaining the proper security clearances to make federal service a career. Additionally, blacks are less likely than Hispanics and nearly as likely as whites to be employed in the private sector. There could be various reasons

for the shortcoming, and consideration must include geographic location, education, occupational skill sets, and family-owned or specialized businesses where federal regulations may not be considered. In addition, few blacks are self-employed—only 3.8 percent reported being self-employed in 2011—making them almost half as likely to be self-employed as whites (7.2 percent).[9]

3. Those who *prayed* for the land, or the clergy and church body—There is great diversity in the religious belief systems and practices represented in the United States in the manner of tithing, prayer, and personal experience. Reportedly, only 40 percent of the American population attends church services on a regular basis.[10] Blacks and Hispanics comprise the largest participating groups among the total US population. Social and economic groups that are challenged have a tendency to look toward a higher power for help. In individual subcategories, the white male is the least likely to attend church on a regular basis.[11]
4. Those who *worked* the land, or the blue/white collar working population—The unemployment rate for African-Americans is substantially greater than whites no matter the economic climate, good or bad. Realistically, many African-Americans hold seasonal jobs that pay minimum wages.[12] The lack of long employment and career opportunities in the mainstream economy undoubtedly put many African-Americans on a path that lead to criminal careers and incarceration.[13]

I think the mutuality of the Strawberry Pie Rule is applicable here. For this text, the social environment is an ecosystem in which there are humans living and surviving at various levels that illustrate the quality of life at a micro level. Therefore, further research of the demographics of the social environment must be conducted to understand roles and responsibilities:

I. Organizational structure
   a. family unit
   b. neighborhood
   c. marriage protocols
II. Health and welfare (public services)
   a. diet
   b. hygiene
   c. housing
   d. clothing
   e. education
   f. medical
III. Religion (spiritual services)
IV. Citizen soldier (civic and military duty/obligation)

Previous research also indicates that there are comparative differences between blacks and whites where there are roles and responsibilities in the unit, availability of public services, religious beliefs and practices, and citizen obligations.[14]

The PBS television series *African American Lives*,[15] hosted by Henry Louis Gates Jr. has created great interest in the genealogical connection between the African-American population and the continent of Africa. A number of celebrities believed to be of African descent have traced their ancestry in front of the camera, realizing the special results of their heritage. A second PBS television series hosted by Henry Louis Gates Jr. is titled *Finding Your Roots*;[16] this storyline extends its discovery to the roots of celebrities of non-African descent as well. I posted my findings to the online forum.

Years after the Negro migrations, Manav Tanneeru, in his report "Family Roots Lure Many African-Americans Back to South," gives notice that many African-Americans are retracing their roots and leaving established homes in the North as its industrial might fades.[17] The mass exodus to the South from northern cities like Detroit has taken an economic toll. The population and tax base decrease, abandoned homes and industrial structures stand for long periods of time, and the loss of occupational expertise is enormous.[18] The goal of many fellows I worked with in the automobile factory was to save money and return home to the South. Hall of Fame football player Earl Campbell exclaimed that he was never unhappy growing up in the country on a Texas farm, he just wanted more out of life.[19] Dad had a great desire to return to the South but my mother did not share it.

Blacks return home to the South, to what Booker T. Washington, the great Negro educator, believed was their strength.[20] Relative to life on the farm, remember the mature farm boy Roy Hobbs,[21] now living out his dream of playing baseball, asking Iris the big question: did she sell the farm? Iris's response to Roy: "No, I will always have that!" Roy replied, "Good. It's home!"

Acknowledging that the ground is considered God's green earth and a gift to man, it still took material resources—livestock and machinery—to work and keep the earth green and make things grow. My father, a Kentucky farm boy, would say you still need a mule to work the land. Booker T. Washington declared that blacks understood the value of home ownership despite living in adverse conditions.[22] It was historian George W. Williams who found that the opportunity to obtain a formal education hastened the move north, as the newly educated believed that agricultural labor was now beneath them.[23]

The present-day economy is different from the segregated economy in full reality during the Negro migration. The Negro of the South had to be self-sufficient because many of the basic human services and products needed to live and raise a family were unavailable outside of the collective community. Not so today—dollars that flow from minority communities are a staple of the present-day economy.[24]

When the Negro population of the nineteenth century was centered in the South, it was Booker T. Washington who said that the Negro should throw down his bucket where he stood and advance his way from there.[25] I find the meaning to be: participate in everything, not just one thing. Everybody can't be Michael Jordan and play his position; find your own name and play your own position. Taking that concept further, no matter where a bucket is laid down, in the concept of individualism it is important to muster individual talents and uniqueness outside the group versus internal to the group, where the attributes may be shelved. That way generosity can be gifted-wrapped.

In the matter of gifts, look at the uniqueness of Ms. Oseola McCarty of Hattiesburg, Mississippi. Ms. McCarty was an eighty-seven-year-old African-American washerwoman who possessed a fifth-grade education and no family. She donated $150,000 of her long-labored life savings to the education of African-American students. Ms. McCarty's generosity will always be put in a positive light; to date, since her death in 1999, her donation has allowed at least forty deserving African-American students the opportunity to change the future.[26] Statistically, educational opportunities have increased for African-Americans[27] since the nineteenth century, as proclaimed by a twenty-first century fictional assassin, Brother Mouzone of *The Wire*, who shared that "the most dangerous thing in America is a nigger with a library card."[28] I surely took advantage of the success. After walking through the annals of libraries around the world and becoming an author myself, I felt lethal. The assumption has been that education is a cornerstone in building a strong African American community. Recall that Williams asserted in the 19th century newly educated Negroes left the farm for good in the 19th century. The same appears true in the 21st century as newly educated blacks forgo their former neighborhoods for opportunities elsewhere.[29] I admit as I became more knowledgeable the less I wanted to return to my former life but I have never shied away from others seeking opportunity or change.

No doubt there will always be a long quest in obtaining the American dream, and that dream will always be surrounded by barriers:[30] social and economic inequality,[31] catastrophe,[32] military pandemics,[33] urban pandemics,[34] civil unrest,[35] and social violence.[36] All difficult, but the quest must continue because if I don't play the game, then how could I possibly win the game? It took a great deal of time, but this is how I found my way out of that parade of knuckleheads. I understood where I had been and with who, and I had been there with them long enough. So the most important person in the change process is the individual standing at the fork in the road—in this case, me.

In the reorientation process, a quick assessment of assets and faculties is a must. I decided to use the trump card God gave me. I found in my assessment of where I was that had no malice in my heart and no criminal record, but I also had one important piece of paper: a high-school diploma, an administrative asset that was a starting point. After talking to God, the first thing was to find out who I was and what I wanted to do with my life before it was too late. Once I learned more about my mental and physical attributes, I began to put them to good use in edifying myself.

My assessment incorporated the seven stages of man's life cycle addressed by Davidson Powell's article.[37] I found that I was raised by a good and caring family throughout my infancy, toddler, childhood, and puberty stages. Then during my adolescence stage, I was greatly influenced by environmental forces that countermanded my upbringing. This diversion impacted my progression into adulthood, as I acted as an adolescent inside the body of an adult. Thankfully, I recovered and accepted my transition into maturity.

It is sad that many friends and family members did not survive the period of transition. As I head toward the subsequent stage, my goal is to lend a helping hand to others. So I developed the "Know Thyself" Rule: I found out who I was as a person, and in the process I started to understand myself and assess my attributes.

Once I began to understand myself, I started to work on where I was going, my dreams and aspirations. One dream was to go to California and visit Disneyland, because I had been seeing pictures of it on television since it opened in 1955. So I was able to go there thirty years after it opened. Using my Disneyland Theory, I found out what my aspirations were. I started to understand what I wanted out of life. I got away from the naysayers and realized I had my own dreams.

I felt stagnant in growth living in Detroit and the blue-collar positions I held. I made a decision to seek other opportunities, and as a result I returned to the Detroit area in the new millennium a different fellow. I had a new family, a new home, a new lifestyle, and a new belief system. I learned that *if* I got off my butt, *then* I could make things happen. Through my "If/Then" Rule, I found out it takes action on my part to make things happen to get where I wanted to go. I learned that nothing is going to happen until I get up and get to it. When I took action, things began to happen for me.

I overcame years of naivety, being a knucklehead, and legislated social impediments by embracing change in my belief system and gaining confidence in my abilities and heritage through service and citizenship. It was because I learned to believe in myself and visualize myself being successful. Most importantly, my most outstanding achievement was getting my immediate family members to the "social water-cooler," as John H. Johnson described it, because that is where the conversations of inclusion are taking place.[38]

Addendum: One Last Spill of Bureaucratic Milk

Typically, the average person with career goals is diligent and meticulous in making preparation for that great opportunity, no matter what industry. For minorities, few dreamers get a free ride, whether they are a legacy or not. There are many glass ceilings to be endured. And no matter the academic standing, mentorship and relationships are extremely important in seeking positions of greater responsibility.

Besides exhaustive preparation and key associations, timing of the opportunity is also understood to be a factor in obtaining success. Although I am nearing the end of my career as a civil servant, a great opportunity was presented to me recently. Regrettably, the timing may have been out of sync with opportunity and the absence of mentorship because of the reorganization taking place in my office due to budgetary considerations.

The federal government is talent-laden, but most of the talent is not exploited in an efficient manner because the federal government is a rank-oriented infrastructure. In this type of organizational structure, the vision and foresight of the person who invented sliced bread would fall to the wayside if the person did not have enough rank. There is a general officer drive to change the management of government talent. This, in my opinion, is a long and arduous task, since much of the talent has been mal-assigned, as I was.

This particular career opportunity was a fellowship with a government agency that was actively recruiting a select workforce of the best technically trained, educated, experienced, and multifunctional civilian personnel. Understanding that the program was highly competitive in nature, seeking entry in this program was a no-brainer for me. I did not have a mentor to confer with about the career opportunity at the time. The official personnel website indicated that I was already prequalified by service record to apply, and I believed my academic records more than met the criteria for selection to the program. I felt this position would revitalize my career and put my acquired expertise at greater use.

In the matter of timing, the program announcement was posted on Thursday September 11, 2014, and the recruitment action was to conclude nine weeks later on Thursday November 13, 2014. After reading the requirements again and again, it was easy for me to assemble the necessary personnel paperwork and credentials, because I maintained a draft of my professional portfolio on hand in both electronic and hard-copy format. So I got right to work on the task.

Both professionally and personally, I've always seen the glass as being half-full, but this is where the glass started to tip over. My immediate supervisor had formally retired the first week of September 2014, a full week before the recruitment announcement was published. Nonetheless, the following Monday, September 15, 2014, during the first full week of recruitment, I made the first overture to my leadership change of command expressing my intent to apply to the program. The e-mail message contained a summary of the eligibility requirements, a draft of my curriculum vitae/resume, and current administrative records for a preliminary review by my chain of command. In addition, I included details of administrative documents that the chain of command was responsible to complete. The e-mail was sent but I received no response.

Notably, this was the same chain of command that a few weeks earlier had returned to me for employee signature my annual review signed by leadership, which had not undergone spell-check. I shook my head in wonderment and then signed on the dotted line as milk dripped from the lip of the container.

Speaking of the efficiency of government administration, in an associated incident, I requested a copy of my retirement benefit estimate as a planning tool in April of 2104. Typically, the administrative process moves at a snail's pace. It generally takes several months to complete as anxious employees making career decisions await the planning document. From their own experience, some government employees tell horror stories of their communications with the government agency responsible for the operational process. My spouse, who is also a civil servant, received a notice stating that she owed money because the required retirement deductions were not properly made from her payroll account. This was years of deductions not made, and the suffocating interest made me perplexed and my wife furious at the proficiency of members of a bureaucracy. Getting such news at the end of a successful career of civil service only amplifies the flaws and imperfections that fester in the federal employment system.

Here is my story. On September 6, 2014, I received an e-mail message informing me that my retirement estimate was available for viewing at the agency website. When I opened the message and followed the direction in the e-mail message, to my surprise, there was no data to review. I told my spouse, who insisted that I call the retirement center that day to find out what happen. I called and spoke to a customer-service representative who listened to my issue and traced the actions of the original preparer while I waited on the phone. The customer-service representative then told me that she would initiate a service ticket and the original preparer would follow up and complete my employee request in a timely manner. Only recently was my request completed after a third customer-service representative committed herself to getting done.

Getting back to the fellowship application, the next e-mail message with attachments was forwarded to my chain of command on Monday, September 29, 2014, in the third week of the program recruitment. The attachment contained a quality draft of my curriculum vitae/resume, personal interest statement, current administrative records, and details completing the administrative documents the chain of command was responsible to complete. The e-mail was sent, but I received no response.

The next e-mail message with attachments was forwarded to my leadership on Thursday, October 2, 2014, in the fourth week of the program recruitment. The e-mail stated that I had created and uploaded the required documents to the online website as required by the recruiting organization. I informed the principals that the fellowship application cannot be forwarded as a partial packet because the administrative documents signed by the chain of command must also be posted for the packet to be complete. The e-mail was sent but I received no response.

Later that week, I got the new chain of command on board. I included them in my next e-mail message dated Monday October 7, 2014. The following day, the new leadership made an inquiry to the administrative group concerning the roles and responsibility of his office in completing the documentation. The new leader was apprehensive in providing approval, because he felt he needed to understand the workload of the organization he had just inherited. Later, it was determined that the new leadership was ineligible to sign the documents because of time on the job and that the obvious choice to prepare and sign the required document was the previous group leader.

At this point, the question becomes, why I did not ask the leadership directly about this request? Arguably, e-mail has become the standard method of professional and personal communication in an office environment, although Sue Shellenbarger in article in the *Wall Street Journal* suggested that the bulk of e-mail traffic is overlooked and worthless.[39] As stated earlier, my office was undergoing reorganization, and my immediate supervisor had formally retired days before the recruitment announcement was made public. My group leader did not feel compelled to respond, and the energy was focused on moving to a less stressful office environment on the opposite end of the floor.

I continued to speak to members of the new crew as they were identified and came on board. The response I received was unexpected and did not answer the question I asked. Instead of leaving my position, I was now assigned to be team leader for a group of fellow employees. In this age of sophisticated gadgets that block out the outside world, how do you manage a team of people wearing headphones who have flexible office hours? When I heard that proclamation, I said to myself, "It is not my destiny to be team leader." From a career perspective, I saw this assignment as regression rather progression.

In the sixth week of the program recruitment, I was in a training class and getting frustrated. Before I left for class, I initiated another follow-up e-mail requesting the status of the two outstanding documents required to complete my packet. I provided the new group leader with more details of what was required and why. In the seventh week, I made another inquiry on the status and provided an example of what could be done to complete the task.

In the eighth week, I was in another training class and totally frustrated. I had learned from previous experience that it is never good when you have to speak to the lead administrator, but in the ninth week, I requested an appointment with the director to discuss this issue. The director directed the old group leader to complete the requirements, but by then it was too late to meet the immutable due date of Thursday, November 13, 2014.

I am really upset at this bureaucratic process that I perceived to be so easy. Most likely my e-mails were never opened by the group leader. I could feel the frustration of Angry Black Man syndrome slowly creep into my bones. I threw water on its ignition. It was more important for a man of significant accomplishment to serve as an example for other African-American males to emulate than to create a social forest fire.

On Thursday, November 13, 2014, I sent an e-mail to the leadership chain of command cancelling my request for their assistance in completing my application because it had taken too long to acquire executive signatures. For me, the multifunctionally of a government employee has long been suspect because there are just too many formal protocols to deal with that negatively impact job satisfaction and career progression.[40] There was now nine weeks of spilled milk gone sour on a bureaucratic floor, reminding me of Freddie Fender's popular song, "Wasted Days and Wasted Nights."[41]

Nonetheless, the year is 2015, and at this point I do not regret my fifteen years of honorable federal service. I feel fortunate to have all my fingers and all my toes. From all of my assignments, I learned that all types of people provide all kinds of basic services in defense of the nation. I was truly grateful for having an opportunity to serve those people and at the same time enhance my lifestyle. I learned that federal service is a great opportunity for employment. This opportunity has made my family proud.

ENDNOTES

Epigraph

1 "William Barclay Quotes," BrainyQuote, accessed February 26, 2015, http://www.brainyquote.com/quotes/quotes/w/williambar186927.html.
2 "Maya Angelou Quotes," BrainyQuote, accessed February 26, 2015, http://www.brainyquote.com/quotes/quotes/m/mayaangelo133956.html.

Preface

1 2014 Global E-Book Winners, accessed 20 July 2015, http://globalebookawards.com/2014-global-ebook-award-winners/
2 Cristina Lourosa-Ricardo, "How America Gives," *Wall Street Journal*, December 15, 2014, R3.
3 Carla Herreria, "This Graduate Stripped Down for All the Right Reasons," *Huffington Post*, December 30, 2014. http://www.huffingtonpost.com/2014/12/30/hawaii-graduate-malo _n _6392902.html.
4 "Ossian Sweet House," National Park Service, accessed November 5, 2013, http://http://www.nps.gov/nr/travel/detroit/d4.htm.
5 Bill O'Reilly, *Talking Points*, Fox News, January 30, 2014, http://www.foxnews.com/on-air/oreilly/2014/01/31/bill-oreilly-liberal-dissatisfaction-president-obama.
6 "Shooting of Michael Brown," *Wikipedia*, accessed May 7, 2015, http://en.wikipedia.org/wiki/Shooting _of _Michael _Brown.
7 "Death of Eric Garner," *Wikipedia*, accessed May 7, 2015, http://en.wikipedia.org/wiki/Death _of _Eric _Garner.
8 "Shooting of Tamir Rice," *Wikipedia*, accessed May 7, 2015, http://en.wikipedia.org/wiki/Shooting _of _Tamir _Rice; Mark Gillispie, "Excessive Force Incidents Spur Overhaul of Cleveland Police Force," *Detroit News*, Friday December 5, 2014, 11A.

9 "Shooting of Walter Scott," *Wikipedia*, accessed May 7, 2015, http://en.wikipedia.org/wiki/Shooting _of _Walter _Scott .

10 Tom Hays and Collen Long, "Protests Grow: Racial Justice, Police Actions Stir Debate," *Detroit News*, December 5, 2014, 1A; Adam Janos and Thomas MacMillan, "Thousands Take to the Streets in Protest: Demonstrators Nationwide Demand Justice After Two Grand Jury Decision Not to Charge Police in Deaths of Black Men," *Wall Street Journal*, Friday, December 5, 2014, A6; Meg Kinnard, "Cop Charged in Unarmed Man's Death: SC Officer's Attorney Says Prosecution Trying to Make Case 'Racial,'" *Detroit News*, Friday December 5, 2014, 11A.

11 "Death of Freddie Gray," *Wikipedia*, accessed May 7, 2015,http://en.wikipedia.org/wiki/Death _of _Freddie _Gray.

12 Zusha Elinson and Dan Frosch, Police-Misconduct Cost soar, Wall Street Journal, Thursday July 16, 2015, 1A.

13 Nolan Finley, "Where Are the Black People?" Editorial, *Detroit News*, December 14, 2014, 22A.

14 Jim Brunner, "Black Lives Matter protesters shut down Bernie Sanders; later rally draws 15,000, Seattle Times, accessed August 12, 2015, http://www.seattletimes.com/seattle-news/politics/black-lives-matter-protesters-shut-down-bernie-sanders-rally/; David Ferguson, "Marissa Janae Johnson doesn't 'give a f*uck' if protest at Seattle Bernie Sanders rally drive people away" Rawstory.com, accessed August 12, 2015, http://www.rawstory.com/2015/08/marissa-janae-johnson-doesnt-give-a-fck-if-protest-at-seattle-bernie-sanders-rally-drives-people-away/.

15 Wayne R. Davidson, *Manufacturing African American Self-Employment: In the Detroit Metropolitan Area* (Saarbrücken, Germany: VDM Verlag Dr. Müller Aktiengesellschaft & Co. KG., 2008), 13.

16 Ralph Ellison, *Invisible Man* (New York: Random House, 1952).

17 "Angry Black Man Syndrome," *Wikibin*, accessed October 15, 2014, http://wikibin.org/articles/angry-black-man-syndrome.html; "Angry Black Man Syndrome," *All the Tropes Wiki*, accessed October 15, 2014, http://allthetropes.wikia.com/wiki/Angry _Black _Man; "Angry Black Man Syndrome," *The Populace Now*, accessed May 5, 2015, http://www.thepopulacenow.com/the-angry-black-man-stereotype.

18 Richard J. Herrnstein and Charles Murray, *The Bell Curve: Intelligence and Class Structure in American Life* (New York: Free Press, 1994).

19 Davidson Powell, "A Man's Life Cycle," Men's Issues, *Ezine Articles*, March 12, 2010, http://ezinearticles.com/?A-Mans-Life-Cycle&id=3920362.

20 Davidson, *Manufacturing*, 10, 46.

21 Davidson, *Manufacturing*, 133.

22 Davidson, *Manufacturing*, 19, 51.

23 Caryl Rivers, "Preconceptions Plague Blacks: Researchers Say Inherent Double Standard Reinforces Prejudices," *Detroit News*, January 1, 2015, 1B.

24 Kellan Howell, Miami judge leaves accused burglar in tears: 'He was the nicest kid in middle school' The Washington Times, Saturday, July 4, 2015, accessed 7 July 2015, http://www.washingtontimes.com/news/2015/jul/4/miami-judge-mindy-glazer-leaves-accused-burglar-in/.

25 Will Meek, "Invisibility Syndrome," *Psychology of Men*, accessed October 15, 2014, http://www.psychologyofmen.org/invisibility-syndrome/.

26 Wayne R. Davidson, *When Clans Collide: The Germination of Adam's Family Tree through Surname, Life Experience, and DNA* (Bloomington, IN: Abbott Press, 2013), 22.

27 Davidson, *When Clans Collide*, 78-80, 102.

28 Robert Lee Hotz, "Tiny Robot Swarm Works on Its Own," *Wall Street Journal*, August 15, 2014, A3.

29 Alan Deutschman, *Change or Die* (New York: Regan/HarperCollins Publishers Inc., 2007).

30 "Improvised Explosive Device," *Wikipedia*, accessed June 12, 2014, http://en.wikipedia.org/wiki/Improvised _explosive _device.

31 "Compound Interest," *Wikipedia*, accessed December 7, 2014, http://en.wikipedia.org/wiki/Compound _interest.

32 John Steele Gordon, "Write What You Know: *Jack London: An American Life* by Earle Labor," *Wall Street Journal*, October 5-6, 2013, C8.

33 Herrnstein and Murray, *The Bell Curve*.

34 Don Lemon et. al., "Within Black Families, Hard Truths Told to Sons Amid Ferguson Unrest," *CNN.com*, August 15, 2014, http://www.cnn.com/2014/08/15/living/parenting-black-sons-ferguson-missouri/.

35 Federal Bureau of Investigation, Expanded Homicide Data Table 6; Murder, accessed July 6, 2015, https://www.fbi.gov/about-us/cjis/ucr/crime-in-the-u.s/2011/crime-in-the-u.s.-2011/tables/expanded-homicide-data-table-6.

36 "What's Going On (Song)," *Wikipedia*, Soul, accessed October 13, 2013, http://en.wikipedia.org/wiki/What's _Going _On _(song).

37 "Flash Light," *Wikipedia*, accessed November 5, 2013, http://en.wikipedia.org/wiki/Flash _Light _(song).

TIMELINE

1 "20th Century," *Wikipedia*, accessed October 2, 2013, http://en.wikipedia.org/wiki/20th _century.

2 "Industrial Revolution," *Wikipedia*, accessed October 2, 2013, http://en.wikipedia.org/wiki/Industrial _Revolution.

3 "Great Migration (African American)," *Wikipedia*, accessed October 2, 2013, http://en.wikipedia.org/wiki/Great _Migration _(African _American).

4 "Atomic Age," *Wikipedia*, accessed October 2, 2013, http://en.wikipedia.org/wiki/Atomic _Age.

5 "Baby Boomers," *Wikipedia*, accessed October 2, 2013, http://en.wikipedia.org/wiki/Baby _Boomer; Sally Kane, "Baby Boomers," *About.com Legal Careers*, accessed March 3, 2014, http://legalcareers.about.com/od/practicetips/a/Babyboomers.htm; "What's a Boomer?," *Baby Boomer Headquarters*, accessed March 3, 2014, http://www.bbhq.com/whatsabm.htm; "Boomer Statistics," *Baby Boomer Headquarters*, accessed March 3, 2014, http://www.bbhq.com/bomrstat.htm; "Famous Boomers," *Baby Boomer Headquarters*, accessed March 3, 2014, http://www.bbhq.com/famousb.htm; P. J. O'Rourke, "Special Report: How the Boomers ~~Ruined~~ Saved America," *AARP: The Magazine*, December 2013/January 2014, 36; Robert Love, "The Generation That Changed the World," *AARP: The Magazine*, December 2013/January 2014, 35; "Youngest Boomer Turning 50," The Year Ahead: U.S, *Wall Street Journal*, January 2, 2014, A7.

6 "Urban Renewal Initiative," *Wikipedia*, accessed October 2, 2013, http://en.wikipedia.org/wiki/Urban _renewal.

7 "Cold War," *Wikipedia*, accessed October 2, 2013, http://en.wikipedia.org/wiki/Cold _War.

8 "Korean War," *Wikipedia*, accessed October 2, 2013, http://en.wikipedia.org/wiki/Korean _War.

9 "Movements for Civil Rights," *Wikipedia*, accessed October 2, 2013, http://en.wikipedia.org/wiki/Movements _for _civil _rights.

10 "Vietnam War," *Wikipedia*, accessed October 2, 2013, http://en.wikipedia.org/wiki/Vietnam _War.

11 "Volunteer Military," *Wikipedia*, accessed October 2, 2013, http://en.wikipedia.org/wiki/Volunteer _military.

12 "Gulf War," *Wikipedia*, accessed October 2, 2013, http://en.wikipedia.org/wiki/Gulf _War.

13 "Information Superhighway," *Wikipedia*, accessed October 2, 2013, http://en.wikipedia.org/wiki/Information _superhighway.

14 "21st Century," *Wikipedia*, accessed October 2, 2013, http://en.wikipedia.org/wiki/21st _century.

15 "September 11 Attacks," *Wikipedia*, accessed October 2, 2013, http://en.wikipedia.org/wiki/September _11 _attacks.

KEY EVENTS AND CONSIDERATIONS (MACRO LEVEL) 1941-1976

1 Darren A. Nichols, "Highs, Lows of Race Relations," Detroit News, July 19, 2007, http://www.detroitnews.com/article/20070719/METRO/707190403.

2 "Executive Order 8802," *Wikipedia*, accessed July 8, 2014, http://en.wikipedia.org/wiki/Executive _Order _8802.

3 "Sojourner Truth Housing Project," *Detroit: The History and Future of the Motor City*, accessed July 8, 2014, http://detroit1701.org/Sojourner%20Truth%20Housing%20Project.html.

4 "Detroit Race Riot of 1943," *Wikipedia*, accessed July 30, 2013, http://en.wikipedia.org/wiki/Detroit _Race _Riot _(1943).

5 "Irene Morgan," *Wikipedia*, accessed July 8, 2014, http://en.wikipedia.org/wiki/Irene _Morgan _v. _Commonwealth _of _Virginia.

6 "Shelley v. Kraemer," *Wikipedia*, accessed July 8, 2014, http://en.wikipedia.org/wiki/Shelley _v. _Kraemer.

7 "Executive Order 9981," *Wikipedia*, accessed July 8, 2014, http://en.wikipedia.org/wiki/Executive _Order _9981.

8 Jean Marie Ernecq, "Urban Renewal History of Detroit 1946-1970," Center for Urban Studies, Wayne State University, Detroit, March, 1972, https://jscholarship.library.jhu.edu/bitstream/handle/1774.2/32400/ErnUrb.pdf?sequence=1.

9 "Branch History," Detroit Branch NAACP, accessed July 8, 2014, http://detroitnaacp.org/about/branch-history/.

10 "Brown v. Board of Education," *Wikipedia*, accessed July 8, 2014, http://en.wikipedia.org/wiki/Brown _v. _Board _of _Education.

11 "Rosa Parks," *Wikipedia*, accessed July 8, 2014, http://en.wikipedia.org/wiki/Rosa _Parks; Larry Copeland, "Parks Not Seated Alone in History," *USA Today*, November 28, 2005, http://usatoday30.usatoday.com/news/

nation/2005-11-28-montgomery-bus-boycott _x.html; Cassandra Spratling, "An Imperfect Hero: Less-Known Colvin Took Stand on Montgomery Bus Before Parks," *Assata Skakur/Detroit Free Press*, accessed May 5, 2015, http://www.assatashakur.org/forum/open-forum/12480-imperfect-hero-colvin-took-stand-against-segregation-montgomery.html.

12 Joseph Turrini, "Phooie on Louie: African American Detroit and the Election of Jerry Cavanagh," *Michigan History Magazine*, November/December 1999, 10–17, http://michigan.gov/documents/dnr/mhc _mag _phooie-on-louie _308397 _7.pdf.

13 "Civil Rights Act of 1964," *Wikipedia*, accessed July 8, 2014, http://en.wikipedia.org/wiki/Civil _Rights _Act _of _1964.

14 "Protests Against the Vietnam War," *Wikipedia*, accessed July 8, 2014, http://en.wikipedia.org/wiki/Protests _against _the _Vietnam _War.

15 "1967 Detroit Riots," *Wikipedia*, accessed July 8, 2014, http://en.wikipedia.org/wiki/1967 _Detroit _riot.

16 "Detroit Tigers," *Wikipedia*, accessed May 26, 2014, http://en.wikipedia.org/wiki/Detroit _Tigers.

17 "Selective Service System," *Wikipedia*, accessed May 26, 2014, http://en.wikipedia.org/wiki/Selective _Service _System; "Conscription in the United States," *Wikipedia*, accessed October 13, 2013, http://en.wikipedia.org/wiki/Conscription _in _the _United _States.

18 "Volunteer Military," *Wikipedia*, accessed October 2, 2013, http://en.wikipedia.org/wiki/Volunteer _military.

19 "Vietnam War," *Wikipedia*, accessed July 8, 2014, http://en.wikipedia.org/wiki/Vietnam _War.

20 "United States Bicentennial," *Wikipedia*, accessed July 8, 2014, http://en.wikipedia.org/wiki/United _States _Bicentennial.

KEY EVENTS AND CONSIDERATIONS (MICRO LEVEL) 1977-1979

1 "1977," *Wikipedia*, accessed May 25, 2014, http://en.wikipedia.org/wiki/1977.

2 "1978," *Wikipedia*, accessed May 25, 2014, http://en.wikipedia.org/wiki/1978.

3 "1979," *Wikipedia*, accessed May 25, 2014, http://en.wikipedia.org/wiki/1979.

CHAPTER 1

1 "1978," Wikipedia, accessed May 25, 2014, http://en.wikipedia.org/wiki/1978.

2 "Brown Hotel (Louisville, Kentucky), *Wikipedia*, accessed 25 May 2014, http://en.wikipedia.org/wiki/Brown _Hotel _(Louisville, _Kentucky); Wayne Rudolph Davidson, Letter to Diane Sawyer and the Brown Hotel, Louisville, Kentucky.

3 "American Dream," *Wikipedia*, accessed November 2, 2013, http://en.wikipedia.org/wiki/American _Dream.

4 "*The Natural* (Film)," *Wikipedia*, accessed July 16, 2014, http://en.wikipedia.org/wiki/The _Natural _(film).

5 Davidson, *When Clans Collide*, 164–165, 167–170, 197.

6 Davidson, *When Clans Collide*, 197–199.

7 Davidson, *Manufacturing*, 159–160.

8 Davidson, *Manufacturing*, 4, 45–46, 65–66.

9 Davidson, *When Clans Collide*, 169.

10 Davidson, *When Clans Collide*, 197–199.

11 Kristi Tanner, "Raw Data: Detroit's population lowest since 1914," *Detroit Free Press*, July 29, 2013, http://archive.freep.com/article/20130728/OPINION05/307280034/detroit-population-decline-loss.

12 Detroit Historical Society, accessed November 2, 2013, http://detroithistorical.org/.

13 Davidson, *When Clans Collide*, 202–203

14 Detroit African-American History Project, 1900-1949, http://www.daahp.wayne.edu/1900 _1949.html, and 1950-1999, http://www.daahp.wayne.edu/1950 _1999.html, Wayne State University, accessed September 22, 2014.

15 John Gallagher, "100 Years Later, Henry Ford's $5 Day Credited with Changing U.S. Culture, Creating Modern Detroit," *Detroit Free Press*, January 5, 2014, http://archive.freep.com/article/20140105/BUSINESS06/301050040/Henry-Ford-5-day.

16 Davidson, *When Clans Collide*, 197–200.

17 "Detroit Race Riot of 1863," *Wikipedia*, accessed June 12, 2014, http://en.wikipedia.org/wiki/Detroit _Race _Riot _(1863); Detroit Historical Society, accessed November 2, 2013, http://detroithistorical.org/.

18 "Encyclopedia of Detroit," Detroit Historical Museum, accessed November 2, 2013, http://detroithistorical.org/learn/encyclopedia-of-detroit/detroit-police-department.

19 Sojourner Truth Housing Project, accessed July 8, 2014, http://detroit1701.org/Sojourner%20Truth%20Housing%20Project.html.

20 Marvin V. Arnett, *Pieces from Life's Crazy Quilt* (Lincoln, NE, and London: University of Nebraska Press, 2003), 165–168.

21 "Belle Isle Park (Michigan)," *Wikipedia*, accessed May 25, 2014, http://en.wikipedia.org/wiki/Belle _Isle _State _Park _(Michigan).

22 Michael H. Hodges, "Statues, Collectibles, Other Valuables Listed in 2012 Financial Report," *Detroit News*, October 24, 2013, Metro Final, 1A; Nathan Bomey and John Gallagher, "How Detroit Went Broke: The Answers May Surprise You—and Don't Blame Coleman Young," *Detroit Free Press*, September 15, 2013, http://www.freep.com/article/20130915/NEWS01/130801004/Detroit-Bankruptcy-history-1950-debt-pension-revenue.

23 "Detroit Race Riot of 1943," *Wikipedia*, accessed July 30, 2013, http://en.wikipedia.org/wiki/Detroit _Race _Riot _(1943); "1943—A Race Riot There Will Be," The Great Rebellion, access July 30, 2013, http://www.detroits-great-rebellion.com/Detroit---1943.html; James Dickson, "One Moment in Time: The 1943 Race Riots," Politics Blog, *The Detroit News*, July 29, 2013, http://blogs.detroitnews.com/politics/2013/07/29/one-moment-in-time-the-1943-race-riots/; "Hatred on the Home Front: The Detroit Race Riots During World War II," *Life*, accessed July 30, 2013, http://life.time.com/history/detroit-race-riots-1943-photos-from-a-city-in-turmoil-during-wwii/; Jeffrey Shantz, *"They Think Their Fannies Are as Good as Ours": The 1943 Detroit Riot*, summary by Andrea Kaczmarek, accessed October 13, 2014, http://detroitanthologics.pbworks.com/w/page/17602568/They%20Think%20Their%20Fannies%20Are%20As%20Good%20As%20Ours%3A%20The%201943%20Detroit%20Riot; Dominic J. Capeci Jr., "Black-Jewish Relations in Wartime Detroit: the Marsh, Loving, Wolf Surveys and the Race Riot of 1943*," *Jewish Social Studies*, Vol. 47, No. 3/4 (Summer–Autumn, 1985), 221-242, http:// www.jstor.org/stable/4467300; Matthew Wilhelm Kapell, "'Miscreants, Be They White or Colored': The Local Press Reactions to the 1943 Detroit 'Race Riots,'" *Michigan Academician*, XXIX (2009), 213-244, https://netforum.avectra.com/eweb/DynamicPage.aspx?Site=MASAL&WebCode=39article12.

24 "1967 Detroit Riot," *Wikipedia*, accessed July 8, 2014, http://en.wikipedia.org/wiki/1967 _Detroit _riot; "Special Reports: Interactive: Timeline for

Detroit's 1967 Riots," *Detroit News*, accessed May 5, 2015, http://www.detroitnews.com/article/20090424/SPECIAL01/90424002;

"Detroit Riot of 1967," *World History Project*, accessed May 5, 2015, http://worldhistoryproject.org/1967/7/23/detroit-riot-of-1967;

"1967: The 12th Street Riot," *History*, accessed May 5, 2015, http://www.history.com/this-day-in-history/the-12th-street-riot; "Starting Point of the July, 1967 Racial Riot: 9125 Twelfth Street at the corner of Twelfth and Clairmont," *Detroit: The History and Future of the Motor City*, accessed May 5, 2015,

http://www.detroit1701.org/Start1967Riot.html; "Encyclopedia of Detroit: Riots of 1967," *Detroit Historical Society*, accessed May 5, 2015, http://detroithistorical.org/learn/encyclopedia-of-detroit/riots-1967; "The Great Rebellion," *Detroit—Blood That Never Dried*, accessed May 5, 2015, http://www.detroits-great-rebellion.com/Index.html; "American Experience: Eyes on the Prize Civil Rights Movement 1954-1985: Riots in Detroit July 1967" *PBS*, accessed May 5, 2015, http://www.pbs.org/wgbh/amex/eyesontheprize/story/13 _detroit.html.

25 "Final Report of Cyrus R. Vance, Special Assistant to the Secretary of Defense, Concerning the Detroit Riots, July 23 through August 2, 1967," accessed April 4, 2012, http://www.lbjlib.utexas.edu/johnson/archives.hom/oralhistory.hom/Vance-C/DetroitReport.asp.

26 Peter Gavrilovich and Bill McGraw, eds., *The Detroit Almanac: 300 Years of Life in the Motor City* (Detroit: Detroit Free Press, 2010), 36.

27 Ernest H. Borden, *Detroit's Paradise Valley* (Mount Pleasant, SC: Arcadia, 2003), 6-11; "Black Bottom, Detroit," *Wikipedia*, accessed December 20, 2006, http://en.wikipedia.org/wiki/Black _Bottom, _Detroit; Frank D. Rashid, "Literary Map of Detroit: Paradise Valley/Black Bottom," Marygrove College, accessed December 20, 2006, http://www.marygrove.edu/academics/institutes/institute-for-detroit-studies/literary-map-of-detroit/item/9-paradise-valleyblack-bottom.html; "Detroit Black Bottom," *Push Nevada Review*, accessed November 6, 2013, http://pushnevahda.com/detroit-black-bottom/; Gavrilovich and McGraw *Detroit Almanac*, 102-111; John Gallagher, "When Detroit Paved Over Paradise: The Story of I-375," *Detroit Free Press*, December 15, 2013, http://archive.freep.com/article/20131215/OPINION05/312150060/Black-Bottom-Detroit-I-375-I-75-paradise-valley-removal; Davidson, *Manufacturing*, 109-111.

28 Davidson, *Manufacturing*, 168-169.

29 Davidson, *Manufacturing*, 109-111.

30 "Urban Renewal," *Wikipedia*, accessed October 2, 2013, http://en.wikipedia.org/wiki/Urban _renewal; Jean Marie Ernecq, "Urban Renewal History of Detroit 1946-1970," Center for Urban Studies, Wayne State University, Detroit, March, 1972, https://jscholarship.library.jhu.edu/bitstream/handle/1774.2/32400/ErnUrb.pdf?sequence=1.

31 "Jefferies Project," *Wikipedia*, accessed November 2, 2013, http://en.wikipedia.org/wiki/Jeffries _Projects.

32 "Brewster-Douglas Housing Projects," *Wikipedia*, accessed November 2, 2013, http://en.wikipedia.org/wiki/Brewster-Douglass _Housing _Projects;

Steve Pardo, "'Bittersweet' End for Detroit's Brewster Housing Project," *Detroit News*, March 19, 2012, http://www.alipac.us/f19/bittersweet-end-detroits-brewster-housing-project-253175/.

33 Davidson, *When Clans Collide*, xlii.

34 Davidson, *Manufacturing*, 5; *When Clans Collide*, 66.

35 PR Newswire, "Woodbridge Estates Honors Motown Legends, April 11 in Detroit; Developer Holds Street Naming and Groundbreaking Celebration," The Free Library, accessed 25 November 25, 2013,

http://www.thefreelibrary.com/Woodbridge+Estates+Honors +Motown+Legends%2c+April+11+in+Detroit %3b... -a085886537.

36 "My Girl (The Temptations Song)," *Wikipedia*, accessed October 9, 2013, http://en.wikipedia.org/wiki/My _Girl _(The _Temptations _song); Marc Myers, "Making Sunshine on a Cloudy Day," *Wall Street Journal*, October 21, 2011, http://online.wsj.com/news/articles/SB10001424052970203476804576615250196742630.

37 "Laminated Glass," *Wikipedia*, accessed May 25, 2014, http://en.wikipedia.org/wiki/Laminated _glass.

38 "*The Graduate*," *Wikipedia*, accessed August 3, 2014, http://en.wikipedia.org/wiki/The _Graduate; Gautam Nik, "Ideas, Slow and Steady: The Creation of Some of Our Greatest Products Is Often Unplanned and Rarely Smooth. Consider Plastics," *Wall Street Journal*, January 11, 1999, R18.

39 "Chaldeans Christians," *Wikipedia*, accessed November 30, 2014, http://en.wikipedia.org/wiki/Chaldean _Christians; "Who Are the Chaldean Christians?: Questions and Answers," Baqofa.com, accessed November 30, 2014, http://www.baqofa.com/chaldean.html.

40 "Redlining," *Wikipedia*, accessed on June 6, 2014, http://en.wikipedia.org/wiki/Redlining.

41 Beryl Satter, *Family Properties: Race, Real Estate, and the Exploitation of Black Urban America* (New York: Metropolitan Books, 2009), 41-63.

42 Davidson, *When Clans Collide*, 159-160.

43 "American Dream," *Wikipedia*, accessed November 2, 2013, http://en.wikipedia.org/wiki/American _Dream.

44 "White Flight," *Wikipedia*, accessed November 2, 2013, http://en.wikipedia.org/wiki/White _flight.

45 "*The Help* (Film)," *Wikipedia*, accessed July 16, 2014, http://en.wikipedia.org/wiki/The _Help _(film).

46 "Orville L. Hubbard," *Wikipedia*, accessed November 2, 2013, http://en.wikipedia.org/wiki/Orville _L. _Hubbard; Zlati Meyer, "This Week in Michigan History: Hubbard Retires as Mayor of Dearborn," *Sunday Free Press*, January 1, 2012, 15A; Stephen Henderson, "A Monument to a Racist: Symbols of past racism cry out for revisiting;" Sunday Free Press, July 12, 2015, 13A.

47 "Dearborn, Michigan," *Wikipedia*, accessed November 2, 2013, http://en.wikipedia.org/wiki/Dearborn, _Michigan.

48 "1973 Oil Crisis," *Wikipedia*, accessed November 2, 2013, http://en.wikipedia.org/wiki/1973 _oil _crisis.

49 Davidson, *When Clans Collide*, 1–2.

50 "W. Eugene Smith's Landmark Photo Essay, 'Nurse Midwife,'" *Life*, accessed May 25, 2014, http://life.time.com/history/w-eugene-smith-life-magazine-1951-photo-essay-nurse-midwife/?iid=lf%7Cmostpop#1.

51 "Detroit Tigers," *Wikipedia*, accessed May 26, 2014, http://en.wikipedia.org/wiki/Detroit _Tigers.

52 Davidson, *When Clans Collide*, xl.

53 "1930 Overview," United States Census Bureau, accessed September 24, 2014, https://www.census.gov/history/www/through _the _decades/overview/1930.html.

54 Ibid.

55 Anita Roddick, "Podium: To Be Poor in the US Is the Bottom: A Speech by the Founder of the Body Shop to the Human Scale Education Conference," *The Independent*, Wednesday, October 7, 1998, http://www.independent.co.uk/arts-entertainment/podium-to-be-poor-in-the-us-is-the-bottom-1176606.html.

56 Davidson, *When Clans Collide*, 167–168.

57 "Murray's Pomade," *Wikipedia*, accessed June 12, 2014, http://en.wikipedia.org/wiki/Murray%27s _Pomade.

58 John Carlisle, "Residents Try to Revive Lost 'Black Eden,'" *Sunday Free Press*, November 30, 2014, 1A.
59 "Irene Morgan," *Wikipedia*, accessed July 8, 2014, http://en.wikipedia.org/wiki/Irene _Morgan _v. _Commonwealth _of _Virginia.
60 "Rosa Parks," *Wikipedia*, accessed November 2, 2013, http://en.wikipedia.org/wiki/Rosa _Parks.
61 "Linus van Pelt," *Wikipedia*, accessed November 2, 2013, http://en.wikipedia.org/wiki/Linus _van _Pelt.
62 "1960 Overview," United States Census Bureau, accessed September 24, 2014, https://www.census.gov/history/www/through _the _decades/overview/1960.html.
63 Gavrilovich and McGraw, *Detroit Almanac*, 32-33; 105–110.
64 Borden, *Detroit's Paradise Valley*, 6–11.
65 Otis Williams with Patricia Romanowski, *Temptations* (New York: First Cooper Press, 2002), 27.
66 Davidson, *Manufacturing*, 52–53.
67 Laura Meckler, "How Churches Are Slowly Becoming Less Segregated," *Wall Street Journal*, October 13, 2014, http://www.wsj.com/articles/a-church-of-many-colors-the-most-segregated-hour-in-america-gets-less-so-1413253801.
68 New Bethel Baptist Church, accessed June 12, 2014, http://www.nbbcdetroit.org/.
69 "C. L. Franklin," *Wikipedia*, accessed June 12, 2014, http://en.wikipedia.org/wiki/C. _L. _Franklin.
70 Smokey Robinson with David Ritz, *Smokey: Inside My Life* (New York: McGraw-Hill Publishing, 1989), 28–30.
71 Borden, *Detroit's Paradise Valley*, 6–11.
72 "Rosewood Massacre," *Wikipedia*, accessed November 2, 2013, http://en.wikipedia.org/wiki/Rosewood _massacre.
73 "Greenwood (Tulsa)," *Wikipedia*, accessed November 2, 2013, http://en.wikipedia.org/wiki/Greenwood, _Tulsa, _Oklahoma.
74 Davidson, *Manufacturing*, 53.
75 Davidson, *Manufacturing*, 168–169.
76 "New Deal," *Wikipedia*, accessed November 5, 2013, http://en.wikipedia.org/wiki/New _Deal.
77 "Fair Deal," *Wikipedia*, accessed November 5, 2013, http://en.wikipedia.org/wiki/Fair _Deal; "Housing Act of 1949," *Wikipedia*, accessed November 5, 2013, http://en.wikipedia.org/wiki/Housing _Act _of _1949; R. H.

Geselbracht, ed., *The Civil Rights Legacy of Harry S. Truman*, The Truman Legacy Series, vol. 2, Truman State University Press, 14–15, May 2004.

78 "Ford River Rouge Complex," *Wikipedia*, accessed 13, 2013, http://en.wikipedia.org/wiki/Ford _River _Rouge _Complex.

79 "Zug Island," Detroit 1701, accessed November 2, 2013, http://www.detroit1701.org/Zug%20Island.html; "Zug Island," *Wikipedia*, accessed November 2, 2013, http://en.wikipedia.org/wiki/Zug _Island.

80 "Michigan Refining Division," Marathon Petroleum Corporation, accessed November 2, 2013, http://www.marathonpetroleum.com/Operations/Refining _and _Marketing/Refining/Michigan _Refining _Division/ .

81 "Bill Kennedy (Actor)," *Wikipedia*, accessed November 2, 2013, http://en.wikipedia.org/wiki/Bill _Kennedy _(actor).

82 "Rita Louise 'Rita Bell' Bell Hansen," Find a Grave, accessed November 2, 2013, http://www.findagrave.com/cgi-bin/fg.cgi?page=gr&GRid=8200764.

83 "Ghoulardi," *Wikipedia*, accessed November 2, 2013, http://en.wikipedia.org/wiki/Ghoulardi.

84 "*Ocean's 11*," *Wikipedia*, accessed May 26, 2014, http://en.wikipedia.org/wiki/Ocean%27s _Eleven _(1960 _film).

85 "Study: White and Black Children Biased toward Lighter Skin," *CNN*, May 14, 2010, http://www.cnn.com/2010/US/05/13/doll.study/index.html; "Kenneth and Mamie Clark," *Wikipedia*, accessed September 4, 2014, http://en.wikipedia.org/wiki/Kenneth _and _Mamie _Clark; "CNN Pilot Demonstration," April 28, 2010, http://i2.cdn.turner.com/cnn/2010/images/05/13/expanded _results _methods _cnn.pdf.

86 "*The Rifleman*," *Wikipedia*, accessed November 13, 2014, http://en.wikipedia.org/wiki/The _Rifleman.

87 "Pat Boone," *Wikipedia*, accessed November 2, 2013, http://en.wikipedia.org/wiki/Pat _Boone.

88 "Little Richard," *Wikipedia*, accessed November 2, 2013, http://en.wikipedia.org/wiki/Little _Richard.

89 "Michigan State Prison," *Wikipedia*, accessed June 12, 2014, http://en.wikipedia.org/wiki/Michigan _State _Prison.

90 "Jefferies Projects," *Wikipedia*, accessed November 2, 2013, http://en.wikipedia.org/wiki/Jeffries _Projects.

91 Williams, *Temptations*, 42.

92 The Cleveland Memory Project, "Public Housing Projects," Cleveland State University, accessed November 2, 2013, http://images.ulib.csuohio.

edu/cdm/search/searchterm/Public%20housing%20projects!unknown/field/subjec!creato/mode/exact!all/conn/and!and/cosuppress/.

93 "Cold War," *Wikipedia*, accessed October 2, 2013, http://en.wikipedia.org/wiki/Cold _War.

94 "Study: White and Black Children Biased toward Lighter Skin," *CNN*, May 14, 2010, http://www.cnn.com/2010/US/05/13/doll.study/index.html; "Kenneth and Mamie Clark," *Wikipedia*, accessed September 4, 2014, http://en.wikipedia.org/wiki/Kenneth _and _Mamie _Clark; "CNN Pilot Demonstration," April 28, 2010, http://i2.cdn.turner.com/cnn/2010/images/05/13/expanded _results _methods _cnn.pdf.

95 "Lemon Law," *Wikipedia*, accessed November 3, 2013, http://en.wikipedia.org/wiki/Lemon _law; "Magnuson-Moss Warranty Act," *Wikipedia*, accessed November 3, 2013, http://en.wikipedia.org/wiki/Magnuson%E2%80%93Moss _Warranty _Act.

96 Davidson, *Manufacturing*, 13–14.

97 Davidson, *Manufacturing*, 65–66.

98 "On June 16 1962," The Baseball Page, accessed October 13, 2014, http://www.thebaseballpage.com/baseball-history/june-16-1962; "'Ball Four': The Book That Changed Baseball," *NPR Books*, April 26, 2012, http://www.npr.org/2012/04/26/151457344/ball-four-the-book-that-changed-baseball.

99 "Let's Go Get Stoned (R&B song)," *Wikipedia*, accessed October 9, 2013, http://en.wikipedia.org/wiki/Let%27s _Go _Get _Stoned _(Ray _Charles _song).

100 "Joe Simon (Musician)," *Wikipedia*, accessed September 4, 2014, http://en.wikipedia.org/wiki/Joe _Simon _(musician).

101 Melinda Beck, "Are Alpha Males Healthy?: Aggressiveness Aids Rise to Top, but the Stress Can Harm a Body," *Wall Street Journal*, September 13, 2011, D1; "Synopsis: The Alpha Male Syndrome," *Worth Ethic Corporation*, accessed May 1, 2015, http://www.worthethic.com/the-alpha-male-syndrome.html;

"How to Become an Alpha Male," *The Modern Man*, accessed May 1, 2015, http://www.themodernman.com/how _to _become _an _alpha _male.html.

102 "Assassination of John F. Kennedy," *Wikipedia*, accessed November 2, 2013, http://en.wikipedia.org/wiki/Assassination _of _John _F. _Kennedy.

103 "Johann Wolfgang von Goethe Quotes," BrainyQuote, accessed October 5, 2014, http://www.brainyquote.com/quotes/quotes/j/johannwolf119889.html.

104 "*Peter and the Wolf*," *Wikipedia*, accessed June 12, 2014, http://en.wikipedia.org/wiki/Peter _and _the _Wolf.

105 "*It Hurts So Good* (Album)," *Wikipedia*, accessed November 2, 2013, http://en.wikipedia.org/wiki/It_Hurts_So_Good_(Millie_Jackson_album).
106 "Jim Brown," *Wikipedia*, accessed November 2, 2013, http://en.wikipedia.org/wiki/Jim_Brown.
107 "1961 Detroit Tigers Season," *Wikipedia*, accessed May 26, 2014, http://en.wikipedia.org/wiki/1961_Detroit_Tigers_season; "Colavito-for-Kuenn Was Peachy for Tigers," *Detroit Free Press*, April 18, 2010, 10D; John Lowe, "Colavito, an Indian for Life," *Detroit Free Press*, August 18, 2013, 10C.
108 "Marvel Comics," *Wikipedia*, accessed November 10, 2014, http://en.wikipedia.org/wiki/Marvel_Comics.
109 "Iceberg Slim," *Wikipedia*, accessed November 10, 2014, http://en.wikipedia.org/wiki/Iceberg_Slim.
110 "Donald Goines," *Wikipedia*, accessed November 10, 2014, http://en.wikipedia.org/wiki/Donald_Goines.
111 Kevin Clark, "Peterson Indicted," *Wall Street Journal*, September 13–14, 2014, A14.
112 "*Leave It to Beaver*," *Wikipedia*, accessed July 16, 2014, http://en.wikipedia.org/wiki/Leave_It_to_Beaver.
113 "*The Adventures of Ozzie and Harriet*," *Wikipedia*, accessed July 16, 2014, http://en.wikipedia.org/wiki/The_Adventures_of_Ozzie_and_Harriet.
114 Chauncy Glover, "Heroin Overdoses Hit Waterford Families Hard," *Click On Detroit*, December, 11, 2014, http://www.clickondetroit.com/news/heroin-overdoses-hit-waterford-families-hard/30189152; Drew Griffin and Nelli Black, "Deadly High: How Synthetic Drugs Are Killing Kids," *CNN*, December 2, 2014, http://www.cnn.com/2014/12/01/us/synthetic-drugs-investigation/index.html; "2014 Pulitzer Prize Nominated Finalist, Local Reporting: Rebecca D. O'Brien and Thomas Mashberg," The Pulitzer Prizes,, accessed September 13, 2014, http://www.pulitzer.org/2014_local_reporting_finalist_2, with links to nine-part series on "Suburbia's Deadly Secret."
115 "*Good Times*," *Wikipedia*, accessed July 16, 2014, http://en.wikipedia.org/wiki/Good_Times.
116 "*The Jeffersons*," *Wikipedia*, accessed July 16, 2014, http://en.wikipedia.org/wiki/The_Jeffersons.
117 "*The Cosby Show*," *Wikipedia*, accessed July 16, 2014, http://en.wikipedia.org/wiki/The_Cosby_Show.

118 Davidson, *When Clans Collide*, xxxiii.
119 "Interstate Highway System," *Wikipedia*, accessed November 2, 2013, http://en.wikipedia.org/wiki/Interstate _Highway _System; Raymond A. Mohl, *The Interstates and the Cities: Highways, Housing, and the Freeway Revolt*, Department of History, University of Alabama at Birmingham Research Report, Poverty and Race Research Action Council, 2002.
120 Williams, *Temptations*, 78-81.
121 Davidson, *When Clans Collide*, 193.
122 "Mammoth Cave National Park," *Wikipedia*, accessed November 2, 2013, http://en.wikipedia.org/wiki/Mammoth _Cave.
123 Associated Press, "Sinkhole Swallows Cars at Museum," *The Detroit News*, February 13, 2014, Section 1E.
124 Davidson, *When Clans Collide*, lviii-lx.
125 George Washington's Mount Vernon, accessed September 24, 2014, http://www.mountvernon.org/.
126 Davidson, *When Clans Collide*, xlv.
127 "*Rocky*," *Wikipedia*, accessed July 16, 2014, http://en.wikipedia.org/wiki/Rocky.
128 "Jesse Owens," *Wikipedia*, accessed May 26, 2014, http://en.wikipedia.org/wiki/Jesse _Owens.
129 "Harrison Dillard," *Wikipedia*, accessed May 26, 2014, http://en.wikipedia.org/wiki/Harrison _Dillard.
130 "(I Can't Get No) Satisfaction," *Wikipedia*, accessed October 9, 2013, http://en.wikipedia.org/wiki/(I _Can%27t _Get _No) _Satisfaction.
131 Larry Getlen, "Mick Jagger on James Brown: 'I copied all his moves" *TIME.com*, July 24, 2014, http://time.com/3025167/mick-jagger-james-brown-interview-legacy/.
132 Williams, *Temptations*, 21.
133 Williams, *Temptations*, 38.
134 "The 20 Grand," *Wikipedia*, accessed May 26, 2014, http://en.wikipedia.org/wiki/The _20 _Grand; George Clinton and Ben Greenman, *Brothas Be, Yo Like George, Ain't That Funkin' Kinda Hard on You?* (New York: Atria Books, 2014), 43.
135 Williams, *Temptations*, 45, 67, 70.
136 Berry Gordy, *To Be Loved: The Music, The Magic, The Memories of Motown*, New York: Warner Books, 1994), 113; Bill Dahl, *Motown: The Golden Years—The Stars and Music That Shaped a Generation* (Iola, Wisconsin: Krause Publications, 2001), 16.

137 Williams, *Temptations*, 27.

138 "White Flight," *Wikipedia*, accessed November 2, 2013 http://en.wikipedia.org/wiki/White _flight.

139 "Decline of Detroit," *Wikipedia*, accessed September 24, 2014, http://en.wikipedia.org/wiki/Decline _of _Detroit; "Racial Segregation in the United States," accessed September 24, 2014, http://en.wikipedia.org/wiki/Racial _segregation _in _the _United _States; D'Vera Cohn, "The Year the Whites Left the City," *Washington Post*, July 19, 1999, http://www.washingtonpost.com/wp-srv/local/2000/flight071999.htm; Eddie Dean, "A Brief History of White People in Southeast," *Washington City Paper*, October 16, 1998, http://www.washingtoncitypaper.com/articles/15999/a-brief-history-of-white-people-in-southeast.

140 Fuller Brush Company, accessed June 12, 2014, http://www.fuller.com/.

141 Davidson, *Manufacturing*, 66.

142 "*Happy Days*," *Wikipedia*, accessed October 9, 2013, http://en.wikipedia.org/wiki/Happy _Days.

143 "Mackenzie High School (Michigan)," *Wikipedia*, accessed May 26, 2014, http://en.wikipedia.org/wiki/Mackenzie _High _School _(Michigan).

144 "Runaway Child, Running Wild," *Wikipedia*, accessed October 9, 2013, http://en.wikipedia.org/wiki/Runaway _Child, _Running _Wild.

145 "(I Know) I'm Losing You," *Wikipedia*, accessed October 9, 2013, http://en.wikipedia.org/wiki/(I _Know) _I%27m _Losing _You.

146 "The Esquires," *Wikipedia*, accessed October 9, 2013, http://en.wikipedia.org/wiki/The _Esquires; "The Esquires—Get On Up," *YouTube*, accessed October 9, 2013, https://www.youtube.com/watch?v=wnQ8yQJROCI.

147 "Your Precious Love," *Wikipedia*, accessed October 9, 2013, http://en.wikipedia.org/wiki/Your _Precious _Love.

148 "Mumford High School," *Wikipedia*, accessed May 26, 2014, http://en.wikipedia.org/wiki/Mumford _High _School.

149 "Jerry Bruckheimer," *Wikipedia*, accessed May 26, 2014, http://en.wikipedia.org/wiki/Jerry _Bruckheimer; Ben Fritz, "Golden Age Fades for Film Producers in Hollywood," *Wall Street Journal*, January 18–19, 2014, A1.

150 "Ivan Boseky," *Wikipedia*, accessed May 26, 2014, http://en.wikipedia.org/wiki/Ivan _Boesky.

151 Robinson, *Smokey*, 131.

152 "Super Bowl III," *Wikipedia*, accessed May 26, 2014, http://en.wikipedia.org/wiki/Super _Bowl _III.

153 "Interstate 96," *Wikipedia*, accessed June 12, 2014, http://en.wikipedia.org/wiki/Interstate _96.

154 "Ford River Rouge Complex," *Wikipedia*, accessed November 13, 2013, http://en.wikipedia.org/wiki/Ford _River _Rouge _Complex.

155 "Gulf War," *Wikipedia*, accessed November 2, 2013, http://en.wikipedia.org/wiki/Gulf _War.

156 "CNN," *Wikipedia*, accessed November 2, 2013, http://en.wikipedia.org/wiki/Cable _News _Network.

157 Ted Sampley, "First Muslim Congressman Excites Crowd in 'Hezbollah City' USA, aka Dearborn, Michigan," *Sodahead.com-U.S. Veteran Dispatch*, accessed May 1, 2015, http://www.sodahead.com/living/first-muslim-congressman-excites-crowd-in-hezbollah-city-usa-aka-dearborn-michigan/question-1446477/?page=3&link=ibaf&q=First+Muslin+Congressman+excites+crowd+in+Hezbollah+City+USA+aka+Dearborn+Michigan.

158 "*Down to Earth* (Stevie Wonder Album)," *Wikipedia*, accessed October 9, 2013, http://en.wikipedia.org/wiki/Down _to _Earth _(Stevie _Wonder _album).

159 "The Artistics," *Wikipedia*, accessed October 9, 2013, http://en.wikipedia.org/wiki/The _Artistics; "The Artistics – I'm Gonna Miss You," *YouTube*, accessed May 1, 2015; https://www.youtube.com/watch?v=dO8hk5pgh6M.

160 "Love Is a Hurtin' Thing," *Wikipedia*, accessed May 26, 2014, http://en.wikipedia.org/wiki/Love _Is _a _Hurtin%27 _Thing.

161 "Hippie," *Wikipedia*, accessed September 24, 2014, http://en.wikipedia.org/wiki/Hippie.

162 "The Monkees," *Wikipedia*, accessed, December 17, 2014, http://en.wikipedia.org/wiki/The _Monkees.

163 Clinton, *Brothors Be, Yo Like George*, 94–95.

164 Dan Austin, "How Our Transit Went from Best to Worst: The Fall of Metro Detroit's Once Prized Transit System," *Detroit Free Press*, February 8, 2015, 13A.

165 "Motortown Revue," *Wikipedia*, accessed November 2, 2013, http://en.wikipedia.org/wiki/Motortown _Revue.

166 "Bobby Taylor & the Vancouvers," *Wikipedia*, accessed October 9, 2013, http://en.wikipedia.org/wiki/Bobby _Taylor _%26 _the _Vancouvers.

167 "Try a Little Tenderness," *Wikipedia*, accessed October 9, 2013, http://en.wikipedia.org/wiki/Try _a _Little _Tenderness.

168 "Cheech & Chong," *Wikipedia*, accessed June 12, 2014, http://en.wikipedia.org/wiki/Cheech _%26 _Chong.

169 "The Underdogs … Love's Gone Bad," *YouTube*, accessed September 1, 2014, www.youtube.com/watch?v=DhkFgklKcT0.

170 "The Temptations," *Wikipedia*, accessed November 2, 2013, http://en.wikipedia.org/wiki/The _Temptations.

171 "CKLW," *Wikipedia*, accessed November 2, 2013, http://en.wikipedia.org/wiki/CKLW; Clinton, *Brothors Be, Yo Like George*, 55.

172 "Robin Seymour," Detroit Memories, accessed May 27, 2010, http://www.detroitmemories.com/robinseymour.html.

173 "The Fantastic Four (Band)," *Wikipedia*, accessed October 9, 2013, http://en.wikipedia.org/wiki/The _Fantastic _Four _(R%26B _Group).

174 Davidson, *Manufacturing*, 65–66.

175 "George Clinton (Musician)," *Wikipedia*, accessed July 20, 2014, http://en.wikipedia.org/wiki/George _Clinton _(musician); "*Funkadelic* (Album)," accessed October 9, 2013, http://en.wikipedia.org/wiki/Funkadelic _(album); Clinton, *Brothors Be, Yo Like George*, 23, 55, 66.

176 "Ol' Man River," *Wikipedia*, accessed October 9, 2013, http://en.wikipedia.org/wiki/Ol%27 _Man _River.

177 "1967 Detroit Riots," *Wikipedia*, accessed July 8, 2014, http://en.wikipedia.org/wiki/1967 _Detroit _riot; "Special Reports: Interactive: Timeline for Detroit's 1967 Riots," *Detroit News*, accessed May 5, 2015, http://www.detroitnews.com/article/20090424/SPECIAL01/90424002;

"Detroit Riot of 1967," *World History Project*, accessed May 5, 2015, http://worldhistoryproject.org/1967/7/23/detroit-riot-of-1967;

"1967: The 12th Street Riot," *History*, accessed May 5, 2015, http://www.history.com/this-day-in-history/the-12th-street-riot; "Starting Point of the July, 1967 Racial Riot: 9125 Twelfth Street at the corner of Twelfth and Clairmont," *Detroit: The History and Future of the Motor City*, accessed May 5, 2015,

http://www.detroit1701.org/Start1967Riot.html; "Encyclopedia of Detroit: Riots of 1967," *Detroit Historical Society*, accessed May 5, 2015, http://detroithistorical.org/learn/encyclopedia-of-detroit/riots-1967; "The Great Rebellion," *Detroit—Blood That Never Dried*, accessed May 5, 2015, http://www.detroits-great-rebellion.com/Index.html; "American Experience: Eyes on the Prize Civil Rights Movement 1954-1985: Riots in Detroit July 1967" *PBS*, accessed May 5, 2015, http://www.pbs.org/wgbh/amex/eyesontheprize/story/13 _detroit.html; "The Detroit Riot: A Profile of 500

Prisoners," U.S. Department of Labor, March 1968, http://bl-libg-doghill.ads.iu.edu/gpd-web/detroit.pdf; "Kerner Commission," *Wikipedia*, accessed July 20, 2014, http://en.wikipedia.org/wiki/Kerner _Commission; "Report of the National Advisory Commission on Civil Disorders," accessed July 20, 2014, http://www.eisenhowerfoundation.org/docs/kerner.pdf; "Final Report of Cyrus R. Vance, Special Assistant to the Secretary of Defense Concerning the Detroit Riots," July 23 through August 2, 1967, http://www.lbjlib.utexas.edu/johnson/archives.hom/oralhistory.hom/Vance-C/DetroitReport.asp.

178 "Vietnam War," *Wikipedia*, accessed November 2, 2013, http://en.wikipedia.org/wiki/Vietnam _War.

179 "Speakeasy," *Wikipedia*, accessed July 20, 2014, http://en.wikipedia.org/wiki/Speakeasy.

180 "15 U.S. Code § 631 - Declaration of Policy," Legal Information Institute, Cornell University Law School, accessed April 27, 2012, http://www.law.cornell.edu/uscode/text/15/631; Jonathon J. Bean, "'Burn Baby Burn': Small Business in the Urban Riots of the 1960s," *Independent Review*, Fall 2000, Vol. 5, No. 2, 165–187, accessed May 1, 2012, http://www.independent.org/pdf/tir/tir _05 _2 _bean.pdf; "Kerner Commission," *Wikipedia*, accessed July 20, 2014, http://en.wikipedia.org/wiki/Kerner _Commission; "Report of the National Advisory Commission on Civil Disorders," accessed July 20, 2014, http://www.eisenhowerfoundation.org/docs/kerner.pdf; "Final Report of Cyrus R. Vance, Special Assistant to the Secretary of Defense Concerning the Detroit Riots," July 23 through August 2, 1967, http://www.lbjlib.utexas.edu/johnson/archives.hom/oralhistory.hom/Vance-C/DetroitReport.asp.

181 Pervaiz Shallwani, Ben Kesling, and Caroline Porter, "Ferguson Businesses Vow to Rebuild," *Wall Street Journal*, November 28, 2014, A7.

182 Gavrilovich and McGraw, *Detroit Almanac*, 36.

183 "*Happy Days*," *Wikipedia*, accessed October 9, 2013, http://en.wikipedia.org/wiki/Happy _Days.

184 Tom Greenwood, "Race Back to 1964 with Video from City Streets," *Detroit News*, February 28, 2014, 2A.

185 "Deon Jackson," *Wikipedia*, accessed June 12, 2014, http://en.wikipedia.org/wiki/Deon _Jackson.

186 "About the Vikings," Motown Vikings AKA Erick and the Vikings Official Website, accessed June 12, 2014, http://www.motownvikings.com/.

187 "*Amen* (TV Series)" *Wikipedia*, accessed, July 16, 2014, http://en.wikipedia.org/wiki/Amen _(TV _series).

188 Alex M. Franquet, "Talking about Detroit: Interviews and Photos, Francisco (Frank) Garcia II," accessed May 1, 2015, http://www.soul-source.co.uk/ _/soul-articles/talking-about-detroit-interviews-and-photos-by-alex-m-franquet-r1698; "Francisco (Frank) Garcia," LinkedIn, accessed June 6, 2014, http://www.linkedin.com/pub/francisco-frank-garcia/18/43A/1B3.

189 Davidson, *When Clans Collide*, xxxviii.

190 National Association of Police Athletic/Activities Leagues, accessed December 26, 2014, http://nationalpal.org/.

191 Roostertail, accessed June 12, 2014. http://roostertail.com/.

192 "Neil Armstrong," *Wikipedia*, accessed July 30, 2014, http://en.wikiquote.org/wiki/Neil _Armstrong.

193 "Vietnam War," *Wikipedia*, accessed November 2, 2013, http://en.wikipedia.org/wiki/Vietnam _War.

194 "African-American Civil Rights Movement (1954–68)," accessed November 2, 2013, http://en.wikipedia.org/wiki/African-American _Civil _Rights _Movement _(1955%E2%80%931968).

195 "Martin Luther King Jr.," *Wikipedia*, accessed November 2, 2013, http://en.wikipedia.org/wiki/Mlk.

196 "Robert F. Kennedy," *Wikipedia*, accessed November 2, 2013, http://en.wikipedia.org/wiki/Robert _F. _Kennedy.

197 "Black Power," *Wikipedia*, accessed November 2, 2013, http://en.wikipedia.org/wiki/Black _power; Leslie Fulbright, "Militant or Activists? Former Black Panthers Work on Positive Image," *Detroit News*, October 13, 2006, 12A.

198 "The Last Poets," *Wikipedia*, accessed December 21, 2014, http://en.wikipedia.org/wiki/The _Last _Poets.

199 "Gil Scott-Heron," *Wikipedia*, accessed December 21, 2014, http://en.wikipedia.org/wiki/Gil _Scott-Heron.

200 "The Revolution Will Not Be Televised," *Wikipedia*, accessed December 21, 2014, http://en.wikipedia.org/wiki/The _Revolution _Will _Not _ Be _Televised.

201 "*The Last Poets* (Album)," *Wikipedia*, accessed December 21, 2014, http://en.wikipedia.org/wiki/The _Last _Poets _(album).

202 "Highland Park Community College," *Wikipedia*, accessed November 2, 2013, http://en.wikipedia.org/wiki/Highland _Park _Community _College.

203 Robinson, *Smokey*, 77.

204 "Alcatraz Island," *Wikipedia*, accessed November 2, 2013, http://en.wikipedia.org/wiki/Alcatraz _Island.

205 "Selective Service System," *Wikipedia*, accessed May 26, 2014, http://en.wikipedia.org/wiki/Selective _Service _System; "Conscription in the United States," *Wikipedia*, accessed October 13, 2013, http://en.wikipedia.org/wiki/Conscription _in _the _United _States; "Selective Service System," accessed 5 May 2015, http://www.sss.gov/lotter1.htm.

206 Wayne County Community College District, accessed May 10, 2015, http://www.wcccd.edu/about/history.htm.

CHAPTER 2

1 "Iron Butterfly," *Wikipedia*, accessed October 9, 2013, http://en.wikipedia.org/wiki/Iron _butterfly.

2 Thomas De Quincey, *Confessions of an English Opium-Eater*, 2nd ed., London: Printed for Taylor and Hessey, Fleet Street, 1823.

3 "*American Gangster* (Film)," *Wikipedia*, accessed July 23, 2014, http://en.wikipedia.org/wiki/American _Gangster _(film); George Clinton and Ben Greenman, *Brothas Be, Yo Like George, Ain't That Funkin' Kinda Hard on You?* (New York: Atria Books, 2014), 28.

4 "Heroin," *Dictionary.com*, accessed October 13, 2014, http://dictionary.reference.com/browse/heroin.

5 "Heroin," Drugs.com, accessed November 1, 2013, http://www.drugs.com/heroin.html; "Chemical Cocktail Affects Humans and the Environment," Phys.org, accessed November 1, 2013, http://phys.org/print189079522.html; "Cocktail," *Wikipedia*, accessed November 1, 2013, http://en.wikipedia.org/wiki/Cocktail; Peter Brush, "Higher and Higher: American Drug Use in Vietnam," *Vietnam*, Vol. 15, No. 4, December 2002, nintharticle.com/vietnam-drug-usage.htm; Erich Goode and Nachman Beh-Yehuda, "The American Drug Panic of the 1980s," Schaffer Library of Drug Policy, accessed November 6, 2013, http://druglibrary.org/schaffer/lsd/panic.htm; Elaine Casey, "History of Drug Use and Drug Users in the United States," Schaffer Library of Drug Policy, accessed March 3, 2005, http://www.druglibrary.org/schaffer/History/CASEY1.htm; "United States," Get the Facts, accessed November 26, 2013, http://drugwarfacts.org/cms/United _States; "Thirty Years of America's Drug War: a Chronology," *Frontline*, PBS, accessed November 10, 2008, http://www.pbs.org/wgbh/pages/frontline/shows/drugs/cron/; "Substance Abuse in the Military," National Institute on Drug Abuse, accessed May 6, 2015, http://www.

drugabuse.gov/publications/drugfacts/substance-abuse-in-military; "Drugs and Alcohol," TGSthethingstheycarried, accessed November 26, 2013, http://tgsthethingstheycarried.wikispaces.com/Drugs+and+Alcohol; Dylan Matthews, "Kathleen Frydl on the Drug War: 'Here We Have Total and Complete Failure,'" Wonkblog, *Washington Post*, April 30, 2013, http://www.washingtonpost.com/blogs/wonkblog/wp/2013/04/30/kathleen-frydl-on-the-drug-war-here-we-have-total-and-complete-failure/.

6 Rumi Kato Price, Nathan K. Risk, Keith S. Murray, Katherine S. Virgo, Edward L. Spitznagel, "Twenty-Five Mortality of US Servicemen Deployed in Vietnam: Predictive Utility of Early Drug Use," *Drug and Alcohol Dependence*, Vol. 64, No. 3, Pages 309–318, 2001.

7 Davidson, *Manufacturing*, 50.

8 Chauncy Glover, "Heroin Overdoses Hit Waterford Families Hard," *Click On Detroit*, December, 11, 2014, http://www.clickondetroit.com/news/heroin-overdoses-hit-waterford-families-hard/30189152; Drew Griffin and Nelli Black, "Deadly High: How Synthetic Drugs Are Killing Kids," *CNN*, December 2, 2014, http://www.cnn.com/2014/12/01/us/synthetic-drugs-investigation/index.html; "2014 Pulitzer Prize Nominated Finalist, Local Reporting: Rebecca D. O'Brien and Thomas Mashberg," The Pulitzer Prizes, accessed September 13, 2014, http://www.pulitzer.org/2014 _local _reporting _finalist _2, with links to nine-part series on "Suburbia's Deadly Secret."

9 "Who Is Tackling the Heroin Problem in Metro Detroit?" *Click On Detroit*, May 12, 2014, http://www.clickondetroit.com/news/investigations/who-is-tackling-the-heroin-problem-in-metro-detroit/25935312.

10 The Vietnam War, *Wikipedia*, accessed October 2, 2013, http://en.wikipedia.org/wiki/Vietnam _War; Robert Freeman, "General Giap, Vietnam, and How David Bested Goliath," *Detroit News*, Thursday, October 24, 2013, Section B1; Max Frankel, "McNamara's Retreat: *In Retrospect: The Tragedy and Lesson of Vietnam*," Book Review, *New York Times*, April 16, 1995, http://www.nytimes.com/1995/04/16/books/mcnamara-s-retreat.html.

11 "The Civil Rights Movement," *Wikipedia*, accessed October 2, 2013, http://en.wikipedia.org/wiki/Movements _for _civil _rights.

12 "American Drug Epidemic," accessed May 26, 2014, http://www.deamuseum.org/museum _idaafde.html; Peter Brush, "Higher and Higher: American Drug Use in Vietnam," *Vietnam*, Vol. 15, No. 4, December 2002, nintharticle.com/vietnam-drug-usage.htm; Erich Goode and Nachman Beh-Yehuda, "The American Drug Panic of the 1980s," Schaffer Library of Drug Policy,

accessed November 6, 2013, http://druglibrary.org/schaffer/lsd/panic.htm; Elaine Casey, "History of Drug Use and Drug Users in the United States," Schaffer Library of Drug Policy, accessed March 3, 2005, http://www.druglibrary.org/schaffer/History/CASEY1.htm; Dylan Matthews, "Kathleen Frydl on the Drug War: 'Here We Have Total and Complete Failure,'" April 30, 2013, http://www.washingtonpost.com/blogs/wonkblog/wp/2013/04/30/kathleen-frydl-on-the-drug-war-here-we-have-total-and-complete-failure/.

13 291 "*Lady Sings the Blues* (Film)," *Wikipedia*, accessed October 9, 2013, http://en.wikipedia.org/wiki/Lady _Sings _the _Blues _(film).

14 "*Shaft* (1971 Film)," *Wikipedia*, accessed July 16, 2014, http://en.wikipedia.org/wiki/Shaft _(1971 _film).

15 "*Super Fly* (film)," *Wikipedia*, accessed July 16, 2014, http://en.wikipedia.org/wiki/Super _Fly _(film).

16 "*Wattstax*," *Wikipedia*, accessed July 16, 2014, http://en.wikipedia.org/wiki/Wattstax.

17 "*Blue Collar* (Film)," *Wikipedia*, accessed July 16, 2014, http://en.wikipedia.org/wiki/Blue _Collar _(film).

18 "Blaxploitation," *Wikipedia*, accessed November 2, 2013, http://en.wikipedia.org/wiki/Blaxploitation.

19 "Motion Picture Production Code," *Wikipedia*, accessed May 2, 2014, http://en.wikipedia.org/wiki/Motion _Picture _Production _Code; "Pre-Code Hollywood," *Wikipedia*, accessed May 2, 2014, http://en.wikipedia.org/wiki/Pre-Code _Hollywood.

20 "Vietnam War," *Wikipedia*, accessed October 2, 2013, http://en.wikipedia.org/wiki/Vietnam _War.

21 "Selective Service System, *Wikipedia*, accessed May 26, 2014, http://en.wikipedia.org/wiki/Selective _Service _System; "Conscription in the United States," *Wikipedia*, accessed October 13, 2013, http://en.wikipedia.org/wiki/Conscription _in _the _United _States.

22 "Kent State Shootings," *Wikipedia*, accessed October 13, 2013, http://en.wikipedia.org/wiki/Kent _State _shootings.

23 "1967 Detroit Riot," *Wikipedia*, accessed July 8, 2014, http://en.wikipedia.org/wiki/1967 _Detroit _riot; "Special Reports: Interactive: Timeline for Detroit's 1967 Riots," *Detroit News*, accessed May 5, 2015, http://www.detroitnews.com/article/20090424/SPECIAL01/90424002;

"Detroit Riot of 1967," *World History Project*, accessed May 5, 2015, http://worldhistoryproject.org/1967/7/23/detroit-riot-of-1967;

"1967: The 12th Street Riot," *History*, accessed May 5, 2015, http://

www.history.com/this-day-in-history/the-12th-street-riot; "Starting Point of the July, 1967 Racial Riot: 9125 Twelfth Street at the corner of Twelfth and Clairmont," *Detroit: The History and Future of the Motor City*, accessed May 5, 2015,

http://www.detroit1701.org/Start1967Riot.html; "Encyclopedia of Detroit: Riots of 1967," *Detroit Historical Society*, accessed May 5, 2015, http://detroithistorical.org/learn/encyclopedia-of-detroit/riots-1967; "The Great Rebellion," *Detroit—Blood That Never Dried*, accessed May 5, 2015, http://www.detroits-great-rebellion.com/Index.html; "American Experience: Eyes on the Prize Civil Rights Movement 1954-1985: Riots in Detroit July 1967" *PBS*, accessed May 5, 2015, http://www.pbs.org/wgbh/amex/eyesontheprize/story/13 _detroit.html.; "Kercheval: It Will Become You," *Detroit—Blood That Never Dried*, accessed July 20, 2014, http://www.detroits-great-rebellion.com/Kercheval---1966.html.

24 "Boy Scouts of America," *Wikipedia*, accessed October 18, 2014, http://en.wikipedia.org/wiki/Boy _Scouts _of _America.

25 "Civil Air Patrol," *Wikipedia*, accessed October 18, 2014, http://en.wikipedia.org/wiki/Civil _Air _Patrol.

26 "Junior Reserve Officers' Training Corps," *Wikipedia*, accessed May 26, 2014, http://en.wikipedia.org/wiki/Junior _Reserve _Officers' _Training _Corps.

27 "Conscription in the United States," *Wikipedia*, accessed October 13, 2013, http://en.wikipedia.org/wiki/Conscription _in _the _United _States.

28 Davidson, *When Clans Collide*, 149-152; 205-206; 211-212.

29 "Rebuilding the Army Vietnam to Desert Storm," *American Military History*, accessed September 23, 2014, http://www.history.army.mil/books/AMH-V2/PDF/Chapter12.pdf; Leo Shane III, "Senator Seeks Official 'Welcome Home' for Iraq and Afghanistan Vets," *Military Times*, June 18, 2014, http://www.militarytimes.com/article/20140618/NEWS05/306180075/Senator-seeks-official-welcome-home-Iraq-Afghanistan-vets.

30 "The Monitors—Greetings (This Is Uncle Sam)," *YouTube*, accessed November 2, 2013, http://www.youtube.com/watch?v=pa6IqbiDIBo.

31 "General Educational Development," *Wikipedia*, accessed May 26, 2014, http://en.wikipedia.org/wiki/General _Educational _Development.

32 "1967 Detroit Riots," *Wikipedia*, accessed July 8, 2014, http://en.wikipedia.org/wiki/1967 _Detroit _riot.

33 Karl Marlantes, "The Truth About Being a Hero," The Saturday Essay, *Wall Street Journal*, August 20, 2011, http://www.wsj.com/articles/SB10001424053111903596904576516302821089790.

34 "Executive Order 9981," *Wikipedia*, accessed July 8, 2014, http://en.wikipedia.org/wiki/Executive _Order _9981.

35 "*Forest Gump*," *Wikipedia*, accessed July 20, 2014, http://en.wikipedia.org/wiki/Forrest _Gump.

36 Elaine Casey, "History of Drug Use and Drug Users in the United States," http://www.druglibrary.org/schaffer/History/CASEY1.htm; "Thirty Years of America's Drug War: a Chronology," *Frontline*, PBS, accessed November 10, 2008, http://www.pbs.org/wgbh/pages/frontline/shows/drugs/cron/; "Substance Abuse in the Military," National Institute on Drug Abuse, accessed May 6, 2015, http://www.drugabuse.gov/publications/drugfacts/substance-abuse-in-military; Rumi Kato Price, Nathan K. Risk, Keith S. Murray, Katherine S. Virgo, Edward L. Spitznagel, "Twenty-Five Mortality of US Servicemen Deployed in Vietnam: Predictive Utility of Early Drug Use," *Drug and Alcohol Dependence*, Vol. 64, No. 3, Pages 309–318, 2001.; Dylan Matthews, "Kathleen Frydl on the Drug War: 'Here We Have Total and Complete Failure,'" Wonkblog, *Washington Post*, April 30, 2013, http://www.washingtonpost.com/blogs/wonkblog/wp/2013/04/30/kathleen-frydl-on-the-drug-war-here-we-have-total-and-complete-failure/.

37 Peter Brush, "Higher and Higher: American Drug Use in Vietnam," *Vietnam*, Vol. 15, No. 4, December 2002, nintharticle.com/vietnam-drug-usage.htm.

38 Frank N. Schubert, *Voices of the Buffalo Soldiers: Records, Reports and Recollection of Military Life and Service in the West* (Albuquerque: University of New Mexico), 221–224, 2010.

39 "WCHB," *Wikipedia*, accessed January 13, 2015, http://en.wikipedia.org/wiki/WCHB _(AM).

40 "WJLB," *Wikipedia*, accessed January 13, 2015, http://en.wikipedia.org/wiki/WJLB.

41 "In the Year 2525," *Wikipedia*, accessed January 13, 2015, http://en.wikipedia.org/wiki/In _the _Year _2525.

42 "American Pie," *Wikipedia*, accessed January 13, 2015, http://en.wikipedia.org/wiki/American _Pie _(song).

43 "Twenty-Five Miles," *Wikipedia*, accessed September 10 2014, http://en.wikipedia.org/wiki/Twenty-Five _Miles.

44 "Universal Service and the Postal Monopoly: A Brief History," United States Postal Service, October 2008, https://about.usps.com/universal-postal-service/universal-service-and-postal-monopoly-history.pdf.

45 "Going Postal," *Wikipedia*, accessed November 5, 2013, http://en.wikipedia.org/wiki/Going_postal; "The Meaning and Origin of the Expression: Go Postal," The Phrase Finder, http://www.phrases.org.uk/meanings/159050.html.

46 "Zug Island," Detroit 1701, accessed November 2, 2013, http://www.detroit1701.org/Zug%20Island.html; "Zug Island," *Wikipedia*, accessed November 2, 2013, http://en.wikipedia.org/wiki/Zug_Island.

47 "Ford River Rouge Complex," *Wikipedia*, accessed 13, 2013, http://en.wikipedia.org/wiki/Ford_River_Rouge_Complex.

48 Davidson, *When Clans Collide*, 197–198.

49 "Battle of the Overpass," *Wikipedia*, accessed November 2, 2013 http://en.wikipedia.org/wiki/The_Battle_of_the_Overpass; Joe Rossiter, "Activist's Death Reminds of Key UAW–Ford Battle," *Detroit Free Press*, September 28, 2008, 2F.

50 "Magic Carpet Ride (Steppenwolf song)," *Wikipedia*, accessed May 26, 2014, http://en.wikipedia.org/wiki/Magic_Carpet_Ride_(Steppenwolf_song).

51 "Born to Be Wild," *Wikipedia*, accessed October 9, 2013, http://en.wikipedia.org/wiki/Born_to_Be_Wild.

52 "Fire (The Jimi Hendrix Experience Song)," *Wikipedia*, accessed October 9, 2013, http://en.wikipedia.org/wiki/Fire_(The_Jimi_Hendrix_Experience_song).

53 "Assembly Line," *Wikipedia*, accessed November 2, 2013, http://en.wikipedia.org/wiki/Assembly_line; "Ford Celebrate Centennial of the Moving Assembly Line," Ford, accessed May 1, 2015, http://corporate.ford.com/innovation/100-years-moving-assembly-line.html.

54 "Absenteeism," *Wikipedia*, accessed November 2, 2013, http://en.wikipedia.org/wiki/Absenteeism; "Appendix B: Productivity and Absenteeism," *The Competitive Status of the U.S. Auto Industry: A Study of the Influences of Technology in Determining International Industrial Competitive Advantage (1982)*, The National Academies Press, accessed September 24, 2014, http://www.nap.edu/openbook.php?record_id=291&page=189; Arian Campo-Flores, "Drug Use at Work Roils Firms," *Wall Street Journal*, October 13, 2014, A3.

55 "1973 Oil Crisis," *Wikipedia*, accessed November 2, 2013, http://en.wikipedia.org/wiki/1973 _oil _crisis.

56 "Martha Jean Steinberg," *Wikipedia*, accessed October 13, 2013, http://en.wikipedia.org/wiki/Martha _Jean _Steinberg.

57 "Plymouth Barracuda," *Wikipedia*, accessed June 6, 2014, http://en.wikipedia.org/wiki/Plymouth _Barracuda.

58 "Walter Payton," *Wikipedia*, accessed May 26, 2014, http://en.wikipedia.org/wiki/Walter _Payton.

59 "*Stir Crazy* (Film), *Wikipedia*, accessed October 13, 2013, http://en.wikipedia.org/wiki/Stir _Crazy _(film).

60 "David Ruffin," *Wikipedia*, accessed October 13, 2013, http://en.wikipedia.org/wiki/David _Ruffin.

61 "Jim Kelly (Martial Artist)," *Wikipedia*, accessed May 26, 2014, http://en.wikipedia.org/wiki/Jim _Kelly _(martial _artist).

62 "*Good Hair* (Film)," *Wikipedia*, accessed October 13, 2013, http://en.wikipedia.org/wiki/Good _Hair _(film).

63 "*Malcolm X* (1992 Film)," *Wikipedia*, accessed October 13, 2013, http://en.wikipedia.org/wiki/Malcolm _X _(1992 _film).

64 Michigan Barber School, accessed June 6, 2014, http://www.michiganbarberschool.org/.

65 "Grande Ballroom," *Wikipedia*, accessed November 2, 2013, http://en.wikipedia.org/wiki/Grande _Ballroom; Tom Long, "Grand Showcase for the Grande," *Detroit News*, April 5, 2012, 10M.

66 "The Who," *Wikipedia*, accessed June 6, 2014, http://en.wikipedia.org/wiki/The _Who.

67 "Bob Seger," *Wikipedia*, accessed May 26, 2014, http://en.wikipedia.org/wiki/Bob _Seger.

68 "Mitch Ryder," *Wikipedia*, accessed June 6, 2014, http://en.wikipedia.org/wiki/Mitch _Ryder.

69 "John F. Kennedy," *Wikipedia*, accessed June 6, 2014, http://en.wikipedia.org/wiki/John _F. _Kennedy.

70 "Tony Curtis," *Wikipedia*, accessed June 6, 2014, http://en.wikipedia.org/wiki/Tony _Curtis.

71 Williams, *Temptations*, 28.

72 "Jheri Curl," *Wikipedia*, accessed June 6, 2014, http://en.wikipedia.org/wiki/Jheri _curl.

73 "*Soul Train*," *Wikipedia*, accessed June 6, 2014, http://en.wikipedia.org/wiki/Soul _Train.

74 "Buick Electra," *Wikipedia*, accessed October 13, 2013, http://en.wikipedia.org/wiki/Buick _Electra.

75 "Taj Mahal," *Wikipedia*, accessed May 25, 2014, http://en.wikipedia.org/wiki/Taj _Mahal.

76 "Curtis Mayfield," *Wikipedia*, accessed May 26, 2014, http://en.wikipedia.org/wiki/Curtis _Mayfield.

77 "Absenteeism," *Wikipedia*, accessed November 2, 2013, http://en.wikipedia.org/wiki/Absenteeism; Arian Campo-Flores, "Drug Use at Work Roils Firms," *Wall Street Journal*, October 13, 2014, A3.

78 "Takin' Care of Business," *Wikipedia*, accessed October 9, 2013, http://en.wikipedia.org/wiki/Takin%27 _Care _of _Business.

79 "Unemployment," *Wikipedia*, accessed June 6, 2014, http://en.wikipedia.org/wiki/Unemployment.

80 Alan S. Blinder, *The Anatomy of Double–Digit Inflation in the 1970s*, The National Bureau of Economic Research, accessed May 1. 2015, http://www.nber.org/chapters/c11462.pdf.

81 Nathan Bomey and John Gallagher, "How Detroit Went Broke: The Answer May Surprise You—and Don't Blame Coleman Young," *Detroit Free Press*, September 15, 2013, 1A; Joel Kluth, Mike Wilkinson, and Louis Aguilar, "Six Decades: How Abandonment, Racial Tension, and Financial Missteps Bankrupted an Iconic American City," *Detroit News*, October 4, 2013, 1S–8S; "From Then Until Now: a Look at Detroit's Corrupt Political Past," *My Fox Detroit*, accessed October 10, 2013, http://www.myfoxdetroit.com/story/23652333/from-then-until-now-a-look-at-detroits-80-year-corruption.

82 "Coleman Young," *Wikipedia*, accessed May 26, 2014, http://en.wikipedia.org/wiki/Coleman _Young.

83 Bomey and Gallagher, "How Detroit Went Broke," *Detroit Free Press*,; Kluth, Wilkinson, and Aguilar, "Six Decades," *Detroit News*; "From Then Until Now," *My Fox Detroit*; J. C. Reindl, "Detroit Planners Try a Softer Approach to Urban Renewal," *Detroit Free Press*, February 10, 2013, http://www.freep.com/article/20130210/NEWS01/302100118/Detroit-planners-try-a-softer-approach-to-urban-renewal.; Cindy Rodriguez, "Detroit's Racial Divide: 40 Years Later, Together, Yet Still Apart," *Detroit News*, July 19, 2007, 1A.

84 "15 U.S. Code § 631—Declaration of Policy," Legal Information Institute, Cornell University Law School, accessed April 27, 2012, http://www.law.cornell.edu/uscode/text/15/631; Jonathon J. Bean, "'Burn, Baby, Burn': Small Business in the Urban Riots of the 1960s," *Independent Review*, Fall 2000,

Vol. 5, No. 2, 165, accessed May 1, 2012, http://www.independent.org/pdf/tir/tir _05 _2 _bean.pdf; "Kerner Commission," *Wikipedia*, accessed July 20, 2014, http://en.wikipedia.org/wiki/Kerner _Commission; "Report of the National Advisory Commission on Civil Disorders," The Eisenhower Foundation, accessed July 20, 2014, http://www.eisenhowerfoundation.org/docs/kerner.pdf; "Final Report of Cyrus R. Vance, Special Assistant to the Secretary of Defense, Concerning the Detroit Riots, July 23 through August 2, 1967," The Lyndon Baines Johnson Presidential Library, accessed April 4, 2012, http://www.lbjlib.utexas.edu/johnson/archives.hom/oralhistory.hom/Vance-C/DetroitReport.asp.

85 Sheena Harrison, "A City Without Chain Grocery Stores," Assignment Detroit, *CNN*, http://money.cnn.com/2009/07/22/smallbusiness/detroit _grocery _stores.smb/.

86 Annalyn Kurtz, "1 in 6 Unemployed Are Substance Abusers," *CNNMoney*, accessed May 1, 2015, http://money.cnn.com/2013/11/26/news/economy/drugs-unemployed/index.html.

87 "Shorty Long," *Wikipedia*, accessed October 21, 2013, http://en.wikipedia.org/wiki/Shorty _Long.

88 "*Monday Night Football*," *Wikipedia*, accessed October 21, 2013, http://en.wikipedia.org/wiki/Monday _Night _Football; "Chicago Bears 14 at Detroit Lions 28," Pro-Football-Reference.com, accessed April 20, 2011, http://www.pro-football-reference.com/boxscores/197010050det.htm.

89 "Hey There Lonely Girl," *Wikipedia*, accessed October 9, 2013, http://en.wikipedia.org/wiki/Hey _There _Lonely _Girl.

90 "*Funkadelic* (Album)," *Wikipedia*, accessed October 9, 2013, http://en.wikipedia.org/wiki/Good _Old _Music; Clinton, *Brothors Be, Yo Like George*, 72–96.

91 "Secobarbital," *Wikipedia*, accessed July 20, 2014, http://en.wikipedia.org/wiki/Secobarbital.

92 "War (Band)," *Wikipedia*, accessed June 6, 2014, http://en.wikipedia.org/wiki/War _(band).

93 "The Isley Brothers," *Wikipedia*, accessed June 6, 2014, http://en.wikipedia.org/wiki/The _Isley _Brothers.

94 "*Funkadelic* (Album)," *Wikipedia*, accessed October 9, 2013, http://en.wikipedia.org/wiki/Good _Old _Music; Clinton, *Brothors Be, Yo Like George*, 72–96.

95 "Organism," *Wikipedia*, accessed June 6, 2014, http://en.wikipedia.org/wiki/Organism.

96 "Cap Peterson," *Wikipedia*, accessed May 26, 2014, http://en.wikipedia.org/wiki/Cap _Peterson.

97 "Detroit Police Department," *Encyclopedia of Detroit*, Detroit Historical Society, accessed October 25, 2013, http://detroithistorical.org/learn/encyclopedia-of-detroit/detroit-police-department.

98 Kevin Dietz, "'White Boy Rick' Shares Details of Working in Drug World for Police," *Click on Detroit*, February 4, 2015, http://www.clickondetroit.com/news/white-boy-rick-shares-details-of-working-in-drug-world-for-police/31094404; Kevin Dietz, "Drug Dealer-Turned-Informant 'White Boy Rick' Wershe Remains Behind Bars: 1980s Kingpin Helped Feds Bust Dirty Cops, Coleman Young's Relatives," *Click on Detroit*, accessed February 1, 2015, http://www.clickondetroit.com/news/drug-dealerturnedinformant-white-boy-rick-werche-remains-behind-bars/31012934; Kevin Dietz, "Former Michigan Parole Board Member Speaks About 'White Boy Rick,'" *Click on Detroit*, February 11, 2015, http://www.clickondetroit.com/news/former-michigan-parole-board-member-speaks-out-about-white-boy-rick/31211442.

99 "*Across 110th Street*," *Wikipedia*, accessed May 26, 2014, http://en.wikipedia.org/wiki/Across _110th _Street.

100 "Bobby Womack," *Wikipedia*, accessed May 26, 2014, http://en.wikipedia.org/wiki/Bobby _Womack.

101 Richard Pryor, *Craps (After Hours)*, Audiocassette (N/A; US: LAFF Record LAFF-2023 Asshole/Lineup, Track 6), Comedy.

102 "*Crown Imperial* (March)," *Wikipedia*, accessed October 9, 2013, http://en.wikipedia.org/wiki/Crown _Imperial _(march).

103 "Immaculate Reception," *Wikipedia*, accessed December 4, 2014, http://en.wikipedia.org/wiki/Immaculate _Reception.

104 "Pam Grier," *Wikipedia*, accessed May 26, 2014, http://en.wikipedia.org/wiki/Pam _Grier.

105 "Saturday Night Special," *Wikipedia*, accessed December 7, 2014, http://en.wikipedia.org/wiki/Saturday _night _special.

106 "1973 Oil Crisis," *Wikipedia*, accessed May 26, 2014, http://en.wikipedia.org/wiki/1973 _oil _crisis

107 "Lee Iacocca," *Wikipedia*, accessed May 26, 2014, http://en.wikipedia.org/wiki/Lee _Iacocca.

108 "History of Chrysler: 1980s," *Wikipedia*, accessed May 26, 2014, http://en.wikipedia.org/wiki/Chrysler _bailout#1980s.

109 "Freddie's Dead," *Wikipedia*, accessed August 8, 2014, http://en.wikipedia.org/wiki/Freddie's _Dead.

110 "Gates Brown," *Wikipedia*, accessed May 26, 2014, http://en.wikipedia.org/wiki/Gates _Brown.

111 "Johann Wolfgang von Goethe Quotes," GoodReads, accessed October 5, 2014, http://www.goodreads.com/author/quotes/285217.Johann _Wolfgang _von _Goethe?page=2.

112 "Lou Rawls," *Wikipedia*, accessed July 20, 2014, http://en.wikipedia.org/wiki/Lou _Rawls.

Key Events and Considerations (Macro Level) 1980-1990-2000

1 "World Economy, 1980–1990: The European Economic Community, the United States and Japan Lead Expansion," *Wikipedia*, accessed July 11, 2014, http://en.wikipedia.org/wiki/World _economy#1980 _.E2.80.93 _1990 _.E2.80.93 _The _European _Economic _Community.2C _the _United _States _and _Japan _lead _expansion; US Department of State, "The Economy in the 1980s," *About.com Economics*, accessed July 11, 2014, http://economics.about.com/od/useconomichistory/a/economy _1980s.htm.

2 "History of the Internet," *Wikipedia*, accessed July 11, 2014, http://en.wikipedia.org/wiki/History _of _the _Internet; "Timeline of Computing 1980–89," accessed July 11, 2014, http://en.wikipedia.org/wiki/Timeline _of _computing _1980%E2%80%9389.

3 "Space Shuttle *Columbia*," *Wikipedia*, accessed July 11, 2014, http://en.wikipedia.org/wiki/Space _Shuttle _Columbia.

4 "Global Warming," *Wikipedia*, accessed July 11, 2014, http://en.wikipedia.org/wiki/Global _Warming.

5 "Dissolution of the Soviet Union," *Wikipedia*, accessed July 11, 2014, http://en.wikipedia.org/wiki/Dissolution _of _the _Soviet _Union.

6 "Multiculturalism," *Wikipedia*, accessed July 11, 2014, http://en.wikipedia.org/wiki/Multiculturalism.

7 "Alternative Media," *Wikipedia*, accessed July 11, 2014, http://en.wikipedia.org/wiki/Alternative _media.

8 "Dot-Com Wealth," *Wikipedia*, accessed July 11, 2014, http://en.wikipedia.org/wiki/Dot-com _bubble.

9 "Hip Hop," *Wikipedia*, accessed July 11, 2014, http://en.wikipedia.org/wiki/Hip _hop.

10 "Globalization," *Wikipedia*, accessed July 11, 2014, http://en.wikipedia.org/wiki/Globalization.

11 "Internet Explosion," *The Free Dictionary*, accessed July 11, 2014, http://encyclopedia2.thefreedictionary.com/Internet+explosion.

12 "Financial crisis of 2007–08," *Wikipedia*, accessed July 11, 2014, http://en.wikipedia.org/wiki/2007%E2%80%932012 _global _financial _crisis.

KEY EVENTS AND CONSIDERATIONS (MICRO LEVEL) 1980-1990-2000

1 "Television," *Wikipedia*, accessed July 11, 2014, http://en.wikipedia.org/wiki/Television.

2 "IBM Personal Computer," *Wikipedia*, accessed July 11, 2014, http://en.wikipedia.org/wiki/IBM _Personal _Computer.

3 "Berlin Wall," *Wikipedia*, accessed July 11, 2014, http://en.wikipedia.org/wiki/Berlin _Wall; "Cold War," *Wikipedia*, accessed July 11, 2014, http://en.wikipedia.org/wiki/Cold _War.

4 "Gulf War," *Wikipedia*, accessed July 11, 2014, http://en.wikipedia.org/wiki/Gulf _War.

5 "Greatest Engineering Achievements of the 20th Century," *Wikipedia*, accessed July 11, 2014, http://en.wikipedia.org/wiki/Greatest _Engineering _ Achievements _of _the _20th _Century.

6 "September 11 Attacks," *Wikipedia*, accessed July 11, 2014, http://en.wikipedia.org/wiki/September _11 _attacks.

7 "War of Terror," *Wikipedia*, accessed July 11, 2014, http://en.wikipedia.org/wiki/War _on _terror.

8 "Barack Obama," *Wikipedia*, accessed July 11, 2014, http://en.wikipedia.org/wiki/Barack _Obama.

CHAPTER 3

1 "Cold War," Wikipedia, accessed October 2, 2013, http://en.wikipedia.org/wiki/Cold _War; Barry Newman, "A Cold Shoulder for Cold-War Vets," Wall Street Journal, November 10-11, 2012, C3.

2 "Fulda Gap," *Wikipedia*, accessed November 2, 2013, http://en.wikipedia.org/wiki/Fulda _Gap.

3 "NATO," *Wikipedia*, accessed November 2, 2013, http://en.wikipedia.org/wiki/NATO.

4 "Warsaw Pact," accessed May 26, 2014, *Wikipedia*, http://en.wikipedia.org/wiki/Warsaw _Pact.

5 Alex Dixon, "July Marks 40th Anniversary of All-Volunteer Army," accessed October 13, 2013, *DoD News*, US Department of Defense, http://www.defense.gov/news/newsarticle.aspx?id=120408; "Issues Paper: Draft Reform and the All-Volunteer Armed Forces," Rand Corporation, accessed July 20, 2014, http://www.rand.org/content/dam/rand/pubs/monographs/MG265/images/webG0533.pdf; "The Evolution of the All-Volunteer Force," Rand Corporation, accessed July 20, 2014, http://www.rand.org/pubs/research _briefs/RB9195/index1.html; Bernard Rostker, "I Want You! The Evolution of the All-Volunteer Force," Rand Corporation, accessed July 20, 2014, http://www.rand.org/content/dam/rand/pubs/monographs/2007/RAND _MG265.pdf; Thomas W. Evans, "The All-Volunteer Army After Twenty Years: Recruiting in the Modern Era," accessed June 19, 2014, http://www.shsu.edu/~his _ncp/VolArm.html.

6 "Slogans of the United States Army," *Wikipedia*, accessed May 26, 2014, http://en.wikipedia.org/wiki/Slogans _of _the _United _States _Army.

7 "Soviet War in Afghanistan," *Wikipedia*, accessed June 12, 2014, http://en.wikipedia.org/wiki/Soviet _war _in _Afghanistan.

8 "World Economy, 1980–1990: The European Economic Community, the United States and Japan Lead Expansion," *Wikipedia*, accessed July 11, 2014, http://en.wikipedia.org/wiki/World _economy#1980 _E2.80.93 _1990 _.E2.80.93 _The _European _Economic _Community.2C _the _United _ States _and _Japan _lead _expansion; US Department of State, "The Economy in the 1980s," *About.com Economics*, accessed July 11, 2014, http://economics.about.com/od/useconomichistory/a/economy _1980s.htm; "1973 Oil Crisis," *Wikipedia*, accessed May 26, 2014, http://en.wikipedia.org/wiki/1973 _oil _crisis; "History of Chrysler: 1980s," *Wikipedia*, accessed May 26, 2014, http://en.wikipedia.org/wiki/Chrysler _bailout#1980s.

9 "Lee Iacocca," *Wikipedia*, accessed May 26, 2014, http://en.wikipedia.org/wiki/Lee _Iacocca.

10 Richard Pryor, *Army Life Go to Jail/Go Army*, Audiocassette, (1968; US: Dove/Reprise#RS-6325 (11/68), Track 7), Comedy.

11 "*Stripes* (Film)" *Wikipedia*, accessed July 16, 2014, http://en.wikipedia.org/wiki/Stripes _(film).

12 Thomas E. Ricks, "US Infantry Surprise: It's Now Mostly White; Blacks Hold Office Jobs," *Wall Street Journal*, Monday, January 6, 1997, A1.

13 Rick Montgomery, "Three in Four Young Americans Unfit for Military Service: Report Has Critics, But It Stirs Concern," *Sunday Free Press*, November 15, 2009, 16A; Miriam Jordan, "Uncle Sam Wants You: Unless You're 71% of Youths," *Wall Street Journal*, June 28-29, 2014, A1; "Too Fat to Fight: Retired Military Leaders Want Junk Food Out of America's School," Mission: Readiness, accessed July 20, 2014, http://cdn.missionreadiness.org/MR _Too _Fat _to _Fight-1.pdf.

14 "G.I. (Military)," *Wikipedia*, accessed November 2, 2013, http://en.wikipedia.org/wiki/G.I. _(military).

15 "0-dark-thirty," *Urban Dictionary*, accessed November 2, 2013, www.urbandictionary.com/define.php?term=o-dark-thirty.

16 Davidson, *When Clans Collide*, 73.

17 "Indian Removal Act," *Primary Documents in American History*, The Library of Congress, accessed October 6, 2014, http://www.loc.gov/rr/program/bib/ourdocs/Indian.html.

18 "GI Glasses," *Wikipedia*, accessed May 26, 2014, http://en.wikipedia.org/wiki/GI _glasses.

19 "*Off the Wall* (Album)," *Wikipedia*, accessed June 12, 2014, http://en.wikipedia.org/wiki/Off _the _Wall _(album).

20 Richard Pryor, *Craps (After Hours)*, Audiocassette, (N/A; US: LAFF Record LAFF-2023 Asshole/Lineup, Track 6), Comedy.

21 *Dallas* (1978 TV Series)," *Wikipedia*, accessed July 16, 2014, http://en.wikipedia.org/wiki/Dallas _(1978 _TV _series).

22 "El Paso (Song)," *Wikipedia*, accessed October 9, 2013, http://en.wikipedia.org/wiki/El _Paso _(song).

23 "Richard Pryor," *Wikipedia*, accessed October 9, 2014, http://en.wikipedia.org/wiki/Richard _Pryor.

24 Pervaiz Shallwani, "Police Discovered Variety of Drugs at Actor's Home," *Wall Street Journal*, February 4, 2014, A5.

25 "Walt Disney Anthology Television Series," *Wikipedia*, accessed July 16, 2014, http://en.wikipedia.org/wiki/Walt _Disney _anthology _television _series.

26 Richard Pryor, *Is It Something I Said? [Mudbone-Little Feets (Ms Ruda)]*, Audiocassette, (1975; US: Reprise Records/Warner Brothers Recording Inc.), Comedy.

27 "Doc Noss," *Wikipedia*, accessed October 13, 2013, http://en.wikipedia.org/wiki/Doc _Noss; Bonnie Wayne McGuire, "The Treasure of Victorio

Peak," The McGuire's Place, accessed October 13, 2013, http://www.mcguiresplace.net/The%20Treasure%20of%20Victorio%20Peak/.

28 "Soldier of the Month—First Board," Army Study Guide, accessed May 26, 2014, http://community.armystudyguide.com/groupee/forums/a/tpc/f/3711043041/m/9541087612.

29 Jeff Jurgensen, "Signal Corps General Contributed to Critical Army Transitions," *Army Communicator,* Summer 2013, http://www.signal.army.mil/ArmyCommunicator/2013/Vol38/No2/African-American%20General.pdf.

30 "Ed 'Too Tall' Jones," *Wikipedia*, accessed June 12, 2014, http://en.wikipedia.org/wiki/Ed _Jones _(American _football).

31 "Wildflecken," *Wikipedia*, accessed May 26, 2014, http://en.wikipedia.org/wiki/Wildflecken.

32 "Elvis Presley," *Wikipedia*, accessed June 6, 2014, http://en.wikipedia.org/wiki/Elvis _Presley.

33 "Shaquille O'Neal," *Wikipedia*, accessed June 6, 2014, http://en.wikipedia.org/wiki/Shaquille _O%27Neal.

34 Oberwiessbrunn, accessed May 26, 2014, http://www.oberweissenbrunn.de/index.htm.

35 "Jack & Diane," *Wikipedia*, accessed October 9, 2013, http://en.wikipedia.org/wiki/Jack _%26 _Diane.

36 "Cold War," *Wikipedia*, accessed October 2, 2013, http://en.wikipedia.org/wiki/Cold _War.

37 Davidson, *When Clans Collide*, 215.

38 "*Hot Buttered Soul*," *Wikipedia*, accessed July 16, 2014, http://en.wikipedia.org/wiki/Hot _Buttered _Soul.

39 "Montserrat (Spain)," *Wikipedia*, accessed November 2, 2013, http://wikitravel.org/en/Montserrat _(Spain).

40 "Palace at Versailles," *Wikipedia*, accessed November 2, 2013, http://en.wikipedia.org/wiki/Versailles.

41 "Neuschwanstein Castle," *Wikipedia*, accessed November 2, 2013, http://en.wikipedia.org/wiki/Neuschwanstein _Castle.

42 "Bless You Boys: A Celebration of the '84 Tigers," Detroit Tigers, accessed October 13, 2013, http://detroit.tigers.mlb.com/det/history/bless _you _boys.jsp.

43 "Fort Huachuca," *Wikipedia*, accessed June 6, 2014, http://en.wikipedia.org/wiki/Fort _Huachuca; "Fort Huachuca: The Traditional Home of the

Buffalo Soldier," *Huachuca Illustrated*, accessed October 13, 2013, http://net.lib.byu.edu/~rdh7/wwi/comment/huachuca/HI1-01.htm.

44 Cochise Stronghold, accessed June 12, 2014, http://cochisestronghold.com/.

45 "Gunfight at the OK Corral," *Wikipedia*, accessed November 2, 2013, http://en.wikipedia.org/wiki/Gunfight _at _the _O.K. _Corral.

46 "*My Darling Clementine*," *Wikipedia*, accessed June 6, 2014, http://en.wikipedia.org/wiki/My _Darling _Clementine.

47 "Old Tucson Studios," *Wikipedia*, accessed November 2, 2013, http://en.wikipedia.org/wiki/Old _Tucson _Studios.

48 "*Three Amigos*," *Wikipedia*, accessed August 10, 2014, http://en.wikipedia.org/wiki/Three _Amigos.

49 "*100 Rifles*," *Wikipedia*, accessed August 10, 2014. http://en.wikipedia.org/wiki/100 _Rifles.

50 Davidson, *When Clans Collide*, 152–157.

51 "Woody Strode," *Wikipedia*, accessed October 13, 2013, http://en.wikipedia.org/wiki/Woody _Strode.

52 "Colin Powell," *Wikipedia*, accessed November 2, 2013, http://en.wikipedia.org/wiki/Colin _Powell.

53 Davidson, *When Clans Collide*, 152–157.

54 Davidson, *When Clans Collide*, 152–157.

55 "25th Infantry Regiment (United States)," *Wikipedia*, accessed September 22, 2014, http://en.wikipedia.org/wiki/25th _Infantry _Regiment _(United _States); "92nd Infantry Division (United States)," *Wikipedia*, accessed September 22, 2014, http://en.wikipedia.org/wiki/92nd _Infantry _Division _(United _States); *Entering 92d Inf. Div. Area 1942-1945*, Published by Information-Education Section, MTOUSA, Compiled by Historical Committee 92d Infantry Division; "93rd Infantry Division (United States)," *Wikipedia*, accessed September 22, 2014, http://en.wikipedia.org/wiki/93rd _Infantry _Division _(United _States).

56 Richard Pryor, *Live on the Sunset Strip, Arizona Prison*, Audiocassette, (1982; US: Warner Brothers Records Inc. Track 2).

57 "Fiber Optic Communication," *Wikipedia*, accessed June 6, 2014, http://en.wikipedia.org/wiki/Fiber-optic _communication; "Optical Fiber," *Wikipedia*, accessed June 6, 2014, http://en.wikipedia.org/wiki/Optical _fiber.

58 "SOC Army Degrees (SOCAD)," *Wikipedia*, accessed June 6, 2014, https://www.goarmyed.com/public/public _earn _degree-soc _army _degrees.aspx.

59 "Color Him Father," *Wikipedia*, accessed July 16, 2014, http://en.wikipedia.org/wiki/Color _Him _Father.

60 "Clarence Carter," *Wikipedia*, accessed October 9, 2013, http://en.wikipedia.org/wiki/Clarence _Carter.

61 "NASA," *Wikipedia*," accessed May 26, 2014, http://en.wikipedia.org/wiki/NASA.

62 "Space Shuttle *Challenger*," *Wikipedia*, accessed October 13, 2013, http://en.wikipedia.org/wiki/Space _Shuttle _Challenger.

63 Davidson, *Manufacturing*, 52–53.

64 "Bobby Jimmy & The Critters – Roaches," YouTube, accessed October 9, 2013, http://www.youtube.com/watch?v=yygrgcOtezM.

65 "USAA," *Wikipedia*, accessed September 8, 2014, http://en.wikipedia.org/wiki/USAA.

66 Davidson, *When Clans Collide*, 131–137.

67 Davidson, *When Clans Collide*, 144–152.

68 Davidson, *When Clans Collide*, 137–144.

69 "Mount Shasta," *Wikipedia*, accessed November 2, 2013, http://en.wikipedia.org/wiki/Mount _Shasta.

70 "*Operation Pacific*," *Wikipedia*, accessed May 26, 2014, http://en.wikipedia.org/wiki/Operation _Pacific.

71 "Midnight Sun," *Wikipedia*, accessed June 6, 2014, http://en.wikipedia.org/wiki/Midnight _sun.

72 "Denali National Park and Preserve," *Wikipedia*, accessed June 6, 2014, http://en.wikipedia.org/wiki/Denali _National _Park _and _Preserve.

73 "Alaska Highway," *Wikipedia*, accessed November 2, 2013, http://en.wikipedia.org/wiki/Alaska _Highway.

74 Roberta Tognetti-Stuff, *Alaska Native Games: A Resource Guide*, Alaska Native Knowledge Network, accessed June 6, 2014, http://www.ankn.uaf.edu/curriculum/NativeGames/index.html; Hannah Karp, "Got a Good Story? Go Tell It to the Eskimos," *Wall Street Journal*, July 19, 2011, D6.

75 "Rodney King," *Wikipedia*, accessed October 13, 2013, http://en.wikipedia.org/wiki/Rodney _King.

76 "Accident Description," Aviation Safety Network, accessed April 6, 2011, http://aviation-safety.net/database/record.php?id=19890129-0; "Fairbanks-Fort Wainwright Airport, AK profile," Aviation Safety Network,, accessed April 6, 2011, http://aviation-safety.net/database/airport/airport.php?id=FBK.

77 Department of the Army, Headquarters 6th Infantry Division (Light) and U.S. Army Garrison, Alaska, Fort Wainwright, Alaska, to Wayne R. Davidson, ORDERS 262-105, promotion from second lieutenant to first lieutenant, December 1988.

78 Department of the Army, United States Military Academy, West Point New York, to CPT Wayne R. Davidson, CS HHC SPT CMD, Ft Richardson, Alaska, regarding candidacy for advanced civil schooling followed by potential position as instructor in the Department of Mathematics, 16 October 1987.

79 "Norman Schwarzkopf, Jr." *Wikipedia*, accessed November 2, 2013, http://en.wikipedia.org/wiki/Norman _Schwarzkopf, _Jr.

80 "Detroit Pistons," *Wikipedia*, accessed May 26 2014, http://en.wikipedia.org/wiki/Detroit _Pistons.

81 Jeep, accessed June 12, 2014, http://www.jeep.com/en/usab/.

82 "*Exxon Valdez* Oil Spill," *Wikipedia*, accessed November 2, 2013, http://en.wikipedia.org/wiki/Exxon _Valdez _oil _spill.

83 Santa Claus House, accessed June 6, 2014, http://www.santaclaushouse.com/.

84 "*Nine Tonight*," *Wikipedia*, accessed October 9, 2013, http://en.wikipedia.org/wiki/Nine _Tonight.

85 "Against the Wind (Bob Seger Song)," *Wikipedia*, accessed October 9, 2013, http://en.wikipedia.org/wiki/Against _the _Wind _(Bob _Seger _song).

86 "Fire Lake," *Wikipedia*, accessed October 9, 2013, http://en.wikipedia.org/wiki/Fire _Lake.

87 *The Milepost*, Alaska Travel Planner and Guide, accessed May 25, 2014 http://www.milepost.com/.

88 "Chilkat River," *Wikipedia*, accessed November 2, 2013, http://en.wikipedia.org/wiki/Chilkat _River.

89 "1989 Loma Prieta Earthquake," *Wikipedia*, accessed November 2, 2013 http://en.wikipedia.org/wiki/1989 _Loma _Prieta _earthquake.

90 "Jerry Buss," *Wikipedia*, accessed May 26, 2014, http://en.wikipedia.org/wiki/Jerry _Buss.

91 "Magic Johnson," *Wikipedia*, accessed May 26, 2014, http://en.wikipedia.org/wiki/Magic _Johnson.

92 "Unified Task Force," *Wikipedia*, accessed November 2, 2013, http://en.wikipedia.org/wiki/Unified _Task _Force.

93 "Maytag: Ol' Lonely," *Wikipedia*, accessed June 6, 2014, http://en.wikipedia.org/wiki/Maytag _Repairman#Ol.27 _Lonely.

94 Wayne R. Davidson, "United Services Automobile Association (USAA): A Case Study," (MBA thesis, Western International University, 1993).

95 "Indian Gaming Regulatory Act," *Wikipedia*, accessed November 2, 2013, http://en.wikipedia.org/wiki/Indian _Gaming _Regulatory _Act; Blaine Harden, "Indian Country Revolt Spawns Wealth," *Detroit News*, September 30, 2004, 8A; "The Social and Economic Impact of Native American Casinos," National Bureau of Economic Research, accessed 2/13/2012, http://www.nber.org/digest/feb03/w9198.html.

96 Lisa Green, "Diversifying Business School Faculties: Ph.D. Project Is Attracting Minorities," *USA Today*, 1993.

97 "Standardized Test," *Wikipedia*, accessed August 24, 2014, http://en.wikipedia.org/wiki/Standardized _test.

98 Harvard University to Wayne R. Davidson, non-acceptance letter, March 21, 1994; University of South Florida to Wayne R. Davidson, non-acceptance letter March 22, 1994. Virginia Polytechnic Institute and State University to Wayne R. Davidson, non-acceptance letter, March 16, 1994. Rensselaer Polytechnic Institute to Wayne R. Davidson, non-acceptance letter, May 1, 1994.

99 "*Monday Night Football*," *Wikipedia*, accessed May 26, 2014, http://en.wikipedia.org/wiki/Monday _Night _Football.

100 "1967 Detroit Riots, *Wikipedia*, accessed July 8, 2014, http://en.wikipedia.org/wiki/1967 _Detroit _riot.

101 "Oklahoma City Bombing," *Wikipedia*, accessed May 7, 2015, http://en.wikipedia.org/wiki/Oklahoma _City _bombing.

102 "105th Anniversary of Springfield's 'Easter Offering,'" Historic Joplin, accessed September 22, 2014, http://www.historicjoplin.org/?p=434.

103 "Strange Fruit," *Wikipedia*, accessed November 2, 2013, http://en.wikipedia.org/wiki/Strange _Fruit.

104 "FBI Investigates Alleged Racially Motivated Hanging," *The Final Call*, January 29, 2003, http://www.finalcall.com/artman/publish/national _news _2/fbi _investigates _alleged _racially _motivated _hangin _418.shtml.

105 "George Washington Carver," *Wikipedia*, accessed November 2, 2013, http://en.wikipedia.org/wiki/George _Washington _Carver.

106 "Fort Smith, Arkansas," *Wikipedia*, accessed September 22, 2014, http://en.wikipedia.org/wiki/Fort _Smith, _Arkansas.

107 Davidson, *When Clans Collide*, 44.

108 "Zig Ziglar," *Wikipedia*, accessed November 2, 2013, http://en.wikipedia.org/wiki/Zig _Ziglar; "How to Attend Zig Ziglar's Automobile University Using Audiobooks," eHow, accessed May 26, 2014, http://www.ehow.com/how _2043426 _attend-zig-ziglars-automobile-university.html.

109 Claude Bristol, *The Magic of Believing* (New York: Pocket Books, 1948).
110 Christopher Marshall, narrator, KJV Marshall Complete Bible on MP3, Amazon, accessed August 21, 2014, http://www.amazon.com/KJV-Marshall-Complete-Bible-MP3/dp/1617154393.
111 "James Brown," *Wikipedia*, accessed November 2, 2013, http://en.wikipedia.org/wiki/James _Brown.
112 Melinda Beck, "Are Alpha Males Healthy: Aggressiveness Aids Rise to Top, But the Stress Can Harm a Body," *Wall Street Journal*, September 13, 2011, D1; "Synopsis: The Alpha Male Syndrome," *Worth Ethic Corporation*, accessed May 1, 2015, http://www.worthethic.com/the-alpha-male-syndrome.html;
"How to Become an Alpha Male," *The Modern Man*, accessed May 1, 2015, http://www.themodernman.com/how _to _becomean _ alpha _male.html.

CHAPTER 4

1 Davidson, Manufacturing, 27.
2 "*My Favorite Martian*," *Wikipedia*, accessed September 22, 2014, http://en.wikipedia.org/wiki/My _Favorite _Martian.
3 Melinda Beck, "Are Alpha Males Healthy: Aggressiveness Aids Rise to Top, But the Stress Can Harm a Body," *Wall Street Journal*, September 13, 2011, D1; "Synopsis: The Alpha Male Syndrome," *Worth Ethic Corporation*, accessed May 1, 2015, http://www.worthethic.com/the-alpha-male-syndrome.html; "How to Become an Alpha Male," *The Modern Man*, accessed May 1, 2015, http://www.themodernman.com/how _to _become _an _alpha _ male.html.
4 "Toastmasters International," *Wikipedia*, accessed November 2, 2013, http://en.wikipedia.org/wiki/Toastmasters _International.
5 "National Speakers Association," *Wikipedia*, accessed November 2, 2013, http://en.wikipedia.org/wiki/National _Speakers _Association.
6 "Les Brown (Speaker)," *Wikipedia*, accessed June 12, 2014, http://en.wikipedia.org/wiki/Leslie _C. _Brown.
7 "Zig Ziglar," *Wikipedia*, accessed November 2, 2013, http://en.wikipedia.org/wiki/Zig _Ziglar.
8 "Og Mandino," *Wikipedia*, accessed June 12, 2014, http://en.wikipedia.org/wiki/Og _Mandino.

9 "Brian Tracy," *Brian Tracy International*, accessed May 1, 2015, http://www.briantracy.com/.

10 Rita Davenport, accessed June 6, 2014, http://www.ritadavenport.com/.

11 "New Thought," *Wikipedia*, accessed May 26, 2014, http://en.wikipedia.org/wiki/New _Thought.

12 "One in 31 U.S. Adults are Behind Bars, on Parole or Probation," The Pew Charitable Trusts, accessed February 28, 2008, http://www.pewtrusts.org/en/about/news-room/press-releases/0001/01/01/one-in-31-us-adults-are-behind-bars-on-parole-or-probation; Carl Bialik, "Why Surveys Should Pay Attention to Prisoners," *Wall Street Journal*, September 8–9, 2012, A2; Megha Satyanarayana, "Group Works to Keep Young Men in School: Boy to Men Links At-Risk Youths with Community Mentors," *Detroit Free Press*, November 15, 2009, 13A; "Nearly Half of Black Males, 40 Percent of White Males Are Arrested by Age 23: Study," *Huffington Post*, January 6, 2014, http://www.huffingtonpost.com/2014/01/06/half-of-blacks-arrested-23 _n _4549620.html.

13 Gary Fields and John R. Emshwiller, "As Arrest Records Mount, Consequences Last a Lifetime," *Wall Street Journal*, August 19, 2014, A1; Gary Fields and John R. Emshwiller, "Long After Arrests Record Live On," *Wall Street Journal*, December 26, 2014, A1; Gary Fields, "Phantom Arrest Record Is Finally Expunged: Retiree Success in Quest to Clear Name of 1963 Report No Court Could Find; Study Wants Low-Level Conviction Sealed," *Wall Street Journal*, December 2, 2014, A7.

14 Davidson, *Manufacturing*, 78, 177.

15 "Institute of Management Consultants USA," *Wikipedia*, accessed November 2, 2013, http://en.wikipedia.org/wiki/Institute _of _Management _Consultants _USA.

16 Davidson, *Manufacturing*, 65–66.

17 John Gallagher, "Plans for $650M Wings Arena, Entertainment District Unveiled," *Detroit Free Press*, June 19, 2013, http://www.freep.com/article/20130619/BUSINESS06/306190099/-650-million-Red-Wings-arena-proposed-near-Woodward-and-I-75; Louis Aguilar, "Reshaping Downtown Detroit: Gilbert, Ilitches: 2 Strategies, 1 Goal for City," *Detroit News*, March 2014, 1A.

18 "Quarterly Retail E-Commerce Sales," 4th Quarter 2014, *US Census Bureau News*, accessed December 2, 2014, http://www.census.gov/retail/mrts/www/data/pdf/ec _current.pdf.

19 Davidson, *When Clans Collide*, xxxiii-xxxiv.

20 "Supreme Headquarters Allied Powers Europe," *Wikipedia*, accessed November 2, 2013, http://en.wikipedia.org/wiki/Supreme _Headquarters _Allied _Powers _Europe.

21 Rob Powers, "Physical Fitness Test, " About.com United States Army, accessed November 2, 2013, http://usmilitary.about.com/od/army/a/afpt.htm.

22 "*Renaissance Man* (Film)," *Wikipedia*, accessed July 16, 2014, http://en.wikipedia.org/wiki/Renaissance _Man _(film).

23 "A *Raisin in the Sun*," *Wikipedia*, accessed July 16, 2014, http://en.wikipedia.org/wiki/A _Raisin _in _the _Sun.

24 "The Colored Museum," *Wikipedia*, accessed July 16, 2014, http://en.wikipedia.org/wiki/The _Colored _Museum.

25 "The Twelfth of Never," *Wikipedia*, accessed October 9, 2013, http://en.wikipedia.org/wiki/The _Twelfth _of _Never.

26 "*Five Guys Named Moe*," *Wikipedia*, accessed October 9, 2013, http://en.wikipedia.org/wiki/Five _Guys _Named _Moe.

27 "Always and Forever (Heatwave Song)," *Wikipedia*, accessed October 9, 2013, http://en.wikipedia.org/wiki/Always _and _Forever _(Heatwave _song).

28 Michael M. Phillips, "Reluctant Draftee Completes Tour of Duty, 42 Years Later," *Wall Street Journal*, November 19, 2014, A6; Charles C. Moskos and John Sibley Butler, *All That We Can Be: Black Leadership and Racial Integration the Army Way* (New York: Basic Books, 1996).

29 Davidson, *When Clans Collide*, xxxii.

30 "Standardized Test," *Wikipedia*, accessed August 24, 2014, http://en.wikipedia.org/wiki/Standardized _test.

31 Jonathan S. Landay, "Fewer Blacks Desire Military Career," *The Christian Science Monitor*, June 3, 1996, http://www.csmonitor.com/1996/0603/060396.us.us.2.html.

32 "Sir Francis Bacon (1561–1626)," The Quotations Page, accessed September 22, 2014, http://www.quotationspage.com/quotes/Sir _Francis _Bacon.

33 "Redlining," *Wikipedia*, accessed June 6, 2014, http://en.wikipedia.org/wiki/Redlining; "1934–1968: FHA Mortgage Insurance Requirements Utilize Redlining," The Fair Housing Center, accessed June 6, 2014, http://www.bostonfairhousing.org/timeline/1934-1968-FHA-Redlining.html.

34 Joel Kluth, Mike Wilkinson, and Louis Aguilar, "Six Decades: How Abandonment, Racial Tension and Financial Missteps Bankrupted an Iconic American City," *Detroit News*, October 4, 2013, 1S-8S.

35 "Tiger Stadium (Detroit)," *Wikipedia*, accessed on June 6, 2014, http://en.wikipedia.org/wiki/Tiger _Stadium _(Detroit).

36 "Comerica Park," *Wikipedia*, accessed on June 6, 2014, http://en.wikipedia.org/wiki/Comerica _Park.

37 "Junior Reserve Officers' Training Corps," *Wikipedia*, accessed May 26, 2014, http://en.wikipedia.org/wiki/Junior _Reserve _Officers' _ Training _Corps.

38 "Kronk Gym," *Wikipedia*, accessed May 26, 2014, http://en.wikipedia.org/wiki/Kronk _Gym.

39 "Emanuel Steward," *Wikipedia*, accessed June 6, 2014, http://en.wikipedia.org/wiki/Emanuel _Steward.

40 "Thomas Hearns," *Wikipedia*, accessed June 6, 2014, http://en.wikipedia.org/wiki/Thomas _Hearns.

41 "Sagging (Fashion)," *Wikipedia*, accessed December 3, 2014, http://en.wikipedia.org/wiki/Sagging _(fashion); "Sagging Pants and the Long History Of 'Dangerous' Street Fashion," *Code Switch*, NPR, http://www.npr.org/blogs/codeswitch/2014/09/11 /347143588/sagging-pants-and-the-long-history-of-dangerous-street-fashion.

42 Karen Bouffard, "Study: Detroit Worst Big City for Childhood Poverty," *Detroit News*, February 19, 2015, http://www.detroitnews.com/story/news/local/wayne-county/2015/02/18/detroit-childhood-poverty-ranking-kids-count-report/23657355/; Karen Bouffard, "Report: 67% of Detroit Kids Live in High-Poverty Areas," *Detroit News*, IRP Poverty Dispatch, accessed July 16, 2014, http://www.irp.wisc.edu/dispatch/children-in-high-poverty-areas/.

43 "Miracle at Michigan," *Wikipedia*, accessed November 2, 2013, http://en.wikipedia.org/wiki/The _Miracle _at _Michigan.

44 "*To Sir, with Love*," *Wikipedia*, accessed July 16, 2014, http://en.wikipedia.org/wiki/To _Sir, _with _Love.

45 "*Dynasty* (TV Series)," *Wikipedia*, accessed July 16, 2014. http://en.wikipedia.org/wiki/Dynasty _(TV _series).

46 Davidson, *When Clans Collide*, 20-21.

47 "Harold McKinney," *Wikipedia*, accessed November 2, 2013, http://de.wikipedia.org/wiki/Harold _McKinney.

48 Susan Whitall, "Music Hall's Jazz Café a High Note for Detroit," *Detroit News*, Winter 2006/2007.

49 "RAH! RAH! Detroit (The Detroit Works Song/Michigan Morn)," *YouTube*, accessed May 25, 2012 http://www.youtube.com/watch?v=jfszIjGh1mI.

50 Davidson, *When Clans Collide*, 21–24.

51 "Demographics of Active Duty U.S. Military," Statistic Brain, accessed August 11, 2014, http://www.statisticbrain.com/

demographics-of-active-duty-u-s-military/; Ed O'Keefe, "Percentage of Minority Federal Workers Up Slightly," Federal Eye, *Washington Post*, June 13, 2011, http://www.washingtonpost.com/blogs/federal-eye/post/percentage-of-minority-federal-workers-up-slightly/2011/06/12/AGJQPzSH _blog.html.

52 "*I'm Gonna Git You Sucka*," *Wikipedia*, accessed July 16, 2014, http://en.wikipedia.org/wiki/I%27m _Gonna _Git _You _Sucka.

53 "*The Brady Bunch*," *Wikipedia*, accessed July 16, 2014, http://en.wikipedia.org/wiki/The _Brady _Bunch.

54 "The Star-Spangled Banner," *Wikipedia*, accessed October 9, 2013, http://en.wikipedia.org/wiki/The _Star _Spangled _Banner.

55 Luchina Fisher, "5 Worst Performances of 'Star Spangled Banner,'" *ABC Good Morning America*, July 3, 2013, http://abcnews.go.com/Entertainment/worst-national-anthem-performances/story?id=19566854#5; Dan Fletcher, "Top 10 Worst National-Anthem Renditions," *Time*, October 6, 2010, http://content.time.com/time/specials/packages/article/0,28804,1889754 _1889752 _1889735,00.html.

56 "World Trade Center," *Wikipedia*, accessed October 13, 2013, http://en.wikipedia.org/wiki/World _Trade _Center.

57 "September 11 Attacks," *Wikipedia*, accessed October 2, 2013, http://en.wikipedia.org/wiki/September _11 _attacks.

58 "B-25 Empire State Building Crash," *Wikipedia*, accessed December 2, 2014, http://en.wikipedia.org/wiki/B-25 _Empire _State _Building _crash.

59 "University of Phoenix," *Wikipedia*, accessed November 2, 2013, http://en.wikipedia.org/wiki/University _of _Phoenix.

60 Robert Snell and Mike Wilkinson, "Kilpatrick Gone, Case Rolls On," *Detroit News*, October 11, 2013, Metro Final, 1A; Tresa Baldas, "The High Cost of Kilpatrick's Crimes: How Corruption Deepened the City's Crisis," *Detroit Free Press*, October 6, 2013, 1A; Ron French, "2008: The Year that Rocked Detroit," Detroit News, Friday December 26, 2008, Section D.

61 "Camelback Mountain," *Wikipedia*, accessed December 22, 2014, http://en.wikipedia.org/wiki/Camelback _Mountain; Kevin Helliker, "Super Bowl Weekend May Bring Mountain Climbing to New Heights: Phoenix Expects Extra Foot Traffic on City Peak; 'Vertical Central Park,'" *Wall Street Journal*, January 31–February 1, 2015, A1, http://www.wsj.com/articles/super-bowl-weekend-may-bring-phoenix-mountain-climbing-to-new-heights-1422674958.

62 "*Do the Right Thing*," *Wikipedia*, accessed July 16, 2014, http://en.wikipedia.org/wiki/Do _the _Right _Thing.

63 Davidson, *Manufacturing*, 6.

64 "Edgar Brazelton," Obituaries 2006, *Crain's Detroit Business*, January 1, 2007, http://www.crainsdetroit.com/article/20070101/SUB/70102008/obituaries-2006; "Edgar Brazelton Jr. Dies," *Michigan Chronicle*, March 14, 2006, High Beam Research, accessed November 3, 2013, http://www.highbeam.com/doc/1P1-122207311.html.

65 "*The Natural* (Film)," *Wikipedia*, accessed July 16, 2014, http://en.wikipedia.org/wiki/The _Natural _(film).

66 Jeffery Zaslow, "Walking Away from a Fantasy," Wall Street Journal, February 2, 2011, D1; Tom Lang, "Knock It Out of the Park: Metro Detroit Residents Step Up to the Plate at Detroit Tigers Fantasy Camp," *Michigan Prime/Detroit Media Partnership*, May 11, 2014, E.

67 Kevin Allen, *The People's Champion: Willie Horton* (Wayne, MI: Immortal Investment Publishing, 2004), 8–16.

68 Allen, *Willie Horton*, 8–16.

69 Terence Moore, "Willie Horton Can Change the World, Sports on Earth," June 24, 2015, accessed June 26, 2015, http://www.sportsonearth.com/article/132442560/detroit-tigers-willie-horton-tries-change-world.

70 "Space Shuttle *Columbia*," *Wikipedia*, accessed November 2, 2013, http://en.wikipedia.org/wiki/Space _Shuttle _Columbia.

71 "Detroit Tigers Baseball Fantasy Camp-2013," *Detroit Tigers Weekly*, Fox Sports Detroit, 2013.

72 "Super Bowl XXXVIII Halftime Show Controversy," *Wikipedia*, accessed October 13, 2013, http://en.wikipedia.org/wiki/Super _Bowl _XXXVIII _halftime _show _controversy.

73 "Comerica Park," *Wikipedia*, accessed on June 6, 2014, http://en.wikipedia.org/wiki/Comerica _Park; "Arizona vs. Detroit, Extended Box How They Scored Game Story," USATODAY, accessed July 21, 2015, http://cgi.usatoday.com/sports/scores105/105142/20050522ML---DETROIT---0nr.htm#.

74 "LASIK," *Wikipedia*, accessed January 21, 2015, http://en.wikipedia.org/wiki/LASIK.

75 "*The Exorcist* (Film)," *Wikipedia*, accessed September 22, 2014, http://en.wikipedia.org/wiki/The _Exorcist _(film).

76 Ben Wallace, JockBio.com, accessed October 13, 2014, http://www.jockbio.com/Bios/Wallace/Wallace _bio.html.

77 "Sir Francis Bacon (1561–1626)," *Wikipedia*, accessed September 22, 2014, http://www.quotationspage.com/quotes/Sir _Francis _Bacon.

78 Davidson, *Manufacturing*, 52–53.

79 Davidson, *Manufacturing*, 62.

80 Davidson, *Manufacturing*, 159–160.

81 "Ballroom Dance," *Wikipedia*, accessed June 6, 2014, http://en.wikipedia.org/wiki/Ballroom _dance.

82 "Arthur Murray," *Wikipedia*, accessed June 12, 2014, http://en.wikipedia.org/wiki/Arthur _Murray _Studios.

83 Davidson, *Manufacturing*, 53.

84 "Kumon," *Wikipedia*, accessed December 14, 2014, http://en.wikipedia.org/wiki/Kumon.

85 "Kumon Learning Centers," *Wikipedia*, accessed December 14, 2014, http://www.kumon.com/aboutkumon/successstories.aspx/.

86 Anita Roddick, "Podium: To Be Poor in the US Is the Bottom: A Speech by the Founder of the Body Shop to the Human Scale Education Conference," *The Independent*, 7 October 1998, http://www.independent.co.uk/arts-entertainment/podium-to-be-poor-in-the-us-is-the-bottom-1176606.html.

87 "Saturday-Morning Cartoon," *Wikipedia*, accessed December 15, 2014, http://en.wikipedia.org/wiki/Saturday-morning _cartoon.

88 Gail Sullivan, "Saturday Cartoons Are No More," *Washington Post*, September 30, 2014, http://www.washingtonpost.com/news/morning-mix/wp/2014/09/30/saturday-morning-cartoons-are-no-more/.

89 "Television & Health," *The Sourcebook for Teaching Science*, accessed December 15, 2014, http://www.csun.edu/science/health/docs/tv&health.html.

90 Davidson, *Manufacturing*, 50.

91 "Nielsen Study: African Americans Watch the Most Television," *EurWeb*, March 31, 2011, http://www.eurweb.com/2011/03/nielsen-study-african-americans-watch-the-most-television/; "Top TV Viewing Facts," *blAck*, October 25, 2012, http://blackamericaweb.com/2012/10/25/top-tv-viewing-facts/; B. Sophia Ford, Tiffany E. McDonald, Ayisha S. Owens, and Thomas N. Robinson, "Primary Care Interventions to Reduce Television Watching in African-American Children," *American Journal of Preventive Medicine*, vol. 22, no. 2 (February 2002): 106–109, http://www.sciencedirect.com/science/article/pii/S074937970100410X.

92 "Digital Video Recorder," *Wikipedia*, accessed December 15, 2014, http://en.wikipedia.org/wiki/Digital _video _recorder.

93 "African-American TV Usage and Buying Power Highlighted," Marketing Charts, October 18, 2007, http://www.marketingcharts.com/television/african-american-tv-usage-and-buying-power-highlighted-2068/;

"African-Americans Spend Most Time with Many TV-Related Media," Marketing Charts, April 6, 2011, http://www.marketingcharts.com/television/african-americans-spend-most-time-with-many-tv-related-media-16872/.

94 "Black Millennials Viewing Fewer Hours of TV Than African-American Baby Boomers," *Target Market News*, September 25, 2012, http://targetmarketnews.com/storyid10011201.htm.

95 Davidson, *When Clans Collide*, xlv.

96 "Idioms: The Apple Doesn't Fall Far from the Tree," Bits: English Language Learning, accessed December 4, 2014, http://esl-bits.net/idioms/id606.htm.

97 Davidson, *Manufacturing*, 13.

98 "Eddie Rickenbacker Quotes," BrainyQuote, accessed January 16, 2015, http://www.brainyquote.com/quotes/authors/e/eddie _rickenbacker.html.

99 Alisa Priddle, "Investors and Travelers Discover a Whole New Motor City," *Detroit Free Press*, November 9, 2014, 1A; "How Detroit was Reborn," *Detroit Free Press*, November 9, 2014, 1X; Daniel Howes, Chad Livengood, and David Shepardson, "Bankruptcy and Beyond," *Detroit News*, November 13, 2014, B1.

100 Deutschman, *Change or Die*, 1-15.

EPILOGUE

1 "Sir Winston Churchill (1874–1965)," The Quotations Page, accessed September 22, 2014, http://www.quotationspage.com/quotes/Sir _Winston _Churchill/.

2 623 Davidson, *When Clans Collide*, 1–11.

3 624 Davidson, *Manufacturing*, 46, 121; Dina Gilio-Whitaker, "Richard Nixon's Influence on American Indian Affairs," About.com Native American History, accessed December 4, 2014, http://nativeamericanhistory.about.com/od/Policies/a/Richard-Nixon-S-Influence-On-American-Indian-Affairs.htm; "Native American Self-Determination," *Wikipedia*, accessed December 4, 2014, http://en.wikipedia.org/wiki/Native _American _self-determination.

4 "*The Butler*," *Wikipedia*, accessed September 9, 2014, http://en.wikipedia.org/wiki/The _Butler.

5 "Demographics of the United States," *Wikipedia*, accessed August 14, 2014, http://en.wikipedia.org/wiki/Demographics _of _the _United _States.

6 "Term Limits in the United States," *Wikipedia*, accessed September 24, 2014, http://en.wikipedia.org/wiki/Term _limits _in _the _United _States; "A

Case against Term Limits," Editorial, *Detroit News*, Thursday, December 25, 2014, 21A.

7 "Demographics of Active Duty U.S. Military," Statistic Brain, accessed August 11, 2014, http://www.statisticbrain.com/demographics-of-active-duty-u-s-military/.

8 Ed O'Keefe, "Percentage of Minority Federal Workers Up Slightly," Federal Eye, *Washington Post*, June 12, 3011, http://www.washingtonpost.com/blogs/federal-eye/post/percentage-of-minority-federal-workers-up-slightly/2011/06/12/AGJQPzSH _blog.html.

9 "The African-American Labor Force in the Recovery," US Department of Labor, accessed August 11, 2014, http://www.dol.gov/ _sec/media/reports/blacklaborforce/.

10 "Church Attendance," *Wikipedia*, accessed August 11, 2014, http://en.wikipedia.org/wiki/Church _attendance.

11 Albert L. Winseman, "U.S. Churches Looking for a Few White Men," Gallup, July 27, 2004, http://www.gallup.com/poll/12463/US-Churches-Looking-Few-White-Men.aspx.

12 Christian E. Weller, "The Black and White Labor Gap in America: Why African Americans Struggle to Find Jobs and Remain Employed Compared to Whites," Center for American Progress, accessed August 11, 2014, http://www.americanprogress.org/issues/labor/report/2011/07/25/9992/the-black-and-white-labor-gap-in-america/.

13 "One in 31 U.S. Adults Are Behind Bars, on Parole or Probation," The Pew Charitable Trusts, accessed February 28, 2008, http://www.pewtrusts.org/en/about/news-room/press-releases/0001/01/01/one-in-31-us-adults-are-behind-bars-on-parole-or-probation; Carl Bialik, "Why Surveys Should Pay Attention to Prisoners," *Wall Street Journal*, September 8–9, 2012, A2; Megha Satyanarayana, "Group Works to Keep Young Men in School: Boy to Men Links At-Risk Youths with Community Mentors," *Detroit Free Press*, November 15, 2009, 13A; "Nearly Half of Black Males, 40 Percent of White Males Are Arrested by Age 23: Study," *Huffington Post*, January 6, 2014, http://www.huffingtonpost.com/2014/01/06/half-of-blacks-arrested-23 _n _4549620.html; John R. Emshwiller and Gary Fields, "Second Chance: Hiring Managers Bedeviled by Flood of Arrest Records," *Wall Street Journal*, December 13–14, 2014.

14 Davidson, *When Clans Collide*, 1–11, 15–32, 61–106.

15 *African American Lives*, PBS, accessed September 22, 2014, http://www.pbs.org/wnet/aalives/.

16 *Finding your Roots with Henry Louis Gates Jr.*, PBS, accessed May 7, 2015, http://www.pbs.org/wnet/finding-your-roots/your-stories/wayne-davidson/.
17 Manav Tanneeru, "Family Roots Lure Many African-Americans Back to South," Black in America 2, *CNN.com*, July 20, 2009, http://www.cnn.com/2009/LIVING/wayoflife/07/10/bia.return.south/index.html; Larry Copeland, "Blacks Return to Southern Roots," July 1, 2011, http://usatoday30.usatoday.com/news/nation/census/2011-06-30-black-south-census-migration _n.htm.
18 Joel Kluth, Mike Wilkinson, and Louis Aguilar, "Six Decades: How Abandonment, Racial Tension and Financial Missteps Bankrupted an Iconic American City," *Detroit News*, October 4, 2013, 1S-8S.
19 "Earl Campbell Talks About His Career in the NFL," Rogers Photo Archives, *YouTube*, December 6, 2012, http://www.youtube.com/watch?v=FvHB9QAIFbs.
20 Davidson, *Manufacturing*, 159–160.
21 "*The Natural* (Film)," *Wikipedia*, http://en.wikipedia.org/wiki/The _Natural _(film).
22 Davidson, *Manufacturing*, 159–160.
23 Davidson, *When Clans Collide*, 169.
24 Davidson, *Manufacturing*, 4.
25 Davidson, *Manufacturing*, 47.
26 "The Unusual Tale of Oseola McCarty," Money, *Wall Street Journal*, Winter 2013, 26.
27 Kim Kozlowski, "Historically Black Colleges See Rise in Enrollment," *Detroit News*, February 12, 2015, http://www.detroitnews.com/story/news/local/michigan/2015/02/12/historically-black-colleges-enrollment/23335687/.
28 "The Wire (Season 2): Episode 12, 'Port in a Storm,'" *Wikipedia*, http://en.wikipedia.org/wiki/The _Wire.
29 Alana Semuels, What Happened to Lincoln Heights, One of America's First Black Suburbs: The Destruction of a Black Suburb, *The Atlantic*, accessed July 13, 2015, http://www.theatlantic.com/business/archive/2015/07/lincoln-heights-black-suburb/398303/.
30 "Two Thirds Feel American Dream Harder to Achieve,", *About News*, accessed May 8, 2015, http://usgovinfo.about.com/od/moneymatters/a/baddream.htm; Jerry Newcombe, "Is the American Dream dead?" *Detroit News*, December 26, 2014, 19A.

31 Robert B. Reich, "The American Dream Has Become Only a Pipe Dream," *Detroit Free Press*, December 31, 2013, http://www.freep.com/article/C4/20140101/OPINION05/301010009/.

32 "How 9/11 Changed America," *Detroit News*, September 9, 2011, 5–8B.

33 Laura I. Haley, *The Poppy Fields of Afghanistan: Another Vietnam?*, Air Command and Staff College Air University, Maxwell Air Force Base, Alabama, April 2006; Margherita Stancati, "Afghanistan, Opium Poppy Cultivation Up 17% This Year, U.N. Says," *Wall Street Journal*, November 12, 2014, A11.

34 Paul Draus, "Heroin and Bare Life: Drugs, Work and Worth in the Post-Industrial City, Conference Papers, American Sociological Association, 2008 Annual Meeting, p1, 30p; Paul J. Draus, Juliette K. Roddy, and Mark Greenwald, "A Hell of a Life: Addition and Marginality in Post-Industrial Detroit," *Social and Cultural Geography*, vol. 11, no.7, November 2010; Arian Campo-Flores and Zusha Elinson, "Heroin Use, and Deaths, Rise: Increased Supply, Purer Batches and Addicts Shifting from Pain Pills Are Blamed," *Wall Street Journal*, February 4, 2014, A5.

35 "Michael Brown Shooting," *NBC News*, accessed December 3, 2014, http://www.nbcnews.com/storyline/michael-brown-shooting.

36 "Reporter Who Commented on 'Black Men Growing Up Without Fathers' Suspended," *Fox News*, http://www.foxnews.com/us/2014/07/16/reporter-who-commented-on-black-men-growing-up-without-fathers-suspended/; Josh Peters, "Former NFL Exec: Teams Hid 'Hundreds' of Abuse Incidents," *USA Today*, October 9, 2014, http://www.msn.com/en-us/sports/nfl/former-nfl-exec-teams-hid-hundreds-of-abuse-incidents/ar-BB8n5N9.

37 Davidson Powell, "A Man's Life Cycle," Men's Issues, *Ezine Articles*, March 12, 2010, http://ezinearticles.com/?A-Mans-Life-Cycle&id=3920362.

38 Davidson, *Manufacturing*, 79–80, 177.

39 Sue Shellenbarger, "Stop Wasting Everyone's Time: Meetings and e-Mail Kill Hours, But You Can Identify the Worst Offenders—Seven Common Mistakes," *Wall Street Journal*, December 3, 2014, D1.

40 Stephanie Castillo, "'I Hate My Job,' Say 70% of US Employees," *Medical Daily*, accessed January 29, 2015, http://www.msn.com/en-us/health/medical/i-hate-my-job-say-70percent-of-us-employees/ar-AA8JEzf?ocid=bb7hp.

41 "Wasted Days and Wasted Nights," *Wikipedia*, accessed December, 22, 2014, http://en.wikipedia.org/wiki/Wasted _Days _and _Wasted _Nights.

Printed in the United States
By Bookmasters